Using Samba

Using Samba

Robert Eckstein, David Collier-Brown,
and Peter Kelly

O'REILLY®

Beijing · Cambridge · Farnham · Köln · Paris · Sebastopol · Taipei · Tokyo

Using Samba

by Robert Eckstein, David Collier-Brown, and Peter Kelly

Published by O'Reilly & Associates, Inc., 101 Morris Street, Sebastopol, CA 95472.

Editor: Andy Oram

Production Editor: Sarah Jane Shangraw

Printing History:

January 2000: First Edition.

ISBN: 1-56592-449-5 [2/00]
[M]

Table of Contents

Preface

It's nine in the morning and you've just arrived at the computer center after a refreshing night's sleep. Your pager hasn't gone off in months. Life is pretty good as a system administrator—and why shouldn't it be, with the network you're running? Two hundred identical machines, all running the same operating system. All of the printers are networked, accessible from anywhere in the building, and the auto-configuration scripts that the manufacturer supplied ensure that everyone in the company has a consistent view of the shared disks you've set up. Yes, this is the good life. You lean back and take that first delicious sip of morning coffee....

And then, the alarm clock jolts you out of your blissful reverie. If you're like most system administrators, this could only be a dream. Your morning probably starts with a tireless struggle to get four different computer platforms running three different operating systems simply to talk to each other—that is, if the phone ever stops ringing. Most of your users don't understand why it's so hard to access a file on another computer or to send a job to a remote printer. The logs show that the backups are late. For some reason the PCs on the second floor can't find the tape server. With all these headaches, what's a network administrator to do?

Easy: take the day off, read this book, and learn Samba!

The Samba Suite

Samba is a suite of tools for sharing resources such as printers and files across a network. This may be a bit of an oversimplification, but Samba is really designed to make your life easier. Samba uses the Server Message Block (SMB) protocol, which is endorsed jointly by Microsoft and IBM, to communicate low-level data between Windows clients and Unix servers on a TCP/IP network.

Four features of Samba make it extremely attractive:

- Samba speaks the same SMB protocol that Microsoft and IBM operating systems have used as their standard since DOS 3.0. This means that almost all Windows machines already understand it and there is no extra client software to install.

- Samba runs on a variety of platforms, including most variants of Unix, Open-VMS, OS/2, AmigaDOS, and NetWare. This means that you can use a single program on the server to provide files and printers to a community of PCs.

- Samba is free. There are several commercial products that duplicate Samba's features, and some of them are quite expensive. Samba offers you an alternative to packages that could gobble up a significant portion of your IS budget. Samba is distributed under the GNU General Public License (GPL), and is considered by its authors to be *Open Source* software. In other words, you can freely download both the application and the accompanying source code to your computer, and even improve on the original Samba programs if you like.

- Samba administration is centralized on the server. You don't have to visit every one of your machines, floppy or CD-ROM in hand, to upgrade the client software.

Samba is a complete solution for local area networks (LANs) of all sizes—everything from the two-computer home network to corporate installations with hundreds of nodes. Samba is simple to set up and to administer, and presents itself as a transparent network environment that offers users access to all of the resources they need to get their work done. Once you've set it up, Samba will let you:

- Serve Unix files to Windows, OS/2, and other OS clients
- Allow Unix clients to access PC files
- Serve network printers to Windows clients
- Provide name services (broadcast and WINS)
- Allow browsing of network resources from Windows clients
- Create Windows workgroups or domains
- Enforce username and password authentication of clients

Audience for this Book

The primary audience of this book is Unix administrators who need to support PCs on their network, and anyone who needs to provide a Unix server in a PC environment. But we don't want to burden you with an endless series of arcane system administration tools and vocabulary. While we assume you are familiar with basic Unix system administration, we will *not* assume you are a networking expert. We'll do our best along the way to help out with unusual definitions and terms.

Because we don't assume a tremendous amount of experience with Microsoft Windows, we will go through the PC side of the installation task in considerable detail and give examples for both Windows 95/98 and Windows NT, which are subtly different. For the Unix side, we will give examples for common Unix operating systems, such as Linux 2.0 or Solaris 2.6.

Samba Installation Checklist

Before you get started, you should have:

- Either the CD-ROM from this book (which contains both source and binary distributions of Samba 2.0.5) or the latest Samba distribution, which you can download directly off the Internet at *http://www.samba.org/*.

- The names and IP addresses of the servers and client machines you plan to use, the netmask of your network, and the names and IP addresses of your domain name (DNS) servers.

Organization

The book can be roughly divided into two sections: Samba installation (Chapter 1 through Chapter 3) and Samba configuration and optimization (Chapter 4 through Chapter 9). Here is a detailed breakdown of each of the chapters:

Chapter 1, *Learning the Samba*
> This chapter introduces each of the Samba components and gives a brief overview of NetBIOS and Windows networking.

Chapter 2, *Installing Samba on a Unix System*
> This chapter covers configuring, compiling, installing, and testing the Samba server on a Unix platform.

Chapter 3, *Configuring Windows Clients*
> This chapter explains how to configure Microsoft Windows 95/98 and NT 4.0 clients to participate in an SMB network. It also gives a brief introduction to the SMB protocol in action.

Chapter 4, *Disk Shares*
> This chapter gets you up to speed with the individual parts of the Samba configuration file and shows you how to configure disk services.

Chapter 5, *Browsing and Advanced Disk Shares*
> This chapter continues the discussion of disk options and examines browsing with Samba.

Chapter 6, *Users, Security, and Domains*
> This chapter discusses how to set up users, introduces you to Samba security, and shows you how to work with encrypted and non-encrypted passwords. We also discuss how to set up Samba as a primary domain controller for Windows 95/98 and NT clients.

Chapter 7, *Printing and Name Resolution*
> This chapter discusses printer and Windows Internet Naming Service (WINS) setup with Samba.

Chapter 8, *Additional Samba Information*
> This chapter bundles several miscellaneous activities associated with Samba, such as configuring Samba shares for programmers, internationalization issues, and backing up with *smbtar.*

Chapter 9, *Troubleshooting Samba*
> If you have problems installing Samba, this comparatively large chapter is packed with troubleshooting hints and strategies as to what might be going wrong.

Appendix A, *Configuring Samba with SSL*
> This appendix shows you the nitty-gritty of setting up Samba with Secure Sockets Layers (SSL) connections between the server and its clients.

Appendix B, *Samba Performance Tuning*
> This appendix discusses various techniques to optimize Samba processing on your network.

Appendix C, *Samba Configuration Option Quick Reference*
> This appendix covers each of the options used in the *smb.conf* file.

Appendix D, *Summary of Samba Daemons and Commands*
> Each of the server daemons and tools that make up the Samba suite are covered in this appendix. In addition, we provide a list of mirror sites on the Internet from which Samba can be downloaded.

Appendix E, *Downloading Samba with CVS*
> This appendix explains how to download the latest version of Samba with CVS.

Appendix F, *Sample Configuration File*
> This appendix provides a large-scale Samba configuration file, which you might find in place at a large corporation. We have embedded comments in the file to explain the more arcane options.

Conventions

The following font conventions are followed throughout this book:

Italic

> Filenames, file extensions, URLs, Internet addresses, executable files, commands, and emphasis.

Constant Width

> Samba configuration options and other code that appear in the text, and command-line information that should be typed verbatim on the screen.

Bold Constant Width

> Commands that are entered by the user, and new configuration options that we wish to bring to the attention of the reader.

Constant Width Italic

> Replaceable content in code and command-line information.

 The owl icon designates a note, which is an important aside to the nearby text.

 The turkey icon designates a warning related to the nearby text.

Request for Comments

We have tested and verified the information in this book to the best of our ability, but you may find that features have changed (or even that we have made mistakes!). Please let us know about any errors you find, as well as your suggestions for future editions, by writing to:

> O'Reilly & Associates, Inc.
> 101 Morris Street
> Sebastopol, CA 95472
> 1-800-998-9938 (in the U.S. or Canada)
> 1-707-829-0515 (international/local)
> 1-707-829-0104 (FAX)

You can also send us messages electronically. To be put on the mailing list or request a catalog, send email to:

info@oreilly.com

To ask technical questions or comment on the book, send email to:

bookquestions@oreilly.com

We have a web site for the book, where we'll list examples, errata, and any plans for future editions. You can access this page at:

http://www.oreilly.com/catalog/samba/

For more information about this book and others, see the O'Reilly web site:

http://www.oreilly.com

Acknowledgments

Robert Eckstein

> I'd first like to recognize Dave Collier-Brown and Peter Kelly for all their help in the creation of this book. I'd also like to thank each of the technical reviewers that helped polish this book into shape on such short notice: Matthew Temple, Jeremy Allison, and of course Andrew Tridgell. Andrew and Jeremy deserve special recognition, not only for creating such a wonderful product, but for providing a tireless amount of support in the final phase of this book—hats off to you, guys! A warm hug goes out to my wife Michelle, who once again put up with a husband loaded down with too much caffeine on a tight schedule. Thanks to Dave Sifry and the people at LinuxCare, San Francisco, for hosting me on such short notice for Andrew Tridgell's visit. And finally, a huge amount of thanks to our editor, Andy Oram, who (very) patiently helped guide this book through its many stages until we got it right.

David Collier-Brown

> I'd especially like to thank Joyce, who put up with me during the sometimes exciting development of the book. My thanks to Andy Oram, who was kind enough to provide the criticism that allowed me to contribute; the crew at Opcom who humored the obvious madman in their midst; and Ian MacMillan, who voluntarily translated several of my early drafts from nerd to English. I would also like to give special thanks to Perry Donham, Drew Sullivan, and Jerry DeRoo.

Peter Kelly

> A few people really made this book possible, and I have to bow to them. Dave Collier-Brown, and then Bob Eckstein, took over my part of this project with style and professionalism and I can't explain how much I owe them for the great work that came out of it. Editor Andy Oram is by far the most patient and pleasant per-

son I have met. Also, I don't think that I would have been involved in this book without the help of Xavier Cazin from O'Reilly, who originally came to me asking for a proposal after reading my Linux Journal article. I also would like to thank all of the JDP.COM consultants (Jerry, Peggyann, Drew, Gord, Jerome, Mark, Rick— too many to list!) for allowing me to continue to work with them. I thank the O'Reilly staff that I have worked with as well; they are a great bunch of people. Also, thanks to the Samba Team for making Samba in the first place. And most importantly, Kate McKay, for staying with me this long!

We would especially like to give thanks to Perry Donham for helping mold the first draft of this book. Although Perry was unable to contribute to subsequent drafts, his material was essential to getting this book off on the right foot. In addition, some of the browsing material came from text originally written by Dan Shearer for O'Reilly.

We are deeply indebted to the production department at O'Reilly for another fantastic job. Sarah Jane Shangraw worked long hours accommodating our seemingly endless edits, and Rob Romano tirelessly edited our images again and again until they were perfect. Special thanks also to Claire Cloutier LeBlanc, Rhon Porter, and Mike Sierra for their help—we couldn't have done it without any of them. It is largely through their collective efforts that this book arrived to you in November 1999 instead of November 2000.

1

Learning the Samba

If you are a typical system administrator, then you know what it means to be *swamped* with work. Your daily routine is filled with endless hardware incompatibility issues, system outages, data backup problems, and a steady stream of angry users. So adding another program to the mix of tools that you have to maintain may sound a bit perplexing. However, if you're determined to reduce the complexity of your work environment, as well as the workload of keeping it running smoothly, Samba may be the tool you've been waiting for.

A case in point: one of the authors of this book used to look after 70 Unix developers sharing 5 Unix servers. His neighbor administered 20 Windows 3.1 users and 5 OS/2 and Windows NT servers. To put it mildly, the Windows 3.1 administrator was swamped. When he finally left—and the domain controller melted—Samba was brought to the rescue. Our author quickly replaced the Windows NT and OS/2 servers with Samba running on a Unix server, and eventually bought PCs for most of the company developers. However, he did the latter without hiring a new PC administrator; the administrator now manages one centralized Unix application instead of fifty distributed PCs.

If you know you're facing a problem with your network and you're sure there is a better way, we encourage you to start reading this book. Or, if you've heard about Samba and you want to see what it can do for you, this is also the place to start. We'll get you started on the path to understanding Samba and its potential. Before long, you can provide Unix services to all your Windows machines—all without spending tons of extra time or money. Sound enticing? Great, then let's get started.

What is Samba?

Samba is a suite of Unix applications that speak the SMB (Server Message Block) protocol. Many operating systems, including Windows and OS/2, use SMB to perform client-server networking. By supporting this protocol, Samba allows Unix servers to get in on the action, communicating with the same networking protocol as Microsoft Windows products. Thus, a Samba-enabled Unix machine can masquerade as a server on your Microsoft network and offer the following services:

- Share one or more filesystems
- Share printers installed on both the server and its clients
- Assist clients with Network Neighborhood browsing
- Authenticate clients logging onto a Windows domain
- Provide or assist with WINS name server resolution

Samba is the brainchild of Andrew Tridgell, who currently heads the Samba development team from his home of Canberra, Australia. The project was born in 1991 when Andrew created a fileserver program for his local network that supported an odd DEC protocol from Digital Pathworks. Although he didn't know it at the time, that protocol later turned out to be SMB. A few years later, he expanded upon his custom-made SMB server and began distributing it as a product on the Internet under the name SMB Server. However, Andrew couldn't keep that name—it already belonged to another company's product—so he tried the following Unix renaming approach:

```
grep -i 's.*m.*b' /usr/dict/words
```

And the response was:

```
salmonberry samba sawtimber scramble
```

Thus, the name "Samba" was born.*

Today, the Samba suite revolves around a pair of Unix daemons that provide shared resources—or *shares*—to SMB clients on the network. (Shares are sometimes called s*ervices* as well.) These daemons are:

smbd

> A daemon that allows file and printer sharing on an SMB network and provides authentication and authorization for SMB clients.

nmbd

> A daemon that looks after the Windows Internet Name Service (WINS), and assists with browsing.

---

* Which is a good thing, because our marketing people highly doubt you would have picked up a book called "Using Salmonberry"!

Samba is currently maintained and extended by a group of volunteers under the active supervision of Andrew Tridgell. Like the Linux operating system, Samba is considered *Open Source software* (OSS) by its authors, and is distributed under the GNU General Public License (GPL). Since its inception, development of Samba has been sponsored in part by the Australian National University, where Andrew Tridgell earned his Ph.D.* In addition, some development has been sponsored by independent vendors such as Whistle and SGI. It is a true testament to Samba that both commercial and non-commercial entities are prepared to spend money to support an Open Source effort.

Microsoft has also contributed materially by putting forward its definition of SMB and the Internet-savvy Common Internet File System (CIFS), as a public Request for Comments (RFC), a standards document. The CIFS protocol is Microsoft's renaming of future versions of the SMB protocol that will be used in Windows products—the two terms can be used interchangeably in this book. Hence, you will often see the protocol written as "SMB/CIFS."

What Can Samba Do For Me?

As explained earlier, Samba can help Windows and Unix machines coexist in the same network. However, there are some specific reasons why you might want to set up a Samba server on your network:

- You don't want to pay for—or can't afford—a full-fledged Windows NT server, yet you still need the functionality that one provides.

- You want to provide a common area for data or user directories in order to transition from a Windows server to a Unix one, or vice versa.

- You want to be able to share printers across both Windows and Unix workstations.

- You want to be able to access NT files from a Unix server.

Let's take a quick tour of Samba in action. Assume that we have the following basic network configuration: a Samba-enabled Unix machine, to which we will assign the name hydra, and a pair of Windows clients, to which we will assign the names phoenix and chimaera, all connected via a local area network (LAN). Let's also assume that hydra also has a local inkjet printer connected to it, lp, and a disk share named network—both of which it can offer to the other two machines. A graphic of this network is shown in Figure 1-1.

---

* At the time of this printing, Andrew had completed his Ph.D. work and had joined San Francisco-based LinuxCare.

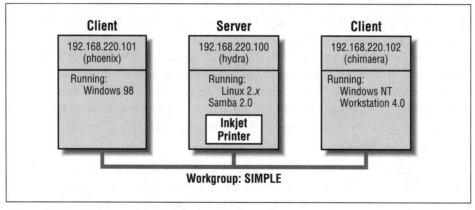

Figure 1-1. A simple network setup with a Samba server

In this network, each of the computers listed share the same *workgroup*. A work-group is simply a group nametag that identifies an arbitrary collection of comput-ers and their resources on an SMB network. There can be several workgroups on the network at any time, but for our basic network example, we'll have only one: the SIMPLE workgroup.

Sharing a Disk Service

If everything is properly configured, we should be able to see the Samba server, **hydra**, through the Network Neighborhood of the **phoenix** Windows desktop. In fact, Figure 1-2 shows the Network Neighborhood of the **phoenix** computer, including **hydra** and each of the computers that reside in the SIMPLE workgroup. Note the Entire Network icon at the top of the list. As we just mentioned, there can be more than one workgroup on an SMB network at any given time. If a user clicks on the Entire Network icon, he or she will see a list of all the workgroups that currently exist on the network.

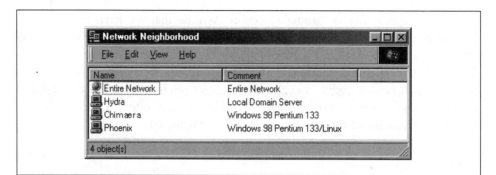

Figure 1-2. The Network Neighborhood directory

We can take a closer look at the **hydra** server by double-clicking on its icon. This contacts **hydra** itself and requests a list of its *shares*—the file and printer resources—that the machine provides. In this case, there is a printer entitled **lp** and a disk share entitled **network** on the server, as shown in Figure 1-3. Note that the Windows display shows hostnames in mixed case (Hydra). Case is irrelevant in hostnames, so you may see hydra, Hydra, and HYDRA in various displays or command output, but they all refer to a single system. Thanks to Samba, Windows 98 sees the Unix server as a valid SMB server, and can access the **network** folder as if it were just another system folder.

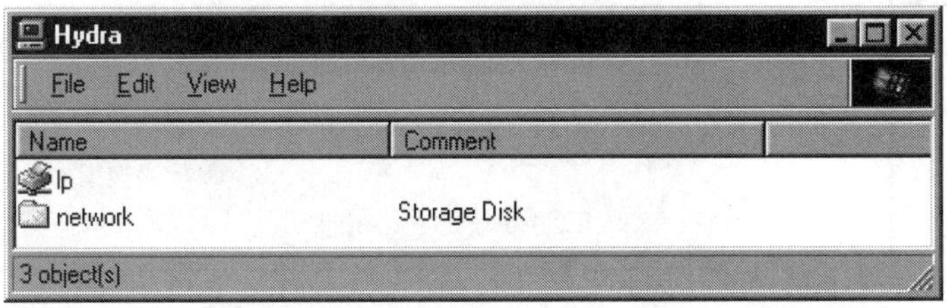

Figure 1-3. Shares available on the hydra sever as viewed from phoenix

One popular feature of Windows 95/98/NT is that you can map a letter-drive to a known network directory using the Map Network Drive option in the Windows Explorer.* Once you do so, your applications can access the folder across the network with a standard drive letter. Hence, you can store data on it, install and run programs from it, and even password-protect it against unwanted visitors. See Figure 1-4 for an example of mapping a letter-drive to a network directory.

Take a look at the Path: entry in the dialog box of Figure 1-4. An equivalent way to represent a directory on a network machine is by using two backslashes, followed by the name of the networked machine, another backslash, and the networked directory of the machine, as shown below:

    \\network-machine\directory

This is known as the *UNC* (Universal Naming Convention) in the Windows world. For example, the dialog box in Figure 1-4 represents the network directory on the **hydra** server as:

    \\HYDRA\network

---

* You can also right-click on the shared resource in the Network Neighborhood, and then select the Map Network Drive menu item.

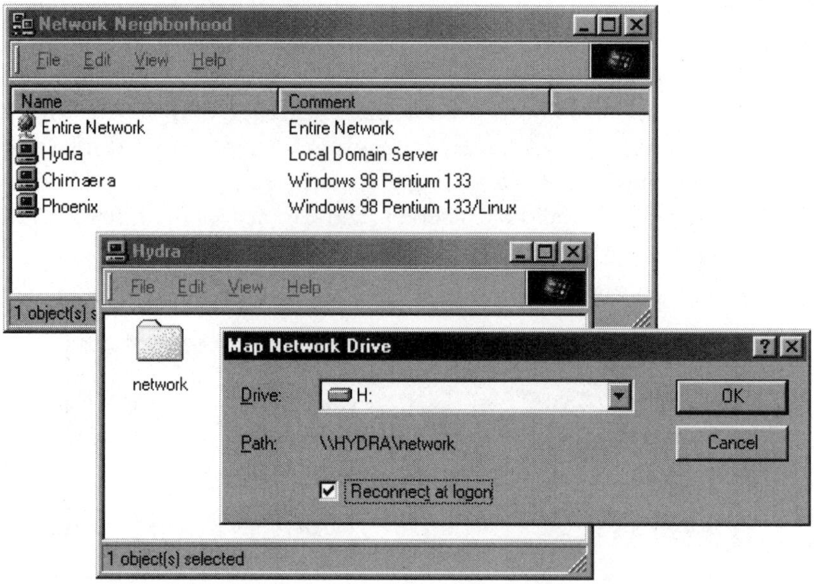

Figure 1-4. Mapping a network drive to a Windows letter-drive

If this looks somewhat familiar to you, you're probably thinking of *uniform resource locators* (URLs), which are addresses that web browsers such as Netscape Navigator and Internet Explorer use to resolve machines across the Internet. Be sure not to confuse the two: web browsers typically use forward slashes instead of back slashes, and they precede the initial slashes with the data transfer protocol (i.e., ftp, http) and a colon (:). In reality, URLs and UNCs are two completely separate things.

Once the network drive is set up, Windows and its programs will behave as if the networked directory was a fixed disk. If you have any applications that support multiuser functionality on a network, you can install those programs on the network drive.* Figure 1-5 shows the resulting network drive as it would appear with other storage devices in the Windows 98 client. Note the pipeline attachment in the icon for the G: drive; this indicates that it is a network drive instead of a fixed drive.

From our Windows NT Workstation machine, **chimaera**, Samba looks almost identical to Windows 98. Figure 1-6 shows the same view of the **hydra** server from the Windows NT 4.0 Network Neighborhood. Setting up the network drive

---

* Be warned that many end-user license agreements forbid installing a program on a network such that multiple clients can access it. Check the legal agreements that accompany the product to be absolutely sure.

Figure 1-5. The Network directory mapped to the client letter-drive G

using the Map Network Drive option in Windows NT Workstation 4.0 would have identical results as well.

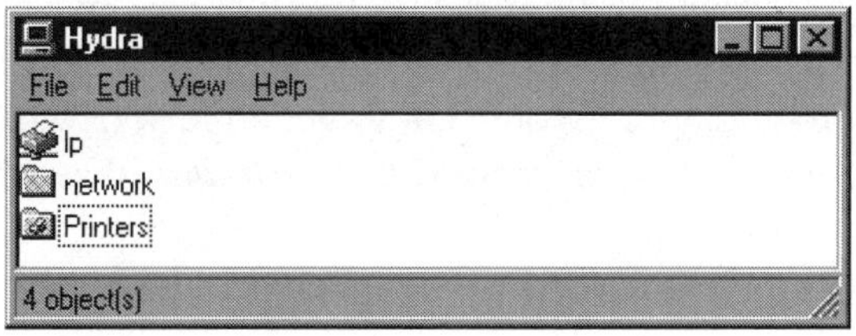

Figure 1-6. Shares available on hydra (viewed from chimaera)

Sharing a Printer

You probably noticed that the printer lp appeared under the available shares for **hydra** in Figure 1-3. This indicates that the Unix server has a printer that can be shared by the various SMB clients in the workgroup. Data sent to the printer from any of the clients will be spooled on the Unix server and printed in the order it is received.

Setting up a Samba-enabled printer on the Windows side is even easier than setting up a disk share. By double-clicking on the printer and identifying the manufacturer and model, you can install a driver for this printer on the Windows client. Windows can then properly format any information sent to the network printer and access it as if it were a local printer (we show you how to do this later in the chapter). Figure 1-7 shows the resulting network printer in the Printers window of Windows 98. Again, note the pipeline attachment below the printer, which identifies it as being on a network.

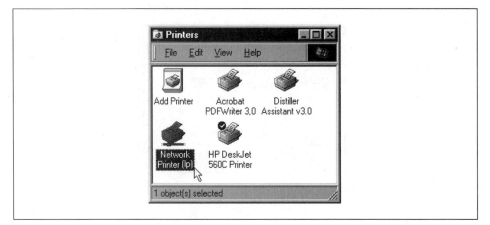

Figure 1-7. A network printer available on hydra (viewed from chimaera)

Seeing things from the Unix side

As mentioned earlier, Samba appears in Unix as a set of daemon programs. You can view them with the Unix **ps** and **netstat** commands, you can read any messages they generate through custom debug files or the Unix **syslog** (depending on how Samba is set up), and you can configure it from a single Samba properties file: *smb.conf.* In addition, if you want to get an idea of what each of the daemons are doing, Samba has a program called *smbstatus* that will lay it all on the line. Here is how it works:

```
# smbstatus
Samba version 2.0.4
Service      uid       gid      pid     machine
-------------------------------------------------
network      davecb    davecb   7470    phoenix  (192.168.220.101) Sun May 16
network      davecb    davecb   7589    chimaera (192.168.220.102) Sun May 16


Locked files:
Pid    DenyMode    R/W        Oplock       Name
--------------------------------------------------
7589   DENY_NONE   RDONLY     EXCLUSIVE+BATCH /home/samba/quicken/inet/common/
system/help.bmp   Sun May 16 21:23:40 1999
7470   DENY_WRITE  RDONLY     NONE            /home/samba/word/office/findfast.exe
Sun May 16 20:51:08 1999
7589   DENY_WRITE  RDONLY     EXCLUSIVE+BATCH /home/samba/quicken/1fbmp70n.dll
Sun May 16 21:23:39 1999
7589   DENY_WRITE  RDWR       EXCLUSIVE+BATCH /home/samba/quicken/inet/qdata/
runtime.dat   Sun May 16 21:23:41 1999
7470   DENY_WRITE  RDONLY     EXCLUSIVE+BATCH /home/samba/word/office/osa.exe
Sun May 16 20:51:09 1999
7589   DENY_WRITE  RDONLY     NONE            /home/samba/quicken/qversion.dll
Sun May 16 21:20:33 1999
```

```
7470   DENY_WRITE RDONLY      NONE                   /home/samba/quicken/
qversion.dll   Sun May 16 20:51:11 1999

Share mode memory usage (bytes):
   1043432(99%) free + 4312(0%) used + 832(0%) overhead = 1048576(100%) total
```

The Samba status from this output provides three sets of data, each divided into separate sections. The first section tells which systems have connected to the Samba server, identifying each client by its machine name (**phoenix** and **chimaera**) and IP address. The second section reports the name and status of the files that are currently in use on a share on the server, including the read/write status and any locks on the files. Finally, Samba reports the amount of memory it has currently allocated to the shares that it administers, including the amount actively used by the shares plus additional overhead. (Note that this is not the same as the total amount of memory that the *smbd* or *nmbd* processes are using.)

Don't worry if you don't understand these statistics; they will become easier to understand as you move through the book.

Getting Familiar with a SMB/CIFS Network

Now that you have had a brief tour of Samba, let's take some time to get familiar with Samba's adopted environment: an SMB/CIFS network. Networking with SMB is significantly different from working with a Unix TCP/IP network, because there are several new concepts to learn and a lot of information to cover. First, we will discuss the basic concepts behind an SMB network, followed by some Microsoft implementations of it, and finally we will show you where a Samba server can and cannot fit into the picture.

Understanding NetBIOS

To begin, let's step back in time. In 1984, IBM authored a simple application programming interface (API) for networking its computers called the *Network Basic Input/Output System* (NetBIOS). The NetBIOS API provided a rudimentary design for an application to connect and share data with other computers.

It's helpful to think of the NetBIOS API as networking extensions to the standard BIOS API calls. With BIOS, each low-level call is confined to the hardware of the local machine and doesn't need any help traveling to its destination. NetBIOS, however, originally had to exchange instructions with computers across IBM PC or Token Ring networks. It therefore required a low-level transport protocol to carry its requests from one computer to the next.

In late 1985, IBM released one such protocol, which it merged with the NetBIOS API to become the *NetBIOS Extended User Interface* (*NetBEUI*). NetBEUI was designed for small local area networks (LANs), and it let each machine claim a name (up to 15 characters) that wasn't already in use on the network. By a "small LAN," we mean fewer than 255 nodes on the network—which was considered a practical restriction in 1985!

The NetBEUI protocol was very popular with networking applications, including those running under Windows for Workgroups. Later, implementations of Net-BIOS over Novell's IPX networking protocols also emerged, which competed with NetBEUI. However, the networking protocols of choice for the burgeoning Internet community were TCP/IP and UDP/IP, and implementing the NetBIOS APIs over those protocols soon became a necessity.

Recall that TCP/IP uses numbers to represent computer addresses, such as 192.168.220.100, while NetBIOS uses only names. This was a major issue when trying to mesh the two protocols together. In 1987, the Internet Engineering Task Force (IETF) published a series of standardization documents, titled RFC 1001 and 1002, that outlined how NetBIOS would work over a TCP/UDP network. This set of documents still governs each of the implementations that exist today, including those provided by Microsoft with their Windows operating systems as well as the Samba suite.

Since then, the standard this document governs has become known as *NetBIOS over TCP/IP*, or NBT for short. The NBT standard (RFC 1001/1002) currently outlines a trio of services on a network:

- A name service
- Two communication services:
  — Datagrams
  — Sessions

The name service solves the name-to-address problem mentioned earlier; it allows each computer to declare a specific name on the network that can be translated to a machine-readable IP address, much like today's DNS on the Internet. The datagram and session services are both secondary communication protocols used to transmit data back and forth from NetBIOS machines across the network.

Getting a Name

For a human being, getting a name is easy. However, for a machine on a Net-BIOS network, it can be a little more complicated. Let's look at a few of the issues.

In the NetBIOS world, when each machine comes online, it wants to claim a name for itself; this is called *name registration*. However, no two machines in the same workgroup should be able to claim the same name; this would cause endless confusion for any machine that wanted to communicate with either machine. There are two different approaches to ensuring that this doesn't happen:

- Use a *NetBIOS Name Server* (NBNS) to keep track of which hosts have registered a NetBIOS name.

- Allow each machine on the network to defend its name in the event that another machine attempts to use it.

Figure 1-8 illustrates a (failed) name registration, with and without a NetBIOS Name Server.

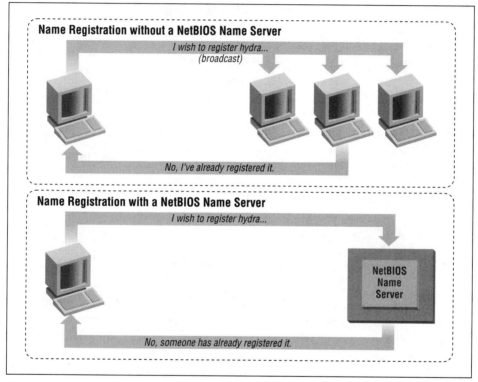

Figure 1-8. NBNS versus non-NBNS name registration

In addition, there must be a way to resolve a NetBIOS name to a specific IP address as mentioned earlier; this is known as *name resolution*. There are two different approaches with NBT here as well:

- Have each machine report back its IP address when it "hears" a broadcast request for its NetBIOS name.

- Use the NBNS to help resolve NetBIOS names to IP addresses.

Figure 1-9 illustrates the two types of name resolution.

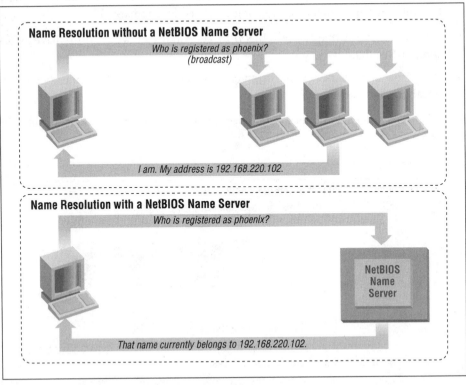

Figure 1-9. NBNS versus non-NBNS name resolution

As you might expect, having an NBNS on your network can help out tremendously. To see exactly why, let's look at the non-NBNS method.

Here, when a client machine boots, it will broadcast a message declaring that it wishes to register a specified NetBIOS name as its own. If nobody objects to the use of the name after multiple registration attempts, it keeps the name. On the other hand, if another machine on the local subnet is currently using the requested name, it will send a message back to the requesting client that the name is already taken. This is known as *defending* the hostname. This type of system comes in handy when one client has unexpectedly dropped off the network—another can take its name unchallenged—but it does incur an inordinate amount of traffic on the network for something as simple as name registration.

With an NBNS, the same thing occurs, except that the communication is confined to the requesting machine and the NBNS server. No broadcasting occurs when the machine wishes to register the name; the registration message is simply sent directly from the client to NBNS server and the NBNS server replies whether or not the name is already taken. This is known as *point-to-point communication*, and is often beneficial on networks with more than one subnet. This is because routers are often preconfigured to block incoming packets that are broadcast to all machines in the subnet.

The same principles apply to name resolution. Without an NBNS, NetBIOS name resolution would also be done with a broadcast mechanism. All request packets would be sent to each computer in the network, with the hope that one machine that might be affected will respond directly back to the machine that asked. At this point, it's clear that using an NBNS server and point-to-point communication for this purpose is far less taxing on the network than flooding the network with broadcasts for every name resolution request.

Node Types

How can you tell what strategy each client on your network will use when performing name registration and resolution? Each machine on an NBT network earns one of the following designations, depending on how it handles name registration and resolution: b-node, p-node, m-node, and h-node. The behaviors of each type of node are summarized in Table 1-1.

Table 1-1. NetBIOS Node Types

Role	Value
b-node	Uses broadcast registration and resolution only.
p-node	Uses point-to-point registration and resolution only.
m-node	Uses broadcast for registration. If successful, it notifies the NBNS server of the result. Uses broadcast for resolution; uses NBNS server if broadcast is unsuccessful.
h-node (hybrid)	Uses NBNS server for registration and resolution; uses broadcast if the NBNS server is unresponsive or inoperative.

In the case of Windows clients, you will usually find them listed as *h-nodes* or *hybrid nodes*. Incidentally, h-nodes were invented later by Microsoft, as a more fault-tolerant route, and do not appear in RFC 1001/1002.

You can find out the node type of a Windows 95/98 machine with the "More Info" button of the *winipcfg* command. On Windows NT, type `ipconfig /all` and search for the line that says `Node Type`.

What's in a Name?

The names NetBIOS uses are quite different from the DNS hostnames you might be familiar with. First, NetBIOS names exist in a flat namespace. In other words, there are no qualifiers such as *ora.com* or *samba.org* to section off hostnames; there is only a single unique name to represent each computer. Second, NetBIOS names are allowed to be only 15 characters, may not begin with an asterisk (*), and can consist only of standard alphanumeric characters (a-z, A-Z, 0-9) and the following:

```
! @ # $ % ^ & ( ) - ' { } . ~
```

Although you are allowed to use a period (.) in a NetBIOS name, we recommend against it because those names are not guaranteed to work in future versions of NetBIOS over TCP/IP.

It's not a coincidence that all valid DNS names are also valid NetBIOS names. In fact, the DNS name for a Samba server is often reused as its NetBIOS name. For example, if you had a machine **phoenix.ora.com**, its NetBIOS name would likely be PHOENIX (followed by 8 blanks).

Resource names and types

With NetBIOS, a machine not only advertises its presence, but also tells others what types of services it offers. For example, **phoenix** can indicate that it's not just a workstation, but is also a file server and can receive WinPopup messages. This is done by adding a 16th byte to the end of the machine (resource) name, called the *resource type*, and registering the name more than once. See Figure 1-10.

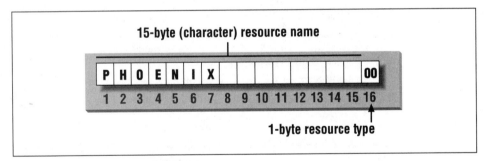

Figure 1-10. The structure of NetBIOS names

The one-byte resource type indicates a unique service the named machine provides. In this book, you will often see the resource type shown in angled brackets (<>) after the NetBIOS name, such as:

```
PHOENIX<00>
```

You can see which names are registered for a particular NBT machine using the Windows command-line NBTSTAT utility. Because these services are unique (i.e., there cannot be more than one registered), you will see them listed as type UNIQUE in the output. For example, the following partial output describes the hydra server:

```
D:\>NBTSTAT -a hydra

        NetBIOS Remote Machine Name Table
     Name               Type        Status
  ---------------------------------------------
     HYDRA          <00>  UNIQUE     Registered
     HYDRA          <03>  UNIQUE     Registered
     HYDRA          <20>  UNIQUE     Registered
     ...
```

This says the server has registered the NetBIOS name hydra as a machine (workstation) name, a recipient of WinPopup messages, and a file server. Some possible attributes a name can have are listed in Table 1-2.

Table 1-2. NetBIOS Unique Resource Types

Named Resource	Hexidecimal Byte Value
Standard Workstation Service	00
Messenger Service (WinPopup)	03
RAS Server Service	06
Domain Master Browser Service (associated with primary domain controller)	1B
Master Browser name	1D
NetDDE Service	1F
Fileserver (including printer server)	20
RAS Client Service	21
Network Monitor Agent	BE
Network Monitor Utility	BF

Note that because DNS names don't have resource types, the designers intentionally made hexidecimal value 20 (an ASCII space) default to the type for a file server.

Group names and types

SMB also uses the concept of groups, with which machines can register themselves. Earlier, we mentioned that the machines in our example belonged to a *workgroup*, which is a partition of machines on the same network. For example, a business might very easily have an ACCOUNTING and a SALES workgroup, each with different servers and printers. In the Windows world, a workgroup and an SMB group are the same thing.

Continuing our NBTSTAT example, the `hydra` Samba server is also a member of the SIMPLE workgroup (the GROUP attribute hex 00), and will stand for election as a browse master (GROUP attribute 1E). Here is the remainder of the NBTSTAT utility output:

```
        NetBIOS Remote Machine Name Table, continued
    Name                    Type     Status
   --------------------------------------------------
    SIMPLE          <00>  GROUP      Registered
    SIMPLE          <1E>  GROUP      Registered
    .._ _MSBROWSE_ _.<01>  GROUP      Registered
```

The possible group attributes a machine can have are illustrated in Table 1-3. More information is available in *Windows NT in a Nutshell* by Eric Pearce, also published by O'Reilly.

Table 1-3. NetBIOS Group Resource Types

Named Resource	Hexidecimal Byte Value
Standard Workstation group	00
Logon Server	1C
Master Browser name	1D
Normal Group name (used in browser elections)	1E
Internet Group name (administrative)	20
<01><02>_ _MSBROWSE_ _<02>	01

The final entry, _ _MSBROWSE_ _, is used to announce a group to other master browsers. The nonprinting characters in the name show up as dots in a NBTSTAT printout. Don't worry if you don't understand all of the resource or group types. Some of them you will not need with Samba, and others you will pick up as you move through the rest of the chapter. The important thing to remember here is the logistics of the naming mechanism.

Datagrams and Sessions

At this point, let's digress to introduce another responsibility of NBT: to provide connection services between two NetBIOS machines. There are actually two services offered by NetBIOS over TCP/IP: the *session service* and the *datagram service*. Understanding how these two services work is not essential to using Samba, but it does give you an idea of how NBT works and how to troubleshoot Samba when it doesn't work.

The datagram service has no stable connection between one machine and another. Packets of data are simply sent or broadcast from one machine to another, without regard for the order that they arrive at the destination, or even if they arrive at all. The use of datagrams is not as network intensive as sessions, although they can bog down a network if used unwisely (remember broadcast name resolution earlier?) Datagrams, therefore, are used for quickly sending simple blocks of data to one or more machines. The datagram service communicates using the simple primitives shown in Table 1-4.

Table 1-4. Datagram Primitives

Primitive	Description
Send Datagram	Send datagram packet to machine or groups of machines.
Send Broadcast Datagram	Broadcast datagram to any machine waiting with a Receive Broadcast Datagram.
Receive Datagram	Receive a datagram from a machine.
Receive Broadcast Datagram	Wait for a broadcast datagram.

The session service is more complex. Sessions are a communication method that, in theory, offers the ability to detect problematic or inoperable connections between two NetBIOS applications. It helps to think of an NBT session in terms of a telephone call.* A full-duplex connection is opened between a caller machine and a called machine, and it must remain open throughout the duration of their conversation. Each side knows who the caller and the called machine is, and can communicate with the simple primitives shown in Table 1-5.

Table 1-5. Session Primitives

Primitive	Description
Call	Initiate a session with a machine listening under a specified name.
Listen	Wait for a call from a known caller or any caller.
Hang-up	Exit a call.
Send	Send data to the other machine.
Receive	Receive data from the other machine.
Session Status	Get information on requested sessions.

Sessions are the backbone of resource sharing on an NBT network. They are typically used for establishing stable connections from client machines to disk or printer shares on a server. The client "calls" the server and starts trading information such as which files it wishes to open, which data it wishes to exchange, etc. These calls can last a long time—hours, even days—and all of this occurs within the context of a single connection. If there is an error, the session software (TCP) will retransmit until the data is received properly, unlike the "punt-and-pray" approach of the datagram service (UDP).

---

* As you can see in RFC 1001, the telephone analogy was strongly evident in the creation of the NBT service.

In truth, while sessions are supposed to be able to handle problematic communications, they often don't. As you've probably already discovered when using Windows networks, this is a serious detriment to using NBT sessions. If the connection is interrupted for some reason, session information that is open between the two computers can easily become invalidated. If that happens, the only way to regain the session information is for the same two computers to call each other again and start over.

If you want more information on each of these services, we recommend you look at RFC 1001. However, there are two important things to remember here:

- Sessions always occur between *two* NetBIOS machines—no more and no less. If a session service is interrupted, the client is supposed to store sufficient state information for it to re-establish the connection. However, in practice, this is rarely the case.

- Datagrams can be broadcast to multiple machines, but they are unreliable. In other words, there is no way for the source to know that the datagrams it sent have indeed arrived at their destinations.

Microsoft Implementations

With that amount of background, we can now talk about some of Microsoft's implementations of the preceding concepts in the CIFS/SMB networking world. And, as you might expect, there are some complex extensions to introduce as well.

Windows Domains

Recall that a workgroup is a collection of SMB computers that all reside on a subnet and subscribe to the same SMB group. A *Windows domain* goes a step further. It is a workgroup of SMB machines that has one addition: a server acting as a *domain controller.* You must have a domain controller in order to have a Windows domain.* Otherwise, it is only a workgroup. See Figure 1-11.

There are currently two separate protocols used by a domain controller (logon server): one for communicating with Windows 95/98 machines and one for communicating with Windows NT machines. While Samba currently implements the domain controller protocol for Windows 95/98 (which allows it to act as a domain controller for Windows 9x machines), it still does not fully support the protocol for Windows NT computers. However, the Samba team promises that support for the Windows NT domain controller protocol is forthcoming in Samba 2.1.

---

* Windows domains are called "Windows NT domains" by Microsoft because they assume that Windows NT machines will take the role of the domain controller. However, because Samba can perform this function as well, we'll simply call them "Windows domains" to avoid confusion.

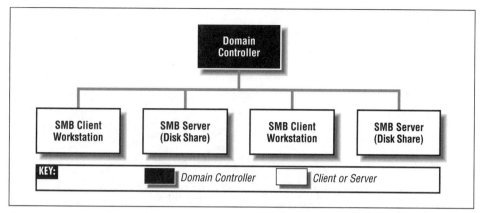

Figure 1-11. A simple Windows domain

 Why all the difficulty? The protocol that Windows domain controllers use to communicate with their clients and other domain controllers is proprietary and has not been released by Microsoft. This has
forced the Samba development team to reverse-engineer the domain
controller protocol to see which codes perform specific tasks.

Domain controllers

The domain controller is the nerve center of a Windows domain, much like an NIS
server is the nerve center of the Unix network information service. Domain controllers have a variety of responsibilities. One responsibility that you need to be
concerned with is *authentication.* Authentication is the process of granting or
denying a user access to a shared resource on another network machine, typically
through the use of a password.

Each domain controller uses a *security account manager* (SAM) to maintain a list
of username-password combinations. The domain controller then forms a central
repository of passwords that are tied to usernames (one password per user), which
is more efficient than each client machine maintaining hundreds of passwords for
every network resource available.

On a Windows domain, when a non-authenticated client requests access to a
server's shares, the server will turn around and ask the domain controller whether
that user is authenticated. If it is, the server will establish a session connection
with the access rights it has for that service and user. If not, the connection is
denied. Once a user is authenticated by the domain controller, a special authenticated token will be returned to the client so that the user will not need to relogin
to other resources on that domain. At this point, the user is considered "logged in"
to the domain itself. See Figure 1-12.

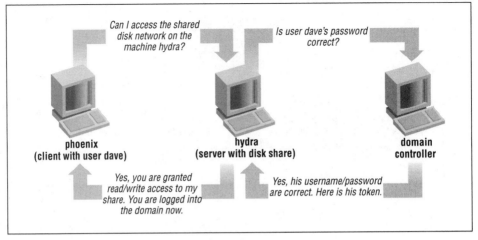

Figure 1-12. Using a domain controller for authentication

Primary and backup domain controllers

Redundancy is a key idea behind a Windows domain. The domain controller that is currently active on a domain is called the *primary domain controller* (PDC). There can be one or more *backup domain controllers* (BDCs) in the domain as well, which will take over in the event that the primary domain controller fails or becomes inaccessible. BDCs frequently synchronize their SAM data with the primary domain controller so that, if the need arises, any one of them can perform DC services transparently without impacting its clients. Note that BDCs, however, have only read-only copies of the SAM; they can update their data only by synchronizing with a PDC. A server in a Windows domain can use the SAM of any primary or backup domain controller to authenticate a user who attempts to access its resources and logon to the domain.

Note that in many aspects, the behaviors of a Windows workgroup and a Windows domain overlap. This is not accidental since the concept of Windows domains did not evolve until Windows NT 3.1 was introduced, and Windows domains were forced to remain backwards compatible with the workgroups present in Windows for Workgroups 3.1. The key thing to remember here is that a Windows domain is simply a Windows workgroup with one or more domain controllers added.

Samba can function as a primary domain controller for Windows 95/98 machines without any problems. However, Samba 2.0 can act as a primary domain controller only for authentication purposes; it currently cannot assume any other PDC responsibilities. (By the time you read this, Samba 2.1 may be available so you can use Samba as a PDC for NT clients.) Also, because of the closed protocol used by Microsoft to synchronize SAM data, Samba currently cannot serve as a backup domain controller.

Browsing

Browsing is a high-level answer to the user question: "What machines are out there on the Windows network?" Note that there is no connection with a World Wide Web browser, apart from the general idea of "discovering what's there." And, like the Web, what's out there can change without warning.

Before browsing, users had to know the name of the specific computer they wanted to connect to on the network, and then manually enter a UNC such as the following into an application or file manager to access resources:

```
\\HYDRA\network\
```

With browsing, however, you can examine the contents of a machine using a standard point-and-click GUI—in this case, the Network Neighborhood window in a Windows client.

Levels of browsing

As we hinted at the beginning of the chapter, there are actually two types of browsing that you will encounter in an SMB/CIFS network:

- Browsing a list of machines (with shared resources)
- Browsing the shared resources of a specific machine

Let's look at the first one. On each Windows workgroup (or domain) subnet, one computer has the responsibility of maintaining a list of the machines that are currently accessible through the network. This computer is called the *local master browser*, and the list that it maintains is called the *browse list*. Machines on a subnet use the browse list in order to cut down on the amount of network traffic generated while browsing. Instead of each computer dynamically polling to determine a list of the currently available machines, the computer can simply query the local master browser to obtain a complete, up-to-date list.

To browse the actual resources on a machine, a user must connect to the specific machine; this information cannot be obtained from the browse list. Browsing the list of resources on a machine can be done by clicking on the machine's icon when it is presented in the Network Neighborhood in Windows 95/98 or NT. As you saw at the opening of the chapter, the machine will respond with a list of shared resources that can be accessed if that user is successfully authenticated.

Each of the servers on a Windows workgroup is required to announce its presence to the local master browser after it has registered a NetBIOS name, and (theoretically) announce that it is leaving the workgroup when it is shut down. It is the local master browser's responsibility to record what the servers have announced. Note that the local master browser is not necessarily the same machine as a NetBIOS name server (NBNS), which we discussed earlier.

The Windows Network Neighborhood can behave oddly: until you select a particular machine to browse, the Network Neighborhood window may contain data that is not up-to-date. That means that the Network Neighborhood window can be showing machines that have crashed, or can be missing machines that haven't been noticed yet. Put succinctly, once you've selected a server and connected to it, you can be a lot more confident that the shares and printers really exist on the network.

Unlike the roles you've seen earlier, almost any Windows machine (NT Server, NT Workstation, 98, 95, or Windows 3.1 for Workgroups) can act as a local master browser. As with the domain controller, the local master browser can have one or more *backup browsers* on the local subnet that will take over in the event that the local master browser fails or becomes inaccessible. To ensure fluid operation, the local backup browsers will frequently synchronize their browse list with the local master browser. Let's update our Windows domain diagram to include both a local master and local backup browser. The result is shown in Figure 1-13.

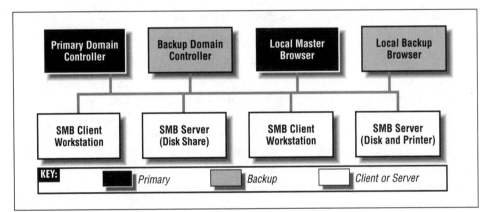

Figure 1-13. A Windows domain with a local master and local backup browser

Here is how to calculate the minimum number of backup browsers that will be allocated on a workgroup:

- If there are between 1 and 32 Windows NT workstations on the network, or between 1 and 16 Windows 95/98 machines on the network, the local master browser allocates one backup browser in addition to the local master browser.

- If the number of Windows NT workstations falls between 33 and 64, or the number of Windows 95/98 workstations falls between 17 and 32, the local master browser allocates two backup browsers.

- For each group of 32 NT workstations or 16 Windows 95/98 machines beyond this, the local master browser allocates another backup browser.

There is currently no upper limit on the number of backup browsers that can be allocated by the local master browser.

Browsing elections

Browsing is a critical aspect of any Windows workgroup. However, not everything runs perfectly on any network. For example, let's say that the Windows NT Server on the desk of a small company's CEO is the local master browser—that is, until he switches it off while plugging in his massage chair. At this point the Windows NT Workstation in the spare parts department might agree to take over the job. However, that computer is currently running a large, poorly written program that has brought its processor to its knees. The moral: browsing has to be very tolerant of servers coming and going. Because nearly every Windows machine can serve as a browser, there has to be a way of deciding at any time who will take on the job. This decision-making process is called an *election*.

An election algorithm is built into nearly all Windows operating systems such that they can each agree who is going to be a local master browser and who will be local backup browsers. An election can be forced at any time. For example, let's assume that the CEO has finished his massage and reboots his server. As the server comes online, it will announce its presence and an election will take place to see if the PC in the spare parts department should still be the master browser.

When an election is performed, each machine broadcasts via datagrams information about itself. This information includes the following:

- The version of the election protocol used
- The operating system on the machine
- The amount of time the client has been on the network
- The hostname of the client

These values determine which operating system has seniority and will fulfill the role of the local master browser. (Chapter 6, *Users, Security, and Domains*, describes the election process in more detail.) The architecture developed to achieve this is not elegant and has built-in security problems. While a browsing domain can be integrated with domain security, the election algorithm does not take into consideration which computers become browsers. Thus it is possible for any machine running a browser service to register itself as participating in the browsing election, and (after winning) being able to change the browse list. Nevertheless, browsing is a key feature of Windows networking and backwards compatibility requirements will ensure that it is in use for years to come.

Can a Windows Workgroup Span Multiple Subnets?

Yes, but most people who have done it have had their share of headaches. Spanning multiple subnets was not part of the initial design of Windows NT 3.5 or Windows for Workgroups. As a result, a Windows domain that spans two or more subnets is, in reality, the "gluing" together of two or more workgroups that share an identical name. The good news is that you can still use a primary domain controller to control authentication across each of the subnets. The bad news is that things are not as simple with browsing.

As mentioned previously, each subnet must have its own local master browser. When a Windows domain spans multiple subnets, a system administrator will have to assign one of the machines as the *domain master browser*. The domain master browser will keep a browse list for the entire Windows domain. This browse list is created by periodically synchronizing the browse lists of each of the local master browsers with the browse list of the domain master browser. After the synchronization, the local master browser and the domain master browser should contain identical entries. See Figure 1-14 for an illustration.

Sound good? Well, it's not quite nirvana for the following reasons:

- If it exists, a primary domain controller always plays the role of the domain master browser. By Microsoft design, the two always share the NetBIOS resource type <1B>, and (unfortunately) cannot be separated.

- Windows 95/98 machines cannot become *or even contact* a domain master browser. The Samba group feels that this is a marketing decision from Microsoft that forces customers to have at least one Windows NT workstation (or Samba server) on each subnet of a multi-subnet workgroup.

Each subnet's local master browser continues to maintain the browse list for its subnet, for which it becomes authoritative. So if a computer wants to see a list of servers within its own subnet, the local master browser of that subnet will be queried. If a computer wants to see a list of servers outside the subnet, it can still go only as far as the local master browser. This works because, at appointed intervals, the authoritative browse list of a subnet's local master browser is synchronized with the domain master browser, which is synchronized with the local master browser of the other subnets in the domain. This is called *browse list propagation*.

Samba can act as a domain master browser on a Windows domain if required. In addition, it can also act as a local master browser for a Windows subnet, synchronizing its browse list with the domain master browser.

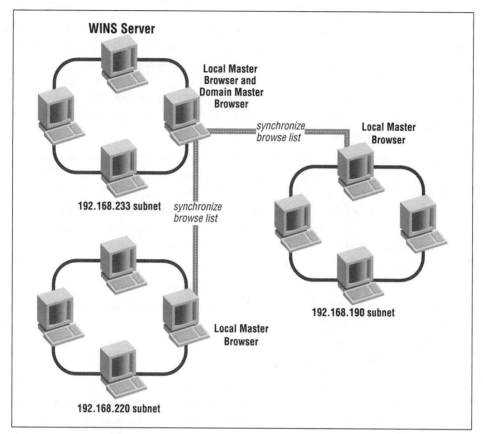

Figure 1-14. A workgroup that spans more than one subnet

The Windows Internet Name Service (WINS)

The Windows Internet Name Service (WINS) is Microsoft's implementation of a NetBIOS name server (NBNS). As such, WINS inherits much of NetBIOS's characteristics. First, WINS is flat; you can only have machines named **fred** or workgroups like CANADA or USA. In addition, WINS is dynamic: when a client first comes online, it is required to report its hostname, its address, and its workgroup to the local WINS server. This WINS server will retain the information so long as the client periodically refreshes its WINS registration, which indicates that it's still connected to the network. Note that WINS servers are not domain or workgroup specific; they can appear anywhere and serve anyone.

Multiple WINS servers can be set to synchronize with each other after a specified amount of time. This allows entries for machines that come online and offline on the network to propagate from one WINS server to another. While in theory this seems efficient, it can quickly become cumbersome if there are several WINS servers covering a network. Because WINS services can cross multiple subnets (you'll either hardcode the address of a WINS server in each of your clients or obtain it via DHCP), it is often more efficient to have each Windows client, no matter how many Windows domains there are, point themselves to the same WINS server. That way, there will only be one authoritative WINS server with the correct information, instead of several WINS servers continually struggling to synchronize themselves with the most recent changes.

The currently active WINS server is known as the *primary WINS server.* You can also install a secondary WINS server, which will take over in the event that the primary WINS server fails or becomes inaccessible. Note that there is no election to determine which machine becomes a primary or backup WINS server—the choice of WINS servers is static and must be predetermined by the system administrator. Both the primary and any backup WINS servers will synchronize their address databases on a periodic basis.

In the Windows family of operating systems, only an NT Workstation or an NT server can serve as a WINS server. Samba can also function as a primary WINS server, but not a secondary WINS server.

What Can Samba Do?

Whew! Bet you never thought Microsoft networks would be that complex, did you? Now, let's wrap up by showing where Samba can help out. Table 1-6 summarizes which roles Samba can and cannot play in a Windows NT Domain or Windows workgroup. As you can see, because many of the NT domain protocols are proprietary and have not been documented by Microsoft, Samba cannot properly synchronize its data with a Microsoft server and cannot act as a backup in most roles. However, with version 2.0.*x*, Samba does have limited support for the primary domain controller's authentication protocols and is gaining more functionality every day.

Table 1-6. Samba Roles (as of 2.0.4b)

Role	Can Perform?
File Server	Yes
Printer Server	Yes
Primary Domain Controller	Yes (Samba 2.1 or higher recommended)
Backup Domain Controller	No
Windows 95/98 Authentication	Yes
Local Master Browser	Yes
Local Backup Browser	No

Table 1-6. Samba Roles (as of 2.0.4b) (continued)

Role	Can Perform?
Domain Master Browser	Yes
Primary WINS Server	Yes
Secondary WINS Server	No

An Overview of the Samba Distribution

As mentioned earlier, Samba actually contains several programs that serve different but related purposes. Let's introduce each of them briefly, and show how they work together. The majority of the programs that come with the Samba distribution center on its two daemons. Let's take a refined look at the responsibilities of each daemon:

smbd

> The *smbd* daemon is responsible for managing the shared resources between the Samba server machine and its clients. It provides file, print, and browser services to SMB clients across one or more networks. *smdb* handles all notifications between the Samba server and the network clients. In addition, it is responsible for user authentication, resource locking, and data sharing through the SMB protocol.

nmbd

> The *nmbd* daemon is a simple nameserver that mimics the WINS and Net-BIOS name server functionality, as you might expect to encounter with the LAN Manager package. This daemon listens for nameserver requests and provides the appropriate information when called upon. It also provides browse lists for the Network Neighborhood and participates in browsing elections.

The Samba distribution also comes with a small set of Unix command-line tools:

smbclient

> An FTP-like Unix client that can be used to connect to Samba shares

smbtar

> A program for backing up data in shares, similar to the Unix *tar* command

nmblookup

> A program that provides NetBIOS over TCP/IP name lookups

smbpasswd

> A program that allows an administrator to change the encrypted passwords used by Samba

smbstatus

> A program for reporting the current network connections to the shares on a Samba server

testparm

A simple program to validate the Samba configuration file

testprns

A program that tests whether various printers are recognized by the *smbd* daemon

Each significant release of Samba goes through a significant exposure test before it's announced. In addition, it is quickly updated afterward if problems or unwanted side-effects are found. The latest stable distribution as of this writing is Samba 2.0.5, the long-awaited production version of Samba 2.0. This book focuses on the functionality supported in Samba 2.0, as opposed to the older 1.9.*x* versions of Samba, which are now obsolete.

How Can I Get Samba?

Samba is available in both binary and source format from a set of mirror sites across the Internet. The primary home site for Samba is located at *http://www. samba.org/.*

However, if you don't want to wait for packets to arrive all the way from Australia, mirror sites for Samba can be found at any of several locations on the Internet. A list of mirrors is given at the primary Samba home page.

In addition, a CD-ROM distribution is available in the back of this book. We strongly encourage you to start with the CD-ROM if this is your first time using Samba. We've included source and binaries up to Samba 2.0.5 with this book. In addition, several of the testing tools that we refer to through the book are conveniently packaged on the CD-ROM.

What's New in Samba 2.0?

Samba 2.0 was an eagerly-awaited package. The big additions to Samba 2.0 are more concrete support for NT Domains and the new Samba Web Administration Tool (SWAT), a browser-based utility for configuring Samba. However, there are dozens of other improvements that were introduced in the summer and fall of 1998.

NT Domains

Samba's support for NT Domains (starting with version 2.0.*x*) produced a big improvement: it allows SMB servers to use its authentication mechanisms, which is essential for future NT compatibility, and to support *NT domain logons*. Domain logons allow a user to log in to a Windows NT domain and use all the computers in the domain without logging into them individually. Previous to version 2.0.0, Samba supported Windows 95/98 logon services, but not NT domain logons. Although domain logons support is not complete is Samba 2.0, it is partially implemented.

Ease of Administration

SWAT, the Samba Web Administration Tool, makes it easy to set up a server and change its configuration, without giving up the simple text-based configuration file. SWAT provides a graphical interface to the resources that Samba shares with its clients. In addition, SWAT saves considerable experimentation and memory work in setting up or changing configurations across the network. You can even create an initial setup with SWAT and then modify the file later by hand, or vice versa. Samba will not complain.

On the compilation side, GNU *autoconf* is now used to make the task of initial compilation and setup easier so you can get to SWAT quicker.

Performance

There are major performance and scalability increases in Samba: the code has been reorganized and *nmbd* (the Samba name service daemon) heavily rewritten:

- Name/browsing service now supports approximately 35,000 simultaneous clients.

- File and print services support 500 concurrent users from a single medium-sized server without noticeable performance degradation.

- Linux/Samba on identical hardware now consistently performs better than NT Server. And best of all, Samba is improving.

- Improved "opportunistic" locking allows client machines to cache entire files locally, greatly improving speed without running the risk of accidentally over-writing the cached files.

More Features

There are several additional features in Samba 2.0. You can now have multiple Samba aliases on the same machine, each pretending to be a different server, a feature similar to virtual hosts in modern web servers. This allows a host to serve multiple departments and groups, or provide disk shares with normal username/password security while also providing printers to everyone without any security. Printing has been changed to make it easier for Unix System V owners: Samba can now find the available printers automatically, just as it does with Berkeley-style printing. In addition, Samba now has the capability to use multiple code pages, so it can be used with non-European languages, and to use the Secure Sockets Layer protocol (SSL) to encrypt all the data it sends across the Internet, instead of just passwords.*

Compatibility Improvements

At the same time as it's becoming more capable, Samba is also becoming more compatible with Windows NT. Samba has always supported Microsoft-style password encryption. It now provides tools and options for changing over to Microsoft encryption, and for keeping the Unix and Microsoft password files synchronized while doing so. Finally, a Samba master browser can be instructed to hunt down and synchronize itself with other SMB servers on different LANs, allowing SMB to work seamlessly across multiple networks. Samba uses a different method of accomplishing this from the Microsoft method, which is undocumented.

Smbwrapper

Finally, there is an entirely new version of the Unix client called *smbwrapper*. Instead of a kernel module that allows Linux to act as a Samba client, there is now a command-line entry to load the library that provides a complete SMB filesystem on some brands of Unix. Once loaded, the command `ls /smb` will list all the machines in your workgroup, and `cd /smb/`*server_name*`/`*share_name* will take you to a particular share (shared directory), similar to the Network File System (NFS). As of this writing, *smbwrapper* currently runs on Linux, Solaris, SunOS 4, IRIX, and OSF/1, and is expected to run on several more operating systems in the near future.

And That's Not All...

Samba is a wonderful tool with potential for even the smallest SMB/CIFS network. This chapter presented you with a thorough introduction to what Samba is, and more importantly, how it fits into a Windows network. The next series of chapters will help you set up Samba on both the Unix server side, where its two daemons reside, as well as configure the Windows 95, 98, and NT clients to work with Samba. Before long, the aches and pains of your heterogeneous network may seem like a thing of the past. Welcome to the wonderful world of Samba!

---

* If you reside in the United States, there are some federal rules and regulations dealing with strong cryptography. We'll talk about his later when we set up Samba and SSL in Appendix A, *Configuring Samba with SSL.*

2

Installing Samba on a Unix System

Now that you know what Samba can do for you and your users, it's time to get your own network set up. Let's start with the installation of Samba itself on a Unix system. When dancing the samba, one learns by taking small steps. It's just the same when installing Samba; we need to teach it step by step. This chapter will help you to start off on the right foot.

For illustrative purposes, we will be installing the 2.0.4 version of the Samba server on a Linux* system running version 2.0.31 of the kernel. However, the installation steps are the same for all of the platforms that Samba supports. A typical installation will take about an hour to complete, including downloading the source files and compiling them, setting up the configuration files, and testing the server.

Here is an overview of the steps:

1. Download the source or binary files.

2. Read the installation documentation.

3. Configure a makefile.

4. Compile the server code.

5. Install the server files.

6. Create a Samba configuration file.

7. Test the configuration file.

8. Start the Samba daemons.

9. Test the Samba daemons.

---

* If you haven't heard of Linux yet, then you're in for a treat. Linux is a freely distributed Unix-like operating system that runs on the Intel x86, Motorola PowerPC, and Sun Sparc platforms. The operating system is relatively easy to configure, extremely robust, and is gaining in popularity. You can get more information on the Linux operating system at *http://www.linux.org/*.

Downloading the Samba Distribution

If you want to get started quickly, the CD-ROM packaged with this book contains both the sources and binaries of Samba that were available as this book went to print. The CD is a mirror image of the files and directories on the Samba download server: *ftp.samba.org*.

On the other hand, if you want to download the latest version, the primary web site for the Samba software is *http://www.samba.org*. Once connected to this page, you'll see links to several Samba mirror sites across the world, both for the standard Samba web pages and sites devoted exclusively to downloading Samba. For the best performance, choose a site that is closest to your own geographic location.

The standard Samba web sites have Samba documentation and tutorials, mailing list archives, and the latest Samba news, as well as source and binary distributions of Samba. The download sites (sometimes called *FTP sites*) have only the source and binary distributions. Unless you specifically want an older version of the Samba server or are going to install a binary distribution, download the latest source distribution from the closest mirror site. This distribution is always named:

```
samba-latest.tar.gz
```

If you choose to use the version of Samba that is located on the CD-ROM packaged with this book, you should find the latest Samba distribution in the base directory.

Binary or Source?

Precompiled packages are also available for a large number of Unix platforms. These packages contain binaries for each of the Samba executables as well as the standard Samba documentation. Note that while installing a binary distribution can save you a fair amount of trouble and time, there are a couple of issues that you should keep in mind when deciding whether to use the binary or compile the source yourself:

- The binary packages can lag behind the latest version of the software by one or two (maybe more) minor releases, especially after a series of small changes and for less popular platforms. Compare the release notes for the source and binary packages to make sure that there aren't any new features that you need on your platform. This is especially true of the sources and binaries on the CD-ROM: at the time this book went to print, they were from the latest production release of Samba. However, development is ongoing, so the beta-test versions on the Internet will be newer.

- If you use a precompiled binary, you will need to ensure that you have the correct libraries required by the executables. On some platforms the executables are statically linked so this isn't an issue, but on modern Unix operating systems (e.g., Linux, SGI Irix, Solaris, HP-UX, etc.), libraries are often dynamically linked. This means that the binary looks for the right version of each library on your system, so you may have to install a new version of a library. The *README* file or *makefile* that accompanies the binary distribution should list any special requirements.*

  Many machines with shared libraries come with a nifty tool called *ldd*. This tool will tell you which libraries a specific binary requires and which libraries on the system satisfy that requirement. For example, checking the *smbd* program on our test machine gave us:

  ```
  $ ldd smbd
  libreadline.so.3 => /usr/lib/libreadline.so.3
  libdl.so.2 => /lib/libdl.so.2
  libcrypt.so.1 => /lib/libcrypt.so.1
  libc.so.6 => /lib/libc.so.6
  libtermcap.so.2 => /lib/libtermcap.so.2
  /lib/ld-linux.so.2 => /lib/ld-linux.so.2
  ```

  If there are any incompatibilities between Samba and specific libraries on your machine, the distribution-specific documentation should highlight those.

- Keep in mind that each binary distribution carries preset values about the target platform, such as default directories and configuration option values. Again, check the documentation and the makefile included in the source directory to see which directives and variables were used when the binary was compiled. In some cases, these will not be appropriate for your situation.

  A few configuration items can be reset with command-line options at runtime instead of at compile time. For example, if your binary tries to place any log, lock, or status files in the "wrong" place (for example, in */usr/local*), you can override this without recompiling.

One point worth mentioning is that the Samba source requires an ANSI C compiler. If you are on a platform with a non-ANSI compiler, such as the *cc* compiler on SunOS version 4, you'll have to install an ANSI-compliant compiler such as *gcc* before you do anything else.† If installing a compiler isn't something you want to wrestle with, you can start off with a binary package. However, for the most flexibility and compatibility on your system, we always recommend compiling from the latest source.

---

* This is especially true with programs that use *glibc-2.1* (which comes standard with Red Hat Linux 6). This library caused quite a consternation in the development community when it was released because it was incompatable with previous versions of *glibc*.

† *gcc* binaries are available for almost every modern machine. See *http://www.gnu.org/* for a list of sites with *gcc* and other GNU software.

Read the Documentation

This sounds like an obvious thing to say, but there have probably been times where you have uncompressed a package, blindly typed `configure`, `make`, and `make install`, and walked away to get another cup of coffee. We'll be the first to admit that we do that, many more times than we should. It's a bad idea— especially when planning a network with Samba.

Samba 2.0 automatically configures itself prior to compilation. This reduces the likelihood of a machine-specific problem, but there may be an option mentioned in the *README* file that you end up wishing for after Samba's been installed. With both source and binary packages you'll find a large number of documents in the *docs* directory, in a variety of formats. The most important files to look at in the distribution are:

```
WHATSNEW.txt
docs/textdocs/UNIX_INSTALL.txt
```

These files tell you what features you can expect in your Samba distribution, and will highlight common installation problems that you're likely to face. Be sure to look over both of them before you start the compilation process.

Configuring Samba

The source distribution of Samba 2.0 and above doesn't initially have a makefile. Instead, one is generated through a GNU *configure* script, which is located in the *samba-2.0.x/source/* directory. The *configure* script, which must be run as root, takes care of the machine-specific issues of building Samba. However, you still may want to decide on some global options. Global options can be set by passing options on the command-line:

```
# ./configure --with-ssl
```

For example, this will configure the Samba makefile with support for the Secure Sockets Layer (SSL) encryption protocol. If you would like a complete list of options, type the following:

```
#./configure --help
```

Each of these options enable or disable various features. You typically enable a feature by specifying the `--with-`*feature* option, which will cause the feature to be compiled and installed. Likewise, if you specify a `--without-`*feature* option, the feature will be disabled. As of Samba 2.0.5, each of the following features is disabled by default:

`--with-smbwrapper`

 Include SMB wrapper support, which allows executables on the Unix side to access SMB/CIFS filesystems as if they were regular Unix filesystems. We recommend using this option. However, at this time this book went to press, there were several incompatibilities between the *smbwrapper* package and the GNU *libc* version 2.1, and it would not compile on Red Hat 6.0. Look for more information on these incompatibilities on the Samba home page.

--with-afs

Include support of the Andrew Filesystem from Carnegie Mellon University. If you're going to serve AFS files via Samba, we recommend compiling Samba once first without enabling this feature to ensure that everything runs smoothly. Once that version is working smoothly, recompile Samba with this feature enabled and compare any errors you might receive against the previous setup.

--with-dfs

Include support for DFS, a later version of AFS, used by OSF/1 (Digital Unix). Note that this is *not* the same as Microsoft DFS, which is an entirely different filesystem. Again, we recommend compiling Samba once first without this feature to ensure that everything runs smoothly, then recompile with this feature to compare any errors against the previous setup.

--with-krb4=*base-directory*

Include support for Kerberos version 4.0, explicitly specifying the base directory of the distribution. Kerberos is a network security protocol from MIT that uses private key cryptography to provide strong security between nodes. Incidentally, Microsoft has announced that Kerberos 5.0 will be the standard authentication mechanism for Microsoft Windows 2000 (NT 5.0). However, the Kerberos 5.0 authentication mechanisms are quite different from the Kerberos 4.0 security mechanisms. If you have Kerberos version 4 on your system, the Samba team recommends that you upgrade and use the **--with-krb5** option (see the next item). You can find more information on Kerberos at *http://web.mit.edu/kerberos/www*.

--with-krb5=*base-directory*

Include support for Kerberos version 5.0, explicitly specifying the base directory of the distribution. Microsoft has announced that Kerberos 5.0 will be the standard authentication mechanism for Microsoft Windows 2000 (NT 5.0). However, there is no guarantee that Microsoft will not extend Kerberos for their own needs in the future. Currently, Samba's Kerberos support only uses a plaintext password interface and not an encrypted one. You can find more information on Kerberos at its home page: *http://web.mit.edu/kerberos/www*.

--with-automount

Include support for automounter, a feature often used on sites that offer NFS.

--with-smbmount

Include *smbmount* support, which is for Linux only. This feature wasn't being maintained at the time the book was written, so the Samba team made it an optional feature and provided *smbwrapper* instead. The *smbwrapper* feature works on more Unix platforms than *smbmount*, so you'll usually want to use --with-smbwrapper instead of this option.

--with-pam

Include support for pluggable authentication modules (PAM), an authentication feature common in the Linux operating system.

--with-ldap

Include support for the Lightweight Directory Access Protocol (LDAP). A future version of LDAP will be used in the Windows 2000 (NT 5.0) operating system; this Samba support is experimental. LDAP is a flexible client-server directory protocol that can carry information such as certificates and group memberships.*

--with-nis

Include support for getting password-file information from NIS (network yellow pages).

--with-nisplus

Include support for obtaining password-file information from NIS+, the successor to NIS.

--with-ssl

Include experimental support for the Secure Sockets Layer (SSL), which is used to provide encrypted connections from client to server. Appendix A, *Configuring Samba with SSL*, describes setting up Samba with SSL support.

--with-nisplus-home

Include support for locating which server contains a particular user's home directory and telling the client to connect to it. Requires --with-nis and, usually, --with-automounter.

--with-mmap

Include experimental memory mapping code. This is not required for fast locking, which already uses mmap or System V shared memory.

--with-syslog

Include support for using the SYSLOG utility for logging information generated from the Samba server. There are a couple of Samba configuration options that you can use to enable SYSLOG support; Chapter 4, *Disk Shares*, discusses these options.

---

* By *directory*, we don't mean a directory in a file system, but instead an indexed directory (such as a phone directory). Information is stored and can be easily retrieved in a public LDAP system.

`--with-netatalk`

Include experimental support for interoperating with the (Macintosh) Netatalk file server.

`--with-quotas`

Include disk-quota support.

Because each of these options is disabled by default, none of these features are essential to Samba. However, you may want to come back and build a modified version of Samba if you discover that you need one at a later time.

In addition, Table 2-1 shows some other parameters that you can give the *configure* script if you wish to store parts of the Samba distribution in different places, perhaps to make use of multiple disks or partitions. Note that the defaults sometimes refer to a prefix specified earlier in the table.

Table 2-1. Additional Configure Options

Option	Meaning	Default
`--prefix=`*directory*	Install architecture-independent files at the base directory specified.	*/usr/local/samba*
`--eprefix=`*directory*	Install architecture-dependent files at the base directory specified.	*/usr/local/samba*
`--bindir=`*directory*	Install user executables in the directory specified.	*eprefix/bin*
`--sbindir=`*directory*	Install administrator executables in the directory specified.	*eprefix/bin*
`--libexecdir=`*directory*	Install program executables in the directory specified.	*eprefix/ libexec*
`--datadir=`*directory*	Install read-only architecture independent data in the directory specified.	*prefix/share*
`--libdir=`*directory*	Install program libraries in the directory specified.	*eprefix/lib*
`--includedir=`*directory*	Install package include files in the directory specified.	*prefix/include*
`--infodir=`*directory*	Install additional information files in the directory specified.	*prefix/info*
`--mandir=`*directory*	Install manual pages in the directory specified.	*prefix/man*

Again, before running the *configure* script, it is important that you are the root user on the system. Otherwise, you may get a warning such as:

```
configure: warning: running as non-root will disable some tests
```

You don't want any test to be disabled when the Samba makefile is being created; this leaves the potential for errors down the road when compiling or running Samba on your system.

Here is a sample execution of the *configure* script, which creates a Samba 2.0.4 makefile for the Linux platform. Note that you must run the configure script in the *source* directory, and that several lines from the middle of the excerpt have been omitted:

```
# cd samba-2.0.4b/source/
# ./configure | tee mylog

loading cache ./config.cache
checking for gcc... (cached) gcc
checking whether the C compiler (gcc -O ) works... yes
checking whether the C compiler (gcc -O ) is a cross-compiler... no
checking whether we are using GNU C... (cached) yes
checking whether gcc accepts -g... (cached) yes
checking for a BSD compatible install... (cached) /usr/bin/install -c

...(content omitted)...

checking configure summary
configure OK
creating ./config.status
creating include/stamp-h
creating Makefile
creating include/config.h
```

In general, any message from *configure* that doesn't begin with the words **checking** or **creating** is an error; it often helps to redirect the output of the configure script to a file so you can quickly search for errors, as we did with the **tee** command above. If there was an error during configuration, more detailed information about it can be found in the *config.log* file, which is written to the local directory by the *configure* script.

If the configuration works, you'll see a **checking configure summary** message followed by a **configure OK** message and four or five file creation messages. So far, so good.... Next step: compiling.

Compiling and Installing Samba

At this point you should be ready to build the Samba executables. Compiling is also easy: in the *source* directory, type **make** on the command line. The *make* utility will produce a stream of explanatory and success messages, beginning with:

```
Using FLAGS = -O -Iinclude ...
```

This build includes compiles for both *smbd* and *nmbd*, and ends in a linking command for *bin/make_printerdef*. For example, here is a sample make of Samba version 2.0.4 on a Linux server:

```
# make
Using FLAGS = -O -Iinclude -I./include -I./ubiqx -I./smbwrapper -DSMBLOGFILE="/
usr/local/samba/var/log.smb" -DNMBLOGFILE="/usr/local/samba/var/log.nmb" -
DCONFIGFILE="/usr/local/samba/lib/smb.conf" -DLMHOSTSFILE="/usr/local/samba/lib/
lmhosts"  -DSWATDIR="/usr/local/samba/swat" -DSBINDIR="/usr/local/samba/bin" -
DLOCKDIR="/usr/local/samba/var/locks" -DSMBRUN="/usr/local/samba/bin/smbrun" -
DCODEPAGEDIR="/usr/local/samba/lib/codepages" -DDRIVERFILE="/usr/local/samba/lib/
printers.def" -DBINDIR="/usr/local/samba/bin" -DHAVE_INCLUDES_H -DPASSWD_
PROGRAM="/bin/passwd" -DSMB_PASSWD_FILE="/usr/local/samba/private/smbpasswd"
Using FLAGS32 =  -O -Iinclude -I./include -I./ubiqx -I./smbwrapper  -
DSMBLOGFILE="/usr/local/samba/var/log.smb" -DNMBLOGFILE="/usr/local/samba/var/log.
nmb" -DCONFIGFILE="/usr/local/samba/lib/smb.conf" -DLMHOSTSFILE="/usr/local/samba/
lib/lmhosts"   -DSWATDIR="/usr/local/samba/swat" -DSBINDIR="/usr/local/samba/bin"
-DLOCKDIR="/usr/local/samba/var/locks" -DSMBRUN="/usr/local/samba/bin/smbrun" -
DCODEPAGEDIR="/usr/local/samba/lib/codepages" -DDRIVERFILE="/usr/local/samba/lib/
printers.def" -DBINDIR="/usr/local/samba/bin" -DHAVE_INCLUDES_H -DPASSWD_
PROGRAM="/bin/passwd" -DSMB_PASSWD_FILE="/usr/local/samba/private/smbpasswd"
Using LIBS = -lreadline -ldl  -lcrypt -lpam
Compiling smbd/server.c
Compiling smbd/files.c
Compiling smbd/chgpasswd.c

...(content omitted)...

Compiling rpcclient/cmd_samr.c
Compiling rpcclient/cmd_reg.c
Compiling rpcclient/cmd_srvsvc.c
Compiling rpcclient/cmd_netlogon.c
Linking bin/rpcclient
Compiling utils/smbpasswd.c
Linking bin/smbpasswd
Compiling utils/make_smbcodepage.c
Linking bin/make_smbcodepage
Compiling utils/nmblookup.c
Linking bin/nmblookup
Compiling utils/make_printerdef.c
Linking bin/make_printerdef
```

If you encounter problems when compiling, check the Samba documentation to see if it is easily fixable. Another possibility is to search or post to the Samba mailing lists, which are given at the end of Appendix D, *Summary of Samba Daemons and Commands*, and on the Samba home page. Most compilation issues are system specific and almost always easy to overcome.

Now that the files have been compiled, you can install them into the directories you identified with the command:

```
# make install
```

If you happen to be upgrading, your old Samba files will be saved with the extension *.old*, and you can go back to that previous version with the command **make revert**. After doing a **make install**, you should copy the *.old* files (if they exist) to a new location or name. Otherwise, the next time you install Samba, the original *.old* will be overwritten without warning and you could lose your earlier version. If you configured Samba to use the default locations for files, the new files will be installed in the directories listed in Table 2-2. Remember that you need to perform the installation from an account that has write privileges on these target directories; this is typically the root account.

Table 2-2. Samba Installation Directories

Directory	Description
/usr/local/samba	Main tree
/usr/local/samba/bin	Binaries
/usr/local/samba/lib	*smb.conf, lmhosts*, configuration files, etc.
/usr/local/samba/man	Samba documentation
/usr/local/samba/private	Samba encrypted password file
/usr/local/samba/swat	SWAT files
/usr/local/samba/var	Samba log files, lock files, browse list info, shared memory files, process ID files

Throughout the remainder of the book, we occasionally refer to the location of the main tree as **samba_dir**. In most configurations, this is the base directory of the installed Samba package: */usr/local/samba*.

Watch out if you've made */usr* a read-only partition. You will want to put the logs, locks, and password files somewhere else.

Here is the installation that we performed on our machine. You can see that we used */usr/local/samba* as the base directory for the distribution (e.g., **samba_dir**):

```
# make install
Using FLAGS = -O -Iinclude -I./include -I./ubiqx -I./smbwrapper  -DSMBLOGFILE="/
usr/local/samba/var/log.smb" -DNMBLOGFILE="/usr/local/samba/var/log.nmb" -
DCONFIGFILE="/usr/local/samba/lib/smb.conf" -
```

...(content omitted)...

```
The binaries are installed. You may restore the old binaries
(if there were any) using the command "make revert". You may
uninstall the binaries using the command "make uninstallbin"
or "make uninstall" to uninstall binaries, man pages and shell
scripts.
```

...(content omitted)...

```
=============================================================
The SWAT files have been installed. Remember to read the
README for information on enabling and using SWAT.
=============================================================
```

If the last message is about SWAT, you've successfully installed all the files. Congratulations! You now have Samba on your system!

Final Installation Steps

There are a couple of final steps to perform. Specifically, add the Samba Web Administration Tool (SWAT) to the */etc/services* and */etc/inetd.conf* configuration files. SWAT runs as a daemon under *inetd* and provides a forms-based editor in your web browser for creating and modifying SMB configuration files.

1. To add SWAT, add the following line to the end of the */etc/services* file:

   ```
   swat    901/tcp
   ```

2. Add these lines to */etc/inetd.conf*. (Check your *inetd.conf* manual page to see the exact format of the *inetd.conf* file if it differs from the following example.) Don't forget to change the path to the SWAT binary if you installed it in a different location from the default */usr/local/samba*.

   ```
   swat    stream tcp nowait.400  root  /usr/local/samba/bin/swat  swat
   ```

And that's pretty much it for the installation. Before you can start up Samba, however, you need to create a configuration file for it.

A Basic Samba Configuration File

The key to configuring Samba is its lone configuration file: *smb.conf.* This configuration file can be very simple or extremely complex, and the rest of this book is devoted to helping you get deeply personal with this file. For now, however, we'll show you how to set up a single file service, which will allow you to fire up the Samba daemons and see that everything is running as it should be. In later chapters, you will see how to configure Samba for more complicated and interesting tasks.

The installation process does not automatically create an *smb.conf* configuration file, although several example files are included in the Samba distribution. To test the server software, though, we'll use the following file. It should be named *smb. conf* and placed in the */usr/local/samba/lib* directory.*

```
[global]
    workgroup = SIMPLE
```

---

* If you did not compile Samba, but instead downloaded a binary, check with the documentation for the package to find out where it expects the *smb.conf* file. If Samba came preinstalled with your Unix system, there is probably already an *smb.conf* file somewhere on your system.

```
[test]
    comment = For testing only, please
    path = /export/samba/test
    read only = no
    guest ok = yes
```

This brief configuration file tells the Samba server to offer the directory */export/samba/test* on the server as an SMB/CIFS share called **test**. The server also becomes part of the named workgroup SIMPLE, which each of the clients must also be a part of. (Use your own workgroup here if you already know what it is.) We'll use the [test] share in the next chapter to set up the Windows clients. For now, you can complete the setup by performing the following commands as root on your Unix server:

```
# mkdir /export/samba/test
# chmod 777 /export/samba/test
```

We should point out that in terms of system security, this is the worst setup possible. For the moment, however, we only wish to test Samba, so we'll leave security out of the picture. In addition, there are some encrypted password issues that we will encounter with Windows clients later on, so this setup will afford us the least amount of headaches.

 If you are using Windows 98 or Windows NT Service Pack 3 or above, you must add the following entry to the [global] section of the Samba configuration file: **encrypt passwords = yes**. In addition, you must use the *smbpasswd* program (typically located in */usr/local/samba/bin/*) to reenter the username/password combinations of those users on the Unix server who should be able to access shares into Samba's encrypted client database. For example, if you wanted to allow Unix user **steve** to access shares from an SMB client, you could type: **smbpasswd -a steve**. The first time a user is added, the program will output an error saying that the encrypted password database does not exist. Don't worry, it will then create the database for you. Make sure that the username/password combinations that you add to the encrypted database match the usernames and passwords that you intend to use on the Windows client side.

Using SWAT

With Samba 2.0, creating a configuration file is even easier than writing a configuration file by hand. You can use your browser to connect to *http://localhost:901*, and log on as the root account, as shown in Figure 2-1.

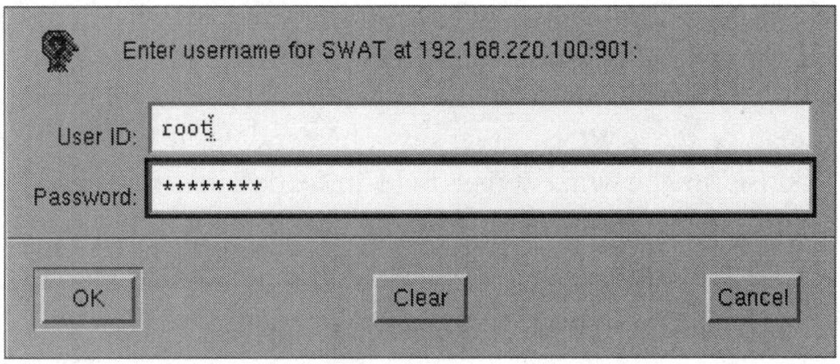

Figure 2-1. SWAT login

After logging in, press the GLOBALS button at the top of the screen. You should
see the Global Variables page shown in Figure 2-2.

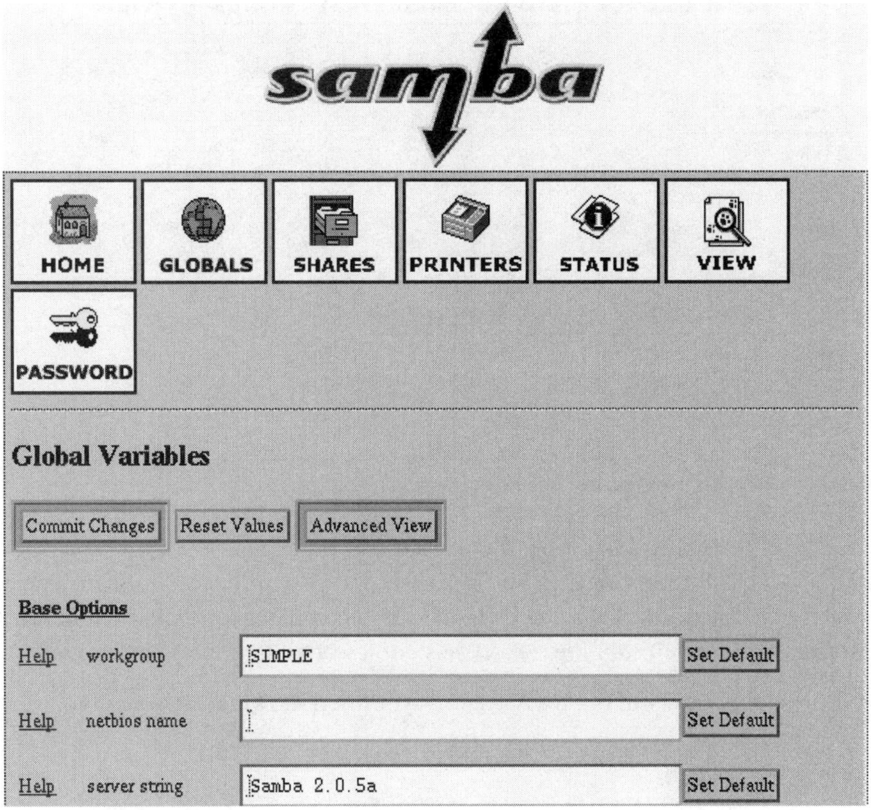

Figure 2-2. SWAT Global Variables page

In this example, set the workgroup field to SIMPLE and the security field to USER. The only other option you need to change from the menu is one determining which system on the LAN resolves NetBIOS addresses; this system is called the *WINS server*. At the very bottom of the page, set the wins support field to Yes, unless you already have a WINS server on your network. If you do, put the WINS server's IP address in the wins server field instead. Then return to the top and press the Commit Changes button to write the changes out to the *smb.conf* file.

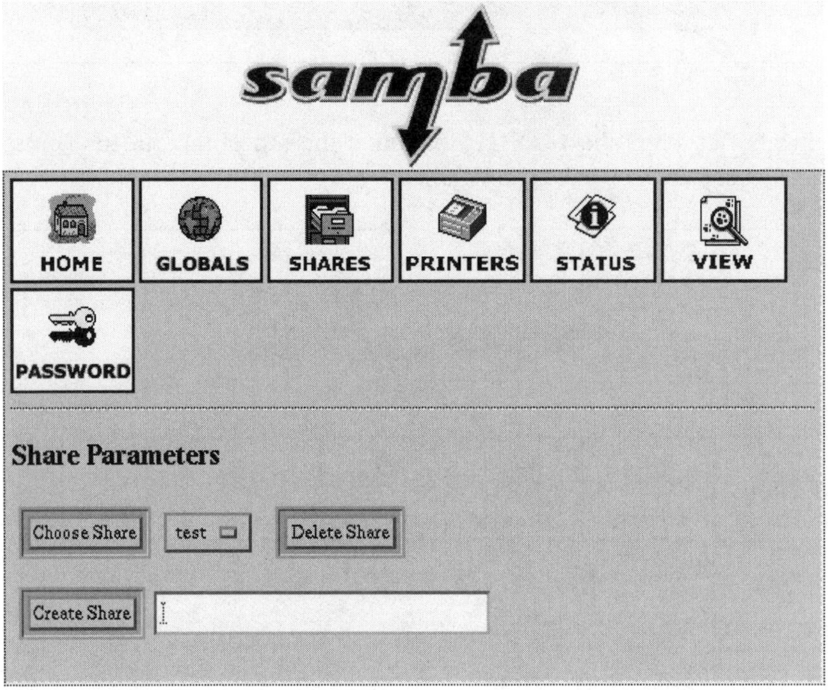

Figure 2-3. SWAT Share Creation screen

Next, press the Shares icon. You should see a page similar to Figure 2-3. Choose Test in the field beside the Choose Share button. You will see the Share Parameters screen, as shown in Figure 2-4. We added a comment to remind us that this is a test share in the *smb.conf* file. SWAT has copies of all that information here.

If you press the View button, SWAT shows you the following *smb.conf* file:

```
# Samba config file created using SWAT
# from localhost (127.0.0.1)
# Date: 1998/11/27 15:42:40

# Global parameters
        workgroup = SIMPLE
```

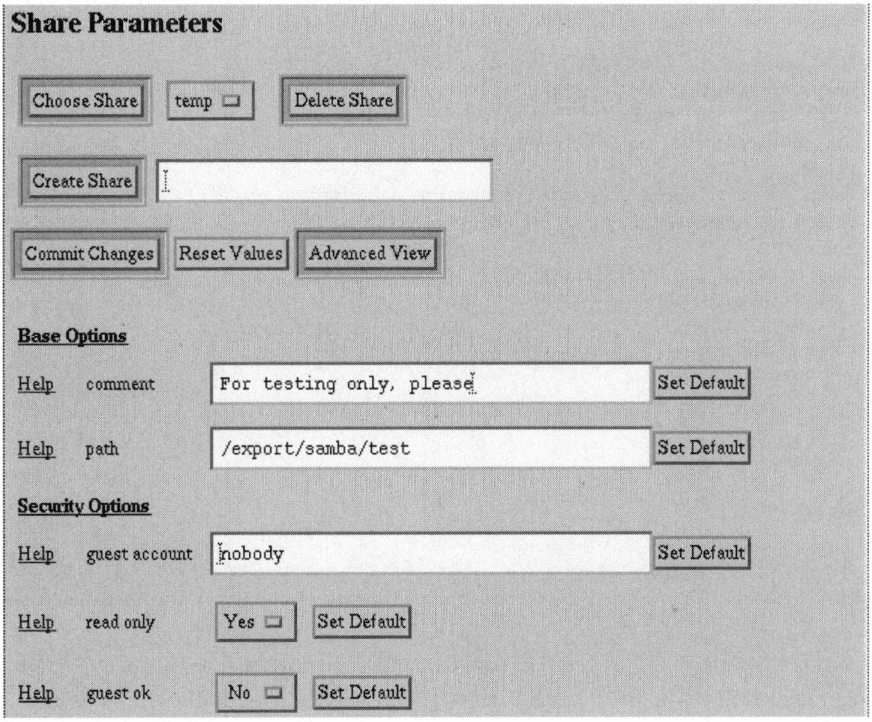

Figure 2-4. SWAT Share Parameters screen

```
[test]
        comment = For testing only, please
        path = /export/samba/test
        read only = no
        guest ok = yes
```

Once this configuration file is completed, you can skip the next step because the output of SWAT is guaranteed to be syntactically correct.

Testing the Configuration File

If you didn't use SWAT to create your configuration file, you should probably test it to ensure that it is syntactically correct. It may seem silly to run a test program against an eight-line configuration file, but it's good practice for the real ones that we'll be writing later on.

The test parser, *testparm*, examines an *smb.conf* file for syntax errors and reports any it finds along with a list of the services enabled on your machine. An example follows; you'll notice that in our haste to get the server running we mistyped

workgroup as **workgrp** (the output is often lengthy, so we recommend capturing the last parts with the **tee** command):

```
Load smb config files from smb.conf
Unknown parameter encountered: "workgrp"
Ignoring unknown parameter "workgrp"
Processing section "[test]"
Loaded services file OK.
Press enter to see a dump of your service definitions
# Global parameters
[global]
        workgroup = WORKGROUP
        netbios name =
        netbios aliases =
        server string = Samba 2.0.5a
        interfaces =
        bind interfaces only = No
```

...(content omitted)...

```
[test]
        comment = For testing only, please
    path = /export/samba/test
        read only = No
        guest ok = Yes
```

The interesting parts are at the top and bottom. The top of the output will flag any syntax errors that you may have made, and the bottom lists the services that the server thinks it should offer. A word of advice: make sure that you and the server have the same expectations.

If everything looks good, then you are ready to fire up the server daemons!

Starting the Samba Daemons

There are two Samba processes, *smbd* and *nmbd*, that need to be running for Samba to work correctly. There are three ways to start:

- By hand
- As stand-alone daemons
- From *inetd*

Starting the Daemons by Hand

If you're in a hurry, you can start the Samba daemons by hand. As root, simply enter the following commands:

```
# /usr/local/samba/bin/smbd -D
# /usr/local/samba/bin/nmbd -D
```

At this point, Samba will be running on your system and will be ready to accept connections.

Stand-alone Daemons

To run the Samba processes as stand-alone daemons, you need to add the commands listed in the previous section to your standard Unix startup scripts. This varies depending on whether you have a BSD-style Unix system or a System V Unix.

BSD Unix

WIth a BSD-style Unix, you need to append the following code to the *rc.local* file, which is typically found in the */etc* or */etc/rc.d* directories:

```
if [ -x /usr/local/samba/bin/smbd]; then
    echo "Starting smbd..."
    /usr/local/samba/bin/smbd -D
    echo "Starting nmbd..."
    /usr/local/samba/bin/nmbd -D
fi
```

This code is very simple; it checks to see if the *smbd* file has execute permissions on it, and if it does, it starts up each of the Samba daemons on system boot.

System V Unix

With System V, things can get a little more complex. System V typically uses scripts to start and stop daemons on the system. Hence, you need to instruct Samba how to operate when it starts and when it stops. You can modify the contents of the */etc/rc.local* directory and add something similar to the following program entitled *smb*:

```
#!/bin/sh

# Contains the "killproc" function on Red Hat Linux
./etc/rc.d/init.d/functions

PATH="/usr/local/samba/bin:$PATH"

case $1 in
    'start')
        echo "Starting smbd..."
        smbd -D
        echo "Starting nmbd..."
        nmbd -D
        ;;
    'stop')
        echo "Stopping smbd and nmbd..."
        killproc smbd
        killproc nmbd
        rm -f /usr/local/samba/var/locks/smbd.pid
```

```
        rm -f /usr/local/samba/var/locks/nmbd.pid
        ;;
*)
        echo "usage: smb {start|stop}"
        ;;
esac
```

With this script, you can start and stop the SMB service with the following commands:

```
# /etc/rc.local/smb start
Starting smbd...
Starting nmbd...
# /etc/rc.local/smb stop
Stopping smbd and nmbd...
```

Starting From Inetd

The *inetd* daemon is a Unix system's Internet "super daemon." It listens on TCP ports defined in */etc/services* and executes the appropriate program for each port, which is defined in */etc/inetd.conf.* The advantage of this scheme is that you can have a large number of daemons ready to answer queries, but they don't all have to be running. Instead, the *inetd* daemon listens in places of all the others. The penalty is a small overhead cost of creating a new daemon process, and the fact that you need to edit two files rather than one to set things up. This is handy if you have only one or two users or your machine has too many daemons already. It's also easier to perform an upgrade without disturbing an existing connection.

If you wish to start from *inetd*, first open */etc/services* in your text editor. If you don't already have them defined, add the following two lines:

```
netbios-ssn     139/tcp
netbios-ns      137/udp
```

Next, edit */etc/inetd.conf.* Look for the following two lines and add them if they don't exist. If you already have **smbd** and **nmbd** lines in the file, edit them to point at the new *smbd* and *nmbd* you've installed. Your brand of Unix may use a slightly different syntax in this file; use the existing entries and the *inetd.conf* manual page as a guide:

```
netbios-ssn stream tcp nowait root /usr/local/samba/bin/smbd smbd
netbios-ns  dgram  udp wait   root /usr/local/samba/bin/nmbd nmbd
```

Finally, kill any *smbd* or *nmbd* processes and send the *inetd* process a hangup (HUP) signal. (The *inetd* daemon rereads its configuration file on a HUP signal.) To do this, use the **ps** command to find its process ID, then signal it with the following command:

```
# kill -HUP process_id
```

After that, Samba should be up and running.

Testing the Samba Daemons

It's hard to believe, but we're nearly done with the Samba server setup. All that's left to do is to make sure that everything is working as we think it should. A convenient way to do this is to use the *smbclient* program to examine what the server is offering to the network. If everything is set up properly, you should be able to do the following:

```
# smbclient -U% -L localhost

Added interface ip=192.168.220.100 bcast=192.168.220.255 nmask=255.255.255.0
Domain=[SIMPLE] OS=[Unix] Server=[Samba 2.0.5a]

        Sharename       Type        Comment
        ---------       ----        -------
        test            Disk        For testing only, please
        IPC$            IPC         IPC Service (Samba 2.0.5a)


        Server                      Comment
        ---------                   -------
        HYDRA                       Samba 2.0.5a


        Workgroup                   Master
        ---------                   -------
        SIMPLE                      HYDRA
```

If there is a problem, don't panic! Try to start the daemons manually, and check the system output or the debug files at */usr/local/samba/var/log.smb* to see if you can determine what happened. If you think it may be a more serious problem, skip to Chapter 7, *Printing and Name Resolution*, for help on troubleshooting the Samba daemons.

If it worked, congratulations! You now have successfully set up the Samba server with a disk share. It's a simple one, but we can use it to set up and test the Windows 95 and NT clients in the next chapter. Then we will start making it more interesting by adding services such as home directories, printers, and security, and seeing how to integrate the server into a larger Windows domain.

3

Configuring Windows Clients

You'll be glad to know that configuring Windows to use your new Samba server is quite simple. SMB is Microsoft's native language for resource sharing on a local area network, so much of the installation and setup on the Windows client side has been taken care of already. The primary issues that we will cover in this chapter involve communication and coordination between Windows and Unix, two completely different operating systems.

Samba uses TCP/IP to talk to its clients on the network. If you aren't already using TCP/IP on your Windows computers, this chapter will show you how to install it. Then you'll need to configure your Windows machines to operate on a TCP/IP network. Once these two requirements have been taken care of, we can show how to access a shared disk on the Samba server.

This chapter is divided into three sections. The first section covers setting up Windows 95/98 computers while the second covers Windows NT 4.0 machines. The final section provides some prerequisite information on how SMB connections are made from Windows clients and servers, which is useful as we move into the later chapters of the book.

Setting Up Windows 95/98 Computers

Unfortunately, Windows 95/98 wasn't designed for a PC to have more than one user; that concept is more inherent to a Unix operating system or Windows NT. However, Windows 95/98 does have *limited* support for multiple users: if you tell it, the operating system will keep a separate profile (desktop layout) and password file for each user. This is a far cry from true multiuser security. In other words, Windows 95/98 won't try to keep one user from destroying the work of another on the local hard drive like Unix, but profiles are a place to start.

Accounts and Passwords

The first thing we need to do is to tell Windows to keep user profiles separate, and to collect usernames and passwords to authenticate anyone trying to access a Samba share. We do so via the Password settings in the Control Panel. If you are not familiar with the Windows Control Panel, you can access it by choosing the Settings menu item from the pop-up menu of the Start button in the lower-left corner of the screen. Alternatively, you'll find it as a folder under the icon in the upper-left corner that represents your computer and is typically labeled My Computer.

After selecting the Passwords icon in the Control Panel, click on the User Profiles tab on the far right. You should see the dialog box shown in Figure 3-1. Then click the lower of the two radio buttons that starts "Users can customize their preferences...." This causes Windows to store a separate profile for each user, and saves the username and password you provide, which it will use later when it connects to an SMB/CIFS server. Finally, check *both* the options under the User Profile Settings border, as shown in the figure.

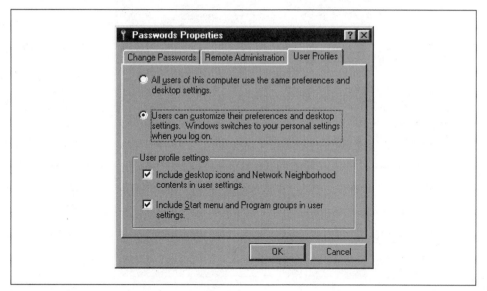

Figure 3-1. The Passwords Properties panel

The next step is to select the Change Passwords tab on the left side of the dialog box. In order for Samba to allow you access to its shares, the username and password you give to Windows must match the account and password on the Samba server. If you don't have this tab in your dialog box, don't worry; it's probably because you haven't given yourself a Windows username and password yet. Simply click the OK button at the bottom and respond Yes when Windows asks to reboot. Then, skip down to the section entitled "Logging in for the first time."

Changing the Windows password

After selecting the Change Passwords tab, the dialog box in Figure 3-2 will appear.

Figure 3-2. The Change Passwords tab

Select the Change Windows Password button. The Change Windows Password dialog box should appear, as shown in Figure 3-3. From here, you can change your password to match the password of the account on the Samba server through which you intend to log in.

Figure 3-3. The Change Windows Password dialog box

Logging in for the first time

If you didn't have a Change Passwords tab in the Passwords Properties window, then after Windows has finished rebooting, it will ask you to log in with a username and a password. Give yourself the same username and password that you have on the Samba server. After confirming your new username and password, or if you already have one, Windows should ask you if you want to have a profile, using the dialog shown in Figure 3-4.

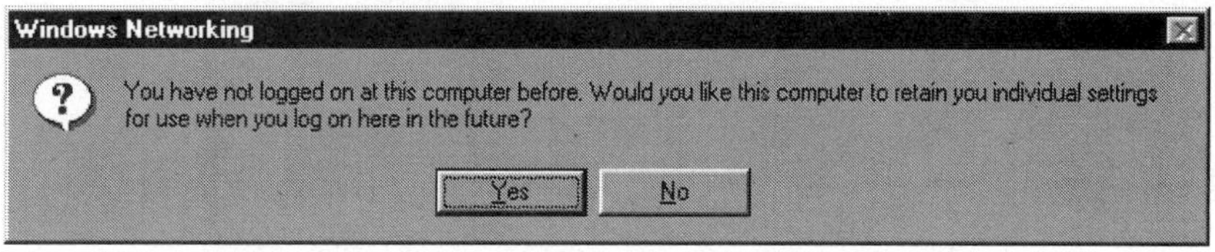

Figure 3-4. Windows Networking profiles

Answer Yes, upon which Windows will create a separate profile and password file for you and save a copy of your password in the file. Now when you connect to Samba, Windows will send its password, which will be used to authenticate you for each share. We won't worry about profiles for the moment; we'll cover them in Chapter 6, *Users, Security, and Domains*. We should point out, however, that there is a small security risk: someone can steal the password file and decrypt the passwords because it's weakly encrypted. Unfortunately, there isn't a solution to this with Windows 95/98. In Windows 2000 (NT 5.0), the password encryption should be replaced with a much better algorithm.

Setting Up the Network

The next thing we need to do is make sure we have the TCP/IP networking protocol set up correctly. To do this, double-click on the Network icon in the Control Panel. You should see the network configuration dialog box, as shown in Figure 3-5.

Microsoft networking works by binding specific protocols, such as IPX or TCP/IP, to a specific hardware device, such as an Ethernet card or a dialup connection. By routing a protocol through a hardware device, the machine can act as a client or server for a particular type of network. For Samba, we are interested in binding the TCP/IP protocol through a networking device, making the machine a client for Microsoft networks. Thus, when the dialog box appears, you should see at least the Client for Microsoft Networks component installed on the machine, and hopefully a networking device (preferably an Ethernet card) bound to the TCP/IP protocol. If there is only one networking hardware device, you'll see the TCP/IP protocol listed below that device. If it appears similar to Figure 3-5, the protocol is bound to the device.

You may also see "File and printer sharing for Microsoft Networks," which is useful. In addition, you might see NetBEUI or Novell Networking, which are standard

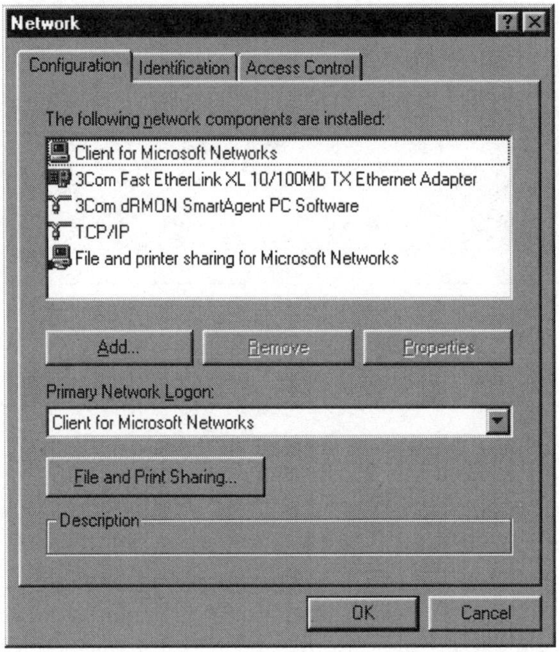

Figure 3-5. The Windows 95/98 Network panel

with Windows installations but undesirable when TCP/IP is running. Remove Net-BEUI if you possibly can—it's unnecessary and makes debugging Windows browsing difficult. If you don't have any Novell servers on your network, you can remove Novell (IPX/SPX) as well.

Adding TCP/IP

If you don't see TCP/IP listed at all, you'll need to install the protocol. If you already have TCP/IP, skip this section, and continue with the section "Setting Your Name and Workgroup," later in this chapter.

Installing TCP/IP isn't difficult since Microsoft distributes its own version of TCP/IP for free on their installation CD-ROM. You can add the protocol by clicking on the Add button below the component window. Indicate that you wish to add a specific protocol by selecting Protocol and clicking Add... on the following dialog box, which should look similar to Figure 3-6.

After that, select the protocol TCP/IP from manufacturer Microsoft, as shown in Figure 3-7, then click OK. After doing so, you will be returned to the network dialog. Click OK there to close the dialog box, upon which Windows will install the necessary components from disk and reboot the machine.

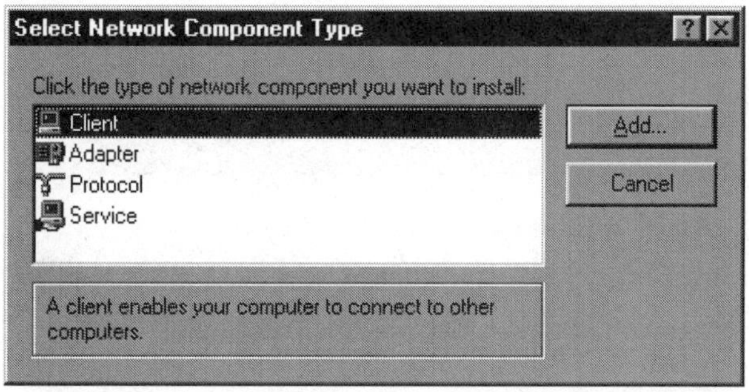

Figure 3-6. Selecting a protocol to install

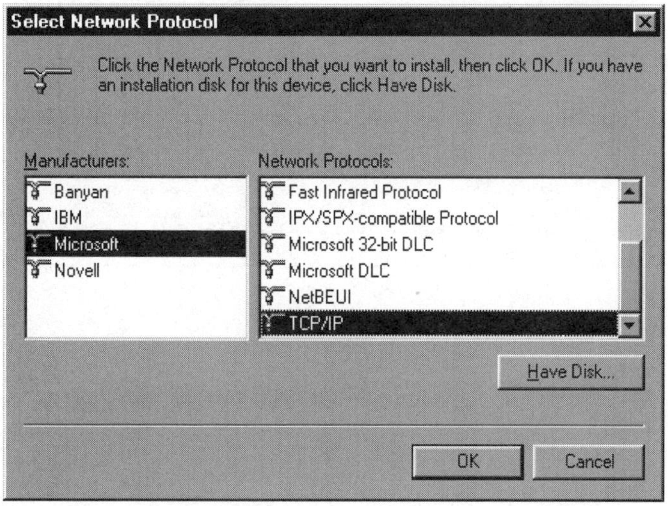

Figure 3-7. Selecting a protocol to install

Configuring TCP/IP

If you have more than one networking device (for example, both an Ethernet card and a dialup networking modem), each appropriate hardware device should be "linked" to the TCP/IP protocol with an arrow, as shown in Figure 3-8. Select the TCP/IP protocol linked to the networking device that will be accessing the Samba network. When it is highlighted, click the Properties button.

After doing so, the TCP/IP Properties panel for that device is displayed, as shown in Figure 3-9.

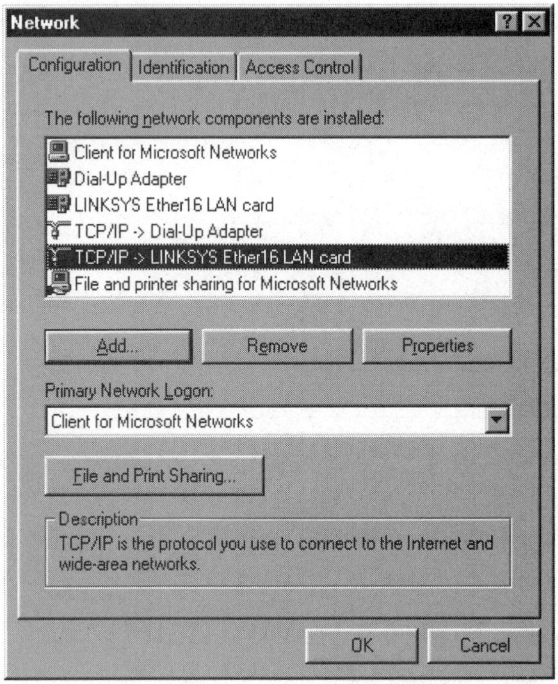

Figure 3-8. Selecting the correct TCP/IP protocol

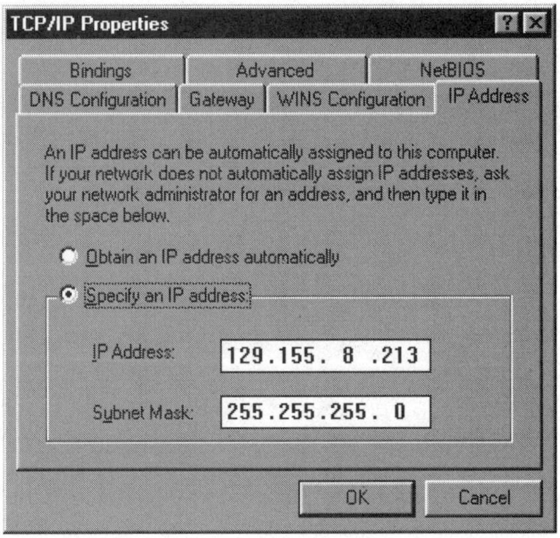

Figure 3-9. STCP/IP Properties panel

There are seven tabs near the top of this panel, and you will need to configure four of them:

- IP address

- DNS configuration

- WINS configuration

- Bindings

IP Address tab

The IP Address tab is shown in Figure 3-9. Press the "Specify an IP address" radio button and enter the client's address and subnet mask in the space provided. You or your network manager should have selected an address for the machine. The values should place the computer on the same subnet as the Samba server. For example, if the server's address is 192.168.236.86, and its network mask 255.255. 255.0, you might use address 192.168.236.10 (if it is available) for the Windows 98 computer, along with the same netmask as the server. If you already use DHCP on your network to provide IP addresses to Windows machines, select the "Obtain an IP address automatically" button.

DNS Configuration tab

Domain Name Service (DNS) is responsible for translating Internet computer names such as *hobbes.example.com* into machine-readable IP addresses such as 192.168.236.10. There are two ways to accomplish this on a Windows 98 machine: you can specify a server to do the translation for you or you can keep a local list of name/address pairs to refer to.

Networks that are connected to the Internet typically use a server, since the hosts files required would otherwise be huge. For an unconnected LAN, the list of possible hosts is small and well-known and might be kept on a Unix machine in the */etc/ hosts* file. If you are in doubt as to whether a DNS server is being used, or what its address might be, look at the file */etc/resolv.conf* on your Unix servers. Any machine using DNS will have this file, which looks like:

```
#resolv.conf
domain example.com
nameserver 127.0.0.1
nameserver 192.168.236.20
```

In the example shown, the second **nameserver** line in the list contains the IP address of another machine on the local network: 192.168.236.20. It's a good candidate for a DNS server.[*]

---

[*] We can disqualify the other address because every Unix machine has a localhost address of 127.0.0.1 whether it is connected to a network or not. This address is required for some system tools to operate correctly.

You must type the correct IP address of one or more DNS servers (note that you *cannot* use its Internet name, such as *dns.oreilly.com*) into the appropriate field in Figure 3-10. Be sure not to use 127.0.0.1—that will never be the correct DNS server address!

Try to select addresses on your own network. Any name servers listed in */etc/resolv.conf* should work, but you'll get better performance by using a server nearby. (If you don't find */etc/resolv.conf* files on your Unix machines, just disable DNS until you can find the address of at least one DNS server.) Let's assume you only have one DNS server, and its address is 192.168.236.20. Click the Enable DNS radio button, as shown in Figure 3-10, and add the server's address to the top DNS Server Search Order field.

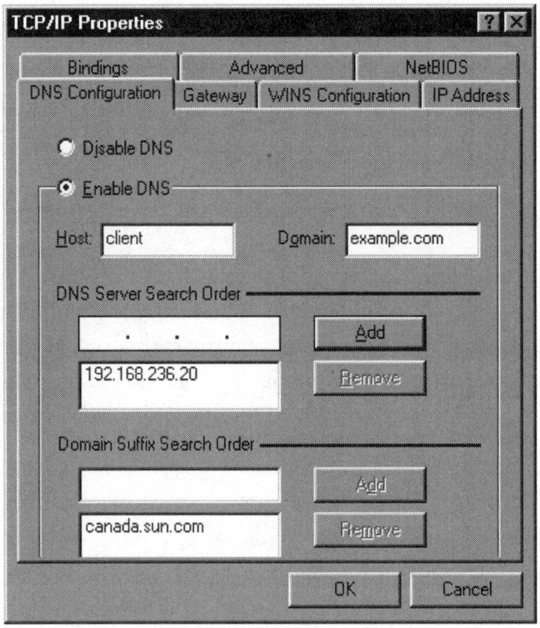

Figure 3-10. The DNS Configuration tab

Also, provide the name of the Windows 95/98 machine and the Internet domain you're in. You can safely ignore the Domain Suffix Search Order field for anything related to Samba.

WINS Configuration tab

WINS is the Windows Internet Name Service, its version of a NetBIOS name server. If you've enabled WINS on Samba, you must tell Windows the Samba server's address. If you are using WINS servers that are entirely Windows NT, enter each of them here as well. The dialog box shown after selecting the WINS Configuration tab is shown in Figure 3-11.

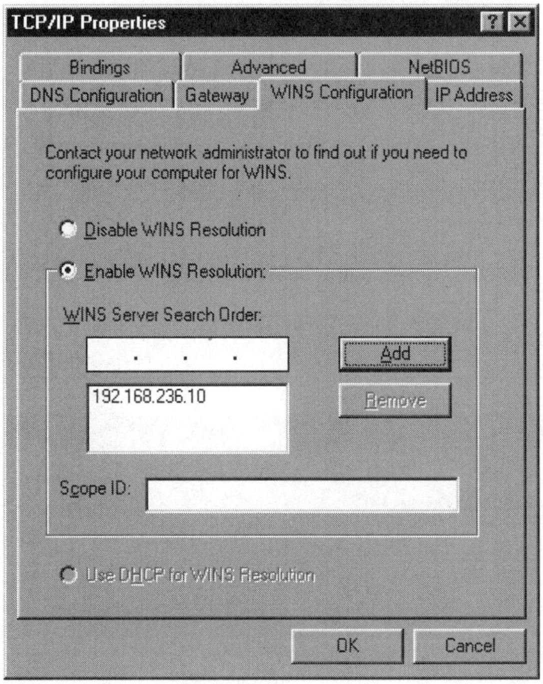

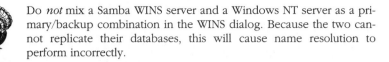

Figure 3-11. The WINS Configuration tab

Do *not* mix a Samba WINS server and a Windows NT server as a primary/backup combination in the WINS dialog. Because the two cannot replicate their databases, this will cause name resolution to perform incorrectly.

From here, select Enable WINS Resolution and enter the WINS server's address in the space provided, then press Add. Do not enter anything in the Scope ID field.

Hosts files

If you do not have either DNS or WINS, and you don't wish to use broadcast resolution, you'll need to provide a table of IP addresses and hostnames, in the standard Unix */etc/hosts* format. On a Windows machine, this goes in \WIN-DOWS\HOSTS under whichever drive you installed Windows on (typically C:\). A sample host file follows:

```
# 127.0.0.1            localhost
192.168.236.1      escrime.example.com escrime
192.168.236.2      riposte.example.com riposte
192.168.236.3      wizzin.example.com wizzin
192.168.236.4      touche.example.com touche
192.168.236.10     hobbes.example.com hobbes
```

You can copy this file directly from any of your Unix machines' */etc/hosts*; the format is identical. However, *you should only use hosts files in Windows as a last resort for name resolution.*

Check the bindings

The final tab to look at is Bindings, as shown in Figure 3-12.

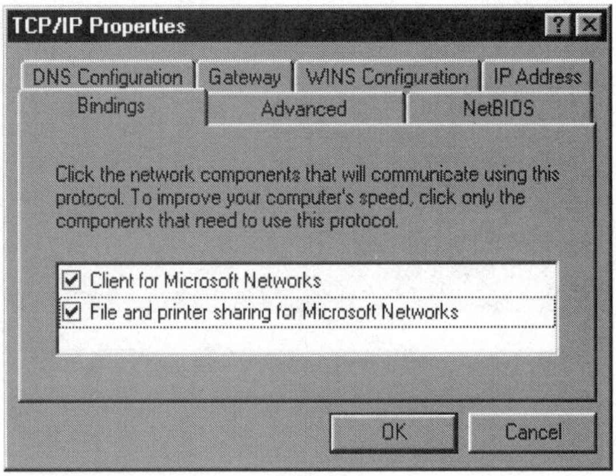

Figure 3-12. The Bindings tab

You should have a check beside Client for Microsoft Networks, indicating that it's using TCP/IP. If you have "File and printer sharing for Microsoft Networks" in the dialog, it should also be checked, as shown in the figure.

Setting Your Name and Workgroup

Finally, press the OK button in the TCP/IP configuration panel, and you'll be taken back to the Network Configuration screen. Then select the Identification tab, which will take you to the dialog box shown in Figure 3-13.

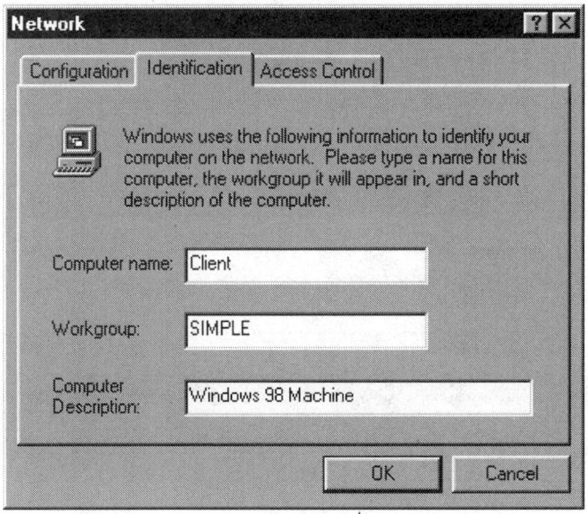

Figure 3-13. The Identification tab

Here, for the second time, set your machine's name. This time, instead of your DNS hostname and domain, you're setting your NetBIOS name. However, it is best to make this the *same* as your hostname. Try not to make a spelling mistake: it can be very confusing to configure a machine if TCP thinks it's `fred` and SMB thinks its `ferd`!

You also set your workgroup name here. In our case, it's SIMPLE, but if you used a different one in Chapter 2, *Installing Samba on a Unix System*, when creating the Samba configuration file, use that here as well. Try to avoid calling it WORKGROUP or you'll be in the same workgroup as every unconfigured (or ill-configured) machine in the world.

Accessing the Samba Server

Click on the OK button to complete the configuration; you will need to reboot in order for your changes to take effect.

Now for the big moment. Your Samba server is running, and you have set up your Windows 95/98 client to communicate with it. After rebooting, log in and double-click the Network Neighborhood icon on the desktop. You should see your Samba server listed as a member of the workgroup, as shown in Figure 3-14.

Double-clicking the server name will show the resources that the server is offering to the network, as shown in Figure 3-15 (in this case a printer and the *test* directory).

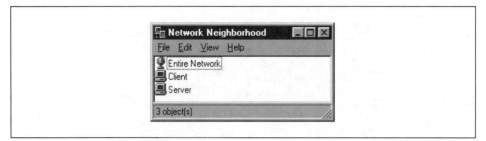

Figure 3-14. Windows Network Neighborhood

Figure 3-15. Shares on Server

 If you are presented with a dialog requesting the password for a user IPC$, then Samba did not accept the password that was sent from the client. In this case, the username and the password that were created on the client side *must* match the username/password combination on the Samba server. If you are using Windows 98 or Windows NT Service Pack 3 or above, this is probably because the client is sending encrypted passwords instead of plaintext passwords. You can remedy this situation by performing two steps on the Samba server. First, add the following entry to the [global] section of your Samba configuration file: encrypt passwords=yes. Second, find the *smbpasswd* program on the samba server (it is located in */usr/local/samba/bin* by default) and use it to add an entry to Samba's encrypted password database. For example, to add user steve to Samba's encrypted password database, type *smbpasswd -a steve*. The first time you enter this password, the program will output an error message indicating that the password database does not exist; it will then create the database, which is typically stored in */usr/local/samba/private/smbpasswd*.

If you don't see the server listed, start Windows Explorer (not Internet Explorer!) and select Map Network Drive from the Tools menu. This will give you a dialog box into which you can type the name of your server and the share test in the Windows UNC format: *server**test*, like we did in the first chapter. This should attempt to contact the Samba server and its temporary share. If things still aren't right, go to Chapter 9, *Troubleshooting Samba*, for troubleshooting assistance.

Setting Up Windows NT 4.0 Computers

Configuring Windows NT is a little different than configuring Windows 95/98. In order to use Samba with Windows NT, you will need both the Workstation service and the TCP/IP protocol. Both come standard with NT, but we'll work through installing and configuring them because they may not be configured correctly.

There are six basic steps:

1. Assign the machine a name.

2. Install the Workstation service.

3. Install the TCP/IP protocol.

4. Set the machine's name and IP address.

5. Configure the DNS and WINS name services.

6. Bind the protocol and service together.

Basic Configuration

This section presents an outline of the steps to follow for getting Windows NT to cooperate with Samba. If you need more details on Windows NT network administration, refer to Craig Hunt and Robert Bruce Thompsom's *Windows NT TCP/IP Network Administration* (O'Reilly), an excellent guide. You should perform these steps as the "Administrator" user.

Name the machine

The first thing you need to do is to give the machine a NetBIOS name. From the Control Panel, double click on the Network icon. This will take you to the Network dialog box for the machine. The first tab in this dialog box should be the Identification tab, as illustrated in Figure 3-16.

Here, you need to identify your machine with a name (we use the name Artish here) and change the default workgroup to the one you specified in the *smb.conf* file of your Samba server. In this case, the workgroup name is SIMPLE. However, you cannot edit either name here (as you could in Windows 95/98), but instead must use the Change button below the two text fields. Pressing this button raises an Identification Changes dialog box, where you can reset the workgroup and the machine name, as shown in Figure 3-17.

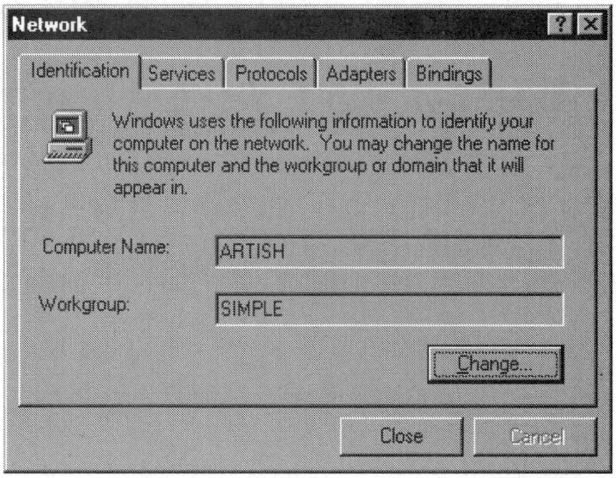

Figure 3-16. Network panel Identification tab

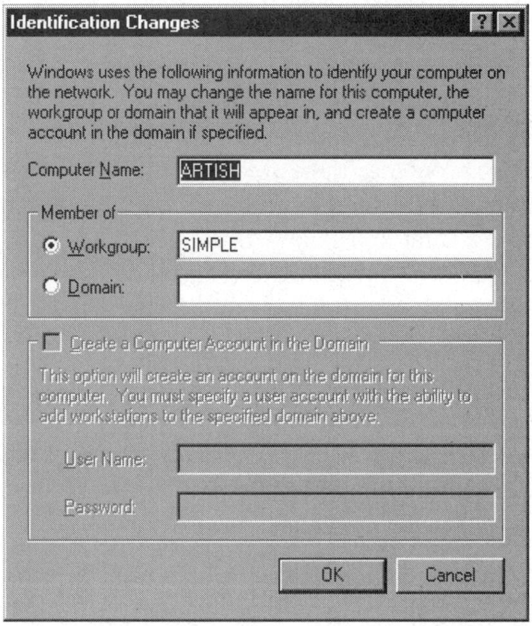

Figure 3-17. Changing the identification

A word of warning: you will have to set the machine name again later while configuring TCP/IP, so be sure that the two names match. The name you set here is the NetBIOS name. You're allowed to make it different from the TCP/IP hostname, but doing so is usually not a good thing. Don't worry that Windows NT forces the computer name and the workgroup to be all capital letters; it's smart enough to figure out what you mean when it connects to the network.

Installing the TCP/IP protocol

Next, select the Protocols tab in the Network dialog box, and look to see if you have the TCP/IP protocol installed, as shown in Figure 3-18.

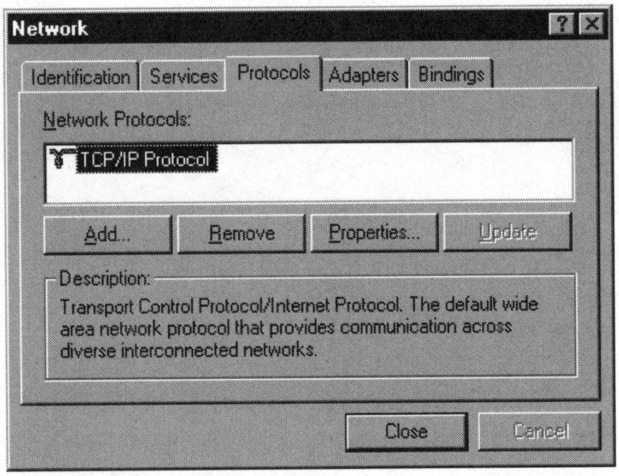

Figure 3-18. The Protocols tab

If the protocol is not installed, you need to add it. Press the Add button, which will display the Select Network Protocol dialog box shown in Figure 3-19. Unlike Windows 95/98, you should immediately see the TCP/IP protocol as one of the last protocols listed.

Select TCP/IP as the protocol and confirm it. If possible, install only the TCP/IP protocol. You usually do not want NetBEUI installed because this causes the machine to look for services under two different protocols, only one of which is likely in use.*

Installing the Workstation service

After installing TCP/IP, press the Services tab in the Network panel and check that you have a Workstation service, as shown at the end of the list in Figure 3-20.

This service is actually the Microsoft Networking Client, which allows the machine to access SMB services. The Workstation service is mandatory. The service is installed by default on both Windows NT Workstation 4.0 and Server 4.0. If it's not

---

* A common occurrence: after looking at the unused protocol for a while, the machine will time out and try the good one. This fruitless searching gives you terrible performance and mysterious delays.

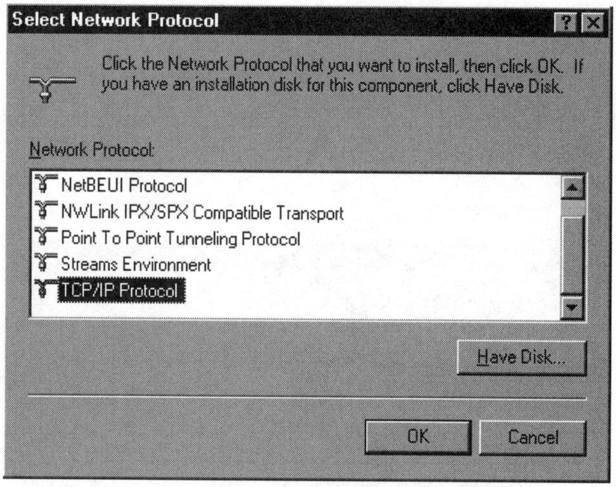

Figure 3-19. Select Network Protocol dialog box

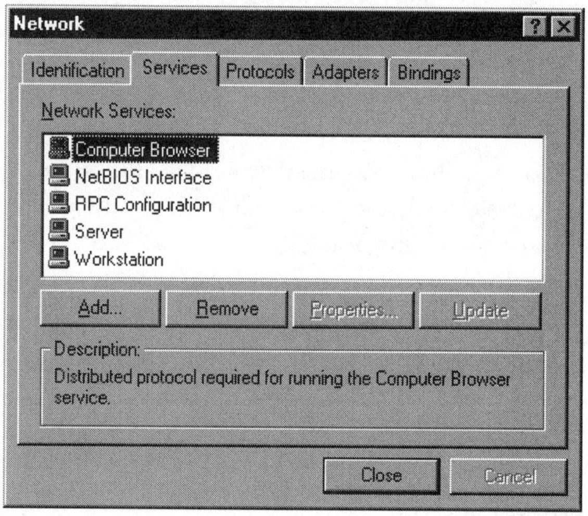

Figure 3-20. Network Services panel dialog box

there, you can install it much like TCP/IP. In this case you need to press the Add button and then select Workstation Service, as shown in Figure 3-21.

Configuring TCP/IP

After you've installed the Workstation service, return to the Protocols tab and select the TCP/IP Protocol entry in the window. Then click the Properties button

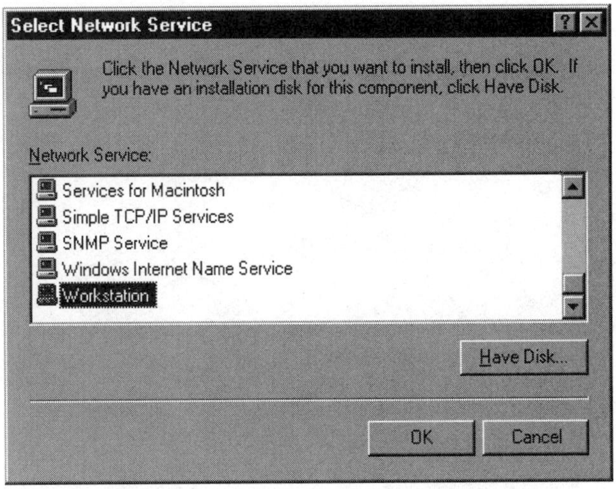

Figure 3-21. Select Network Service dialog box

below the window. The Microsoft TCP/IP Protocol panel will be displayed. There are five tabs on the Windows NT panel, and (like Windows 95/98) you will need to work on three of them:

- IP address

- DNS

- WINS address

IP Address tab

The IP Address tab is shown in Figure 3-22.

Select the "Specify an IP address" radio button and enter the computer's address and subnet mask in the space provided for the proper adapter (Ethernet card). You or your network manager should have selected an address for the client on the same subnet (LAN) as the Samba server. For example, if the server's address is 192.168.236.86 and its network mask 255.255.255.0, you might use the address 192.168.236.10, if it is available, for the NT workstation, along with the same netmask. If you use DHCP on your network, select the "Obtain an IP Address from a DHCP server" button.

If you don't have an IP address to use, and you are on a network by yourself, steal ours, as the 192.168.*x.x* subnet is specifically reserved by the Internic for LANs. If you're not by yourself, see your system administrator for some available addresses on your network.

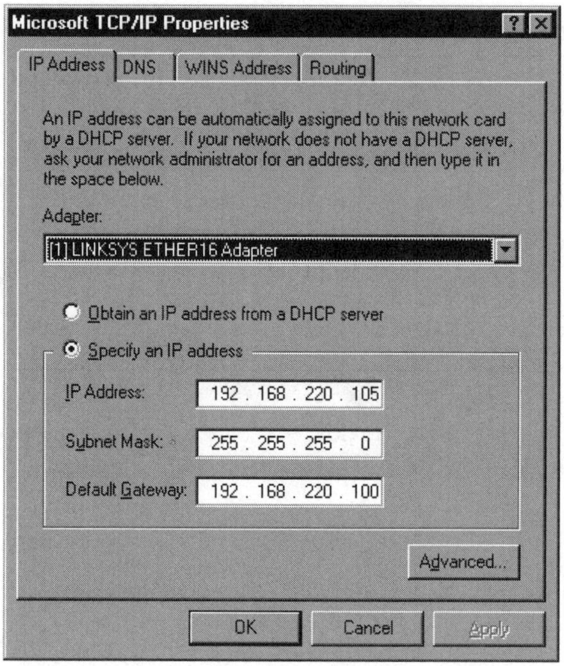

Figure 3-22. Microsoft TCP/IP Properties for Windows NT

The gateway field refers to a machine typically known as a *router*. If you have routers connecting multiple networks, you should put in the IP address of the one on your subnet.

DNS tab

Next we go to the tab for DNS, as shown in Figure 3-23. This brings up the DNS panel.

The Domain Name System (DNS) is responsible for translating human-readable computer names such as *atrish.example.com* into IP addresses such as 192.168. 236.10. There are two ways to accomplish this on a NT machine. First, you can specify a DNS server to do the translation for you, or you can keep a local list of name/address pairs for your workstation to refer to.

For a LAN that's not on the Internet, the list of possible hosts is typically small and well known, and may be kept in a file locally. Networks that are connected to the Internet typically use DNS service since it isn't possible to guess ahead of time what addresses you might be accessing out on the net. If you are in doubt as to whether a DNS server is being used, or what its address might be, look at the file

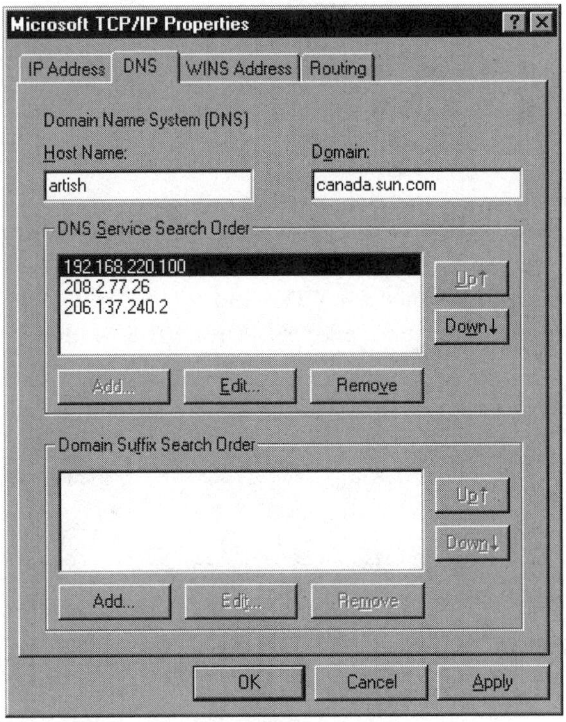

Figure 3-23. The DNS panel

/etc/resolv.conf on your Samba server: any machine using DNS will have this file. It looks like the following:

```
#resolv.conf
domain example.com
nameserver 127.0.0.1
nameserver 192.168.236.20
```

In this example, the first nameserver in the list is 127.0.0.1, which indicates that the Samba server is also a DNS server for this LAN.* In that case, you would use its network IP address (not 127.0.0.1, its localhost address) when filling in the DNS Configuration dialog box. Otherwise, use the other addresses you find in the lines beginning with **nameserver**. Try to select ones on your own network. Any name servers listed in */etc/resolv.conf* should work, but you'll get better performance by using a server nearby.

---

* The address 127.0.0.1 is known as the *localhost* address, and always refers to itself. For example, if you type **ping 127.0.0.1** on a Unix server, you should always get a response, as you're pinging the host itself.

Finally, enter the machine name once more, making sure that it's the same one listed in the Identification tab of the Network dialog box (before the NetBIOS name). Also, enter the DNS domain on which this machine resides. For example, if your workstation has a domain name such as *example.com*, enter it here. You can safely ignore the other options.

WINS Address tab

If you are not using a DNS server, you still need a way of translating NetBIOS names to addresses and back again. We recommend that you configure both DNS and WINS; NT has a preference for WINS and WINS can use DNS as a fallback if it cannot resolve any machine address. The WINS Address tab is shown in Figure 3-24.

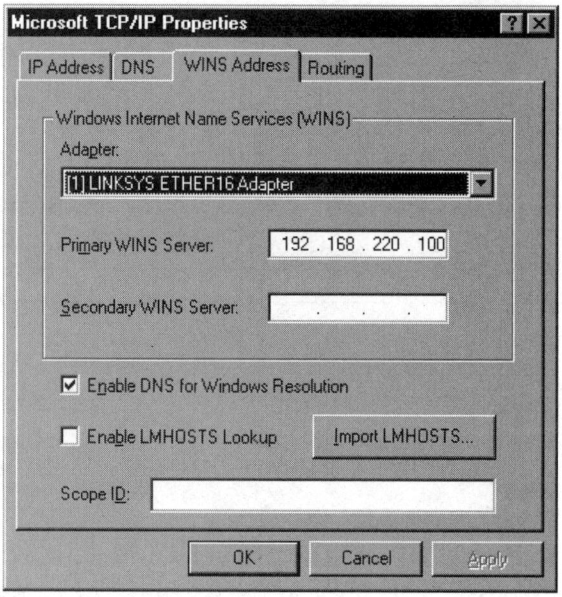

Figure 3-24. The WINS Address tab

If you have a WINS server, enter its address in the space marked Primary WINS Server. If your Samba server is providing WINS service (in other words, you have the line `wins service = yes` in the *smb.conf* file of your Samba server), provide the Samba server's IP address here. Otherwise, provide the address of another WINS server on your network.

You probably noticed that there is a field here for the adaptor; this field must specify the Ethernet adaptor that you're running TCP/IP on so that WINS will provide name service on the correct network. If you have both a LAN and a dialup adaptor, make sure you have the LAN's adaptor here.

Finally, select the "Enable DNS for Windows Resolution" checkbox, so WINS will try DNS as a fallback if it can't find a name. You can safely ignore the other options.

Hosts files

If you don't have either DNS or WINS, and you don't wish to use broadcast name resolution, you'll need to provide a table of IP addresses and hosts names, in standard Unix */etc/hosts* format. We recommend against this because maintenance of this file on any dynamic network is troublesome, but we will explain it just the same. If Windows NT is installed in the directory C:\WINNT, the host file is C:\WINNT\System32\drivers\etc\HOSTS. A sample follows:

```
127.0.0.1        localhost
192.168.236.1    escrime     escrime.example.com
192.168.236.2    riposte     riposte.example.com
192.168.236.3    wizzin      wizzin.example.com
192.168.236.4    touche      touche.example.com
192.168.236.5    gurgi       gurgi.example.com
192.168.236.6    jessiac     jessiac.example.com
192.168.236.7    skyline     skyline.example.com
```

If you wish, you can copy the contents directly from the Samba server's */etc/hosts*. The format is identical. This file will then serve the same purpose as the hosts file on the Unix server. Again, *hosts* files on Windows should only be used as a last resort.

Bindings

The term *bindings* is a way of saying "connected together at configuration time." It means that the TCP/IP protocol will channel through the Ethernet card (instead of, say, a dialup connection), and is actually connected properly. If you return to the Network dialog box and set the Show field to "all services" and click on all the + buttons in the tree, you should see a display similar to Figure 3-25.

This means that the Workstation, Server, and NetBIOS interface services are connected to the WINS client. This is the correct binding for Microsoft TCP/IP.

Connecting to the Samba Server

You can safely leave the default values for the remainder of the tabs in the Network dialog box. Click on the OK button to complete the configuration. Once the proper files are loaded (if any), you will need to reboot in order for your changes to take effect.

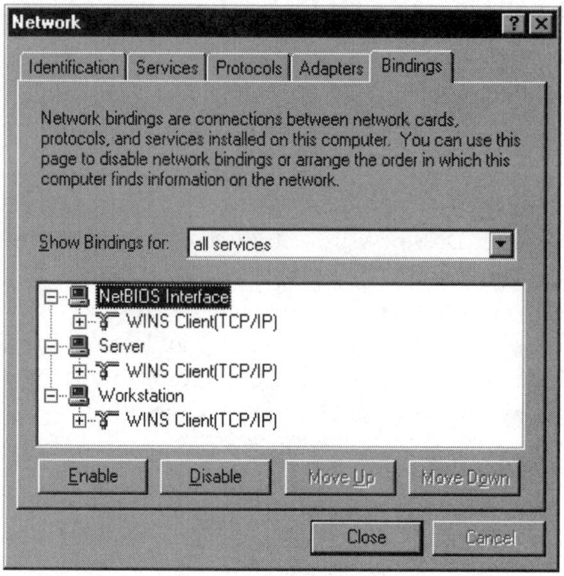

Figure 3-25. Service bindings

Now for the big moment. Your Samba server is running and you have set up your NT client to communicate with it. After the machine reboots, login and double-click the Network Neighborhood icon on the desktop, and you should see your Samba server listed as a member of the workgroup, as shown in Figure 3-26.

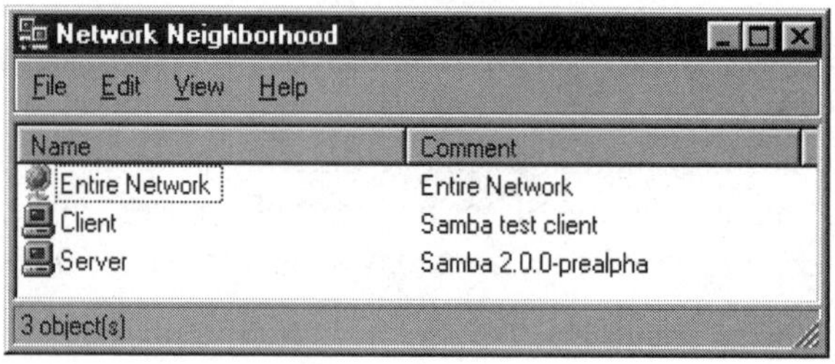

Figure 3-26. Windows NT Network Neighborhood

Double-clicking the server name will show the resources that the server is offering to the network, as shown in Figure 3-27. In this case, the test and the default printer are offered to the Window NT workstation. For more information, see the warning under the "Accessing the Samba Server" section, earlier in this chapter.

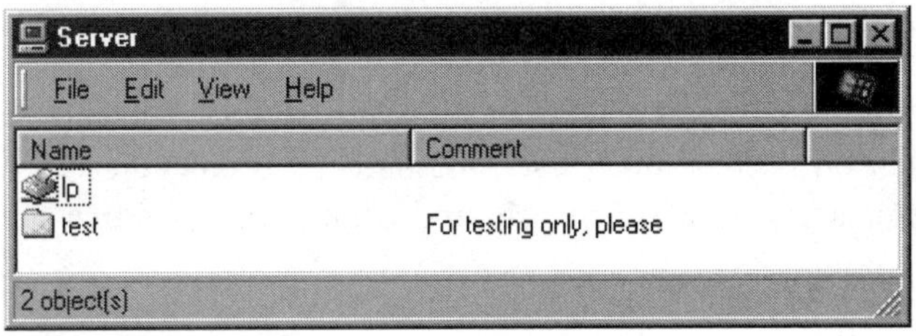

Server

File Edit View Help

Name	Comment
lp	
test	For testing only, please

2 object(s)

Figure 3-27. Server's shares

 If you are presented with a dialog requesting the password for a user IPC$, then Samba did not accept the password that was sent from the client. In this case, the username and the password that were created on the client side *must* match the username/password combination on the Samba server. If you are using Windows 98 or Windows NT Service Pack 3 or above, this is probably because the client is sending encrypted passwords instead of plaintext passwords. You can remedy this situation by performing two steps on the Samba server. First, add the following entry to the [global] section of your Samba configuration file: encrypt passwords=yes. Second, find the *smbpasswd* program on the samba server (it is located in */usr/local/samba/bin* by default) and use it to add an entry to Samba's encrypted password database. For example, to add user steve to Samba's encrypted password database, type *smbpasswd -a steve*. The first time you enter this password, the program will output an error message indicating that the password database does not exist; it will then create the database, which is typically stored in */usr/local/samba/private/smbpasswd*.

If you don't see the server listed, don't panic. Start the Windows NT Explorer (not Internet Explorer!) and select Map Network Drive from the Tools menu. A dialog box appears that allows you to type the name of your server and its share directory in Windows format. For example, you would enter *server**temp* if your server happened to be named "server." If things still aren't right, go directly to the section "The Fault Tree" in Chapter 9, to see if you can troubleshoot what is wrong with the network.

If it works, congratulations! Try writing to the server and sending data to the network printer. You will be pleasantly surprised how seamlessly everything works! Now that you've finished setting up the Samba server and its clients, we can starting talking about how Samba works and how to configure it to your liking.

An Introduction to SMB/CIFS

We'll wrap up this chapter with a short tutorial on SMB/CIFS. SMB/CIFS is the protocol that Windows 95/98 and NT machines use to communicate with the Samba server and each other. At a high level, the SMB protocol suite is relatively simple. It includes commands for all of the file and print operations that you might do on a local disk or printer, such as:

- Opening and closing a file

- Creating and deleting files and directories

- Reading and writing a file

- Searching for files

- Queueing and dequeueing files to a print spool

Each of these operations can be encoded into an SMB message and transmitted to and from a server. The original name SMB comes from their data format: these are versions of the standard DOS system-call data structures, or *Server Message Blocks*, redesigned for transmitting to another machine across a network.

SMB Format

Richard Sharpe of the Samba team defines SMB as a "request-response" protocol.[*] In effect, this means that a client sends an SMB request to a server, and the server sends an SMB response back to the client. Rarely does a server send a message that is not in response to a client.

An SMB message is not as complex as you might think. Let's take a closer look at the internal structure of such a message. It can be broken down into two parts: the *header*, which is a fixed size, and the *command string*, whose size can vary dramatically based on the contents of the message.

SMB header format

Table 3-1 shows the format of an SMB header. SMB commands are not required to use all the fields in the SMB header. For example, when a client first attempts to connect to a server, it does not yet have a tree identifier (TID) value—one is assigned after it successfully connects—so a null TID (0xFFFF) is placed in its header field. Other fields may be padded with zeros when not used.

---

[*] See *http://anu.samba.org/cifs/docs/what-is-smb.html* for Richard's excellent summary of SMB.

The fields of the SMB header are listed in Table 3-1.

Table 3-1. SMB Header Fields

Field	Size (bytes)	Description
0xFF 'SMB'	1	Protocol identifier
COM	1	Command code, from 0x00 to 0xFF
RCLS	1	Error class
REH	1	Reserved
ERR	2	Error code
REB	1	Reserved
RES	14	Reserved
TID	2	Tree identifier; a unique ID for a resource in use by client
PID	2	Caller process ID
UID	2	User identifier
MID	2	Multiplex identifier; used to route requests inside a process

SMB command format

Immediately after the header is a variable number of bytes that constitute an SMB command or reply. Each command, such as Open File (COM field identifier: SMBopen) or Get Print Queue (SMBsplretq), has its own set of parameters and data. Like the SMB header fields, not all of the command fields need to be filled, depending on the specific command. For example, the Get Server Attributes (SMBdskattr) command sets the WCT and BCC fields to zero. The fields of the command segment are shown in Table 3-2.

Table 3-2. SMB Command Contents

Field	Size in Bytes	Description
WCT	1	Word count
VWV	Variable	Parameter words (size given by WCT)
BCC	2	Parameter byte count
DATA	Variable	Data (size given by BCC)

Don't worry if you don't understand each of these fields; they are not necessary for using Samba at an administrator level. However, they do come in handy when debugging system messages. We will show you some of the more common SMB messages that clients and servers send using a modified version of *tcpdump* later in this section. (If you would like an SMB sniffer with a graphical interface, try "ethereal," which uses the GTK libraries; see the Samba homepage for more information on this tool.)

If you would like more information on each of the commands for
the SMB protocol, see the SMB/CIFS documentation at *ftp://ftp.*
microsoft.com/developr/drg/CIFS/.

SMB variations

The SMB protocol has been extended with new commands several times since its
inception. Each new version is backwards compatible with the previous versions.
This makes it quite possible for a LAN to have various clients and servers running
different versions of the SMB protocol at once.

Table 3-3 outlines the major versions of the SMB protocol. Within each "dialect" of
SMB are many sub-versions that include commands supporting particular releases
of major operating systems. The ID string is used by clients and servers to determine what level of the protocol they will speak to each other.

Table 3-3. SMB Protocol Dialects

Protocol Name	ID String	Used By
Core	`PC NETWORK PROGRAM 1.0`	
Core Plus	`MICROSOFT NETWORKS 1.03`	
LAN Manager 1.0	`LANMAN1.0`	
LAN Manager 2.0	`LM1.2X002`	
LAN Manager 2.1	`LANMAN2.1`	
NT LAN Manager 1.0	`NT LM 0.12`	Windows NT 4.0
Samba's NT LM 0.12	`Samba`	Samba
Common Internet File System	`CIFS 1.0`	Windows 2000

Samba implements the `NT LM 0.12` specification for NT LAN Manager 1.0. It is
backwards compatible with all of the other SMB variants. The CIFS specification is,
in reality, LAN Manager 0.12 with a few specific additions.

SMB Clients and Servers

As mentioned earlier, SMB is a client/server protocol. In the purest sense, this
means that a client sends a request to a server, which acts on the request and
returns a reply. However, the client/server roles can often be reversed, sometimes
within the context of a single SMB session. For example, consider the two Windows 95/98 computers in Figure 3-28. The computer named WIZZIN shares a
printer to the network, and the computer named ESCRIME shares a disk directory.
WIZZIN is in the client role when accessing ESCRIME's network drive, and in the
server role when printing a job for ESCRIME.

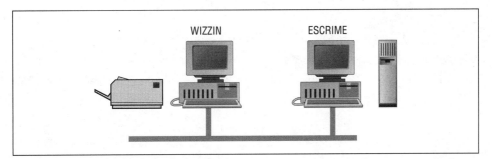

Figure 3-28. Two computers that both have resources to share

This brings out an important point in Samba terminology:

- A *server* is a machine with a resource to share.

- A *client* is a machine that wishes to use that resource.

- A server can be a client (of another computer's resource) at any given time.

Note that there are no implications as to the amount of resources that make up a server, or whether it has a large disk space or fast processor. A server could be an old 486 with a printer attached to it, or it could be an UltraSparc station with a 10 gigabyte disk service.

Microsoft Windows products have both the SMB client and server built in to the operating system. Wndows NT 4.0 uses a newer SMB protocol than Windows for Workgroups, and it offers an enhanced form of network security which will be discussed in Chapter 6. In addition, there are a large number of commercial SMB server products available from companies such as Sun, Compaq, SCO, Hewlett-Packard, Syntax, and IBM. Unfortunately, on the client side there are far fewer offerings, limited mainly to Digital Equipment's Pathworks product, and of course, Samba.

A Simple SMB Connection

Before we close this chapter, let's take a look at a simple SMB connection. This is some pretty technical data—which isn't really necessary to administer Samba—so you can skip over it if you like. We present this information largely as a way to help you get familiar with how the SMB protocol negotiates connections with other computers on the network.

There are four steps that the client and server must complete in order to establish a connection to a resource:

1. Establish a virtual connection.

2. Negotiate the protocol variant to speak.

3. Set session parameters.

4. Make a tree connection to a resource.

We will examine each of these steps through the eyes of a useful tool that we mentioned earlier: the modified *tcpdump* that is available from the Samba web site.

You can download this program at *samba.org* in the *samba/ftp/ tcpdump-smb* directory; the latest version as of this writing is 3.4-5. Use this program as you would use the standard *tcpdump* application, but add the -s 1500 switch to ensure that you get the whole packet and not just the first few bytes.

Establishing a virtual connection

When a user first makes a request to access a network disk or send a print job to a remote printer, NetBIOS takes care of making a connection at the session layer. The result is a bidirectional virtual channel between the client and server. In reality, there are only two messages that the client and server need to establish this connection. This is shown in the following example session request and response, as captured by *tcpdump*:

```
>>> NBT Packet
NBT Session Request
Flags=0x81000044
Destination=ESCRIME      NameType=0x20 (Server)
Source=WIZZIN           NameType=0x00 (Workstation)

>>> NBT Packet
NBT Session Granted
Flags=0x82000000
```

Negotiating the Protocol Variant

At this point, there is an open channel between the client and server. Next, the client sends a message to the server to negotiate an SMB protocol. As mentioned earlier, the client sets its tree identifier (TID) field to zero, since it does not yet know what TID to use. A *tree identifier* is a number that represents a connection to a share on a server.

The command in the message is SMBnegprot, a request to negotiate a protocol variant that will be used for the entire session. Note that the client sends to the server a list of all of the variants that it can speak, not vice versa.

The server responds to the **SMBnegprot** request with an index into the list of variants that the client offered, starting with index 0, or with the value 0xFF if none of the protocol variants are acceptable. Continuing this example, the server responds with the value 5, which indicates that the **NT LM 0.12** dialect will be used for the remainder of the session:

```
>>> NBT Packet
NBT Session Packet
Flags=0x0
Length=154

SMB PACKET: SMBnegprot (REQUEST)
SMB Command   =  0x72
Error class   =  0x0
Error code    =  0
Flags1        =  0x0
Flags2        =  0x0
Tree ID       =  0
Proc ID       =  5371
UID           =  0
MID           =  385
Word Count    =  0
Dialect=PC NETWORK PROGRAM 1.0
Dialect=MICROSOFT NETWORKS 3.0
Dialect=DOS LM1.2X002
Dialect=DOS LANMAN2.1
Dialect=Windows for Workgroups 3.1a
Dialect=NT LM 0.12

>>> NBT Packet
NBT Session Packet
Flags=0x0
Length=69

SMB PACKET: SMBnegprot (REPLY)
SMB Command   =  0x72
Error class   =  0x0
Error code    =  0
Flags1        =  0x0
Flags2        =  0x1
Tree ID       =  0
Proc ID       =  5371
UID           =  0
MID           =  385
Word Count    =  02
[000] 05 00
```

Set Session and Login Parameters

The next step is to transmit session and login parameters for the session. This includes the account name and password (if there is one), the workgroup name, the maximum size of data that can be transferred, and the number of pending requests that may be in the queue at any one time.

In the following example, the Session Setup command presented allows for an additional SMB command to be piggybacked onto it. The letter X at the end of the command name indicates this, and the hexadecimal code of the second command is given in the Com2 field. In this case the command is 0x75, which is the Tree Connect and X command. The SMBtconX message looks for the name of the resource in the *smb_buf* buffer. (This is the last field listed in the following request.) In this example, *smb_buf* contains the string \\ESCRIME\PUBLIC, which is the full pathname to a shared directory on node ESCRIME. Using the "and X" commands like this speeds up each transaction, since the server doesn't have to wait on the client to make a second request.

Note that the TID is still zero. The server will provide a TID to the client once the session has been established and a connection has been made to the requested resource. In addition, note that the password is sent in the open. We can change this later using encrypted passwords:

```
>>> NBT Packet
NBT Session Packet
Flags=0x0
Length=139

SMB PACKET: SMBsesssetupX (REQUEST)
SMB Command    =  0x73
Error class    =  0x0
Error code     =  0
Flags1         =  0x10
Flags2         =  0x0
Tree ID        =  0
Proc ID        =  5371
UID            =  1
MID            =  385
Word Count     =  13
Com2=0x75
Res1=0x0
Off2=106
MaxBuffer=2920
MaxMpx=2
VcNumber=0
SessionKey=0x1FF2
CaseInsensitivePasswordLength=1
CaseSensitivePasswordLength=1
Res=0x0
Capabilities=0x1
Pass1&Pass2&Account&Domain&OS&LanMan=
  KRISTIN PARKSTR Windows 4.0 Windows 4.0
```

```
PassLen=2
Passwd&Path&Device=
smb_bcc=22
smb_buf[]=\\ESCRIME\PUBLIC
```

Making Connection to a Resource

For the final step, the server returns a TID to the client, indicating that the user has been authorized access and that the resource is ready to be used. It also sets the *ServiceType* field to "A" to indicate that this is a file service. Available service types are:

- "A" for a disk or file

- "LPT1" for a spooled output

- "COMM" for a direct-connect printer or modem

- "IPC" for a named pipe

The output is:

```
>>> NBT Packet
NBT Session Packet
Flags=0x0
Length=78

SMB PACKET: SMBsesssetupX (REPLY)
SMB Command    =  0x73
Error class    =  0x0
Error code     =  0
Flags1         =  0x80
Flags2         =  0x1
Tree ID        =  121
Proc ID        =  5371
UID            =  1
MID            =  385
Word Count     =  3
Com2=0x75
Off2=68
Action=0x1
[000] Unix Samba 1.9.1
[010] PARKSTR

SMB PACKET: SMBtconX (REPLY) (CHAINED)
smbvwv[]=
Com2=0xFF
Off2=78
smbbuf[]=
ServiceType=A:
```

Now that a TID has been assigned, the client may issue any sort of command that it would use on a local disk drive. It can open files, read and write to them, delete them, create new files, search for filenames, and so on.

4

Disk Shares

In the previous three chapters, we showed you how to install Samba on a Unix server and set up Windows clients to use a simple disk share. This chapter will show you how Samba can assume more productive roles on your network.

Samba's daemons, *smbd* and *nmbd*, are controlled through a single ASCII file, *smb.conf*, that can contain over 200 unique options. These options define how Samba reacts to the network around it, including everything from simple permissions to encrypted connections and NT domains. The next five chapters are designed to help you get familiar with this file and its options. Some of these options you will use and change frequently; others you may never use—it all depends on how much functionality you want Samba to offer its clients.

This chapter introduces the structure of the Samba configuration file and shows you how to use these options to create and modify disk shares. Subsequent chapters will discuss browsing, how to configure users, security, domains, and printers, and a host of other myriad topics that you can implement with Samba on your network.

Learning the Samba Configuration File

Here is an example of a Samba configuration file. If you have worked with a Windows .INI file, the structure of the *smb.conf* file should look very familiar:

```
[global]
    log level = 1
    max log size = 1000
    socket options = TCP_NODELAY IPTOS_LOWDELAY
    guest ok = no
[homes]
    browseable = no
    map archive = yes
```

```
[printers]
    path = /usr/tmp
    guest ok = yes
    printable = yes
    min print space = 2000
[test]
    browseable = yes
    read only = yes
    guest ok = yes
    path = /export/samba/test
```

Although you may not understand the contents yet, this is a good configuration file to grab if you're in a hurry. (If you're not, we'll create a new one from scratch shortly.) In a nutshell, this configuration file sets up basic debug logging in a default log file not to exceed 1MB, optimizes TCP/IP socket connections between the Samba server and any SMB clients, and allows Samba to create a disk share for each user that has a standard Unix account on the server. In addition, each of the printers registered on the server will be publicly available, as will a single read-only share that maps to the */export/samba/test* directory. The last part of this file is similar to the disk share you used to test Samba in Chapter 2, *Installing Samba on a Unix System.*

Configuration File Structure

Let's take another look at this configuration file, this time from a higher level:

```
[global]
    ...
[homes]
    ...
[printers]
    ...
[test]
    ...
```

The names inside the square brackets delineate unique sections of the *smb.conf* file; each section names the *share* (or service) that the section refers to. For example, the [test] and [homes] sections are each unique disk shares; they contain options that map to specific directories on the Samba server. The [printers] share contains options that map to various printers on the server. All the sections defined in the *smb.conf* file, with the exception of the [global] section, will be available as a disk or printer share to clients connecting to the Samba server.

The remaining lines are individual configuration options unique to that share. These options will continue until a new bracketed section is encountered, or until the end of the file is reached. Each configuration option follows a simple format:

```
option = value
```

Options in the *smb.conf* file are set by assigning a value to them. We should warn you up front that some of the option names in Samba are poorly chosen. For example, `read only` is self-explanatory, and is typical of many recent Samba options. `public` is an older option, and is vague; it now has a less-confusing synonym `guest ok` (may be accessed by guests). We describe some of the more common historical names in this chapter in sections that highlight each major task. In addition, Appendix C, *Samba Configuration Option Quick Reference*, contains an alphabetical index of all the configuration options and their meanings.

Whitespaces, quotes, and commas

An important item to remember about configuration options is that all whitespaces in the `value` are significant. For example, consider the following option:

```
volume = The Big Bad Hard Drive Number 3543
```

Samba strips away the spaces between the final `e` in `volume` and the first `T` in `The`. These whitespaces are insignificant. The rest of the whitespaces are significant and will be recognized and preserved by Samba when reading in the file. Space is not significant in option names (such as `guest ok`), but we recommend you follow convention and keep spaces between the words of options.

If you feel safer including quotation marks at the beginning and ending of a configuration option's value, you may do so. Samba will ignore these quotation marks when it encounters them. Never use quotation marks around an option itself; Samba will treat this as an error.

Finally, you can use whitespaces to separate a series of values in a list, or you can use commas. These two options are equivalent:

```
netbios aliases = sales, accounting, payroll
netbios aliases = sales accounting payroll
```

In some values, however, you must use one form of separation—spaces in some cases, commas in others.

Capitalization

Capitalization is not important in the Samba configuration file except in locations where it would confuse the underlying operating system. For example, let's assume that you included the following option in a share that pointed to */export/samba/simple*:

```
PATH = /EXPORT/SAMBA/SIMPLE
```

Samba would have no problem with the `path` configuration option appearing entirely in capital letters. However, when it tries to connect to the given directory, it would be unsuccessful because the Unix filesystem in the underlying operating system *is* case sensitive. Consequently, the path listed would not be found and clients would be unable to connect to the share.

Line continuation

You can continue a line in the Samba configuration file using the backslash, as follows:

```
comment = The first share that has the primary copies \
        of the new Teamworks software product.
```

Because of the backslash, these two lines will be treated as one line by Samba. The second line begins at the first non-whitespace character that Samba encounters; in this case, the o in of.

Comments

You can insert comments in the *smb.conf* configuration file by preceding a line with either a hash mark (#) or a semicolon (;). Both characters are equivalent. For example, the first three lines in the following example would be considered comments:

```
#   This is the printers section. We have given a minimum print
;   space of 2000 to prevent some errors that we've seen when
;   the spooler runs out of space.

[printers]
    public = yes
    min print space = 2000
```

Samba will ignore all comment lines in its configuration file; there are no limitations to what can be placed on a comment line after the initial hash mark or semicolon. Note that the line continuation character (\) will *not* be honored on a commented line. Like the rest of the line, it is ignored.

Changes at runtime

You can modify the *smb.conf* configuration file and any of its options at any time while the Samba daemons are running. By default, Samba checks the configuration file every 60 seconds for changes. If it finds any, the changes are immediately put into effect. If you don't wish to wait that long, you can force a reload by either sending a SIGHUP signal to the *smbd* and *nmbd* processes, or simply restarting the daemons.

For example, if the *smbd* process was 893, you could force it to reread the configuration file with the following command:

```
# kill -SIGHUP 893
```

Not all changes will be immediately recognized by clients. For example, changes to a share that is currently in use will not be registered until the client disconnects and reconnects to that share. In addition, server-specific parameters such as the workgroup or NetBIOS name of the server will not register immediately either. This keeps active clients from being suddenly disconnected or encountering unexpected access problems while a session is open.

Variables

Samba includes a complete set of variables for determining characteristics of the Samba server and the clients to which it connects. Each of these variables begins with a percent sign, followed by a single uppercase or lowercase letter, and can be used only on the right side of a configuration option (e.g., after the equal sign):

```
[pub]
    path = /home/ftp/pub/%a
```

The `%a` stands for the client machine's architecture (e.g., `WinNT` for Windows NT, `Win95` for Windows 95 or 98, or `WfWg` for Windows for Workgroups). Because of this, Samba will assign a unique path for the `[pub]` share to client machines running Windows NT, a different path for client machines running Windows 95, and another path for Windows for Workgroups. In other words, the paths that each client would see as its share differ according to the client's architecture, as follows:

```
/home/ftp/pub/WinNT
/home/ftp/pub/Win95
/home/ftp/pub/WfWg
```

Using variables in this manner comes in handy if you wish to have different users run custom configurations based on their own unique characteristics or conditions. Samba has 19 variables, as shown in Table 4-1.

Table 4-1. Samba Variables

Variable	Definition
Client variables	
`%a`	Client's architecture (e.g., Samba, WfWg, WinNT, Win95, or UNKNOWN)
`%I`	Client's IP address (e.g., 192.168.220.100)
`%m`	Client's NetBIOS name
`%M`	Client's DNS name
User variables	
`%g`	Primary group of `%u`
`%G`	Primary group of `%U`
`%H`	Home directory of `%u`
`%u`	Current Unix username
`%U`	Requested client username (not always used by Samba)

Table 4-1. Samba Variables (continued)

Variable	Definition
Share variables	
%p	Automounter's path to the share's root directory, if different from %P
%P	Current share's root directory
%S	Current share's name
Server variables	
%d	Current server process ID
%h	Samba server's DNS hostname
%L	Samba server's NetBIOS name
%N	Home directory server, from the automount map
%v	Samba version
Miscellaneous variables	
%R	The SMB protocol level that was negotiated
%T	The current date and time

Here's another example of using variables: let's say that there are five clients on your network, but one client, **fred**, requires a slightly different [homes] configuration loaded when it connects to the Samba server. With Samba, it's simple to attack such a problem:

```
[homes]
    ...
    include = /usr/local/samba/lib/smb.conf.%m
    ...
```

The **include** option here causes a separate configuration file for each particular NetBIOS machine (%m) to be read in addition to the current file. If the hostname of the client machine is **fred**, and if a *smb.conf.fred* file exists in the *samba_dir/lib/* directory (or whatever directory you've specified for your configuration files), Samba will insert that configuration file into the default one. If any configuration options are restated in *smb.conf.fred*, those values will override any options previously encountered in that share. Note that we say "previously." If any options are restated in the main configuration file after the **include** option, Samba will honor those restated values for the share in which they are defined.

Here's the important part: if there is no such file, Samba will not generate an error. In fact, it won't do anything at all. This allows you to create only one extra configuration file for **fred** when using this strategy, instead of one for each Net-BIOS machine that is on the network.

Machine-specific configuration files can be used both to customize particular clients and to make debugging Samba easier. Consider the latter; if we have one client with a problem, we can use this approach to give it a private log file with a more verbose logging level. This allows us to see what Samba is doing without slowing down all the other clients or overflowing the disk with useless logs. Remember, with large networks you may not always have the option to restart the Samba server to perform debugging!

You can use each of the variables in Table 4-1 to give custom values to a variety of Samba options. We will highlight several of these options as we move through the next few chapters.

Special Sections

Now that we've gotten our feet wet with variables, there are a few special sections of the Samba configuration file that we should talk about. Again, don't worry if you do not understand each and every configuration options listed below; we'll go over each of them over the course of the upcoming chapters.

The [globals] Section

The [globals] section appears in virtually every Samba configuration file, even though it is not mandatory to define one. Any option set in this section of the file will apply to all the other shares, as if the contents of the section were copied into the share itself. There is one catch: other sections can list the same option in their section with a new value; this has the effect of overriding the value specified in the [globals] section.

To illustrate this, let's again look at the opening example of the chapter:

```
[global]
    log level = 1
    max log size = 1000
    socket options = TCP_NODELAY IPTOS_LOWDELAY
    guest ok = no
[homes]
    browseable = no
    map archive = yes
[printers]
    path = /usr/tmp
    guest ok = yes
    printable = yes
    min print space = 2000
[test]
    browseable = yes
    read only = yes
    guest ok = yes
    path = /export/samba/test
```

In the previous example, if we were going to connect a client to the [test] share, Samba would first read in the [globals] section. At that point, it would set the option guest ok = no as the global default for each share it encounters throughout the configuration file. This includes the [homes] and [printers] shares. When it reads in the [test] share, however, it would then find the configuration option guest ok = yes, and override the default from the [globals] section with the value yes.

Any option that appears outside of a section (before the first marked section) is also assumed to be a global option.

The [homes] Section

If a client attempts to connect to a share that doesn't appear in the *smb.conf* file, Samba will search for a [homes] share in the configuration file. If one exists, the unidentified share name is assumed to be a Unix username, which is queried in the password database of the Samba server. If that username appears, Samba assumes the client is a Unix user trying to connect to his or her home directory on the server.

For example, assume a client machine is connecting to the Samba server hydra for the first time, and tries to connect to a share named [alice]. There is no [alice] share defined in the *smb.conf* file, but there is a [homes], so Samba searches the password database file and finds an alice user account is present on the system. Samba then checks the password provided by the client against user alice's Unix password—either with the password database file if it's using non-encrypted passwords, or Samba's *smbpasswd* file if encrypted passwords are in use. If the passwords match, then Samba knows it has guessed right: the user alice is trying to connect to her home directory. Samba will then create a share called [alice] for her.

The process of using the [homes] section to create users (and dealing with their passwords) is discussed in more detail in the Chapter 6, *Users, Security, and Domains.*

The [printers] Section

The third special section is called [printers] and is similar to [homes]. If a client attempts to connect to a share that isn't in the *smb.conf* file, and its name can't be found in the password file, Samba will check to see if it is a printer share. Samba does this by reading the printer capabilities file (usually */etc/printcap*) to see if the share name appears there.* If it does, Samba creates a share named after the printer.

Like [homes], this means you don't have to maintain a share for each of your system printers in the *smb.conf* file. Instead, Samba honors the Unix printer registry if you request it to, and provides the registered printers to the client machines. There is, however, an obvious limitation: if you have an account named fred and a printer named fred, Samba will always find the user account first, even if the client really needed to connect to the printer.

The process of setting up the [printers] share is discussed in more detail in Chapter 7, *Printing and Name Resolution*.

Configuration Options

Options in the Samba configuration files fall into one of two categories: *global* or *share*. Each category dictates where an option can appear in the configuration file.

Global

> Global options *must* appear in the [global] section and nowhere else. These are options that typically apply to the behavior of the Samba server itself, and not to any of its shares.

Share

> Share options can appear in specific shares, or they can appear in the [global] section. If they appear in the [global] section, they will define a default behavior for all shares, unless a share overrides the option with a value of its own.

In addition, the values that a configuration option can take can be divided into four categories. They are as follows:

Boolean

> These are simply yes or no values, but can be represented by any of the following: yes, no, true, false, 0, 1. The values are case insensitive: YES is the same as yes.

Numerical

> An integer, hexidecimal, or octal number. The standard 0x*nn* syntax is used for hexadecimal and 0*nnn* for octal.

String

> A string of case-sensitive characters, such as a filename or a username.

---

* Depending on your system, this file may not be */etc/printcap*. You can use the *testparm* command that comes with Samba to determine the value of the printcap name configuration option; this was the default value chosen when Samba was compiled.

Enumerated list

> A finite list of known values. In effect, a boolean is an enumerated list with only two values.

Configuration File Options

Samba has well over 200 configuration options at its disposal. So let's start off easy by introducing some of the options you can use to modify the configuration file itself.

As we hinted earlier in the chapter, configuration files are by no means static. You can instruct Samba to include or even replace configuration options as it is processing them. The options to do this are summarized in Table 4-2.

Table 4-2. Configuration File Options

Option	Parameters	Function	Default	Scope
config file	string (fully-qualified name)	Sets the location of a configuration file to use instead of the current one.	None	Global
include	string (fully-qualified name)	Specifies an additional segment of configuration options to be included at this point in the configuration file.	None	Global
copy	string (name of share)	Allows you to clone the configuration options of another share in the current share.	None	Share

config file

The global **config file** option specifies a replacement configuration file that will be loaded when the option is encountered. If the target file exists, the remainder of the current configuration file, as well as the options encounter so far, will be discarded; Samba will configure itself entirely with the options in the new file. The **config file** option takes advantage of the variables above, which is useful in the event that you want load a special configuration file based on the machine name or user of the client that it connecting.

For example, the following line instructs Samba to use a configuration file specified by the NetBIOS name of the client connecting, if such a file exists. If it does, options specified in the original configuration file are ignored. The following example attempts to lead a new configuration file based on the client's NetBIOS name:

```
[global]
    config file = /usr/local/samba/lib/smb.conf.%m
```

If the configuration file specified does not exist, the option is ignored and Samba will continue to configure itself based on the current file.

include

This option, discussed in greater detail earlier, copies the target file into the current configuration file at the point specified, as shown in Figure 4-1. This option also takes advantage of the variables specified earlier in the chapter, which is useful in the event that you want load configuration options based on the machine name or user of the client that it connecting. You can use this option as follows:

```
[global]
    include = /usr/local/samba/lib/smb.conf.%m
```

If the configuration file specified does not exist, the option is ignored. Remember that any option specified previously is overridden. In Figure 4-1, all three options will override their previous values.

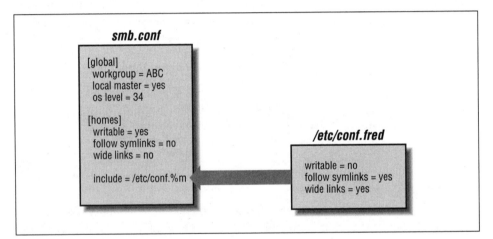

Figure 4-1. The include option in a Samba configuration file

The `include` option cannot understand the variables `%u` (user), `%p` (current share's rout directory), or `%s` (current share) because they are not set at the time the file is read.

copy

The `copy` configuration option allows you to clone the configuration options of the share name that you specify in the current share. The target share must appear earlier in the configuration file than the share that is performing the copy. For example:

```
[template]
    writable = yes
```

```
        browsable = yes
        valid users = andy, dave, peter

    [data]
        path = /usr/local/samba
        copy = template
```

Note that any options in the share that invoked the **copy** directive will override those in the cloned share; it does not matter whether they appear before or after the **copy** directive.

Server Configuration

Now it's time to begin configuring your Samba server. Let's introduce three basic configuration options that can appear in the [**global**] section of your *smb.conf* file:

```
    [global]
        #  Server configuration parameters
        netbios name = HYDRA
        server string = Samba %v on (%L)
        workgroup = SIMPLE
```

This configuration file is pretty simple; it advertises the Samba server on a NBT network under the NetBIOS name **hydra**. In addition, the machine belongs to the workgroup SIMPLE and displays a description to clients that includes the Samba version number as well as the NetBIOS name of the Samba server.

If you had to enter **encrypt passwords=yes** in your earlier configuration file, you should do so here as well.

Go ahead and try this configuration file. Create a file named *smb.conf* under the */usr/local/samba/lib* directory with the text listed above. Then reset the Samba server and use a Windows client to verify the results. Be sure that your Windows clients are in the SIMPLE workgroup as well. After clicking on the Network Neighborhood on a Windows client, you should see a window similar to Figure 4-2. (In this figure, **phoenix** and **chimaera** are our Windows clients.)

You can verify the **server string** by listing the details of the Network Neighborhood window (select the Details menu item under the View menu), at which point you should see a window similar to Figure 4-3.

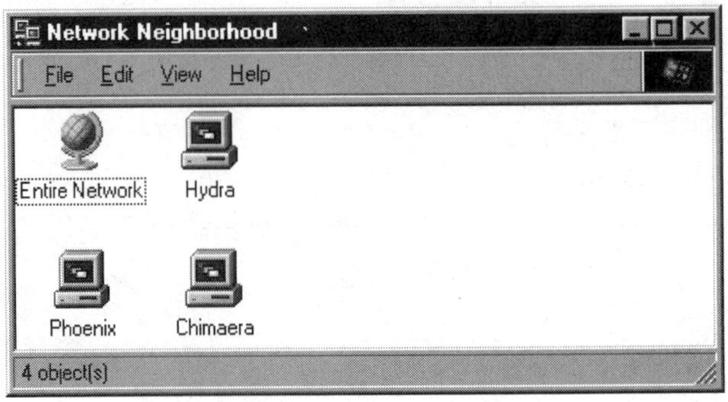

Figure 4-2. Network Neighborhood showing the Samba server

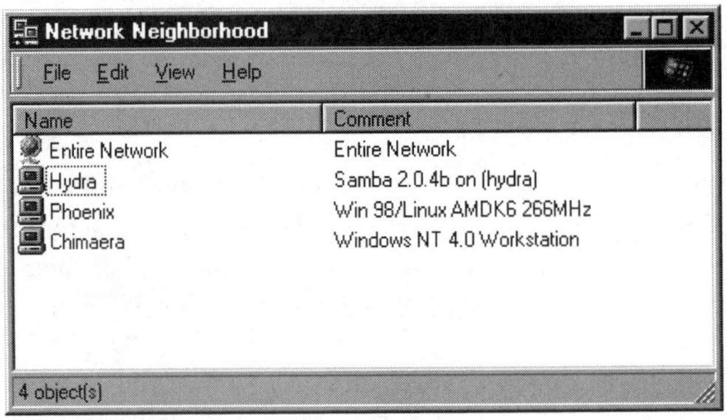

Figure 4-3. Network Neighborhood details listing

If you were to click on the Hydra icon, a window should appear that shows the services that it provides. In this case, the window would be completely empty because there are no shares on the server yet.

Server Configuration Options

Table 4-3 summarizes the server configuration options introduced previously. Note that all three of these options are global in scope; in other words, they must appear in the [global] section of the configuration file.

Table 4-3. Server Configuration Options

Option	Parameters	Function	Default	Scope
netbios name	string	Sets the primary NetBIOS name of the Samba server.	Server DNS hostname	Global

Table 4-3. Server Configuration Options (continued)

Option	Parameters	Function	Default	Scope
`server string`	string	Sets a descriptive string for the Samba server.	`Samba %v`	Global
`workgroup`	string	Sets the NetBIOS group of machines that the server belongs to.	Defined at compile time	Global

netbios name

The `netbios name` option allows you to set the NetBIOS name of the server. For example:

```
netbios name = YORKVM1
```

The default value for this configuration option is the server's hostname; that is, the first part of its complete DNS machine name. For example, a machine with the DNS name `ruby.ora.com` would be given the NetBIOS name `RUBY` by default. While you can use this option to restate the machine's NetBIOS name in the configuration file (as we did previously), it is more commonly used to assign the Samba server a NetBIOS name other than its current DNS name. Remember that the name given must follow the rules for valid NetBIOS machine names as outlines in Chapter 1, *Learning the Samba*.

Changing the NetBIOS name of the server is not recommended unless you have a good reason. One such reason might be if the hostname of the machine is not unique because the LAN is divided over two or more DNS domains. For example, YORKVM1 is a good NetBIOS candidate for *vm1.york.example.com* to differentiate it from *vm1.falkirk.example.com*, which has the same hostname but resides in a different DNS domain.

Another use of this option is for relocating SMB services from a dead or retired machine. For example, if `SALES` is the SMB server for the department, and it suddenly dies, you could immediately reset `netbios name = SALES` on a backup Samba machine that's taking over for it. Users won't have to change their drive mappings to a different machine; new connections to `SALES` will simply go to the new machine.

server string

The `server string` parameter defines a comment string that will appear next to the server name in both the Network Neighborhood (when shown with the Details menu) and the comment entry of the Microsoft Windows print manager. You can use the standard variables to provide information in the description. For example, our entry earlier was:

```
[global]
    server string = Samba %v on (%h)
```

The default for this option simply presents the current version of Samba and is equivalent to:

```
server string = Samba %v
```

workgroup

The **workgroup** parameter sets the current workgroup where the Samba server will advertise itself. Clients that wish to access shares on the Samba server should be on the same NetBIOS workgroup. Remember that workgroups are really just NetBIOS group names, and must follow the standard NetBIOS naming conventions outlined in Chapter 1. For example:

```
[global]
    workgroup = SIMPLE
```

The default option for this parameter is set at compile time. If the entry is not changed in the makefile, it will be WORKGROUP. Because this tends to be the workgroup name of every unconfigured NetBIOS network, we recommend that you always set your workgroup name in the Samba configuration file.*

Disk Share Configuration

We mentioned in the previous section that there were no disk shares on the **hydra** server. Let's continue with the configuration file and create an empty disk share called [**data**]. Here are the additions that will do it:

```
[global]
    netbios name = HYDRA
    server string = Samba %v on (%L)
    workgroup = SIMPLE

[data]
    path = /export/samba/data
    comment = Data Drive
    volume = Sample-Data-Drive
    writeable = yes
    guest ok = yes
```

The [**data**] share is typical for a Samba disk share. The share maps to a directory on the Samba server: */export/samba/data*. We've also provided a comment that describes the share as a **Data Drive**, as well as a volume name for the share itself.

The share is set to writeable so that users can write data to it; the default with Samba is to create a read-only share. As a result, this option needs to be explicitly set for each disk share you wish to make writeable.

---

* We should also mention that it is an inherently bad idea to have a workgroup that shares the same name as a server.

You may have noticed that we set the guest ok parameter to yes. While this isn't very security-conscious, there are some password issues that we need to understand before setting up individual users and authentication. For the moment, this will sidestep those issues and let anyone connect to the share.

Go ahead and make these additions to your configuration file. In addition, create the */export/samba/data* directory as root on your Samba machine with the following commands:

```
# mkdir /export/samba/data
# chmod 777 /export/samba/data
```

Now, if you connect to the hydra server again (you can do this by clicking on its icon in the Windows Network Neighborhood), you should see a single share listed entitled data, as shown in Figure 4-4. This share should also have read/write access to it. Try creating or copying a file into the share. Or, if you're really feeling adventurous, you can even try mapping a network drive to it!

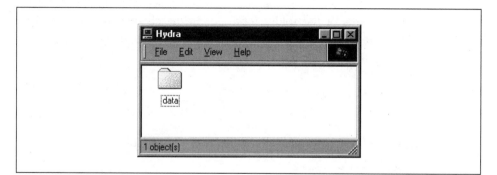

Figure 4-4. The initial data share on the Samba server

Disk Share Configuration Options

The basic Samba configuration options for disk shares previously introduced are listed in Table 4-4.

Table 4-4. Basic Share Configuration Options

Option	Parameters	Function	Default	Scope
path (directory)	string (fully-qualified pathname)	Sets the Unix directory that will be provided for a disk share or used for spooling by a printer share	/tmp	Share
guest ok (public)	boolean	If set to yes, authentication is not needed to access this share	no	Share
comment	string	Sets the comment that appears with the share	None	Share

Table 4-4. Basic Share Configuration Options (continued)

Option	Parameters	Function	Default	Scope
volume	string	Sets the volume name: the DOS name of the physical drive	Share name	Share
read only	boolean	If yes, allows read only access to a share.	yes	Share
writeable (write ok)	boolean	If no, allows read only access to a share.	no	Share

path

This option, which has the synonym **directory**, indicates the pathname at the root of the file or printing share. You can choose any path on the Samba server, so long as the owner of the Samba process that is connecting has read and write access to that directory. If the path is for a printing share, it should point to a temporary directory where files can be written on the server before being spooled to the target printer (*/tmp* and */var/spool* are popular choices). If this path is for a disk share, the contents of the folder representing the share name on the client will match the content of the directory on the Samba server. For example, if we have the following disk share listed in our configuration file:

```
[network]
    path = /export/samba/network
    writable = yes
    guest ok = yes
```

And the contents of the directory */usr/local/network* on the Unix side are:

```
$ ls -al /export/samba/network
drwxrwxrwx  9  root    nobody  1024  Feb 16 17:17  .
drwxr-xr-x  9  nobody nobody  1024  Feb 16 17:17  ..
drwxr-xr-x  9  nobody nobody  1024  Feb 16 17:17  quicken
drwxr-xr-x  9  nobody nobody  1024  Feb 16 17:17  tax98
drwxr-xr-x  9  nobody nobody  1024  Feb 16 17:17  taxdocuments
```

Then we should see the equivalent of Figure 4-5 on the client side.

guest ok

This option (which has an older synonym **public**) allows or prohibits guest access to a share. The default value is **no**. If set to **yes**, it means that no username or password will be needed to connect to the share. When a user connects, the access rights will be equivalent to the designated guest user. The default account to which Samba offers the share is **nobody**. However, this can be reset with the

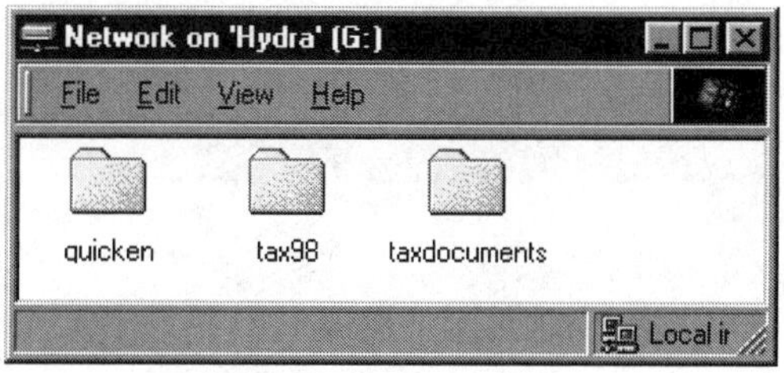

Figure 4-5. Windows client view of a network filesystem specified by path

guest account configuration option. For example, the following lines allow guest user access to the [accounting] share with the permissions of the *ftp* account:

```
. [global]
     guest account = ftp
[accounting]
     path = /usr/local/account
     guest ok = yes
```

Note that users can still connect to the share using a valid username/password combination. If successful, they will hold the access rights granted by their own account and not the guest account. If a user attempts to log in and fails, however, he or she will default to the access rights of the guest account. You can mandate that every user who attaches to the share will be using the guest account (and will have the permissions of the guest) by setting the option **guest only = yes**.

comment

The **comment** option allows you to enter a comment that will be sent to the client when it attempts to browse the share. The user can see the comment by listing Details on the share folder under the appropriate computer in the Windows Network Neighborhood, or type the command **NET VIEW** at an MS-DOS prompt. For example, here is how you might insert a comment for a [network] share:

```
[network]
     comment = Network Drive
     path = /export/samba/network
```

This yields a folder similar to Figure 4-6 on the client side. Note that with the current configuration of Windows, this comment will not be shown once a share is mapped to a Windows network drive.

Be sure not to confuse the **comment** option, which documents a Samba server's shares, with the **server string** option, which documents the server itself.

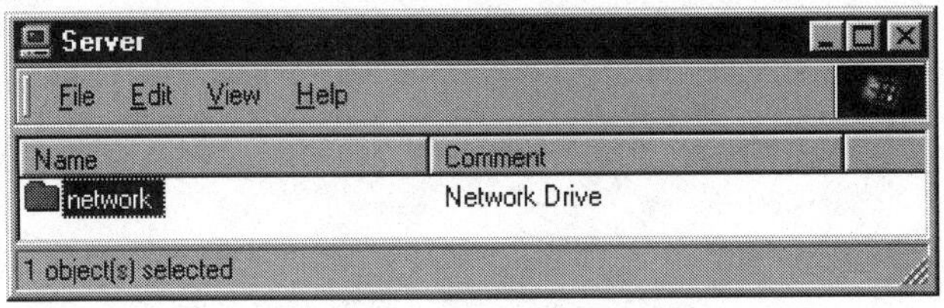

Figure 4-6. Windows client view of a share comment

volume

This option allows you to specify the volume name of the share as reported by SMB. This normally resolves to the name of the share given in the *smb.conf* file. However, if you wish to name it something else (for whatever reason) you can do so with this option.

For example, an installer program may check the volume name of a CD-ROM to make sure the right CD-ROM is in the drive before attempting to install it. If you copy the contents of the CD-ROM into a network share, and wish to install from there, you can use this option to get around the issue:

```
[network]
    comment = Network Drive
    volume = ASVP-102-RTYUIKA
    path = /home/samba/network
```

read only and writeable

The options **read only** and **writeable** (or **write ok**) are really two ways of saying the same thing, but approached from opposite ends. For example, you can set either of the following options in the **[global]** section or in an individual share:

```
read only = yes
writeable = no
```

If either option is set as shown, data can be read from a share, but cannot be written to it. You might think you would need this option only if you were creating a read-only share. However, note that this read-only behavior is the *default* action for shares; if you want to be able to write data to a share, you must explicitly specify one of the following options in the configuration file for each share:

```
read only = no
writeable = yes
```

Note that if you specify more than one occurrence of either option, Samba will adhere to the last value it encounters for the share.

Networking Options with Samba

If you're running Samba on a multi-homed machine (that is, one on multiple subnets), or even if you want to implement a security policy on your own subnet, you should take a close look at the networking configuration options:

For the purposes of this exercise, let's assume that our Samba server is connected to a network with more than one subnet. Specifically, the machine can access both the 192.168.220.* and 134.213.233.* subnets. Here are our additions to the ongoing configuration file for the networking configuration options:

```
[global]
    netbios name = HYDRA
    server string = Samba %v on (%L)
    workgroup = SIMPLE

    # Networking configuration options
    hosts allow = 192.168.220. 134.213.233. localhost
    hosts deny = 192.168.220.102
    interfaces = 192.168.220.100/255.255.255.0 \
                 134.213.233.110/255.255.255.0
    bind interfaces only = yes

[data]
    path = /home/samba/data
    guest ok = yes
    comment = Data Drive
    volume = Sample-Data-Drive
    writeable = yes
```

Let's first talk about the **hosts allow** and **hosts deny** options. If these options sound familiar, you're probably thinking of the *hosts.allow* and *hosts.deny* files that are found in the */etc* directories of many Unix systems. The purpose of these options is identical to those files; they provide a means of security by allowing or denying the connections of other hosts based on their IP addresses. Why not just use the *hosts.allow* and *hosts.deny* files themselves? Because there may be services on the server that you want others to access without giving them access Samba's disk or printer shares

With the **hosts allow** option above, we've specified a cropped IP address: 192. 168.220. (Note that there is still a third period; it's just missing the fourth number.) This is equivalent to saying: "All hosts on the 192.168.220 subnet." However, we've explicitly specified in a hosts deny line that 192.168.220.102 is not to be allowed access.

You might be wondering: why will 192.168.220.102 be denied even though it is still in the subnet matched by the **hosts allow** option? Here is how Samba sorts out the rules specified by **hosts allow** and **hosts deny**:

1. If there are no **allow** or **deny** options defined anywhere in *smb.conf*, Samba will allow connections from any machine allowed by the system itself.

2. If there are **hosts allow** or **hosts deny** options defined in the [global] section of *smb.conf*, they will apply to all shares, even if the shares have an overriding option defined.

3. If there is only a **hosts allow** option defined for a share, only the hosts listed will be allowed to use the share. All others will be denied.

4. If there is only a **hosts deny** option defined for a share, any machine which is not on the list will be able to use the share.

5. If both a **hosts allow** and **hosts deny** option are defined, a host must appear in the allow list and not appear in the deny list (in any form) in order to access the share. Otherwise, the host will not be allowed.

 Take care that you don't explicitly allow a host to access a share, but then deny access to the entire subnet of which the host is part.

Let's look at another example of that final item. Consider the following options:

```
hosts allow = 111.222.
hosts deny = 111.222.333.
```

In this case, only the hosts that belong to the subnet 111.222.*.* will be allowed access to the Samba shares. However, if a client belongs to the 111.222.333.* subnet, it will be denied access, even though it still matches the qualifications outlined by **hosts allow**. The client must appear on the **hosts allow** list and *must not* appear on the **hosts deny** list in order to gain access to a Samba share. If a computer attempts to access a share to which it is not allowed access, it will receive an error message.

The other two options that we've specified are the **interfaces** and the **bind interface only** address. Let's look at the **interfaces** option first. Samba, by default, sends data only from the primary network interface, which in our example is the 192.168.220.100 subnet. If we would like it to send data to more than that one interface, we need to specify the complete list with the **interfaces** option. In the previous example, we've bound Samba to interface with both subnets (192.168.220 and 134.213.233) on which the machine is operating by specifying the other network interface address: 134.213.233.100. If you have more than one interface on your computer, you should always set this option as there is no guarantee that the primary interface that Samba chooses will be the right one.

Finally, the `bind interfaces only` option instructs the *nmbd* process not to accept any broadcast messages other than those subnets specified with the `interfaces` option. Note that this is different from the `hosts allow` and `hosts deny` options, which prevent machines from making connections to services, but not from receiving broadcast messages. Using the `bind interfaces only` option is a way to shut out even datagrams from foreign subnets from being received by the Samba server. In addition, it instructs the *smbd* process to bind to only the interface list given by the *interfaces* option. This restricts the networks that Samba will serve.

Networking Options

The networking options we introduced above are summarized in Table 4-5.

Table 4-5. Networking Configuration Options

Option	Parameters	Function	Default	Scope
hosts allow (allow hosts)	string (list of hostnames)	Specifies the machines that can connect to Samba.	none	Share
hosts deny (deny hosts)	string (list of hostnames)	Specifies the machines that cannot connect to Samba.	none	Share
interfaces	string (list of IP/netmask combinations)	Sets the network interfaces Samba will respond to. Allows correcting defaults.	system-dependent	Global
bind interfaces only	boolean	If set to **yes**, Samba will bind only to those interfaces specified by the `interfaces` option.	no	Global
socket address	string (IP address)	Sets IP address to listen on, for use with multiple virtual interfaces on a server.	none	Global

hosts allow

The `hosts allow` option (sometimes written as `allow hosts`) specifies the machines that have permission to access shares on the Samba server, written as a comma- or space-separated list of names of machines or their IP addresses. You can gain quite a bit of security by simply placing your LAN's subnet address in this option. For example, we specified the following in our example:

```
hosts allow = 192.168.220. localhost
```

Note that we placed `localhost` after the subnet address. One of the most common mistakes when attempting to use the `hosts allow` option is to accidentally disallow the Samba server from communicating with itself. The *smbpasswd* program will occasionally need to connect to the Samba server as a client in order to change a user's encrypted password. In addition, local browsing propagation requires local host access. If this option is enabled and the localhost address is not specified, the locally-generated packets requesting the change of the encrypted password will be discarded by Samba, and browsing propagation will not work properly. To avoid this, explicitly allow the loopback address (either `localhost` or `127.0.0.1`) to be used.[*]

You can specify any of the following formats for this option:

- Hostnames, such as `ftp.example.com`.

- IP addresses, like `130.63.9.252`.

- Domain names, which can be differentiated from individual hostnames because they start with a dot. For example, `.ora.com` represents all machines within the *ora.com* domain.

- Netgroups, which start with an at-sign, such as `@printerhosts`. Netgroups are available on systems running yellow pages/NIS or NIS+, but rarely otherwise. If netgroups are supported on your system, there should be a `netgroups` manual page that describes them in more detail.

- Subnets, which end with a dot. For example, `130.63.9.` means all the machines whose IP addresses begin with 130.63.9.

- The keyword `ALL`, which allows any client access.

- The keyword `EXCEPT` followed by more one or more names, IP addresses, domain names, netgroups, or subnets. For example, you could specify that Samba allow all hosts except those on the 192.168.110 subnet with `hosts allow = ALL EXCEPT 192.168.110.` (remember the trailing dot).

Using the `ALL` keyword is almost always a bad idea, since it means that anyone on any network can browse your files if they guess the name of your server.

Note that there is no default value for the `hosts allow` configuration option, although the default course of action in the event that neither option is specified is to allow access from all sources. In addition, if you specify this option in the `[global]` section of the configuration file, it will override any `hosts allow` options defined shares.

---

[*] Starting with Samba 2.0.5, `localhost` will automatically be allowed unless it is explicitly denied.

hosts deny

The `hosts deny` option (also `deny hosts`) specifies machines that do not have permission to access a share, written as a comma- or space-separated list of machine names or their IP addresses. Use the same format as specifying clients as the `hosts allow` option above. For example, to restrict access to the server from everywhere but *example.com*, you could write:

```
hosts deny = ALL EXCEPT .example.com
```

Like `hosts allow`, there is no default value for the `hosts deny` configuration option, although the default course of action in the event that neither option is specified is to allow access from all sources. Also, if you specify this option in the `[global]` section of the configuration file, it will override any `hosts deny` options defined in shares. If you wish to deny *hosts* access to specific shares, omit both the `hosts allow` and `hosts deny` options in the `[global]` section of the configuration file.

interfaces

The `interfaces` option outlines the network addresses to which you want the Samba server to recognize and respond. This option is handy if you have a computer that resides on more than one network subnet. If this option is not set, Samba searches for the primary network interface of the server (typically the first Ethernet card) upon startup and configures itself to operate on only that subnet. If the server is configured for more than one subnet and you do not specify this option, Samba will only work on the first subnet it encounters. You must use this option to force Samba to serve the other subnets on your network.

The value of this option is one or more sets of IP address/netmask pairs, such as the following:

```
interfaces = 192.168.220.100/255.255.255.0 192.168.210.30/255.255.255.0
```

You can optionally specify a CIDR format bitmask, as follows:

```
interfaces = 192.168.220.100/24 192.168.210.30/24
```

The bitmask number specifies the first number of bits that will be turned on in the netmask. For example, the number 24 means that the first 24 (of 32) bits will be activated in the bit mask, which is the same as saying 255.255.255.0. Likewise, 16 would be equal to 255.255.0.0, and 8 would be equal to 255.0.0.0.

This option may not work correctly if you are using DHCP.

bind interfaces only

The bind interfaces only option can be used to force the *smbd* and *nmbd* processes to serve SMB requests to only those addresses specified by the interfaces option. The *nmbd* process normally binds to the all addresses interface (0.0.0.0.) on ports 137 and 138, allowing it to receive broadcasts from anywhere. However, you can override this behavior with the following:

```
bind interfaces only = yes
```

This will cause both Samba processes to ignore any packets whose origination address does not match the broadcast address(es) specified by the interfaces option, including broadcast packets. With *smbd*, this option will cause Samba to not serve file requests to subnets other than those listed in the interfaces option. You should avoid using this option if you want to allow temporary network connections, such as those created through SLIP or PPP. It's very rare that this option is needed, and it should only be used by experts.

> If you set bind interfaces only to yes, you should add the localhost address (127.0.01) to the "interfaces" list. Otherwise, *smbpasswd* will be unable to connect to the server using its default mode in order to change a password.

socket address

The socket address option dictates which of the addresses specified with the interfaces parameter Samba should listen on for connections. Samba accepts connections on all addresses specified by default. When used in an *smb.conf* file, this option will force Samba to listen on only one IP address. For example:

```
interfaces = 192.168.220.100/24 192.168.210.30/24
socket address = 192.168.210.30
```

This option is a programmer's tool and we recommend that you do not use it.

Virtual Servers

Virtual servers are a technique for creating the illusion of multiple NetBIOS servers on the network, when in reality there is only one. The technique is simple to implement: a machine simply registers more than one NetBIOS name in association with its IP address. There are tangible benefits to doing this.

The accounting department, for example, might have an accounting server, and clients of it would see just the accounting disks and printers. The marketing department could have their own server, **marketing**, with their own reports, and so on. However, all the services would be provided by one medium-sized Unix workstation (and one relaxed administrator), instead of having one small server and one administrator per department.

Samba will allow a Unix server to use more than one NetBIOS name with the **netbios aliases** option. See Table 4-6.

Table 4-6. Virtual Server Configuration Options

Option	Parameters	Function	Default	Scope
netbios aliases	List of Net-BIOS names	Additional NetBIOS names to respond to, for use with multiple "virtual" Samba servers.	None	Global

netbios aliases

The **netbios aliases** option can be used to give the Samba server more than one NetBIOS name. Each NetBIOS name listed as a value will be displayed in the Network Neighborhood of a browsing machine. When a connection is requested to any machine, however, it will connect to the same Samba server.

This might come in handy, for example, if you're transferring three departments' data to a single Unix server with modern large disks, and are retiring or reallocating the old NT servers. If the three servers are called **sales**, **accounting**, and **admin**, you can have Samba represent all three servers with the following options:

```
[global]
    netbios aliases = sales accounting admin
    include = /usr/local/samba/lib/smb.conf.%L
```

See Figure 4-7 for what the Network Neighborhood would display from a client. When a client attempts to connect to Samba, it will specify the name of the server that it's trying to connect to, which you can access through the **%L** variable. If the requested server is **sales**, Samba will include the */usr/local/samba/lib/smb.conf. sales* file. This file might contain global and share declarations exclusively for the sales team, such as the following:

```
[global]
    workgroup = SALES
    hosts allow = 192.168.10.255

[sales1998]
    path = /usr/local/samba/sales/sales1998/
...
```

This particular example would set the workgroup to SALES as well, and set the IP address to allow connections only from the SALES subnet (192.168.10). In addition, it would offer shares specific to the sales department.

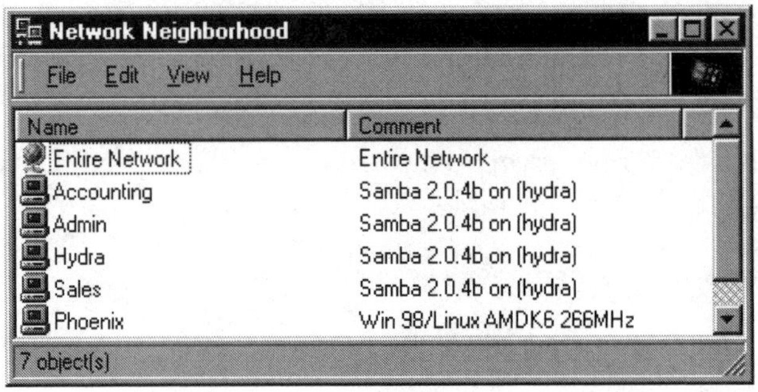

Figure 4-7. Using NetBIOS aliases for a Samba server

Logging Configuration Options

Occasionally, we need to find out what Samba is up to. This is especially true when Samba is performing an unexpected action or is not performing at all. To find out this information, we need to check Samba's log files to see exactly why it did what it did.

Samba log files can be as brief or verbose as you like. Here is an example of what a Samba log file looks like:

```
[1999/07/21 13:23:25, 3] smbd/service.c:close_cnum(514)
  phoenix (192.168.220.101) closed connection to service IPC$
[1999/07/21 13:23:25, 3] smbd/connection.c:yield_connection(40)
  Yielding connection to IPC$
[1999/07/21 13:23:25, 3] smbd/process.c:process_smb(615)
  Transaction 923 of length 49
[1999/07/21 13:23:25, 3] smbd/process.c:switch_message(448)
  switch message SMBread (pid 467)
[1999/07/21 13:23:25, 3] lib/doscalls.c:dos_ChDir(336)
  dos_ChDir to /home/samba
[1999/07/21 13:23:25, 3] smbd/reply.c:reply_read(2199)
  read fnum=4207 num=2820 nread=2820
[1999/07/21 13:23:25, 3] smbd/process.c:process_smb(615)
  Transaction 924 of length 55
[1999/07/21 13:23:25, 3] smbd/process.c:switch_message(448)
  switch message SMBreadbraw (pid 467)
[1999/07/21 13:23:25, 3] smbd/reply.c:reply_readbraw(2053)
  readbraw fnum=4207 start=130820 max=1276 min=0 nread=1276
[1999/07/21 13:23:25, 3] smbd/process.c:process_smb(615)
  Transaction 925 of length 55
[1999/07/21 13:23:25, 3] smbd/process.c:switch_message(448)
  switch message SMBreadbraw (pid 467)
```

Many of these options are of use only to Samba programmers. However, we will go over the meaning of some of these entries in more detail in Chapter 9, *Trouble-shooting Samba.*

Samba contains six options that allow users to describe how and where logging information should be written. Each of these options are global options and cannot appear inside a share definition. Here is an up-to-date configuration file that covers each of the share and logging options that we've seen so far:

```
[global]
        netbios name = HYDRA
        server string = Samba %v on (%I)
        workgroup = SIMPLE

        #  Networking configuration options
        hosts allow = 192.168.220. 134.213.233. localhost
        hosts deny = 192.168.220.102
        interfaces = 192.168.220.100/255.255.255.0 \
                        134.213.233.110/255.255.255.0
        bind interfaces only = yes

        # Debug logging information
        log level = 2
        log file = /var/log/samba.log.%m
        max log size = 50
        debug timestamp = yes

[data]
        path = /home/samba/data
        browseable = yes
        guest ok = yes
        comment = Data Drive
        volume = Sample-Data-Drive
        writeable = yes
```

Here, we've added a custom log file that reports information up to debug level 2. This is a relatively light debugging level. The logging level ranges from 1 to 10, where level 1 provides only a small amount of information and level 10 provides a plethora of low-level information. Level 2 will provide us with useful debugging information without wasting disk space on our server. In practice, you should avoid using log levels greater than 3 unless you are programming Samba.

This file is located in the */var/log* directory thanks to the **log file** configuration option. However, we can use variable substitution to create log files specifically for individual users or clients, such as with the **%m** variable in the following line:

```
log file = /usr/local/logs/samba.log.%m
```

Isolating the log messages can be invaluable in tracking down a network error if you know the problem is coming from a specific machine or user.

We've added another precaution to the log files: no one log file can exceed 50 kilobytes in size, as specified by the **max log size** option. If a log file exceeds this size, the contents are moved to a file with the same name but with the suffix

.old appended. If the *.old* file already exists, it is overwritten and its contents are lost. The original file is cleared, waiting to receive new logging information. This prevents the hard drive from being overwhelmed with Samba log files during the life of our daemons.

For convenience, we have decided to leave the debug timestamp in the logs with the **debug timestamp** option, which is the default behavior. This will place a timestamp next to each message in the logging file. If we were not interested in this information, we could specify **no** for this option instead.

Using syslog

If you wish to use the system logger (*syslog*) in addition to or in place of the standard Samba logging file, Samba provides options for this as well. However, to use *syslog*, the first thing you will have to do is make sure that Samba was built with the **configure --with-syslog** option. See Chapter 2 for more information on configuring and compiling Samba.

Once that is done, you will need to configure your */etc/syslog.conf* to accept logging information from Samba. If there is not already a **daemon.*** entry in the */etc/syslog.conf* file, add the following:

```
daemon.*        /var/log/daemon.log
```

This specifies that any logging information from system daemons will be stored in the */var/log/daemon.log* file. This is where the Samba information will be stored as well. From there, you can specify the following global option in your configuration file:

```
syslog = 2
```

This specifies that any logging messages with a level of 1 will be sent to both the *syslog* and the Samba logging files. (The mappings to *syslog* priorities are described in the upcoming section "syslog.") Let's assume that we set the regular **log level** option above to 4. Any logging messages with a level of 2, 3, or 4 will be sent to the Samba logging files, but not to the *syslog*. Only level 1 logging messages will be sent to both. If the **syslog** value exceeds the **log level** value, nothing will be written to the *syslog*.

If you want to specify that messages be sent only to *syslog*—and not to the standard Samba logging files—you can place this option in the configuration file:

```
syslog only = yes
```

If this is the case, any logging information above the number specified in the **syslog** option will be discarded, just like the **log level** option.

Logging Configuration Options

Table 4-7 lists each of the logging configuration options that Samba can use.

Table 4-7. Global Configuration Options

Option	Parameters	Function	Default	Scope
log file	string (fully-qualified filename)	Sets the name and location of the log file that Samba is to use. Uses standard variables.	Specified in Samba makefile	Global
log level (debug level)	numerical (0–10)	Sets the amount of log/debug messages that are sent to the log file. 0 is none, 3 is considerable.	1	Global
max log size	numerical (size in KB)	Sets the maximum size of log file. After the log exceeds this size, the file will be renamed to *.old* and a new log file started.	5000	Global
debug timestamp (timestamp logs)	boolean	If no, doesn't timestamp logs, making them easier to read during heavy debugging.	yes	Global
syslog	numerical (0–10)	Sets level of messages sent to *syslog*. Those levels below syslog level will be sent to the system logger.	1	Global
syslog only	boolean	If yes, uses *syslog* entirely and sends no output to the standard Samba log files.	no	Global

log file

On our server, Samba outputs log information to text files in the *var* subdirectory of the Samba home directory, as set by the makefile during the build. The log file option can be used to reset the name of the log file to another location. For example, to reset the name and location of the Samba log file to */usr/local/logs/samba.log*, you could use the following:

```
[global]
    log file = /usr/local/logs/samba.log
```

You may use variable substitution to create log files specifically for individual users or clients.

You can override the default log file location using the -1 command-line switch when either daemon is started. However, this does not override the log file option. If you do specify this parameter, initial logging information will be sent to the file specified after -1 (or the default specified in the Samba makefile) until the daemons have processed the *smb.conf* file and know to redirect it to a new log file.

log level

The log level option sets the amount of data to be logged. Normally this is left at 0 or 1. However, if you have a specific problem you may want to set it at 3, which provides the most useful debugging information you would need to track down a problem. Levels above 3 provide information that's primarily for the developers to use for chasing internal bugs, and slows down the server considerably. Therefore, we recommend that you avoid setting this option to anything above 3.

```
[global]
log file = /usr/local/logs/samba.log.%m
log level = 3
```

max log size

The max log size option sets the maximum size, in kilobytes, of the debugging log file that Samba keeps. When the log file exceeds this size, the current log file is renamed to add an *.old* extension (erasing any previous file with that name) and a new debugging log file is started with the original name. For example:

```
[global]
log file = /usr/local/logs/samba.log.%m
max log size = 1000
```

Here, if the size of any log file exceeds one megabyte in size, Samba renames the log file *samba.log.machine-name.old* and a new log file is generated. If there was a file there previously with the *.old* extension, Samba deletes it. We highly recommend setting this option in your configuration files because debug logging (even at lower levels) can covertly eat away at your available disk space. Using this option protects unwary administrators from suddenly discovering that most of their disk space has been swallowed up by a single Samba log file.

debug timestamp or timestamp logs

If you happen to be debugging a network problem and you find that the date-stamp and timestamp information within the Samba log lines gets in the way, you can turn it off by giving either the timestamp logs or the debug timestamp option (they're synonymous) a value of no. For example, a regular Samba log file presents its output in the following form:

```
12/31/98 12:03:34 hydra (192.168.220.101) connect to server network as user davecb
```

With a **no** value for this option, the output would appear without the datestamp or the timestamp:

```
hydra (192.168.220.101) connect to server network as user davecb
```

syslog

The **syslog** option causes Samba log messages to be sent to the Unix system logger. The type of log information to be sent is specified as the parameter for this argument. Like the **log level** option, it can be a number from 0 to 10. Logging information with a level less than the number specified will be sent to the system logger. However, debug logs equal to or above the **syslog** level, but less than log level, will still be sent to the standard Samba log files. To get around this, use the **syslog only** option. For example:

```
[global]
    log level = 3
    syslog = 1
```

With this, all logging information with a level of 0 would be sent to the standard Samba logs and the system logger, while information with levels 1, 2, and 3 would be sent only to the standard Samba logs. Levels above 3 are not logged at all. Note that all messages sent to the system logger are mapped to a priority level that the *syslog* process understands, as shown in Table 4-8. The default level is 1.

Table 4-8. Syslog Priority Conversion

Log Level	Syslog Priority
0	LOG_ERR
1	LOG_WARNING
2	LOG_NOTICE
3	LOG_INFO
4 and above	LOG_DEBUG

If you wish to use *syslog*, you will have to run **configure --with-syslog** when compiling Samba, and you will need to configure your */etc/syslog.conf* to suit. (See the section "Using syslog," earlier in this chapter.)

syslog only

The **syslog only** option tells Samba not to use the regular logging files—the system logger only. To enable this, specify the following option in the global ection of the Samba configuration file:

```
[global]
    syslog only = yes
```

5

Browsing and Advanced Disk Shares

This chapter continues our discussion of disk shares from the previous chapter. Here, we will discuss various differences between the Windows and Unix filesystems—and how Samba works to bridge the gap. There are a surprising number of inconsistencies between a DOS filesystem and a Unix filesystem. In addition, we will talk briefly about name mangling, file locking, and a relatively new feature for Samba: opportunistic locking, or oplocks. However, before we move into that territory, we should first discuss the somewhat arcane topic of browsing with Samba.

Browsing

Browsing is the ability to examine the servers and shares that are currently available on your network. On a Windows NT 4.0 or 95/98 client, a user can browse network servers through the Network Neighborhood folder. By double-clicking the icon representing the server, the user should be able to see the printer and disk share resources available on that machine as well. (If you have Windows NT 3.*x*, you can use the Disk-Connect Network Drive menu in the File Manager to display the available shares on a server.)

From the Windows command line, you can also use the **net view** option to see which servers are currently on the network. Here is an example of the **net view** command in action:

```
C:\>net view
Servers available in workgroup SIMPLE
Server name         Remark
---------------------------------------------------------
\\CHIMAERA          Windows NT 4.0
\\HYDRA             Samba 2.0.4 on (hydra)
\\PHOENIX           Windows 98
```

Preventing Browsing

You can restrict a share from being in a browse list by using the **browseable** option. This boolean option prevents a share from being seen in the Network Neighborhood at all. For example, to prevent the **[data]** share from the previous chapter from being visible, we could write:

```
[data]
    path = /home/samba/data
    browseable = no
    guest ok = yes
    comment = Data Drive
    volume = Sample-Data-Drive
    writeable = yes
```

Although you typically don't want to do this to an ordinary disk share, the browseable option is useful in the event that you need to create a share with contents that you do not want others to see, such as a **[netlogin]** share for storing logon scripts for Windows domain control (see Chapter 6, *Users, Security, and Domains* for more information on logon scripts).

Another example is the **[homes]** share. This share is often marked non-browsable so that a share named **[homes]** won't appear when its machine's resources are browsed. However, if a user **alice** logs on and looks at the machine's shares, an **[alice]** share will appear under the machine. What if we wanted to make sure **alice**'s share appeared to everyone before she logs in? This could be done with the global **auto services** option. This option preloads shares into the browse list to ensure that they are always visible:

```
[global]
    ...
    auto services = alice
    ...
```

Default Services

In the event that a user cannot successfully connect to a share, you can specify a default share to which they can connect. Since you do not know who will default to this share at any time, you will probably want to set the **guest ok** option to **yes** for this share. Specifying a **default service** can be useful when sending the utterly befuddled to a directory of help files. For example:

```
[global]
    ...
    default service = helpshare
    ...

[helpshare]
    path = /home/samba/helpshare/%S
    browseable = yes
```

```
guest ok = yes
comment = Default Share for Unsuccessful Connections
volume = Sample-Data-Drive
writeable = no
```

Note that we used the %S variable in the **path** option. If you use the %S variable, it will refer to the requested nonexistent share (the original share requested by the user), not the name of the resulting default share. This allows us to create different paths with the names of each server, which can provide more customized help files for users. In addition, any underscores (_) specified in the requested share will be converted to slashes (/) when the %S variable is used.

Browsing Elections

As mentioned in Chapter 1, *Learning the Samba,* one machine in each subnet always keeps a list of the currently active machines. This list is called the *browse list* and the server that maintains it is called the *local master browser.* As machines come on and off the network, the local master browser continually updates the information in the browse list and provides it to any machine that requests it.

A computer becomes a local master browser by holding a browsing election on the local subnet. Browsing elections can be called at any time. Samba can rig a browsing election for a variety of outcomes, including always becoming the local master browser of the subnet or never becoming it. For example, the following options, which we've added to the configuration file from Chapter 4, *Disk Shares,* will ensure that Samba always wins the election for local master browser no matter which machines are also present:

```
[global]
    netbios name = HYDRA
    server string = Samba %v on (%L)
    workgroup = SIMPLE

    # Browsing election options
    os level = 34
    local master = yes

    # Networking configuration options
    hosts allow = 192.168.220. 134.213.233. localhost
    hosts deny = 192.168.220.102
    interfaces = 192.168.220.100/255.255.255.0 \
                 134.213.233.110/255.255.255.0

    # Debug logging information
    log level = 2
    log file = /var/log/samba.log.%m
    max log size = 50
    debug timestamp = yes
```

```
[data]
    path = /home/samba/data
    browseable = yes
    guest ok = yes
    comment = Data Drive
    volume = Sample-Data-Drive
    writable = yes
```

However, what if we didn't always want to win the election? What if we wanted to yield browsing to a Windows NT Server if present? In order to do that, we need to learn how browsing elections work. As you already know, each machine that takes place in the election must broadcast information about itself. This information includes the following:

- The version of the election protocol used

- The operating system on the machine

- The amount of time the client has been on the network

- The hostname of the client

Here is how the election is decided. Operating systems are assigned a binary value according to their version, as shown in Table 5-1.

Table 5-1 . Operating System Values in an Election

Operating System	Value
Windows NT Server 4.0	33
Windows NT Server 3.51	32
Windows NT Workstation 4.0	17
Windows NT Workstation 3.51	16
Windows 98	2
Windows 95	1
Windows 3.1 for Workgroups	1

Following that, each computer on the network is assigned a separate value according to its role, as shown in Table 5-2.

Table 5-2. Computer Role Settings in an Election

Role	Value
Primary Domain Controller	128
WINS Client	32
Preferred Master Browser	8
Active Master Browser	4
Standby Browser	2
Active Backup Browser	1

Elections are decided in the following order:

1. The machine with the highest version of the election protocol will win. (So far, this is meaningless, as all Windows clients have version 1 of the election protocol.)

2. The machine with the highest operating system value wins the election.

3. If there is a tie, the machine with the setting of Preferred Master Browser (role 8) wins the election.

4. If there is still a tie, the client who has been online the longest wins the election.

5. And finally, if there is still a tie, the client name that comes first alphabetically wins.

6. The machine that is the "runner-up" can become a backup browser.

As a result, if you want Samba to take the role of a local master browser, but only if there isn't a Windows NT Server (4.0 or 3.51) on the network, you could change the os level parameter in the previous example to:

```
os level = 31
```

This will cause Samba to immediately lose the election to a Windows NT 4.0 or Windows NT 3.5 Server, both of which have a higher operating systems level. On the other hand, if you wanted to decide the local master browser on the basis of the network role, such as which machine is the primary domain controller, you could set the os level to match the highest type of operating system on the network and let the election protocol fall down to the next level.

How can you can tell if a machine is a local master browser? By using the nbtstat command. Place the NetBIOS name of the machine you wish to check after the -a option:

```
C:\>nbtstat -a hydra

        NetBIOS Remote Machine Name Table

    Name                        Type       Status
    ---------------------------------------------------------
    HYDRA                <00>   UNIQUE     Registered
    HYDRA                <03>   UNIQUE     Registered
    HYDRA                <20>   UNIQUE     Registered
    .._ _MSBROWSE_ _.    <01>   GROUP      Registered
    SIMPLE               <00>   GROUP      Registered
    SIMPLE               <1D>   UNIQUE     Registered
    SIMPLE               <1E>   GROUP      Registered

    MAC Address = 00-00-00-00-00-00
```

The resource entry that you're looking for is the `.._ _MSBROWSE_ _.<01>`. This indicates that the server is currently acting as the local master browser for the current subnet. In addition, if the machine is a Samba server, you can check the Samba *nmbd* log file for an entry such as:

```
nmbd/nmbd_become_lmb.c:become_local_master_stage2(406)
*****
Samba name server HYDRA is now a local master browser for
workgroup SIMPLE on subnet 192.168.220.100
****
```

Finally, Windows NT servers serving as primary domain controllers contain a sneak that allows them to assume the role of the local master browser in certain conditions; this is called the *preferred master browser* bit. Earlier, we mentioned that Samba could set this bit on itself as well. You can enable it with the **preferred master** option:

```
#  Browsing election options
os level = 33
local master = yes
preferred master = yes
```

If the preferred master bit is set, the machine will force a browsing election at startup. Of course, this is needed only if you set the **os level** option to match the Windows NT machine. We recommend that you don't use this option if another machine also has the role of preferred master, such as an NT server.

Domain Master Browser

In the opening chapter, we mentioned that in order for a Windows workgroup or domain to extend into multiple subnets, one machine would have to take the role of the *domain master browser*. The domain master browser propagates browse lists across each of the subnets in the workgroup. This works because each local master browser periodically synchronizes its browse list with the domain master browser. During this synchronization, the local master browser passes on any server that the domain master browser does not have in its browse list, and vice versa. In a perfect world, each local master browser would eventually have the browse list for the entire domain.

Unlike the local master browser, there is no election to determine which machine assumes the role of the domain master browser. Instead, the administrator has to set it manually. By Microsoft design, however, the domain master browser and the primary domain controller (PDC) both register a resource type of <1B>, so the roles—and the machines—are inseparable.

If you have a Windows NT server on the network acting as a PDC, we recommend that you do not use Samba to become the domain master browser. The reverse is true as well: if Samba is taking on the responsibilities of a PDC, we recommend making it the domain master browser as well. Although it is possible to split the roles with Samba, this is not a good idea. Using two different machines to serve as the PDC and the domain master browser can cause random errors to occur on a Windows workgroup.

Samba can assume the role of a domain master browser for all subnets in the workgroup with the following option:

```
domain master = yes
```

You can verify that a Samba machine is in fact the domain master browser by checking the *nmbd* log file:

```
nmbd/nmbd_become_dmb.c:become_domain_master_stage2(118)
*****
Samba name server HYDRA is now a domain master browser for
workgroup SIMPLE on subnet 192.168.220.100
*****
```

Or you can use the **nmblookup** command that comes with the Samba distribution to query for a unique <1B> resource type in the workgroup:

```
# nmblookup SIMPLE#1B
Sending queries to 192.168.220.255
192.168.220.100 SIMPLE<1b>
```

Multiple subnets

There are three rules that you must remember when creating a workgroup/domain that spans more than one subnet:

- You must have either a Windows NT or Samba machine acting as a local master browser on each subnet in the workgroup/domain.

- You must have a Windows NT Server or a Samba machine acting as a domain master browser somewhere in the workgroup.

- Each local master browser must be instructed to synchronize with the domain master browser.

Samba has a few other features in this arena in the event that you don't have or want a domain master browser on your network. Consider the subnets shown in Figure 5-1.

First, a Samba server that is a local master browser can use the **remote announce** configuration option to make sure that computers in different subnets are sent broadcast announcements about the server. This has the effect of ensuring that the Samba server appears in the browse lists of foreign subnets. To achieve this, however, the directed broadcasts must reach the local master browser on the other subnet. Be aware that many routers do not allow directed broadcasts by default;

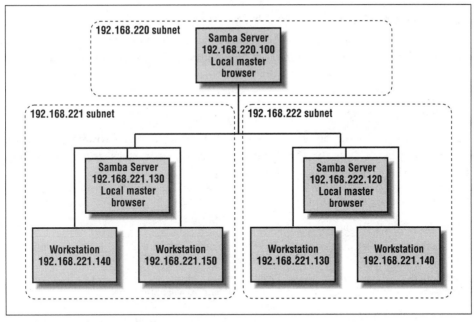

Figure 5-1. Multiple subnets with Samba servers

you may have to change this setting on the router for the directed broadcasts to get through to its subnet.

With the **remote announce** option, list the subnets and the workgroup that should receive the broadcast. For example, to ensure that machines in the 192.168.221 and 192.168.222 subnets and SIMPLE workgroup are sent broadcast information from our Samba server, we could specify the following:

```
#  Browsing election options
os level = 34
local master = yes
remote announce = 192.168.221.255/SIMPLE \
    192.168.222.255/SIMPLE
```

In addition, you are allowed to specify the exact address to send broadcasts to if the local master browser on the foreign subnet is guaranteed to always have a fixed IP address.

A Samba local master browser can synchronize its browse list directly with another Samba server acting as a local master browser on a different subnet. For example, let's assume that Samba is configured as a local master browser, and Samba local master browsers exist at 192.168.221.130 and 192.168.222.120. We can use the **remote browse sync** option to sync directly with the Samba servers, as follows:

```
#  Browsing election options
os level = 34
```

```
local master = yes
remote browse sync = 192.168.221.130 192.168.222.120
```

In order for this to work, the other Samba machines must also be local master browsers. You can also use directed broadcasts with this option if you do not know specific IP addresses of local master browsers.

Browsing Options

Table 5-3 shows 14 options that define how Samba handles browsing tasks. We recommend the defaults for a site that prefers to be easy on its users with respect to locating shares and printers.

Table 5-3. Browsing Configuration Options

Option	Parameters	Function	Default	Scope
announce as	NT or Win95 or WfW	Sets the operating system that Samba will announce itself as.	NT	Global
announce version	numerical	Sets the version of the operating system that Samba will announce itself as.	4.2	Global
browseable (browsable)	boolean	Allows share to be displayed in list of machine resources.	yes	Share
browse list	boolean	If yes, Samba will provide a browse list on this server.	yes	Global
auto services (preload)	string (share list)	Sets a list of shares that will always appear in the browse list.	None	Global
default service (default)	string (share name)	Names a share (service) that will be provided if the client requests a share not listed in *smb.conf*.	None	Global
local master	boolean	If yes, Samba will try to become a master browser on the local subnet.	yes	Global
lm announce	yes or no or auto	Enables or disables LAN Manager style host announcements.	auto	Global
lm interval	numerical	Specifies the frequency in seconds that LAN Manager announcements will be made if activated.	60	Global
preferred master (prefered master)	boolean	If yes, Samba will use the preferred master browser bit to attempt to become the local master browser.	no	Global
domain master	boolean	If yes, Samba will try to become the main browser master for the workgroup.	no	Global

Table 5-3. Browsing Configuration Options (continued)

Option	Parameters	Function	Default	Scope
os level	numerical	Sets the operating system level of Samba in an election for local master browser.	0	Global
remote browse sync	string (list of IP addresses)	Lists Samba servers to synchronize browse lists with.	None	Global
remote announce	string (IP address/ workgroup pairs)	Lists subnets and workgroups to send directed broadcast packets to, allowing Samba to appear to browse lists.	None	Global

announce as

This global configuration option specifies the type of operating system that Samba will announce to other machines on the network. The default value for this option is **NT**, which represents a Windows NT operating system. Other possible values are **Win95**, which represents a Windows 95 operating system, and **WfW** for a Windows for Workgroup operating system. You can override the default value with the following:

```
[global]
    announce as = Win95
```

We recommend against changing the default value of this configuration option.

announce version

This global option is frequently used with the **announce as** configuration option; it specifies the version of the operating system that Samba will announce to other machines on the network. The default value of this options is 4.2, which places itself above the current Windows NT version of 4.0. You can specify a new value with a global entry such as the following:

```
[global]
    announce version = 4.3
```

We recommend against changing the default value of this configuration option.

browseable

The **browseable** option (also spelled **browsable**) indicates whether the share referenced should appear in the list of available resources of the machine on which it resides. This option is always set to **yes** by default. If you wish to prevent the share from being seen in a client's browser, you can reset this option to **no**.

Note that this does not prevent someone from accessing the share using other means, such as specifying a UNC location (**server****accounting**) in Windows

Explorer. It only prevents the share from being listed under the machine's resources when being browsed.

browse list

You should never need to change this parameter from its default value of **yes**. If your Samba server is acting as a local master browser (i.e., it has won the browsing election), you can use the global **browse list** option to instruct Samba to provide or withhold its browse list to all clients. By default, Samba always provides a browse list. You can withhold this information by specifying the following:

```
[global]
    browse list = no
```

If you disable the browse list, clients cannot browse the names of other machines, their services, and other domains currently available on the network. Note that this won't make any particular machine inaccessible; if someone knows a valid machine name/address and a share on that machine, they can still connect to it explicitly using NET USE or by mapping a drive letter to it using Windows Explorer. It simply prevents information in the browse list from being retrieved by any client that requests it.

auto services

The global **auto services** option, which is also called **preload**, ensures that the specified shares are always visible in the browse list. One common use for this option is to advertise specific user or printer shares that are created by the [**homes**] or [**printers**] shares, but are not otherwise browsable.

This option works best with disk shares. If you wish to force each of your system printers (i.e., those listed in the printer capabilities file) into the browse list using this option, we recommend using the **load printers** option instead. Any shares listed .with the **auto services** option will not be displayed if the **browse list** option is set to **no**.

default service

The global **default service** option (sometimes called **default**) names a "last-ditch" share. If set to an existing share name, and a client requests a nonexistent disk or printer share, Samba will attempt to connect the user to the share specified by this option instead. The option is specified as follows:

```
default service = helpshare
```

Note that there are no braces surrounding the share name **helpshare**, even though the definition of the share later in the Samba configuration file will have braces. Also, if you use the **%S** variable in the share specified by this option, it will represent the requested, nonexistent share, not the default service. Any underscores (_) specified in the request share will be converted to slashes (/) when the variable is used.

local master

This global option specifies whether Samba will attempt to become the local master browser for the subnet when it starts up. If this option is set to **yes**, Samba will take place in elections. However, setting this option by itself does not guarantee victory. (Other parameters, such as **preferred master** and **os level** help Samba win browsing elections.) If this option is set to **no**, Samba will lose all browsing elections, no matter which values are specified by the other configuration options. The default value is **yes**.

lm announce

The global **lm announce** option tells Samba's *nmbd* whether or not to send LAN Manager host announcements on behalf of the server. These host announcements may be required by older clients, such as IBM's OS/2 operating system. This announcement allows the server to be added to the browse lists of the client. If activated, Samba will announce itself repetitively at the number of seconds specified by the **lm interval** option.

This configuration option takes the standard boolean values, **yes** and **no**, which engage or disengage LAN Manager announcements, respectively. In addition, there is a third option, **auto**, which causes *nmbd* to passively listen for LAN Manager announcements, but not send any of its own initially. If LAN Manager announcements are detected for another machine on the network, *nmbd* will start sending its own LAN Manager announcements to ensure that it is visible. You can specify the option as follows:

```
[global]
    lm announce = yes
```

The default value is **auto**. You probably won't need to change this value from its default.

lm interval

This option, which is used in conjunction with **lm announce**, indicates the number of seconds *nmbd* will wait before repeatedly broadcasting LAN Manager-style announcements. Remember that LAN Manager announcements must be activated in order for this option to be used. The default value is 60 seconds. If you set this value to 0, Samba will not send any LAN Manager host announcements, no matter what the value of the lm announce option. You can reset the value of this option as follows:

```
[global]
    lm interval = 90
```

preferred master

The **preferred master** option requests that Samba set the preferred master bit when participating in an election. This gives the server a higher preferred status in the workgroup than other machines at the same operating system level. If you are configuring your Samba machine to become the local master browser, it is wise to set the following value:

```
[global]
    preferred master = yes
```

Otherwise, you should leave it set to its default, **no**. If Samba is configured as a preferred master browser, it will force an election when it first comes online.

os level

The global **os level** option dictates the operating system level at which Samba will masquerade during a browser election. If you wish to have Samba win an election and become the master browser, you can set the level above that of the operating system on your network with the highest current value. The values are shown in Table 5-1. The default level is 0, which means that Samba will lose all elections. If you wish Samba to win all elections, you can reset its value as follows:

```
os level = 34
```

This means that the server will vote for itself 34 times each time an election is called, which ensures a victory.

domain master

If Samba is the primary domain controller for your workgroup or NT domain, it should also be the domain master browser. The domain master browser is a special machine that has the NetBIOS resource type <1B> and is used to propagate browse lists to and from each of the local master browsers in individual subnets across the domain. To force Samba to become the domain master browser, set the following in the [global] section of the *smb.conf:*

```
[global]
    domain master = yes
```

If you have a Windows NT server on the network acting as a primary domain controller (PDC), we recommend that you do not use Samba to become the domain master browser. The reverse is true as well: if Samba is taking on the responsibilities of a PDC, we recommend making it the domain master browser. Splitting the PDC and the domain master browser will cause unpredictable errors to occur on the network.

remote browse sync

The global **remote browse sync** option specifies that Samba should synchronize its browse lists with local master browsers in other subnets. However, the synchronization can occur only with other Samba servers, and not with Windows computers. For example, if your Samba server was a master browser on the subnet 192.168.235, and Samba local master browsers existed on other subnets at 192.168.234.92 and 192.168.236.2, you could specify the following:

```
remote browse sync = 192.168.234.92 192.168.236.2
```

The Samba server would then directly contact the other machines on the address list and synchronize browse lists. You can also say:

```
remote browse sync = 192.168.234.255 192.168.236.255
```

This forces Samba to broadcast queries to determine the IP addresses of the local master browser on each subnet, with which it will then synchronize browse lists. This only works, however, if your router doesn't block directed broadcast requests ending in 255.

remote announce

Samba servers are capable of providing browse lists to foreign subnets with the **remote announce** option. This is typically sent to the local master browser of the foreign subnet in question. However, if you do not know the address of the local master browser, you can do the following:

```
[global]
    remote announce = 192.168.234.255/ACCOUNTING \
                      192.168.236.255/ACCOUNTING
```

With this, Samba will broadcast host announcements to all machines on subnets 192.168.234 and 192.168.236, which will hopefully reach the local master browser of the subnet. You can also specify exact IP addresses, if they are known.

Filesystem Differences

One of the biggest issues for which Samba has to correct is the difference between Unix and non-Unix filesystems. This includes items such as handling symbolic links, hidden files, and dot files. In addition, file permissions can also be a headache if not accounted for properly. This section describes how to use Samba to make up for some of those annoying differences, and even how to add some new functionality of its own.

Hiding and Vetoing Files

There are some cases when we need to ensure that a user cannot see or access a file at all. Other times, we don't want to keep a user from accessing a file—we just want to hide it when they view the contents of the directory. On Windows systems, an attribute of files allows them to be hidden from a folder listing. With Unix, the traditional way of hiding files in a directory is to precede them with a dot (.). This prevents items such as configuration files or defaults from being seen when performing an ordinary `ls` command. Keeping a user from accessing a file at all, however, involves working with permissions on files and or directories.

The first option we should discuss is the boolean **hide dot files**. This option does exactly what it says. When set to **yes**, the option treats files beginning with a period (.) as hidden. If set to **no**, those files are always shown. The important thing to remember is that the files are only hidden. If the user has chosen to show all hidden files while browsing (e.g., using the Folder Options menu item under the View menu in Windows 98), they will still be able to see the files, as shown in Figure 5-2.

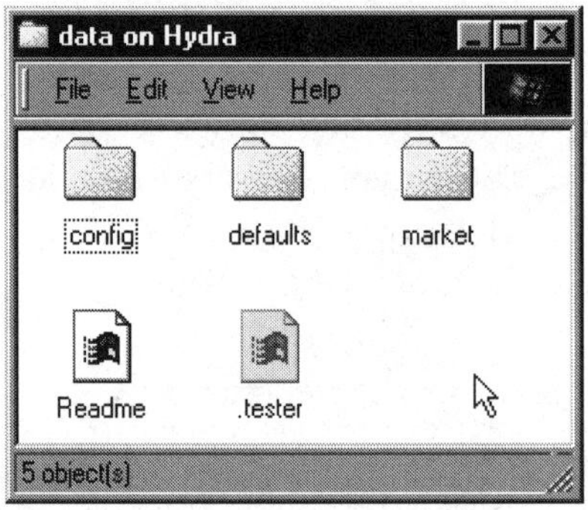

Figure 5-2. Hidden files in the [data] share

Instead of simply hiding files beginning with a dot, you can also specify a string pattern to Samba for files to hide, using the **hide files** option. For example, let's assume that we specified the following in our example [**data**] share:

```
[data]
    path = /home/samba/data
    browseable = yes
```

```
        guest ok = yes
        writeable = yes
        case sensitive = no
        hide files = /*.java/*README*/
```

Each entry for this option must begin, end, or be separated from another with a slash (/) character, even if there is only one pattern listed. This convention allows spaces to appear in filenames. In this example, the share directory would appear as shown in Figure 5-3. Again, note that we have set the Windows 98 option to view hidden files for the window.

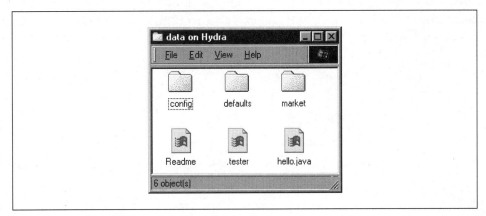

Figure 5-3. Hiding files based on filename patterns

If we want to prevent users from seeing files at all, we can instead use the **veto files** option. This option, which takes the same syntax as the **hide files** option, specifies a list of files that should never be seen by the user. For example, let's change the **[data]** share to the following:

```
[data]
        path = /home/samba/data
        browseable = yes
        guest ok = yes
        writeable = yes
        case sensitive = no
        veto files = /*.java/*README*/
```

The syntax of this option is identical to the **hide files** configuration option: each entry must begin, end, or be separated from another with a slash (/) character, even if there is only one pattern listed. By doing so, the files **hello.java** and **README** will simply disappear from the directory, and the user will not be able to access them through SMB.

There is one other question that we need to address. What happens if the user tries to delete a directory that contains vetoed files? This is where the **delete veto files** option comes in. If this boolean option is set to **yes**, the user is allowed to delete both the regular files and the vetoed files in the directory, and the directory itself will be removed. If the option is set to **no**, the user will not be able to delete the vetoed files, and consequently the directory will not be deleted either. From the user's perspective, the directory will appear to be empty, but cannot be removed.

The **dont descend** directive specifies a list of directories whose contents Samba should not allow to be visible. Note that we say *contents*, not the directory itself. Users will be able to enter a directory marked as such, but they are prohibited from descending the directory tree any farther—they will always see an empty folder. For example, let's use this option with a more basic form of the share that we defined earlier in the chapter:

```
[data]
    path = /home/samba/data
    browseable = yes
    guest ok = yes
    writeable = yes
    case sensitive = no
    dont descend = config defaults
```

In addition, let's assume that the */home/samba/data* directory has the following contents:

```
drwxr-xr-x    6 tom        users      1024 Jun 13 09:24 .
drwxr-xr-x    8 root       root       1024 Jun 10 17:53 ..
-rw-r--r--    2 tom        users      1024 Jun  9 11:43 README
drwxr-xr-x    3 tom        users      1024 Jun 13 09:28 config
drwxr-xr-x    3 tom        users      1024 Jun 13 09:28 defaults
drwxr-xr-x    3 tom        users      1024 Jun 13 09:28 market
```

If the user then connects to the share, he or she would see the directories shown in Figure 5-4. However, the contents of the */config* and */defaults* directories would appear empty to the user, even if other folders or files existed in them. In addition, users cannot write any data to the folder (which prevents them from creating a file or folder with the same name as one that is already there but invisible). If a user attempts to do so, he or she will receive an "Access Denied" message. **dont descend** is an administrative option, not a security option, and is not a substitute for good file permissions.

Links

DOS and NT filesystems don't have symbolic links; Windows 95/98/NT systems approximate this with "shortcuts" instead. Therefore, when a client tries to open a symbolic link on a Samba server share, Samba attempts to follow the link to find

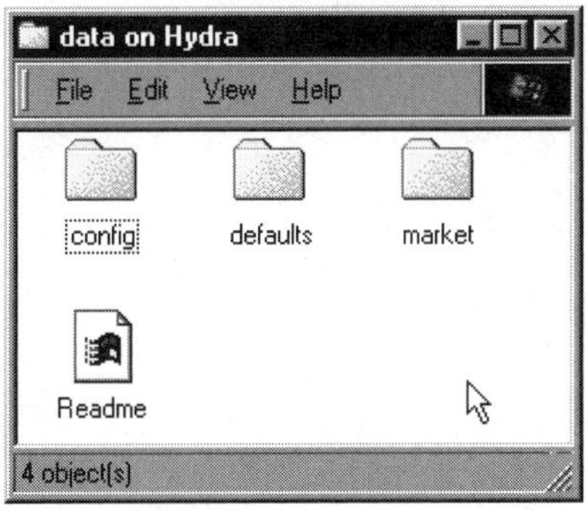

Figure 5-4. Contents of the [data] share with dont descend

the real file and let the client open it, as if he or she were on a Unix machine. If you don't want to allow this, set the `follow symlinks` option:

```
[data]
    path = /home/samba/data
    browseable = yes
    guest ok = yes
    writeable = yes
    case sensitive = no
    follow symlinks = no
```

You can test this by creating a directory on the Unix server inside the share as the user that you are logging in with. Enter the following commands:

```
% mkdir hello; cd hello
% cat "This is a test" >hello.txt
% ln -s hello.txt "Link to hello"
```

This results in the two files shown in the window in Figure 5-5. Normally, if you click on either one, you will receive a file which has the text "This is a test" inside of it. However, with the `follow symlinks` option set to `no`, you should receive an error similar to the dialog in Figure 5-5 if you click on "Link to hello."

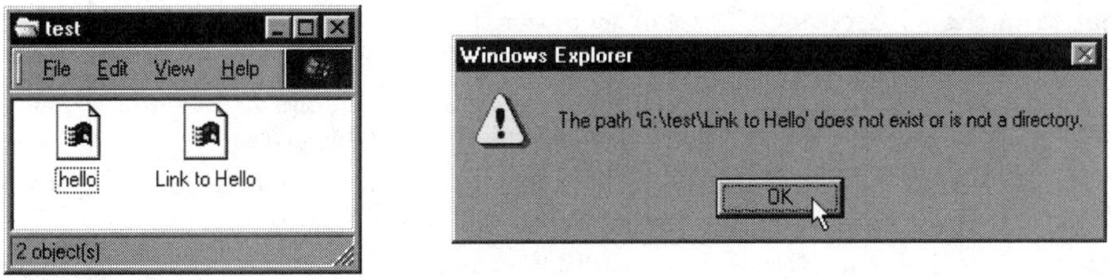

Figure 5-5. An error dialog trying to follow symbolic links when forbidden by Samba

Finally, let's discuss the **wide links** option. This option, if set to **yes**, allows the client user to follow symbolic links that point outside the shared directory tree, including files or directories at the other end of the link. For example, let's assume that we modified the **[data]** share as follows:

```
[data]
    path = /home/samba/data
    browseable = yes
    guest ok = yes
    writeable = yes
    case sensitive = no
    follow symlinks = yes
    wide links = yes
```

As long as the **follow symlinks** option is enabled, this will cause Samba to follow all symbolic links outside the current share tree. If we create a file outside the share (for example, in someone's home directory) and then create a link to it in the share as follows:

```
ln -s ~tom/datafile ./datafile
```

then you will be able to open the file in Tom's directory as per the target file's permissions.

Filesystem Options

Table 5-4 shows a breakdown of the options we discussed earlier. We recommend the defaults for most, except those listed in the following descriptions.

Table 5-4. Filesystem Configuration Options

Option	Parameters	Function	Default	Scope
unix realname	boolean	Provides Unix user's full name to client.	no	Global
dont descend	string (list of directories)	Indicates a list of directories whose contents Samba should make invisible to clients.	None	Share
follow symlinks	boolean	If set to no, Samba will not honor symbolic links.	yes	Share
getwd cache	boolean	If set to yes, Samba will use a cache for getwd() calls.	yes	Global
wide links	boolean	If set to yes, Samba will follow symbolic links outside the share.	yes	Share
hide dot files	boolean	If set to yes, treats Unix hidden files as hidden files in Windows.	yes	Share
hide files	string (list of files)	List of file patterns to treat as hidden.	None	Share

Table 5-4. *Filesystem Configuration Options (continued)*

Option	Parameters	Function	Default	Scope
`veto files`	string (list of files)	List of file patterns to never show.	None	Share
`delete veto files`	boolean	If set to **yes**, will delete files matched by `veto files` when the directory they reside in is deleted.	no	Share

unix realname

Some programs require a full username in order to operate. For example, a Windows email program often needs to associate a username with a given real name. If your system password file contains the real names of users in the GCOS field, the `unix realname` option instructs Samba to provide this information to clients. Without it, the name of the user will simply be his or her login ID. For example, if your Unix password file contains the following line:

```
rcollins:/KaBfco47Rer5:500:500:Robert Collins:
/home/rcollins:/bin/ksh
```

And the option in the configuration file is:

```
[global]
    unix realname = yes
```

then the name Robert Collins will be provided to any client that requests the real name of user **rcollins**. You typically don't need to bother with this option.

dont descend

The **dont descend** option can be used to specify various directories that should appear empty to the client. Note that the directory itself will still appear. However, Samba will not show any of the contents of the directory to the client user. This is not a good option to use as a security feature (a user could probably find a way around it); it really is meant only as a convenience to keep client users from browsing into directories that might have sensitive files. See our example earlier in this section.

follow symlinks

This option, which is discussed in greater detail earlier, controls whether Samba will follow a symbolic link in the Unix operating system to the target, or if it should return an error to the client user. If the option is set to **yes**, the target of the link will be interpreted as the file.

getwd cache

This global option specifies whether Samba should use a local cache for the Unix `getwd()` (get current working directory) system call. You can override the default value of **yes** as follows:

```
[global]
    getwd cache = no
```

Setting this option to **yes** can significantly increase the time it takes to resolve the working directory, especially if the **wide links** option is set to **no**. You should normally not need to alter this option.

wide links

This option specifies whether the client user can follow symbolic links that point outside the shared directory tree. This includes any files or directories at the other end of the link, as long as the permissions are correct for the user. The default value for this option is **yes**. Note that this option will not be honored if the **follow symlinks** options is set to **no**. Setting this option to **no** slows *smbd* considerably.

hide files

The **hide files** option provides one or more directory or filename patterns to Samba. Any file matching this pattern will be treated as a hidden file from the perspective of the client. Note that this simply means that the DOS hidden attribute is set, which may or may not mean that the user can actually see it while browsing.

Each entry in the list must begin, end, or be separated from another entry with a slash (/) character, even if there is only one pattern listed. This allows spaces to appear in the list. Asterisks can be used as a wildcard to represent zero or more characters. Questions marks can be used to represent exactly one character. For example:

```
hide files = /.jav*/README.???/
```

hide dot files

The **hide dot files** option hides any files on the server that begin with a dot (.) character, in order to mimic the functionality behind several shell commands that are present on Unix systems. Like **hide files**, those files that begin with a dot have the DOS hidden attribute set, which doesn't necessarily guarantee that a client cannot view them. The default value for this option is **yes**.

veto files

More stringent than the hidden files state is the state provided by the **veto files** configuration option. Samba won't even admit these files exist. You cannot list or open them from the client. In reality, this isn't a trustworthy security option. It is actually a mechanism to keep PC programs from deleting special files, such as ones used to store the resource fork of a Macintosh file on a Unix filesystem. If both Windows and Macs are sharing the same files, this can prevent ill-advised power users from removing files the Mac users need.

The syntax of this option is identical to that of the `hide files` configuration option: each entry must begin, end, or be separated from another with a slash (/) character, even if only one pattern is listed. Asterisks can be used as a wildcard to represent zero or more characters. Questions marks can be used to represent exactly one character. For example:

```
veto files = /*config/*default?/
```

This option is primarily administrative—not a substitute for good file permissions.

delete veto files

This option tells Samba to delete vetoed files when a user attempts to delete the directory in which they reside. The default value is **no**. This means if a user tries to delete a directory that contains a vetoed file, the file (and the directory) will not be deleted. Instead, the directory will remain and appear to be empty from the perspective of the user. If set to **yes**, the directory and the vetoed files will be deleted.

File Permissions and Attributes on MS-DOS and Unix

DOS was never intended to be a multiuser, networked operating system. Unix, on the other hand, was designed that way from the start. Consequently, there are inconsistencies and gaps in coverage between the two filesystems that Samba must not only be aware of, but also provide solutions for. One of the biggest gaps is how Unix and DOS handle permissions with files.

Let's take a look at how Unix assigns permissions. All Unix files have read, write, and execute bits for three classifications of users: owner, group, and world. These permissions can be seen at the extreme left-hand side when a `ls -al` command is issued in a Unix directory. For example:

```
-rwxr--r--   1 tom     users   2014 Apr 13 14:11 access.conf
```

Windows, on the other hand, has four principal bits that it uses with any file: read-only, system, hidden, and archive. You can view these bits by right-clicking on the

file and choosing the Properties menu item. You should see a dialog similar to
Figure 5-6.*

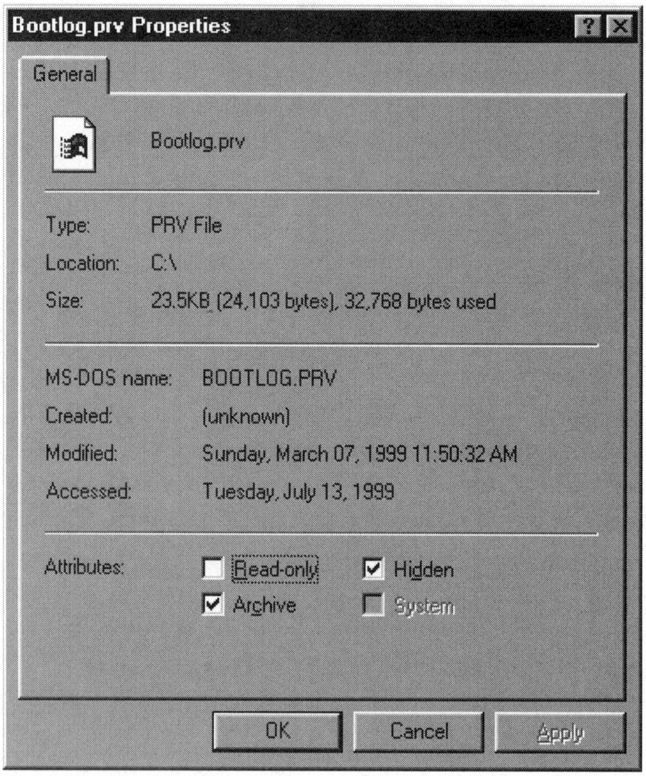

Figure 5-6. DOS and Windows file properties

The definition of each of those bits follows:

Read-only

 The file's contents can be read by a user but cannot be written to.

System

 This file has a specific purpose required by the operating system.

Hidden

 This file has been marked to be invisible to the user, unless the operating systems is explicitly set to show it.

---

* The system checkbox will probably be greyed for your file. Don't worry about that—you should still be
able to see when the box is checked and when it isn't.

Archive

This file has been touched since the last DOS backup was performed on it.

Note that there is no bit to specify that a file is executable. DOS and Windows NT filesystems identify executable files by giving them the extensions .EXE, .COM, .CMD, or .BAT.

Consequently, there is no use for any of the three Unix executable bits that are present on a file in a Samba disk share. DOS files, however, have their own attributes that need to be preserved when they are stored in a Unix environment: the archive, system, and hidden bits. Samba can preserve these bits by reusing the executable permission bits of the file on the Unix side—if it is instructed to do so. Mapping these bits, however, has an unfortunate side-effect: if a Windows user stores a file in a Samba share, and you view it on Unix with the `ls -al` command, some of the executable bits won't mean what you'd expect them to.

Three Samba options decide whether the bits are mapped: **map archive**, **map system**, and **map hidden**. These options map the archive, system, and hidden attributes to the owner, group, and world execute bits of the file, respectively. You can add these options to the [**data**] share, setting each of their values as follows:

```
[data]
    path = /home/samba/data
    browseable = yes
    guest ok = yes
    writeable = yes
    map archive = yes
    map system = yes
    map hidden = yes
```

After that, try creating a file in the share under Unix—such as `hello.java`—and change the permissions of the file to 755. With these Samba options set, you should be able to check the permissions on the Windows side and see that each of the three values has been checked in the Properties dialog box. What about the read-only attribute? By default, Samba 2.0 sets this whenever a file does not have the Unix owner write permission bit set. In other words, you can set this bit by changing the permissions of the file to 555.

We should warn you that the default value of the **map archive** option is **yes**, while the other two options have a default value of **no**. This is because many programs do not work properly if the archive bit is not stored correctly for DOS and Windows files. The system and hidden attributes, however, are not critical for a program's operation and are left to the discretion of the administrator.

Figure 5-7 summarizes the Unix permission bits and illustrates how Samba maps those bits to DOS attributes. Note that the group read/write and world read/write bits do not directly translate to a DOS attribute, but they still retain their original Unix definitions on the Samba server.

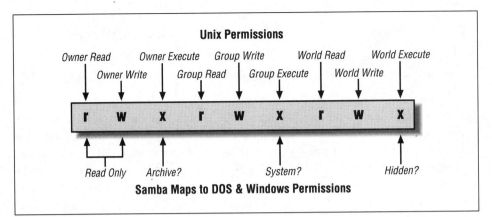

Figure 5-7. How Samba and Unix view the permissions of a file

Creation masks

Samba has several options to help with file creation masks. File creation masks (or *umasks*) help to define the permissions a file or directory will receive at the time it is created. In Unix, this means that you can control what permissions a file or directory does not have when it is created. For files accessed from Windows, this means you can disable the read-only, archive, system, and hidden attributes of a file as well.

For example, the **create mask** option will force the permissions of a file created by a Windows client to be at most 744:

```
[data]
    path = /home/samba/data
    browseable = yes
    guest ok = yes
    writeable = yes
    create mask = 744
```

while the **directory mask** option shown here will force the permissions of a newly created directory to be at most 755:

```
[data]
    path = /home/samba/data
    browseable = yes
    guest ok = yes
    writeable = yes
    directory mask = 755
```

Alternatively, you can also force various bits with the **force create mode** and **force directory mode** options. These options will perform a logical OR against the file and directory creation masks, ensuring that those bits that are specified will always be set. You would typically set these options globally in order to ensure that group and world read/write permissions have been set appropriately for new files or directories in each share.

In the same spirit, if you wish to explicitly set the Unix user and group attributes of a file that is created on the Windows side, you can use the force user and force group options. For example:

```
[data]
     path = /home/samba/data
     browseable = yes
     guest ok = yes
     writeable = yes

     create mask = 744
     directory mask = 755
     force user = joe
     force group = accounting
```

These options actually assign a static Unix user and group to each connection that is made to a share. However, this occurs *after* the client authenticates; it does not allow free access to a share. These options are frequently used for their side effects of assigning a specific user and group to each new file or directory that is created in a share. Use these options with discretion.

Finally, one of the capabilities of Unix that DOS lacks is the ability to delete a read-only file from a writable directory. In Unix, if a directory is writable, a read-only file in that directory can still be removed. This could permit you to delete files in any of your directories, even if the file was left by someone else.

DOS filesystems are not designed for multiple users, and so its designers decided that read-only means "protected against accidental change, including deletion," rather than "protected against some other user on a single-user machine." So the designers of DOS prohibited removal of a read-only file. Even today, Windows file systems exhibit the same behavior.

Normally, this is harmless. Windows programs don't try to remove read-only files because they know it's a bad idea. However, a number of source-code control programs—which were first written for Unix—run on Windows and require the ability to delete read-only files. Samba permits this behavior with the delete readonly option. In order to enable this functionality, set the option to yes:

```
[data]
     path = /home/samba/data
     browseable = yes
     guest ok = yes
     writeable = yes

     create mask = 744
     directory mask = 755
     force user = joe
     force group = accounting
     delete readonly = yes
```

File and Directory Permission Options

The options for file and directory permissions are summarized in Table 5-5; each option is then described in detail.

Table 5-5. File and Directory Permission Options

Option	Parameters	Function	Default	Scope
map archive	boolean	Preserve DOS archive attribute in user execute bit (0100).	yes	Share
map system	boolean	Preserve DOS system attribute in group execute bit (0010).	no	Share
map hidden	boolean	Preserve DOS hidden attribute in world execute bit (0001).	no	Share
create mask (create mode)	numeric	Sets the maximum permissions for files created by Samba.	0744	Share
directory mask (directory mode)	numeric	Sets the maximum permissions for directories created by Samba.	0755	Share
force create mode	numeric	Forces the specified permissions (bitwise or) for directories created by Samba.	0000	Share
force directory mode	numeric	Forces the specified permissions (bitwise or) for directories created by Samba.	0000	Share
force group (group)	string (group name)	Sets the effective group for a user accessing this share.	None	Share
force user	string (username)	Sets the effective username for a user accessing this share.	None	Share
delete readonly	boolean	Allows a user to delete a read-only file from a writable directory.	no	Share

create mask

The argument for this option is an octal number indicating which permission flags may be set at file creation by a client in a share. The default is 0755, which means the Unix owner can at most read, write, and optionally execute his or her own files, while members of the user's group and others can only read or execute them. If you need to change it for non-executable files, we recommend 0644, or rw-r--r--. Keep in mind that the execute bits may be used by the server to map certain DOS file attributes, as described earlier. If you're altering the create mask, those bits have to be part of the create mask as well.

directory mask

The argument for this option is an octal number indicating which permission flags may be set at directory creation by a client in a share. The default is 0755, which allows everyone on the Unix side to at most read and traverse the directories, but allows only you to modify them. We recommend the mask 0750, removing access by world users.

force create mode

This option sets the permission bits that Samba will force to be set when a file permission change is made. It's often used to force group permissions, mentioned previously. It can also be used to preset any of the DOS attributes we mentioned: archive (0100), system (0010), or hidden (0001). This option always takes effect after the **map archive**, **map system**, **map hidden**, and **create mask** options.

Many Windows applications rename their data files to *datafile.bak* and create new ones, thus changing their ownership and permissions so that members of the same Unix group can't edit them. Setting **force create mode = 0660** will keep the new file editable by members of the group.

---

force directory mode

This option sets the permission bits which Samba will force when a directory permission change is made or a directory is created. It's often used to force group permissions, as mentioned previously. This option defaults to 0000, and can be used just like the **force create mode** to add group or other permissions if needed. This option always takes effect after the **map archive**, **map system**, **map hidden**, and **directory mask** options.

force group

This option, sometimes called **group**, assigns a static group ID that will be used on all connections to a service after the client has successfully authenticated. This assigns a specific group to each new file or directory created from an SMB client.

force user

The **force user** option assigns a static user ID that will be used on all connections to a service after the client has successfully authenticated. This assigns a specific user to each new file or directory created from an SMB client.

delete readonly

This option allows a user to delete a directory containing a read-only file. By default, DOS and Windows will not allow such an operation. You probably will want to leave this option turned off unless a program needs this capability; many Windows users would be appalled to find that they'd accidentally deleted a file which they had set read-only. In fact, even the Unix rm command will ask users if they really want to override the protection and delete read-only files. It's a good idea to have Samba be at least as cautious.

map archive

The DOS archive bit is used to flag a file that has been changed since it was last archived (e.g., backed up with the DOS archive program.) Setting the Samba option map archive = yes causes the DOS archive flag to be mapped to the Unix execute-by-owner (0100) bit. It's best to leave this option on if your Windows users are doing their own backups, or are using programs that require the archive bit. Unix lacks the notion of an archive bit entirely. Backup programs typically keep a file that lists what files were backed up on what date, so comparing file modification dates serves the same purpose.

Setting this option to yes causes an occasional surprise on Unix when a user notices that a data file is marked as executable, but rarely causes harm. If a user tries to run it, he or she will normally get a string of error messages as the shell tries to execute the first few lines as commands. The reverse is also possible; an executable Unix program looks like it hasn't been backed up recently on Windows. But again, this is rare, and is usually harmless.

map system

The DOS system attribute is used to indicate files that are required by the operating system, and should not be deleted, renamed, or moved without special effort. Set this option only if you need to store Windows system files on the Unix file server. Executable Unix programs will appear to be non-removable special Windows files when viewed from Windows clients. This may prove mildly inconvenient if you want to move or remove one. For most sites, however, this is fairly harmless.

map hidden

DOS uses the hidden attribute to indicate that a file should not ordinarily be visible in directory listings. Unix doesn't have such a facility; it's up to individual programs (notably the shell) to decide what to display and what not to display. Normally, you won't have any DOS files that need to be hidden, so the best thing to do is to leave this option turned off.

Setting this option to **yes** causes the server to map the hidden flag onto the executable-by-others bit (0001). This feature can produce a rather startling effect. Any Unix program that is executable by world seems to vanish when you look for it from a Windows client. If this option is not set, however, and a Windows user attempts to mark a file hidden on a Samba share, it will not work—Samba has no place to store the hidden attribute!

Name Mangling and Case

Back in the days of DOS and Windows 3.1, every filename was limited to eight upper-case characters, followed by a dot, and three more uppercase characters. This was known as the *8.3 format*, and was a huge nuisance. Windows 95/98, Windows NT, and Unix have since relaxed this problem by allowing many more case-sensitive characters to make up a filename. Table 5-6 shows the current naming state of several popular operating systems.

Table 5-6. Operating System Filename Limitations

Operating System	File Naming Rules
DOS 6.22 or below	Eight characters followed by a dot followed by a three-letter extension (8.3 format); case insensitive
Windows 3.1 for Workgroups	Eight characters followed by a dot followed by a three-letter extension (8.3 format); case insensitive
Windows 95/98	255 characters; case sensitive but case preserving
Windows NT	255 characters; case sensitive but case preserving
Unix	255 characters; case sensitive

Samba still has to remain backwards compatible with network clients who store files only in the 8.3 format, such as Windows for Workgroups. If a user creates a file on a share called *antidisestablishmentarianism.txt*, a Windows for Workgroups client couldn't tell it apart from another file in the same directory called *antidisease.txt*. Like Windows 95/98 and Windows NT, Samba has to employ a special methodology of translating a long filename to an 8.3 filename in such a way that similar filenames will not cause collisions. This is called *name mangling*, and Samba deals with this in a manner that is similar, but not identical to, Windows 95 and its successors.

The Samba Mangling Operation

Here is how Samba mangles a long filename into an 8.3 filename:

- If the original filename does not begin with a dot, up to the first five alphanumeric characters that occur before the last dot (if there is one) are converted to uppercase. These characters are used as the first five characters of the 8.3 mangled filename.

- If the original filename begins with a dot, the dot is removed and up to the first five alphanumeric characters that occur before the last dot (if there is one) are converted to uppercase. These characters are used as the first five characters of the 8.3 mangled filename.

- These characters are immediately followed a special mangling character: by default, a tilde (~), although Samba allows you to change this character.

- The base of the long filename before the last period is hashed into a two-character code; parts of the name after the last dot may be used if necessary. This two character code is appended to the 8.3 filename after the mangling character.

- The first three characters after the last dot (if there is one) of the original filename are converted to uppercase and appended onto the mangled name as the extension. If the original filename began with a dot, three underscores (_ _ _) are used as the extension instead.

Here are some examples:

```
virtuosity.dat                      VIRTU~F1.DAT
.htaccess                           HTACC~U0._ _ _
hello.java                          HELLO~1F.JAV
team.config.txt                     TEAMC~04.TXT
antidisestablishmentarianism.txt    ANTID~E3.TXT
antidiseast.txt                     ANTID~9K.TXT
```

Using these rules will allow Windows for Workgroups to differentiate the two files on behalf of the poor individual who is forced to see the network through the eyes of that operating system. Note that the same long filename should always hash to the same mangled name with Samba; this doesn't always happen with Windows. The downside of this approach is that there can still be collisions; however, the chances are greatly reduced.

You generally want to use the mangling configuration options with only the oldest clients. We recommend doing this without disrupting other clients by adding an **include** directive to the *smb.conf* file:

```
[global]
    include = /ucsr/local/samba/lib/smb.conf.%m
```

This resolves to *smb.conf.WfWg* when a Window for Workgroups client attaches. Now you can create a file */usr/local/samba/lib/smb.conf.WfWg* which might contain these options:

```
[global]
    case sensitive = no
    default case = upper
    preserve case = no
```

```
short preserve case = no
mangle case = yes
mangled names= yes
```

If you are not using Windows for Workgroups 3.1, then you probably do not need to change any of these options from their defaults.

Representing and resolving filenames with Samba

Another item that we should point out is that there is a difference between how an operating system *represents* a file and how it *resolves* it. For example, if you've used Windows 95/98/NT, you have likely run across a file called *README.TXT*. The file can be represented by the operating system entirely in uppercase letters. However, if you open an MS-DOS prompt and enter the command `edit readme.txt`, the all-caps file is loaded into the editing program, even though you typed the name in lowercase letters!

This is because the Windows 95/98/NT family of operating systems resolves files in a case-insensitive manner, even though the files are represented it in a case-sensitive manner. Unix-based operating systems, on the other hand, always resolve files in a case-sensitive manner; if you try to edit *README.TXT* with the command `vi readme.txt`, you will likely be editing the empty buffer of a new file.

Here is how Samba handles case: if the **preserve case** is set to **yes**, Samba will always use the case provided by the operating system for representing (not resolving) filenames. If it is set to **no**, it will use the case specified by the **default case** option. The same is true for **short preserve case**. If this option is set to **yes**, Samba will use the default case of the operating system for representing 8.3 filenames; otherwise it will use the case specified by the **default case** option. Finally, Samba will always resolve filenames in its shares based on the value of the **case sensitive** option.

Mangling Options

Samba allows you to give it more refined instructions on how it should perform name mangling, including those controlling the case sensitivity, the character inserted to form a mangled name, and the ability to manually map filenames from one format to another. These options are shown in Table 5-7.

Table 5-7. Name Mangling Options

Option	Parameters	Function	Default	Scope
case sensitive (casesignames)	boolean	If **yes**, Samba will treat filenames as case-sensitive (Windows doesn't).	no	Share
default case	(upper or lower)	Case to assume as default (only used when preserve case is no).	Lower	Share

Table 5-7. Name Mangling Options (continued)

Option	Parameters	Function	Default	Scope
preserve case	boolean	If yes, keep the case the client supplied (i.e., do not convert to default case).	yes	Share
short preserve case	boolean	If yes, preserve case of 8.3-format names that the client provides.	yes	Share
mangle case	boolean	Mangle a name if it is mixed case.	no	Share
mangled names	boolean	Mangles long names into 8.3 DOS format.	yes	Share
mangling char	string (single character)	Gives mangling character.	~	Share
mangled stack	numerical	Number of mangled names to keep on the local mangling stack.	50	Global
mangled map	string (list of patterns)	Allows mapping of filenames from one format into another.	None	Share

case sensitive

This share-level option, which has the obtuse synonym casesignames, specifies whether Samba should preserve case when resolving filenames in a specific share. The default value for this option is no, which is how Windows handles file resolution. If clients are using an operating system that takes advantage of case-sensitive filenames, you can set this configuration option to yes as shown here:

```
[accounting]
    case sensitive = yes
```

Otherwise, we recommend that you leave this option set to its default.

default case

The default case option is used with preserve case. This specifies the default case (upper or lower) that Samba will use when it creates a file on one of its shares on behalf of a client. The default case is lower, which means that newly created files will use the mixed-case names given to them by the client. If you need to, you can override this global option by specifying the following:

```
[global]
    default case = upper
```

If you specify this value, the names of newly created files will be translated into uppercase, and cannot be overridden in a program. We recommend that you use the default value unless you are dealing with a Windows for Workgroups or other 8.3 client, in which case it should be **upper**.

preserve case

This option specifies whether a file created by Samba on behalf of the client is created with the case provided by the client operating system, or the case specified by the **default case** configuration option above. The default value is **yes**, which uses the case provided by the client operating system. If it is set to **no**, the value of the **default case** option is used.

Note that this option does not handle 8.3 file requests sent from the client—see the **short preserve case** option below. You may want to set this option to **yes** if applications that create files on the Samba server are sensitive to the case used when creating the file. If you want to force Samba, for example, to mimic the behavior of a Windows NT filesystem, you can leave this option to its default, **yes**.

short preserve case

This option specifies whether an 8.3 filename created by Samba on behalf of the client is created with the default case of the client operating system, or the case specified by the **default case** configuration option. The default value is **yes**, which uses the case provided by the client operating system. You can let Samba choose the case through the **default case** option by setting it as follows:

```
[global]
    short preserve case = no
```

If you want to force Samba to mimic the behavior of a Windows NT filesystem, you can leave this option set to its default, **yes**.

mangled names

This share-level option specifies whether Samba will mangle filenames for 8.3 clients in that share. If the option is set to **no**, Samba will not mangle the names and (depending on the client), they will either be invisible or appear truncated to those using 8.3 operating systems. The default value is **yes**. You can override it per share as follows:

```
[data]
    mangled names = no
```

mangle case

This option tells Samba whether it should mangle filenames that are not composed entirely of the case specified using the **default case** configuration option. The default for this option is no. If you set it to **yes**, you should be sure that all clients will be able to handle the mangled filenames that result. You can override it per share as follows:

```
[data]
    mangle case = yes
```

We recommend that you leave this option alone unless you have a well-justified need to change it.

mangling char

This share-level option specifies the mangling character used when Samba mangles filenames into the 8.3 format. The default character used is a tilde (~). You can reset it to whatever character you wish, for instance:

```
[data]
    mangling char = #
```

mangled stack

Samba maintains a local stack of recently mangled 8.3 filenames; this stack can be used to reverse map mangled filenames back to their original state. This is often needed by applications that create and save a file, close it, and need to modify it later. The default number of long filename/mangled filename pairs stored on this stack is 50. However, if you want to cut down on the amount of processor time used to mangle filenames, you can increase the size of the stack to whatever you wish, at the expense of memory and slightly slower file access.

```
[global]
    mangled stack = 100
```

mangled map

If the default behavior of name mangling is not sufficient, you can give Samba further instructions on how to behave using the **mangled map** option. This option allows you to specify mapping patterns that can be used before or even in place of name mangling performed by Samba. For example:

```
[data]
    mangled map =(*.database *.db) (*.class *.cls)
```

Here, Samba is instructed to search each file it encounters for characters that match the first pattern specified in the parenthesis and convert them to the modified second pattern in the parenthesis for display on an 8.3 client. This is useful in the event that name mangling converts the filename incorrectly or to a format that the client cannot understand readily. Patterns are separated by whitespaces.

Locks and Oplocks

Concurrent writes to a single file are not desirable in any operating system. To prevent this, most operating systems use *locks* to guarantee that only one process can write to a file at a time. Operating systems traditionally lock entire files, although newer ones allow a range of bytes within a file to be locked. If another process attempts to write to a file (or section of one) that is already locked, it will receive an error from the operating system and will wait until the lock is released.

Samba supports the standard DOS and NT filesystem (deny-mode) locking requests, which allow only one process to write to an entire file on a server at a give time, as well as byte-range locking. In addition, Samba supports a new locking mechanism known in the Windows NT world as *opportunistic locking—oplock* for short.

Opportunistic Locking

Opportunistic locking allows a client to notify the Samba server that it will not only be the exclusive writer of a file, but will also cache its changes to that file on its own machine (and not on the Samba server) in order to speed up file access for that client. When Samba knows that a file has been opportunistically locked by a client, it marks its version as having an opportunistic lock and waits for the client to complete work on the file, at which point it expects the client to send the final changes back to the Samba server for synchronization.

If a second client requests access to that file before the first client has finished working on it, Samba can send an *oplock break* request to the first client. This tells the client to stop caching its changes and return the current state of the file to the server so that the interrupting client can use it as it sees fit. An opportunistic lock, however, is not a replacement for a standard deny-mode lock. It is not unheard of for the interrupting process to be granted an oplock break only to discover that the original process also has a deny-mode lock on a file as well. Figure 5-8 illustrates this opportunistic locking process.

In terms of locks, we highly recommend using the defaults provided by Samba: standard DOS/Windows deny-mode locks for compatibility and oplocks for the extra performance that local caching allows. If your operating system can take advantage of oplocks, it should provide significant performance improvements. Unless you have a specific reason for changing any of these options, it's best to leave them as they are.

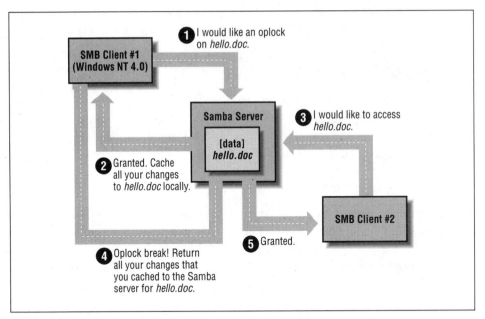

Figure 5-8. Opportunistic locking

Unix and Locking

Windows systems cooperate well to avoid overwriting each other's changes. But if a file stored on a Samba system is accessed by a Unix process, this process won't know a thing about Windows oplocks and could easily ride roughshod over a lock. Some Unix systems have been enhanced to understand the Windows oplocks maintained by Samba. Currently the support exists only in SGI Irix 6.5.2f and later; Linux and FreeBSD should soon follow.

If you have a system that understands oplocks, set **kernel oplocks = yes** in the Samba configuration file. That should eliminate conflicts between Unix processes and Windows users.

If your system does not support kernel oplocks, you could end up with corrupted data when somebody runs a Unix process that reads or writes a file that Windows users also access. However, Samba provides a rough protection mechanism in the absence of kernel oplocks: the **veto oplock files** option. If you can anticipate which Samba files are used by both Windows users and Unix users, set their names in a **veto oplock files** option. This will suppress the use of oplocks on matching filenames, which will supress client caching, and let the Windows and Unix programs use system locking or update times to detect competition for the same file. A sample option is:

```
veto oplock files = /*.dbm/
```

This option allows both Unix processes and Windows users to edit files ending in the suffix *.dbm*. Note that the syntax of this option is similar to `veto files`.

Samba's options for locks and oplocks are given in Table 5-8.

Table 5-8. Locks and Oplocks Configuration Options

Option	Parameters	Function	Default	Scope
share modes	boolean	If set to **yes**, turns on support for DOS-style whole-file locks.	yes	Share
locking	boolean	If **yes**, turns on byte-range locks.	yes	Share
strict locking	boolean	If **yes**, denies access to an entire file if a byte-range lock exists in it.	no	Share
oplocks	boolean	If **yes**, turn on local caching of files on the client for this share.	yes	Share
kernel oplocks	boolean	If **yes**, indicates that the kernel supports oplocks.	yes	Global
fake oplocks	boolean	If **yes**, tells client the lock was obtained, but doesn't actually lock it.	no	Share
blocking locks	boolean	Allows lock requestor to wait for the lock to be granted.	yes	Share
veto oplock files	string (list of filenames)	Does not oplock specified files.	None	Share
lock directory	string (fully-qualified pathname)	Sets the location where various Samba files, including locks, are stored.	As specified in Samba makefile	Global

share modes

The most primitive locks available to Samba are deny-mode locks, known as *share modes*, which are employed by programs such as text editors to avoid accidental overwriting of files. For reference, the deny-mode locks are listed in Table 5-9.

Table 5-9. SMB Deny-Mode Locks

Lock	Description
DENY_NONE	Do not deny any other file requests.
DENY_ALL	Deny all open requests on the current file.
DENY_READ	Deny any read-only open requests on the current file.
DENY_WRITE	Deny any write-only open requests on the current file.
DENY_DOS	If opened for reading, others can read but cannot write to the file. If opened for writing, others cannot open the file at all.
DENY_FCB	Obsolete.

The **share modes** parameter, which enforces the use of these locks, is enabled by default. To disable it, use the following command:

```
[accounting]
     share modes = no
```

We highly recommend against disabling the default locking mechanism unless you have a justifiable reason for doing so. Most Windows and DOS applications rely on these locking mechanisms in order to work correctly, and will complain bitterly if this functionality is taken away.

locking

The **locking** option can be used to tell Samba to engage or disengage server-side byte-range locks on behalf of the client. Samba implements byte-range locks on the server side with normal Unix advisory locks and will consequently prevent other properly-behaved Unix processes from overwriting a locked byte range.

This option can be specified per share as follows:

```
[accounting]
     locking = yes
```

If the **locking** option is set to **yes**, the requestor will be delayed until the holder of either type of lock releases it (or crashes). If, however, the option is set to **no**, no byte-range locks will be kept for the files, although requests to lock and unlock files will appear to succeed. The option is set to **yes** by default; however, you can turn this option off if you have read-only media.

strict locking

This option checks every file access for a byte-range lock on the range of bytes being accessed. This is typically not needed if a client adheres to all the locking mechanisms in place. This option is set to **no** by default; however, you can reset it per share as follows:

```
[accounting]
     strict locking = yes
```

If this option is set to **yes**, mandatory locks are enforced on any file with byte-range locks.

blocking locks

Samba also supports *blocking locks*, a minor variant of range locks. Here, if the range of bytes is not available, the client specifies an amount of time that it's willing to wait. The server then caches the lock request, periodically checking to see if the file is available. If it is, it notifies the client; however, if time expires, Samba will tell the client that the request has failed. This strategy prevents the client from continually polling to see if the lock is available.

You can disable this option per share as follows:

```
[accounting]
    blocking locks = no
```

When set to **yes**, blocking locks will be enforced on the file. If this option is set to no, Samba behaves as if normal locking mechanisms are in place on the file. The default is **yes**.

oplocks

This option enables or disables support for oplocks on the client. The option is enabled by default. However, you can disable it with the following command:

```
[data]
    oplocks = no
```

If you are in an extremely unstable network environment or have many clients that cannot take advantage of opportunistic locking, it may be better to shut this Samba feature off. Oplocks should be disabled if you are accessing the same files from both Unix applications (such as *vi*) and SMB clients (unless you are lucky enough to have an operating system that supports kernel oplocks as discussed earlier).

fake oplocks

Before opportunistic locking was available on Samba, the Samba daemons pretended to allow oplocks via the **fake oplocks** option. If this option was enabled, all clients were told that the file is available for opportunistic locking, and never warned of simultaneous access. This option is deprecated now that real oplocks are available on Samba.

kernel oplocks

If a Unix application separate from Samba tries to update a file that Samba has oplocked to a Windows client, it will likely succeed (depending on the operating system) and both Samba and the client will never be aware of it. However, if the local Unix operating system supports it, Samba can warn it of oplocked files, which can suspend the Unix process, notify the client via Samba to write its copy back, and only then allow the open to complete. Essentially, this means that the operating system kernel on the Samba system has the ability to handle oplocks as well as Samba.

You can enable this behavior with the **kernel oplocks** option, as follows:

```
[global]
    kernel oplocks = yes
```

Samba can automatically detect kernel oplocks and use them if present. At the time of this writing, this feature is supported only by SGI Irix 6.5.2f and later. However, Linux and FreeBSD support are expected in the near future. A system without kernel oplocks will allow the Unix process to update the file, but the client programs will notice the change only at a later time, if at all.

veto oplock files

You can provide a list of filenames that are never granted opportunistic locks with the `veto oplock files` option. This option can be set either globally or on a per-share basis. For example:

```
veto oplock files = /*.bat/*.htm/
```

The value of this option is a series of patterns. Each pattern entry must begin, end, or be separated from another with a slash (/) character, even if there is only one pattern listed. Asterisks can be used as a wildcard to represent zero or more characters. Questions marks can be used to represent exactly one character.

We recommend that you disable oplocks on any files that are meant to be updated by Unix or are intended to be shared by several processes simultaneously.

lock directory

This option (sometimes called `lock dir`) specifies the location of a directory where Samba will store SMB deny-mode lock files. Samba stores other files in this directory as well, such as browse lists and its shared memory file. If WINS is enabled, the WINS database is written to this directory as well. The default for this option is specified in the Samba makefile; it is typically */usr/local/samba/var/locks*. You can override this location as follows:

```
[global]
    lock directory = /usr/local/samba/locks
```

You typically would not need to override this option, unless you want to move the lock files to a more standardized location, such as */var/spool/locks*.

6

Users, Security, and Domains

This chapter discusses how to configure users with the Samba server. This topic may seem straightforward at first, but you'll soon discover that there are several ancillary problems that can crop up. One issue that Samba administrators have difficulty with is user authentication—password and security problems are by far the most common support questions on the Samba mailing lists. Learning why various authentication mechanisms work on certain architectures (and don't on others) can save you a tremendous amount of time testing and debugging Samba users in the future.

Users and Groups

Before we start, we need to warn you up front that if you are connecting to Samba with a Windows 98 or NT 4.0 Workstation SP3, you need to configure your server for encrypted passwords before you can make a connection; otherwise, the clients will refuse to connect to the Samba server. This is because each of those Windows clients sends encrypted passwords, and Samba needs to be configured to expect and decrypt them. We'll show you how to set up Samba for this task later in the chapter, assuming you haven't already tackled this problem in Chapter 2, *Installing Samba on a Unix System*.

Let's start with a single user. The easiest way to set up a client user is to create a Unix account (and home directory) for that individual on the server, and notify Samba of the user's existence. You can do the latter by creating a disk share that maps to the user's home directory in the Samba configuration file, and restricting access to that user with the **valid users** option. For example:

```
[dave]
        path = /home/dave
        comment = Dave's home directory
```

```
writeable = yes
valid users = dave
```

The **valid users** option lists the users that will be allowed to access the share. In this case, only the user **dave** is allowed to access the share. In the previous chapters, we specified that any user could access a disk share using the **guest ok** parameter. Because we don't wish to allow guest access, that option is absent here. We could grant both authenticated users and guest users access to a specific share if we wanted to. The difference between the two typically involves access rights for each of the files.

Remember that you can abbreviate the user's home directory by using the %H variable. In addition, you can use the Unix username variable %u and/or the client username variable %U in your options as well. For example:

```
[dave]
    comment = %U home directory
    writeable = yes
    valid users = dave
    path = %H
```

Both of these examples work as long as the Unix user that Samba uses to represent the client has read/write access to the directory referenced by the **path** option. In other words, a client must first pass Samba's security mechanisms (e.g., encrypted passwords, the **valid users** option, etc.) as well as the normal Unix file and directory permissions of its Unix-side user *before* it can gain read/write access to a share.

With a single user accessing a home directory, access permissions are taken care of when the operating system creates the user account. However, if you're creating a shared directory for group access, there are a few more steps you need to perform. Let's take a stab at a group share for the accounting department in the *smb.conf* file:

```
[accounting]
    comment = Accounting Department Directory
    writeable = yes
    valid users = @account
    path = /home/samba/accounting
    create mode = 0660
    directory mode = 0770
```

The first thing that you might notice we did differently is to specify **@account** as the valid user instead of one or more individual usernames. This is shorthand for saying that the valid users are represented by the Unix group **account**. These users will need to be added to the group entry **account** in the system group file (*/etc/group* or equivalent) to be recognized as part of the group. Once they are, Samba will recognize those users as valid users for the share.

In addition, you will need to create a shared directory that the members of the group can access, which is pointed to by the `path` configuration option. Here are the Unix commands that create the shared directory for the accounting department (assuming */home/samba* already exists):

```
# mkdir /home/samba/accounting
# chgrp account /home/samba/accounting
# chmod 770 /home/samba/accounting
```

There are two other options in this *smb.conf* example, both of which we saw in the previous chapter. These options are `create mode` and `directory mode`. These options set the maximum file and directory permissions that a new file or directory can have. In this case, we have denied all world access to the contents of this share. (This is reinforced by the *chmod* command, shown earlier.).

The [homes] Share

Let's return to user shares for a moment. If we have several users to set up home directory shares for, we probably want to use the special [homes] share that we introduced in Chapter 5, *Browsing and Advanced Disk Shares*. With the [homes] share, all we need to say is:

```
[homes]
     browsable = no
     writable = yes
```

The [homes] share is a special section of the Samba configuration file. If a user attempts to connect to an ordinary share that doesn't appear in the *smb.conf* file (such as specifying it with a UNC in Windows Explorer), Samba will search for a [homes] share. If one exists, the incoming share name is assumed to be a username and is queried as such in the password database (*/etc/passwd* or equivalent) file of the Samba server. If it appears, Samba assumes the client is a Unix user trying to connect to his or her home directory.

As an illustration, let's assume that `sofia` is attempting to connect to a share called [sofia] on the Samba server. There is no share by that name in the configuration file, but a [homes] share exists and user `sofia` is present in the password database, so Samba takes the following steps:

1. Samba creates a new disk share called [sofia] with the `path` specified in the [homes] section. If there is no `path` option specified in [homes], Samba initializes it to her home directory.

2. Samba initializes the new share's options from the defaults in [globals], and any overriding options in [homes] with the exception of `browseable`.

3. Samba connects `sofia`'s client to that share.

The [homes] share is a fast, painless way to create shares for your user community without having to duplicate the information from the password database file in the *smb.conf* file. It does have some peculiarities, however, that we need to point out:

- The [homes] section can represent any account on the machine, which isn't always desirable. For example, it can potentially create a share for *root*, *bin*, *sys*, *uucp*, and the like. (You can set a global invalid users option to protect against this.)

- The meaning of the **browseable** configuration option is different from other shares; it indicates only that a [homes] section won't show up in the local browse list, not that the [alice] share won't. When the [alice] section is created (after the initial connection), it will use the browsable value from the [globals] section for that share, not the value from [homes].

As we mentioned, there is no need for a path statement in [homes] if the users have Unix home directories in the server's */etc/passwd* file. You should ensure that a valid home directory does exist, however, as Samba will not automatically create a home directory for a user, and will refuse a tree connect if the user's directory does not exist or is not accessible.

Controlling Access to Shares

Often you will need to restrict the users who can access a specific share for security reasons. This is very easy to do with Samba since it contains a wealth of options for creating practically any security configuration. Let's introduce a few configurations that you might want to use in your own Samba setup.

Again, if you are connecting with Windows 98 or NT 4.0 with Service Pack 3 (or above), those clients will send encrypted passwords to the Samba server. If Samba is not configured for this, it will continually refuse the connection. This chapter describes how to set up Samba for encrypted passwords. See the "Passwords" section.

We've seen what happens when you specify valid users. However, you are also allowed to specify a list of invalid users—users who should never be allowed access to Samba or its shares. This is done with the invalid users option. We hinted at one frequent use of this option earlier: a global default with the [homes] section to ensure that various system users and superusers cannot be forged for access. For example:

```
[global]
      invalid users = root bin daemon adm sync shutdown \
```

```
                        halt mail news uucp operator gopher
        auto services = dave peter bob

[homes]
    browsable = no
    writeable = yes
```

The invalid users option, like valid users, can take group names as well as usernames. In the event that a user or group appears in both lists, the invalid users option takes precedence and the user or group will be denied access to the share.

At the other end of the spectrum, you can explicitly specify users who will be allowed superuser (root) access to a share with the admin users option. An example follows:

```
[sales]
        path = /home/sales
        comment = Fiction Corp Sales Data
        writeable = yes
        valid users = tom dick harry
        admin users = mike
```

This option takes both group names and usernames. In addition, you can specify NIS netgroups by preceding them with an @ as well; if the netgroup is not found, Samba will assume that you are referring to a standard Unix group.

Be careful if you assign an entire group administrative privileges to a share. The Samba team highly recommends you avoid using this option, as it essentially gives root access to the specified users or groups for that share.

If you wish to force read-only or read-write access to users who access a share, you can do so with the read list and write list options, respectively. These options can be used on a per-share basis to restrict a writable share or grant write access to specific users in a read-only share, respectively. For example:

```
[sales]
        path = /home/sales
        comment = Fiction Corp Sales Data
        read only = yes
        write list = tom dick
```

The write list option cannot override Unix permissions. If you've created the share without giving the write-list user write permission on the Unix system, he or she will be denied write access regardless of the setting of write list.

Guest Access

As mentioned earlier, you can specify users who have guest access to a share. The options that control guest access are easy to work with. The first option, guest account, specifies the Unix account that guest users should be assigned when connecting to the Samba server. The default value for this is set during compilation, and is typically nobody. However, you may want to reset the guest user to ftp if you have trouble accessing various system services.

If you wish to restrict access in a share only to guests—in other words, all clients connect as the guest account when accessing the share—you can use the guest only option in conjunction with the guest ok option, as shown in the following example:

```
[sales]
        path = /home/sales
        comment = Fiction Corp Sales Data
        writeable = yes
        guest ok = yes
        guest account = ftp
        guest only = yes
```

Make sure you specify yes for both guest only and guest ok in this scenario; otherwise, Samba will not use the guest acount that you specify.

Access Control Options

Table 6-1 summarizes the options that you can use to control access to shares.

Table 6-1. Share-level Access Options

Option	Parameters	Function	Default	Scope
admin users	string (list of usernames)	Specifies a list of users who can perform operations as root.	None	Share
valid users	string (list of usernames)	Specifies a list of users that can connect to a share.	None	Share
invalid users	string (list of usernames)	Specifies a list of users that will be denied access to a share.	None	Share
read list	string (list of usernames)	Specifies a list of users that have read-only access to a writable share.	None	Share
write list	string (list of usernames)	Specifies a list of users that have read-write access to a read-only share.	None	Share
max connections	numerical	Indicates the maximum number of connections for a share at a given time.	0	Share
guest only (only guest)	boolean	Specifies that this share allows only guest access.	no	Share
guest account	string (name of account)	Names the Unix account that will be used for guest access.	nobody	Share

admin users

This option specifies a list of users that perform file operations as if they were root. This means that they can modify or destroy any other user's work, no matter what the permissions. Any files that they create will have root ownership and will use the default group of the admin user. The admin users option is used to allow PC users to act as administrators for particular shares. We urge you to avoid this option.

valid users and invalid users

These two options let you enumerate the users and groups who are granted or denied access to a particular share. You can enter a list of comma-delimited users, or indicate an NIS or Unix group name by prefixing the name with an at-sign (@).

The important rule to remember with these options is that any name or group in the invalid users list will *always* be denied access, even if it is included (in any form) in the valid users list. By default, neither option has a value associated with it. If both options have no value, any user is allowed to access the share.

read list and write list

Like the valid users and invalid users options, this pair of options specifies which users have read-only access to a writeable share and read-write access to a read-only share, respectively. The value of either options is a list of users. read list overrides any other Samba permissions granted—as well as Unix file permissions on the server system—to deny users write access. write list overrides other Samba permissions to grant write access, but cannot grant write access if the user lacks write permissions for the file on the Unix system. You can specify NIS or Unix group names by prefixing the name with an at sign (such as @users). Neither configuration option has a default value associated with it.

max connections

This option specifies the maximum number of client connections that a share can have at any given time. Any connections that are attempted after the maximum is reached will be rejected. The default value is 0, which means that an unlimited number of connections are allowed. You can override it per share as follows:

```
[accounting]
    max connections = 30
```

This option is useful in the event that you need to limit the number of users who are accessing a licensed program or piece of data concurrently.

guest only

This share-level option (sometimes called `only guest`) forces a connection to a share to be performed with the user specified by the `guest account` option. The share to which this is applied must explicitly specify `guest ok = yes` in order for this option to be recognized by Samba. The default value for this option is `no`.

guest account

This option specifies the name of account to be used for guest access to shares in Samba. The default for this option varies from system to system, but it is often set to **nobody**. Some default user accounts have trouble connecting as guest users. If that occurs on your system, the Samba team recommends using the ftp account as the guest user.

Username Options

Table 6-2 shows two additional options that Samba can use to correct for incompatibilities in usernames between Windows and Unix.

Table 6-2. Username Options

Option	Parameters	Function	Default	Scope
username map	string (fully-qualified pathname)	Sets the name of the username mapping file.	None	Global
username level	numerical	Indicates the number of capital letters to use when trying to match a username.	0	Global

username map

Client usernames on an SMB network can be relatively large (up to 255 characters), while usernames on a Unix network often cannot be larger than eight characters. This means that an individual user may have one username on a client and another (shorter) one on the Samba server. You can get past this issue by *mapping* a free-form client username to a Unix username of eight or fewer characters. It is placed in a standard text file, using a format that we'll describe shortly. You can then specify the pathname to Samba with the global **username map** option. Be sure to restrict access to this file; make the root user the file's owner and deny write access to others. Otherwise, an untrusted user who can access the file can easily map their client username to the root user of the Samba server.

You can specify this option as follows:

```
[global]
    username map = /etc/samba/usermap.txt
```

Each of the entries in the username map file should be listed as follows: the Unix username, followed by an equal sign (=), followed by one or more whitespace-separated SMB client usernames. Note that unless instructed otherwise, (i.e., a guest connection), Samba will expect both the client and the server user to have the same password. You can also map NT groups to one or more specific Unix groups using the @ sign. Here are some examples:

```
jarwin = JosephArwin
manderso = MarkAnderson
users = @account
```

Also, you can use the asterisk to specify a wildcard that matches any free-form client username as an entry in the username map file:

```
nobody = *
```

Comments in the file can be specified as lines beginning with (#) and (;).

Note that you can also use this file to redirect one Unix user to another user. Be careful if you do so because Samba and your client may not notify the user that the mapping has been made and Samba may be expecting a different password.

username level

SMB clients (such as Windows) will often send usernames in SMB connection requests entirely in capital letters; in other words, client usernames are not necessarily case sensitive. On a Unix server, however, usernames *are* case sensitive: the user **ANDY** is different from the user **andy**. By default, Samba attacks this problem by doing the following:

1. Checking for a user account with the exact name sent by the client

2. Testing the username in all lowercase letters

3. Testing the username in lowercase letters with only the first letter capitalized

If you wish to have Samba attempt more combinations of uppercase and lowercase letters, you can use the **username level** global configuration option. This option takes an integer value that specifies how many letters in the username should be capitalized when attempting to connect to a share. You can specify this options as follows:

```
[global]
    username level = 3
```

In this case, Samba will then attempt all permutations of usernames it can compute having three capital letters. The larger the number, the more computations Samba will have to perform to match the username and the longer the authentication will take.

Authentication Security

At this point, we should discuss how Samba authenticates users. Each user who attempts to connect to a share that does not allow guest access must provide a password to make a successful connection. What Samba does with that password—and consequently the strategy Samba will use to handle user authentication—is the arena of the `security` configuration option. There are currently four security levels that Samba supports on its network: *share, user, server,* and *domain.*

Share-level security

> Each share in the workgroup has one or more passwords associated with it. Anyone who knows a valid password for the share can access it.

User-level security

> Each share in the workgroup is configured to allow access from certain users. With each initial tree connection, the Samba server verifies users and their passwords to allow them access to the share.

Server-level security

> This is the same as user-level security, except that the Samba server uses a separate SMB server to validate users and their passwords before granting access to the share.

Domain-level security

> Samba becomes a member of a Windows domain and uses the domain's primary domain controller (PDC) to perform authentication. Once authenticated, the user is given a special token that allows him or her access to any share with appropriate access rights. With this token, the PDC will not have to revalidate the user's password each time he or she attempts to access another share within the domain.

Each of these security policies can be implemented with the global `security` option, as shown in Table 6-3.

Table 6-3. Security Option

Option	Parameters	Function	Default	Scope
security	domain, server, share, or user	Indicates the type of security that the Samba server will use.	user (Samba 2.0) or share (Samba 1.9)	Global

Share-level Security

With share-level security, each share has one or more passwords associated with it. This differs from the other modes of security in that there are no restrictions as to whom can access a share, as long as that individual knows the correct password. Shares often have multiple passwords. For example, one password may grant read-only access, while another may grant read-write access, and so on. Security is maintained as long as unauthorized users do not discover the password for a share to which they shouldn't have access.

OS/2 and Window 95/98 both support share-level security on their resources. You can set up share-level security with Windows 95/98 by first enabling share-level security using the Access Control tab of the Network Control Panel dialog. Then select the Share-level Access Control radio button (which deselects the user-level access control radio button), as shown in Figure 6-1, and press the OK button.

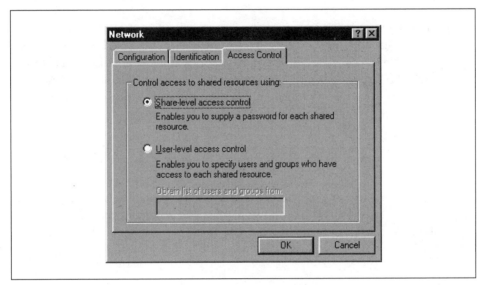

Figure 6-1. Selecting share-level security on a Windows machine

Next, right click on a resource—such as a hard drive or a CD-ROM—and select the Properties menu item. This will bring up the Resource Properties dialog box. Select the Sharing tab at the top of the dialog box and enable the resource as Shared As. From here, you can configure how the shared resource will appear to individual users, as well as assigning whether the resource will appear as read-only, read-write, or a mix, depending on the password that is supplied.

You might be thinking that this security model is not a good fit for Samba—and you would be right. In fact, if you set the `security = share` option in the Samba configuration file, Samba will still reuse the username/passwords combinations in the system password files to authenticate access. More precisely, Samba will take the following steps when a client requests a connection using share-level security:

1. When a connection is requested, Samba will accept the password and (if sent) the username of the client.

2. If the share is `guest only`, the user is immediately granted access to the share with the rights of the user specified by the `guest account` parameter; no password checking is performed.

3. For other shares, Samba appends the username to a list of users who are allowed access to the share. It then attempts to validate the password given in association with that username. If successful, Samba grants the user access to the share with the rights assigned to that user. The user will not need to authenticate again unless a `revalidate = yes` option has been set inside the share.

4. If the authentication is unsuccessful, Samba will attempt to validate the password against the list of users it has previously compiled throughout the attempted connections, as well as any specified under the share in the configuration file. If the password does not match any usernames (as specified in the system password file, typically */etc/passwd*), the user is not granted access to the share under that username.

5. However, if the share has a `guest ok` or `public` option set, the user will default to access with the rights of the user specified by the `guest account` option.

You can indicate in the configuration file which users should be initially placed on the share-level security user list by using the **username** configuration option, as shown below:

```
[global]
    security = share
[accounting1]
    path = /home/samba/accounting1
    guest ok = no
    writable = yes
    username = davecb, pkelly, andyo
```

Here, when a user attempts to connect to a share, Samba will verify the password that was sent against each of the users in its own list, in addition to the passwords of users **davecb**, **pkelly**, and **andyo**. If any of the passwords match, the connection will be verified and the user will be allowed. Otherwise, connection to the specific share will fail.

Share Level Security Options

Table 6-4 shows the options typically associated with share-level security.

Table 6-4. Share-Level Access Options

Option	Parameters	Function	Default	Scope
only user	boolean	Indicates whether usernames specified by **username** will be the only ones allowed.	no	Share
username (user or users)	string (list of usernames)	Specifies a list of users against which a client's password will be tested.	None	Share

only user

This boolean option indicates whether Samba will allow connections to a share using share-level security based solely on the individuals specified in the **username** option, instead of those users compiled on Samba's internal list. The default value for this option is **no**. You can override it per share as follows:

```
[global]
    security = share
[data]
    username = andy, peter, valerie
    only user = yes
```

username

This option presents a list of users against which Samba will test a connection password to allow access. It is typically used with clients that have share-level security to allow connections to a particular service based solely on a qualifying password—in this case, one that matches a password set up for a specific user:

```
[global]
    security = share
[data]
    username = andy, peter, terry
```

We recommend against using this option unless you are implementing a Samba server with share-level security.

User-level Security

The preferred mode of security with Samba is *user-level security*. With this method, each share is assigned specific users that can access it. When a user requests a connection to a share, Samba authenticates by validating the given username and password with the authorized users in the configuration file and the passwords in the password database of the Samba server. As mentioned earlier in the chapter, one way to isolate which users are allowed access to a specific share is by using the **valid users** option for each share:

```
[global]
    security = user
[accounting1]
    writable = yes
    valid users = bob, joe, sandy
```

Each of the users listed will be allowed to connect to the share if the password provided matches the password stored in the system password database on the server. Once the initial authentication succeeds, the user will not need to re-enter a password again to access that share unless the **revalidate = yes** option has been set.

Passwords can be sent to the Samba server in either an encrypted or a non-encrypted format. If you have both types of systems on your network, you should ensure that the passwords represented by each user are stored both in a traditional account database and Samba's encrypted password database. This way, authorized users can gain access to their shares from any type of client.* However, we recommend that you move your system to encrypted passwords and abandon non-encrypted passwords if security is an issue. The "Passwords" section of this chapter explains how to use encrypted as well as non-encrypted passwords.

Server-level Security

Server-level security is similar to user-level security. However, with server-level security, Samba delegates password authentication to another SMB password server, typically another Samba server or a Windows NT Server acting as a PDC on the network. Note that Samba still maintains its list of shares and their configuration in its *smb.conf* file. When a client attempts to make a connection to a particular share, Samba validates that the user is indeed authorized to connect to the share. Samba will then attempt to validate the password by contacting the SMB password server through a known protocol and presenting the username and password to the SMB password server. If the password is accepted, a session will be established with the client. See Figure 6-2 for an illustration of this setup.

You can configure Samba to use a separate password server under server-level security with the use of the **password server** global configuration option, as follows:

---

* Having both encrypted and non-encrypted password clients on your network is another reason why Samba allows you to include (or not include) various options in the Samba configuration file based on the client operating system or machine name variables.

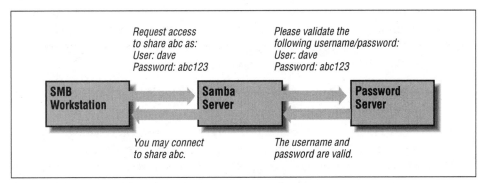

Figure 6-2. A typical system setup using server level security

```
[global]
        security = server
        password server = PHOENIX120 HYDRA134
```

Note that you can specify more than one machine as the target of the **password server**; Samba will move down the list of servers in the event that its first choice is unreachable. The servers identified by the **password server** option are given as NetBIOS names, not their DNS names or equivalent IP addresses. Also, if any of the servers reject the given password, the connection will automatically fail—Samba will not attempt another server.

One caveat: when using this option, you will still need an account representing that user on the regular Samba server. This is because the Unix operating system needs a username to perform various I/O operations. The preferable method of handling this is to give the user an account on the Samba server but disable the account's password by replacing it in the system password file (e.g., */etc/passwd*) with an asterisk (*).

Domain-level Security

Domain-level security is similar to server-level security. However, with domain-level security, the Samba server is acting as a member of a Windows domain. Recall from Chapter 1 that each domain has a *domain controller*, which is usually a Windows NT server offering password authentication. Including these controllers provides the workgroup with a definitive password server. The domain controllers keep track of users and passwords in their own security authentication module (SAM), and authenticates each user when he or she first logs on and wishes to access another machine's shares.

As mentioned earlier in this chapter, Samba has a similar ability to offer user-level security, but this option is Unix-centric and assumes that the authentication occurs via Unix password files. If the Unix machine is part of a NIS or NIS+ domain,

Samba will authenticate the users transparently against a shared password file, in typical Unix fashion. Samba then provides access to the NIS or NIS+ domain from Windows. There is, of course, no relationship between the NIS concept of a domain and the Windows concept of a domain.

With domain-level security, we now have the option of using the native NT mechanism. This has a number of advantages:

- It provides far better integration with NT: there are fewer "kludges" in the *smb.conf* options dealing with domains than with most Windows features. This allows more extensive use of NT management tools, such as the User Manager for Domains tool allowing PC support individuals to treat Samba servers as if they were large NT machines.

- With the better integration comes protocol and code cleanups, allowing the Samba team to track the evolving NT implementation. NT Service Pack 4 corrects several problems in the protocol, and Samba's better integration makes it easier to track and adapt to these changes.

- There is less overhead on the PDC because there is one less permanent network connection between it and the Samba server. Unlike the protocol used by the **security = server** option, the Samba server can make a Remote Procedure Call (RPC) call only when it needs authentication information. It can not keep a connection permanently up just for that.

- Finally, the NT domain authentication scheme returns the full set of user attributes, not just success or failure. The attributes include a longer, more network-oriented version of the Unix uid, NT groups, and other information. This includes:

  — Username

  — Full name

  — Description

  — Security identifier (a domain-wide extension of the Unix uid)

  — NT group memberships

  — Logon hours, and whether to force the user to log out immediately

  — Workstations the user is allowed to use

  — Account expiration date

  — Home directory

  — Login script

  — Profile

  — Account type

- The Samba developers used domain-level security in Samba version 2.0.4 to add and delete domain users on Samba servers semi-automatically. In addition, it adds room for other NT-like additions, such as supporting access control lists and changing permissions of files from the client.

The advantage to this approach is less administration; there is only one authentication database to keep synchronized. The only local administration required on the Samba server will be creating directories for users to work in and */etc/passwd* entries to keep their UIDs and groups in.

Adding a Samba server to a Windows NT Domain

If you already have an NT domain, you can easily add a Samba server to it. First, you will need to stop the Samba daemons. Then, add the Samba server to the NT domain on the PDC using the "Windows NT Server Manager for Domains" tool. When it asks for the computer type, choose "Windows NT Workstation or Server," and give it the NetBIOS name of the Samba server. This creates the machine account on the NT server.

Next, generate a Microsoft-format machine password using the *smbpasswd* tool, which is explained in further detail in the next section. For example, if our domain is SIMPLE and the Windows NT PDC is `beowulf`, we could use the following command on the Samba server to accomplish this:

```
smbpasswd -j SIMPLE -r beowulf
```

Finally, add the following options to the `[global]` section of your *smb.conf* and restart the Samba daemons.

```
[global]
    security = domain
    domain logins = yes
    workgroup = SIMPLE
    password server = beowulf
```

Samba should now be configured for domain-level security. The `domain logins` option is explained in more detail later in this chapter.

Passwords

Passwords are a thorny issue with Samba. So much so, in fact, that they are almost always the first major problem that users encounter when they install Samba, and generate by far the most questions sent to Samba support groups. In previous chapters, we've gotten around the need for passwords by placing the `guest ok` option in each of our configuration files, which allows connections without authenticating passwords. However, at this point, we need to delve deeper into Samba to discover what is happening on the network.

Passwords sent from individual clients can be either encrypted or non-encrypted. Encrypted passwords are, of course, more secure. A non-encrypted password can be easily read with a packet sniffing program, such as the modified *tcpdump* program for Samba that we used in Chapter 3, *Configuring Windows Clients*. Whether passwords are encrypted depends on the operating system that the client is using to connect to the Samba server. Table 6-5 lists which Windows operating systems encrypt their passwords before sending them to the primary domain controller for authentication. If your client is not Windows, check the system documentation to see if SMB passwords are encrypted.

Table 6-5. Windows Operating Systems with Encrypted Passwords

Operating System	Encrypted or Non-encrypted
Windows 95	Non-encrypted
Windows 95 with SMB Update	Encrypted
Windows 98	Encrypted
Windows NT 3.*x*	Non-encrypted
Windows NT 4.0 before SP 3	Non-encrypted
Windows NT 4.0 after SP 3	Encrypted

There are actually two different encryption methods used: one for Windows 95 and 98 clients that reuses Microsoft's LAN Manager encryption style, and a separate one for Windows NT clients and servers. Windows 95 and 98 use an older encryption system inherited from the LAN Manager network software, while Windows NT clients and servers use a newer encryption system.

If encrypted passwords are supported, Samba stores the encrypted passwords in a file called *smbpasswd*. By default, this file is located in the *private* directory of the Samba distribution (*/usr/local/samba/private*). At the same time, the client stores an encrypted version of a user's password on its own system. The plaintext password is never stored on either system. Each system encrypts the password automatically using a known algorithm when the password is set or changed.

When a client requests a connection to an SMB server that supports encrypted passwords (such as Samba or Windows NT), the two computers undergo the following negotiations:

1. The client attempts to negotiate a protocol with the server.

2. The server responds with a protocol and indicates that it supports encrypted passwords. At this time, it sends back a randomly-generated 8-byte challenge string.

3. The client uses the challenge string as a key to encrypt its already encrypted password using an algorithm predefined by the negotiated protocol. It then sends the result to the server.

4. The server does the same thing with the encrypted password stored in its database. If the results match, the passwords are equivalent and the user is authenticated.

Note that even though the original passwords are not involved in the authentication process, you need to be very careful that the encrypted passwords located inside of the *smbpasswd* file are guarded from unauthorized users. If they are compromised, an unauthorized user can break into the system by replaying the steps of the previous algorithm. The encrypted passwords are just as sensitive as the plaintext passwords—this is known as *plaintext-equivalent* data in the cryptography world. Of course, you should also ensure that the clients safeguard their plaintext-equivalent passwords as well.

You can configure Samba to accept encrypted passwords with the following global additions to *smb.conf.* Note that we explicitly name the location of the Samba password file:

```
[global]
    security = user
    encrypt passwords = yes
    smb passwd file = /usr/local/samba/private/smbpasswd
```

Samba, however, will not accept any users until the *smbpasswd* file has been initialized.

Disabling encrypted passwords on the client

While Unix authentication has been in use for decades, including the use of *telnet* and *rlogin* access across the Internet, it embodies well-known security risks. Plaintext passwords are sent over the Internet and can be retrieved from TCP packets by malicious snoopers. However, if you feel that your network is secure and you wish to use standard Unix */etc/passwd* authentication for all clients, you can do so, but you must disable encrypted passwords on those Windows clients that default to using them.

In order to do this, you must modify the Windows registry by installing two files on each system. Depending on the platform involved, the files are either *NT4_PlainPassword.reg* or *Win95_PlainPassword.reg.* You can perform this installation by copying the appropriate *.reg* files from the Samba distribution's */docs* directory to a DOS floppy, and running it from the Run menu item on the client's Start Menu button. Incidentally, the Windows 95 *.reg* file works fine on Windows 98 as well.

After you reboot the machine, the client will not encrypt its hashed passwords before sending them to the server. This means that the plaintext-equivalent passwords can been seen in the TCP packets that are broadcast across the network. Again, we encourage you not to do this unless you are absolutely sure that your network is secure.

If passwords are not encrypted, you can indicate as much in your Samba configuration file:

```
[global]
    security = user
    encrypt passwords = no
```

The smbpasswd File

Samba stores its encrypted passwords in a file called *smbpasswd*, which by default resides in the */usr/local/samba/private* directory. The *smbpasswd* file should be guarded as closely as the *passwd* file; it should be placed in a directory to which only the root user has read/write access. All other users should not be able to read from the directory at all. In addition, the file should have all access closed off to all users except for root.

Before you can use encrypted passwords, you will need to create an entry for each Unix user in the *smbpasswd* file. The structure of the file is somewhat similar to a Unix *passwd* file, but has different fields. Figure 6-3 illustrates the layout of the *smbpasswd* file; the entry shown is actually one line in the file.

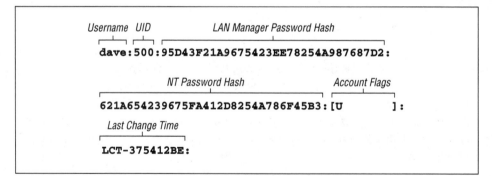

Figure 6-3. Structure of the smbpasswd file entry (actually one line)

Here is a breakdown of the individual fields:

Username

This is the username of the account. It is taken directly from the system password file.

UID

This is the user ID of the account. Like the username, it is taken directly from the system password file and must match the user it represents there.

LAN Manager Password Hash

This is a 32-bit hexadecimal sequence that represents the password Windows 95 and 98 clients will use. It is derived by encrypting the string KGS!@#$% with a 56-bit DES algorithm using the user's password (forced to 14 bytes and converted to capital letters) twice repeated as the key. If there is currently no password for this user, the first 11 characters of the hash will consist of the sequence NO PASSWORD followed by X characters for the remainder. Anyone can access the share with no password. On the other hand, if the password has been disabled, it will consist of 32 X characters. Samba will not grant access to a user without a password unless the **null passwords** option has been set.

NT Password Hash

This is a 32-bit hexadecimal sequence that represents the password Windows NT clients will use. It is derived by hashing the user's password (represented as a 16-bit little-endian Unicode sequence) with an MD4 hash. The password is not converted to uppercase letters first.

Account Flags

This field consists of 11 characters between two braces ([ ]). Any of the following characters can appear in any order; the remaining characters should be spaces:

U This account is a standard user account.

D This account is currently disabled and Samba should not allow any logins.

N This account has no password associated with it.

W This is a workstation trust account that can be used to configure Samba as a primary domain controller (PDC) when allowing Windows NT machines to join its domain.

Last Change Time

This code consists of the characters LCT- followed by a hexidecimal representation of the amount of seconds since the epoch (midnight on January 1, 1970) that the entry was last changed.

Adding entries to smbpasswd

There are a few ways you can add a new entry to the *smbpasswd* file:

- You can use the *smbpasswd* program with the **-a** option to automatically add any user that currently has a standard Unix system account on the server. This program resides in the */usr/local/samba/bin* directory.

- You can use the *addtosmbpass* executable inside the */usr/local/samba/bin* directory. This is actually a simple *awk* script that parses a system password file and extracts the username and UID of each entry you wish to add to the SMB password file. It then adds default fields for the remainder of the user's entry, which can be updated using the *smbpasswd* program later. In order to use this program, you will probably need to edit the first line of the file to correctly point to *awk* on your system.

- In the event that the neither of those options work for you, you can create a default entry by hand in the *smbpasswd* file. The entry should be entirely on one line. Each field should be colon-separated and should look similar to the following:

```
dave:500:XXXXXXXXXXXXXXXXXXXXXXXXXXXXXXXX:XXXXXXXXXXXXXXXXXXXXXXXXXXXXXXXX:[U
]:LCT-00000000:
```

This consists of the username and the UID as specified in the system password file, followed by two sets of exactly 32 X characters, followed by the account flags and last change time as it appears above. After you've added this entry, you must use the *smbpasswd* program to change the password for the user.

Changing the encrypted password

If you need to change the encrypted password in the *smbpasswd* file, you can also use the *smbpasswd* program. Note that this program shares the same name as the encrypted password file itself, so be sure not to accidentally confuse the password file with the password-changing program.

The *smbpasswd* program is almost identical to the *passwd* program that is used to change Unix account passwords. The program simply asks you to enter your old password (unless you're the root user), and duplicate entries of your new password. No password characters are shown on the screen.

```
# smbpasswd dave
Old SMB password:
New SMB password:
Retype new SMB password:
Password changed for user dave
```

You can look at the *smbpasswd* file after this command completes to verify that both the LAN Manager and the NT hashes of the passwords have been stored in their respective positions. Once users have encrypted password entries in the database, they should be able to connect to shares using encrypted passwords!

Password Synchronization

Having a regular password and an encrypted version of the same password can be troublesome when you need to change both of them. Luckily, Samba affords you a limited ability to keep your passwords synchronized. Samba has a pair of configuration options that can be used to automatically update a user's regular Unix password when the encrypted password is changed on the system. The feature can be activated by specifying the **unix password sync** global configuration option:

```
[global]
    encrypt passwords = yes
    smb passwd file = /usr/local/samba/private/smbpasswd

    unix password sync = yes
```

With this option enabled, Samba will attempt to change the user's regular password (as **root**) when the encrypted version is changed with *smbpasswd*. However, there are two other options that have to be set correctly in order for this to work.

The easier of the two is **passwd program**. This option simply specifies the Unix command used to change a user's standard system password. It is set to **/bin/passwd %u** by default. With some Unix systems, this is sufficient and you do not need to change anything. Others, such as Red Hat Linux, use */usr/bin/passwd* instead. In addition, you may want to change this to another program or script at some point in the future. For example, let's assume that you want to use a script called **changepass** to change a user's password. Recall that you can use the variable **%u** to represent the current Unix username. So the example becomes:

```
[global]
    encrypt passwords = yes
    smb passwd file = /usr/local/samba/private/smbpasswd

    unix password sync = yes
    passwd program = changepass %u
```

Note that this program will be called as the **root** user when the **unix password sync** option is set to **yes**. This is because Samba does not necessarily have the plaintext old password of the user.

The harder option to configure is **passwd chat**. The **passwd chat** option works like a Unix chat script. It specifies a series of strings to send as well as responses to expect from the program specified by the **passwd program** option. For example, this is what the default **passwd chat** looks like. The delimiters are the spaces between each groupings of characters:

```
passwd chat = *old*password* %o\n *new*password* %n\n *new*password* %n\n
*changed*
```

The first grouping represents a response expected from the password-changing program. Note that it can contain wildcards (*), which help to generalize the chat programs to be able to handle a variety of similar outputs. Here, ***old*password*** indicates that Samba is expecting any line from the password program containing the letters old followed by the letters **password**, without regard for what comes on either side or between them. Once instructed to, Samba will wait indefinitely for such a match. Is Samba does not receive the expected response, the password will fail.

The second grouping indicates what Samba should send back once the data in the first grouping has been matched. In this case, you see %o\n. This response is actually two items: the variable %o represents the old password, while the \n is a newline character. So, in effect, this will "type" the old password into the standard input of the password changing program, and then "press" Enter.

Following that is another response grouping, followed by data that will be sent back to the password changing program. (In fact, this response/send pattern continues indefinitely in any standard Unix *chat* script.) The script continues until the final pattern is matched.*

You can help match the response strings sent from the password program with the characters listed in Table 6-6. In addition, you can use the characters listed in Table 6-7 to help formulate your response.

Table 6-6. Password Chat Response Characters

Character	Definition
*	Zero or more occurrences of any character.
" "	Allows you to include matching strings that contain spaces. Asterisks are still considered wildcards even inside of quotes, and you can represent a null response with empty quotes.

Table 6-7. Password Chat Send Characters

Character	Definition
%o	The user's old password
%n	The user's new password
\n	The linefeed character
\r	The carriage-return character
\t	The tab character
\s	A space

For example, you may want to change your password chat to the following entry. This will handle scenarios in which you do not have to enter the old password. In

---

* This may not work under Red Hat Linux, as the password program typically responds "All authentication tokens updated successfully," instead of "Password changed." We provide a fix for this later in this section.

addition, this will also handle the new `all tokens updated successfully` string that Red Hat Linux sends:

```
passwd chat = *new password* %n\n *new password* %n\n *success*
```

Again, the default chat should be sufficient for many Unix systems. If it isn't, you can use the **passwd chat debug** global option to set up a new chat script for the password change program. The **passwd chat debug** option logs everything during a password chat. This option is a simple boolean, as shown below:

```
[global]
    encrypted passwords = yes
    smb passwd file = /usr/local/samba/private/smbpasswd

    unix password sync = yes
    passwd chat debug = yes
    log level = 100
```

After you activate the password chat debug feature, all I/O received by Samba through the password chat will be sent to the Samba logs with a debug level of 100, which is why we entered a new log level option as well. As this can often generate multitudes of error logs, it may be more efficient to use your own script, by setting the **passwd program** option, in place of */bin/passwd* to record what happens during the exchange. Also, make sure to protect your log files with strict file permissions and to delete them as soon as you've grabbed the information you need, because they contain the passwords in plaintext.

The operating system on which Samba is running may have strict requirements for valid passwords in order to make them more impervious to dictionary attacks and the like. Users should be made aware of these restrictions when changing their passwords.

Earlier we said that password synchronization is limited. This is because there is no reverse synchronization of the encrypted *smbpasswd* file when a standard Unix password is updated by a user. There are various strategies to get around this, including NIS and freely available implementations of the pluggable authentication modules (PAM) standard, but none of them really solve all the problems yet. In the future, when Windows 2000 emerges, we will see more compliance with the Lightweight Directory Access Protocol (LDAP), which promises to make password synchronization a thing of the past.

Password Configuration Options

The options in Table 6-8 will help you work with passwords in Samba.

Table 6-8. Password Configuration Options

Option	Parameters	Function	Default	Scope
encrypt passwords	boolean	Turns on encrypted passwords.	no	Global
unix password sync	boolean	If **yes**, Samba updates the standard Unix password database when a user changes his or her encrypted password.	no	Global
passwd chat	string (chat commands)	Sets a sequence of commands that will be sent to the password program.	See earlier section on this option	Global
passwd chat debug	boolean	Sends debug logs of the password-change process to the log files with a level of 100.	no	Global
passwd program	string (Unix command)	Sets the program to be used to change passwords.	/bin/passwd %u	Global
password level	numeric	Sets the number of capital letter permutations to attempt when matching a client's password.	None	Global
update encrypted	boolean	If **yes**, Samba updates the encrypted password file when a client connects to a share with a plaintext password.	no	Global
null passwords	boolean	If **yes**, Samba allows access for users with null passwords.	no	Global
smb passwd file	string (fully-qualified pathname)	Specifies the name of the encrypted password file.	/usr/local/ samba/ private/ smbpasswd	Global
hosts equiv	string (fully-qualified pathname)	Specifies the name of a file that contains hosts and users that can connect without using a password.	None	Global
use rhosts	string (fully-qualified pathname)	Specifies the name of an *.rhosts* file that allows users to connect without using a password.	None	Global

unix password sync

The **unix password sync** global option allows Samba to update the standard Unix password file when a user changes his or her encrypted password. The encrypted password is stored on a Samba server in the *smbpasswd* file, which is located in */usr/local/samba/private* by default. You can activate this feature as follows:

```
[global]
    unix password sync = yes
```

If this option is enabled, Samba changes the encrypted password and, in addition, attempts to change the standard Unix password by passing the username and new password to the program specified by the **passwd program** option (described earlier). Note that Samba does not necessarily have access to the plaintext password for this user, so the password changing program must be invoked as **root**.* If the Unix password change does not succeed, for whatever reason, the SMB password will not be changed either.

encrypt passwords

The **encrypt passwords** global option switches Samba from using plaintext passwords to encrypted passwords for authentication. Encrypted passwords will be expected from clients if the option is set to **yes**:

```
encrypt passwords = yes
```

By default, Windows NT 4.0 with Service Pack 3 or above and Windows 98 transmit encrypted passwords over the network. If you are enabling encrypted passwords, you must have a valid *smbpasswd* file in place and populated with usernames that will authenticate with encrypted passwords. (See the section "The smbpasswd File," earlier in this chapter.) In addition, Samba must know the location of the *smbpasswd* file; if it is not in the default location (typically */usr/local/samba/private/smbpasswd*), you can explicitly name it using the **smb passwd file** option.

If you wish, you can use the **update encrypted** to force Samba to update the *smbpasswd* file with encrypted passwords each time a client connects to a non-encrypted password.

A common strategy to ensure that hosts who need encrypted password authentication indeed receive it is with the **include** option. With this, you can create individual configuration files that will be read in based on OS-type (**%a**) or client name (**%m**). These host-specific or OS-specific configuration files can contain an **encrypted passwords = yes** option that will activate only when those clients are connecting to the server.

---

* This is because the Unix *passwd* program, which is the usual target for this operation, allows **root** to change a user's password without the security restriction that requests the old password of that user.

passwd program

The **passwd program** is used to specify a program on the Unix Samba server that Samba can use to update the standard system password file when the encrypted password file is updated. This option defaults to the standard *passwd* program, usually located in the */bin* directory. The **%u** variable is typically used here as the requesting user when the command is executed. The actual handling of input and output to this program during execution is handled through the **passwd chat** option. The "Password Synchronization" section, earlier in this chapter, covers this option in detail.

passwd chat

This option specifies a series of send/response strings similar to a Unix chat script, which are used to interface with the password-changing program on the Samba server. The "Password Synchronization" section, earlier in this chapter, covers this option in detail.

passwd chat debug

If set to **yes**, the **passwd chat debug** global option logs everything sent or received by Samba during a password chat. All the I/O received by Samba through the password chat is sent to the Samba logs with a debug level of 100; you will need to specify **log level = 100** in order for the information to be recorded. The "Password Synchronization" section, earlier in this chapter, describes this option in more detail. Be aware that if you do set this option, the plaintext passwords will be visible in the debugging logs, which could be a security hazard if they are not properly secured.

password level

With SMB, non-encrypted (or plaintext) passwords are sent with capital letters, just like the usernames mentioned previously. Many Unix users, however, choose passwords with both uppercase and lowercase letters. Samba, by default, only attempts to match the password entirely in lowercase letters, and not capitalizing the first letter.

Like **username level**, there is a **password level** option that can be used to attempt various permutations of the password with capital letters. This option takes an integer value that specifies how many letters in the password should be capitalized when attempting to connect to a share. You can specify this options as follows:

```
[global]
    password level = 3
```

In this case, Samba will then attempt all permutations of the password it can compute having three capital letters. The larger the number, the more computations Samba will have to perform to match the password, and the longer a connection to a specific share may take.

update encrypted

For sites switching over to the encrypted password format, Samba provides an option that should help with the transition. The **update encrypted** option allows a site to ease into using encrypted passwords from plaintext passwords. You can activate this option as follows:

```
[global]
    update encrypted = yes
```

This instructs Samba to create an encrypted version of each user's Unix password in the *smbpasswd* file each time he or she connects to a share. When this option is enabled, you must have the **encrypt passwords** option set to **no** so that the client will pass plaintext passwords to Samba to use to update the files. Once each user has connected at least once, you can set **encrypted passwords = yes**, allowing you to use only the encrypted passwords. The user must already have a valid entry in the *smbpasswd* file for this option to work.

null passwords

This global option tells Samba whether or not to allow access from users that have null passwords (encrypted or non-encrypted) set in their accounts. The default value is **no**. You can override it as follows:

```
null passwords = yes
```

We highly recommend against doing so unless you are familiar with the security risks this option can present to your system, including inadvertent access to system users (such as *bin*) in the system password file who have null passwords set.

smb passwd file

This global option identifies the location of the encrypted password database. By default, it is set to */usr/local/samba/private/smbpasswd*. You can override it as follows:

```
[global]
    smb passwd file = /etc/smbpasswd
```

This location, for example, is common on many Red Hat distributions.

hosts equiv

This global option specifies the name of a standard Unix *hosts.equiv* file that will allow hosts or users to access shares without specifying a password. You can specify the location of such a file as follows:

```
[global]
     hosts equiv = /etc/hosts.equiv
```

The default value for this option does not specify any *hosts.equiv* file. Because using such a file is essentially a huge security risk, we highly recommend that you do not use this option unless you are confident in the security of your network.

use rhosts

This global option specifies the name of a standard Unix user's *.rhosts* file that will allow foreign hosts to access shares without specifying a password. You can specify the location of such a file as follows:

```
[global]
     use rhosts = /home/dave/.rhosts
```

The default value for this option does not specify any *.rhosts* file. Like the `hosts equiv` option above, using such a file is a security risk. We highly recommend that you do use this option unless you are confident in the security of your network.

Windows Domains

Now that you are comfortable with users and passwords on a Samba server, we can show you how to set up Samba to become a primary domain controller for Windows 95/98 and NT machines. Why use domains? The answer probably isn't obvious until you look behind the scenes, especially with Windows 95/98.

Recall that with traditional workgroups, Windows 95/98 simply accepts each username and password that you enter when logging on to the system. There are no unauthorized users with Windows 95/98; if a new user logs on, the operating system simply asks for a new password and authenticates the user against that password from then on. The only time that Windows 95/98 attempts to use the password you entered is when connecting to another share.

Domain logons, on the other hand, are similar to Unix systems. In order to log on to the domain, a valid username and password must be presented at startup, which is then authenticated against the primary domain controller's password database. If the password is invalid, the user is immediately notified and they cannot log on to the domain.

There's more good news: once you have successfully logged on to the domain, you can access any of the shares in the domain to which you have rights without having to reauthenticate yourself. More precisely, the primary domain controller returns a token to the client machine that allows it to access any share without consulting the PDC again. Although you probably won't notice the shift, this can be beneficial in cutting down network traffic. (You can disable this behavior if you wish by using the `revalidate` option.)

Configuring Samba for Windows Domain Logons

If you wish to allow Samba to act as a domain controller, use the following sections to configure Samba and your clients to allow domain access.

 If you would like more information on how to set up domains, see the *DOMAINS.TXT* file that comes with the Samba distribution.

Windows 95/98 clients

Setting up Samba as a PDC for Windows 95/98 clients is somewhat anticlimactic. All you really need to do on the server side is ensure that:

- Samba is the only primary domain controller for the current workgroup.
- There is a WINS server available on the network, either a Samba machine or a Windows NT server. (See Chapter 7, *Printing and Name Resolution,* for more information on WINS.)
- Samba is using user-level security (i.e., it doesn't hand off password authentication to anyone else). You do not want to use domain-level security if Samba itself is acting as the PDC.

At that point, you can insert the following options into your Samba configuration file:

```
[global]
    workgroup = SIMPLE
    domain logons = yes

# Be sure to set user-level security!

    security = user

# Be sure to become the primary domain controller!

    os level = 34
    local master = yes
    preferred master = yes
    domain master = yes
```

The `domain logons` option enables Samba to perform domain authentication on behalf of other clients that request it. The name of the domain will be the same as the workgroup listed in the Samba configuration file, in this case: SIMPLE.

After that, you need to create a non-writable, non-public, non-browsable disk share called [`netlogon`] (it does not matter where this share points to as long as each Windows client can connect to it):

```
[netlogon]
     comment = The domain logon service
     path = /export/samba/logon
     public = no
     writeable = no
     browsable = no
```

Windows NT clients

If you have Window NT clients on your system, there are a few more steps that need to be taken in order for Samba to act as their primary domain controller.

 You will need to use at least Samba 2.1 to ensure that PDC functionality for Windows NT clients is present. Prior to Samba 2.1, only limited user authentication for NT clients was present. At the time this book went to press, Samba 2.0.5 was the latest version, but Samba 2.1 was available through CVS download. Instructions on downloading alpha versions of Samba are given in Appendix E, *Downloading Samba with CVS*.

As before, you need to ensure that Samba is a primary domain controller for the current workgroup and is using user-level security. However, you must also ensure that Samba is using encrypted passwords. In other words, alter the [`global`] options the previous example to include the `encrypted passwords = yes` option, as shown here:

```
[global]
     workgroup = SIMPLE
     encrypted passwords = yes
     domain logons = yes

     security = user
```

Creating trust accounts for NT clients

This step is exclusively for Windows NT clients. All NT clients that connect to a primary domain controller make use of *trust accounts*. These accounts allow a machine to log in to the PDC itself (not one of its shares), which means that the PDC can trust any further connections from users on that client. For all intents and purposes, a trust account is identical to a user account. In fact, we will be using standard Unix user accounts to emulate trust accounts for the Samba server.

The login name of a machine's trust account is the name of the machine with a dollar sign appended to it. For example, if our Windows NT machine is named `chimaera`, the login account would be `chimaera$`. The initial password of the account is simply the name of the machine in lowercase letters. In order to forge the trust account on the Samba server, you need to create a Unix account with the appropriate machine name, as well as an encrypted password entry in the *smbpasswd* database.

Let's tackle the first part. Here, we only need to modify the */etc/passwd* file to support the trust account; there is no need to create a home directory or assign a shell to the "user" because the only part we are interested in is whether a login is permitted. Therefore, we can create a "dummy" account with the following entry:

```
chimaera$:*:1000:900:Trust Account:/dev/null:/dev/null
```

Note that we have also disabled the password field by placing a * in it. This is because Samba will use the *smbpasswd* file to contain the password instead, and we don't want anyone to telnet into the machine using that account. In fact, the only value other than the account name that is used here is the UID of the account for the encrypted password database (1000). This number must map to a unique resource ID on the NT server and cannot conflict with any other resource IDs. Hence, no NT user or group should map to this number or a networking error will occur.

Next, add the encrypted password using the *smbpasswd* command, as follows:

```
# smbpasswd -a -m chimaera
Added user chimaera$
Password changed for user chimaera$
```

The `-m` option specifies that a machine trust account is being generated. The *smbpasswd* program will automatically set the initial encrypted password as the NetBIOS name of the machine in lowercase letters; you don't need to enter it. When specifying this option on the command line, do not put a dollar sign after the machine name—it will be appended automatically. Once the encrypted password has been added, Samba is ready to handle domain logins from a NT client.

Configuring Windows Clients for Domain Logons

Once you have Samba configured for domain logons, you need to set up your Windows clients to log on to the domain at startup.

Windows 95/98

With Windows 95/98, this can be done by raising the Network configuration dialog in the Windows Control Panel and selecting the Properties for "Client for Microsoft Networks." At this point, you should see a dialog box similar to Figure 6-4. Select the "Logon to Windows Domain" checkbox at the top of the dialog box, and enter the workgroup that is listed in the Samba configuration file as the Windows NT domain. Then click on OK and reboot the machine when asked.

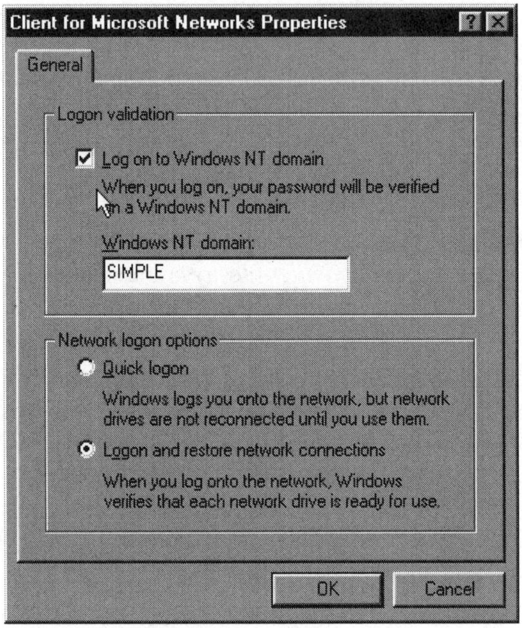

Figure 6-4. Configuring a Windows 95/98 client for domain logons

If Windows complains that you are already logged into the domain, you probably have an active connection to a share in the workgroup (such as a mapped network drive). Simply disconnect the resource temporarily by right-clicking on its icon and choosing the Disconnect pop-up menu item.

When Windows reboots, you should see the standard login dialog with an addition: a field for a domain. The domain name should already be filled in, so simply enter your password and click on the OK button. At this point, Windows should consult the primary domain controller (Samba) to see if the password is correct. (You can check the log files if you want to see this in action.) If it worked, congratulations! You have properly configured Samba to act as a domain controller for Windows 95/98 machines and your client is successfully connected.

Windows NT 4.0

To configure Windows NT for domain logons, open the Network configuration dialog in the Windows NT Control Panel. The first tab that you see should list the identification of the machine.

Press the Change button and you should see the dialog box shown in Figure 6-5. In this dialog box, you can choose to have the Windows NT client become a member of the domain by selecting the radio button marked Domain in the "Member of" box. Then, type in the domain that you wish the client to login to; it should be the same as the workgroup that you specified in the Samba configuration file. Do not check the box marked "Create a Computer Account in the Domain"—Samba does not currently support this functionality.

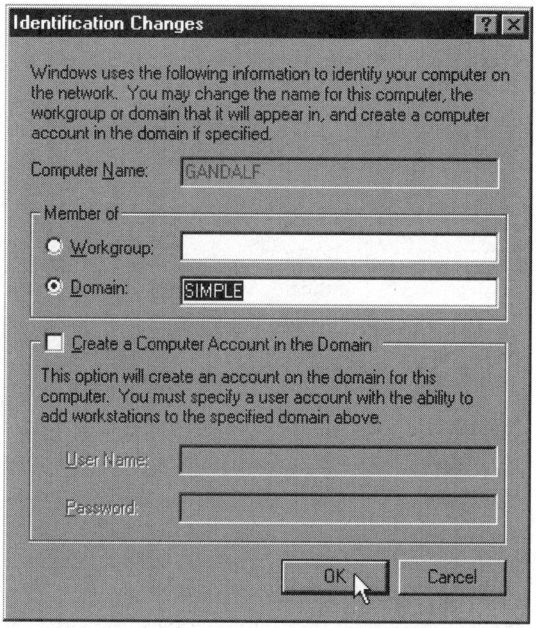

Figure 6-5. Configuring a Windows NT client for domain logons

 Like Windows 95/98, if NT complains that you are already logged in, you probably have an active connection to a share in the workgroup (such as a mapped network drive). Disconnect the resource temporarily by right-clicking on its icon and choosing the Disconnect pop-up menu item.

After you press the OK button, Windows should present you with a small dialog box welcoming you to the domain. At this point, you will need to reset the Windows NT machine. Once it comes up again, the machine will automatically present you with a log on screen similar to the one for Windows 95/98 clients. You can now log in using any account that you have already on the Samba server that is configured to accept logins.

Be sure to select the correct domain in the Windows NT logon dialog box. Once selected, it may take a moment for Windows NT to build the list of available domains.

After you enter the password, Windows NT should consult the primary domain controller (Samba) to see if the password is correct. Again, you can check the log files if you want to see this in action. If it worked, you have successfully configured Samba to act as a domain controller for Windows NT machines.

Domain Options

Table 6-9 shows the options that are commonly used in association with domain logons.

Table 6-9. Windows 95/98 Domain Logon Options

Option	Parameters	Function	Default	Scope
domain logons	boolean	Indicates whether Windows domain logons are to be used.	no	Global
domain group map	string (fully-qualified pathname)	Name of the file used to map Unix to Windows NT domain groups.	None	Global
domain user map	string (fully-qualified pathname)	Name of the file used to map Unix to Windows NT domain users.	None	Global
local group map	string (fully-qualified pathname)	Name of the file used to map Unix to Windows NT local groups.	None	Global
revalidate	boolean	If yes, Samba forces users to authenticate themselves with each connection to a share.	no	Share

domain logons

This option configures Samba to accept domain logons as a primary domain controller. When a client successfully logs on to the domain, Samba will return a special token to the client that allows the client to access domain shares without consulting the PDC again for authentication. Note that the Samba machine must be in user-level security (`security = user`) and must be the PDC in order for this option to function. In addition, Windows machines will expect a [`netlogon`] share to exist on the Samba server (see the section "Configuring Samba for Windows Domain Logons," earlier in this chapter).

domain group map

This option specifies the location of a mapping file designed to translate Windows NT domain group names to Unix group names. The file should reside on the Samba server. For example:

```
/usr/local/samba/private/groups.mapping
```

The file has a simple format:

```
UnixGroup = NTGroup
```

An example is:

```
admin = Administrative
```

The specified Unix group should be a valid group in the */etc/group* file. The NT group should be the name to which you want the Unix group to map on an NT client. This option will work only with Windows NT clients.

domain user map

This option specifies the location of a mapping file designed to translate Unix usernames to Windows NT domain usernames. The file should reside on the Samba server. For example:

```
/usr/local/samba/private/domainuser.mapping
```

The file has a simple format:

```
UnixUsername = [\\Domain\\]NTUserName
```

An example entry is:

```
joe = Joseph Miller
```

The Unix name specified should be a valid username in the */etc/passwd* file. The NT name should be the username to which you want to Unix username to map on an NT client. This option will work with Windows NT clients only.

If you would like more information on how Windows NT uses domain usernames and local groups, we recommend Eric Pearce's *Windows NT in a Nutshell*, published by O'Reilly.

local group map

This option specifies the location of a mapping file designed to translate Windows NT local group names to Unix group names. Local group names include those such as Administrator and Users. The file should reside on the Samba server. For example:

```
/usr/local/samba/private/localgroup.mapping
```

The file has a simple format:

```
UnixGroup = [BUILTIN\]NTGroup
```

An example entry is:

```
root = BUILTIN\Administrators
```

This option will work with Windows NT clients only. For more information, see Eric Pearce's *Windows NT in a Nutshell* (O'Reilly).

revalidate

This share-level option tells Samba to force users to authenticate with passwords each time they connect to a different share on a machine, no matter what level of security is in place on the Samba server. The default value is no, which allows users to be trusted once they successfully authenticate themselves. You can override it as:

```
revalidate = yes
```

You can use this option to increase security on your system. However, you should weigh it against the inconvenience of having users revalidate themselves to every share.

Logon Scripts

Samba supports the execution of Windows logon scripts, which are scripts (.BAT or .CMD) that are executed on the client when a user logs on to a Windows domain. Note that these scripts are stored on the Unix side, but are transported across the network to the client side and executed once a user logs on. These scripts are invaluable for dynamically setting up network configurations for users when they log on. The downside is that because they run on Windows, they must use the Windows network configuration commands.

If you would like more information on NET commands, we recommend the following O'Reilly handbooks: *Windows NT in a Nutshell,* *Windows 95 in a Nutshell,* and *Windows 98 in a Nutshell.*

You can instruct Samba to use a logon script with the **logon script** option, as follows:

```
[global]
    domain logons = yes
    security = user
    workgroup = SIMPLE

    os level = 34
    local master = yes
    preferred master = yes
    domain master = yes
    logon script = %U.bat

[netlogon]
    comment = The domain logon service
    path = /export/samba/logon
    public = no
    writeable = no
    browsable = no
```

Note that this example uses the **%U** variable, which will individualize the script based on the user that is logging in. It is common to customize logon scripts based on the user or machine name that is logging onto the domain. These scripts can then be used to configure individual settings for users or clients.

Each logon script should be stored at the base of the **[netlogon]** share. For example, if the base of the **[netlogon]** share is */export/samba/logon* and the logon script is *jeff.bat*, the file should be located at */export/samba/logon/jeff.bat*. When a user logs on to a domain that contains a startup script, he or she will see a small dialog that informs them that the script is executing, as well as any output the script generates in an MS-DOS-like box.

One warning: because these scripts are loaded by Windows and executed on the Windows side, they must consist of DOS formatted carriage-return/linefeed characters instead of Unix carriage returns. It's best to use a DOS- or Windows-based editor to create them.

Here is an example of a logon script that sets the current time to match that of the Samba server and maps two network drives, **h** and **i**, to individual shares on the server:

```
# Reset the current time to that shown by the server.
# We must have the "time server = yes" option in the
# smb.conf for this to work.

echo Setting Current Time...
net time \\hydra /set /yes

# Here we map network drives to shares on the Samba
# server
```

```
echo Mapping Network Drives to Samba Server Hydra...
net use h: \\hydra\data
net use i: \\hydra\network
```

Roaming profiles

In Windows 95 and NT, each user can have his or her own *profile*. A profile bundles information such as: the appearance of a user's desktop, the applications that appear on the start menus, the background, and other miscellaneous items. If the profile is stored on a local disk, it's called a *local profile*, since it describes what a user's environment is like on one machine. If the profile is stored on a server, on the other hand, the user can download the same profile to any client machine that is connected to the server. The latter is called a *roaming profile* because the user can roam around from machine to machine and still use the same profile. This makes it particularly convenient when someone might be logging in from his or her desk one day and from a portable in the field the next. Figure 6-6 illustrates local and roaming profiles.

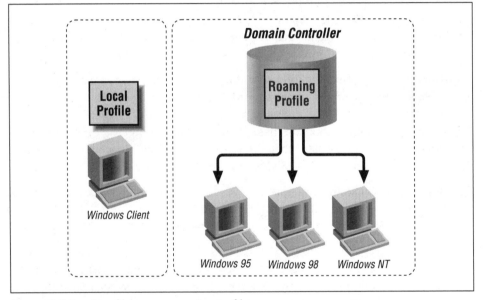

Figure 6-6. Local profiles versus roaming profiles

Samba will provide roaming profiles if it is configured for domain logons and you provide a tree of directories pointed to by the **logon path** option. This option is typically used with one of the user variables, as shown in this example:

```
[global]
    domain logons = yes
    security = user
    workgroup = SIMPLE
```

```
os level = 34
local master = yes
preferred master = yes
domain master = yes

logon path = \\hydra\profile\%U
```

We need to create a new share to support the profiles, which is a basic disk share accessible only by the Samba process' user (**root**). This share must be writeable, but should not be browseable. In addition, we must create a directory for each user who wishes to log on (based on how we specified our **logon path** in the example above), which is accessible only by that user. For an added measure of security, we use the **directory mode** and **create mode** options to keep anyone who connects to it from viewing or altering the files created in those directories:

```
[profile]
  comment = User profiles
  path = /export/samba/profile
  create mode = 0600
  directory mode = 0700
  writable = yes
  browsable = no
```

Once a user initially logs on, the Windows client will create a *user.dat* or *ntuser. dat* file—depending on which operating system the client is running. The client then uploads the contents of the desktop, the Start Menu, the Network Neighborhood, and the programs folders in individual folders in the directory. When the user subsequently logs on, those contents will be downloaded from the server and activated for the client machine with which the user is logging on. When he or she logs off, those contents will be uploaded back on the server until the next time the user connects. If you look at the directory listing of a profile folder, you'll see the following:

```
# ls -al

total 321
drwxrwxr-x  9 root  simple   Jul 21 20:44 .
drwxrwxr-x  4 root  simple   Jul 22 14:32 ..
drwxrwx---  3 fred  develope Jul 12 07:15 Application Data
drwxrwx---  3 fred  develope Jul 12 07:15 Start Menu
drwxrwx---  2 fred  develope Jul 12 07:15 cookies
drwxrwx---  2 fred  develope Jul 12 07:15 desktop
drwxrwx---  7 fred  develope Jul 12 07:15 history
drwxrwx---  2 fred  develope Jul 12 07:15 nethood
drwxrwx---  2 fred  develope Jul 19 21:05 recent
-rw-------  1 fred  develope Jul 21 21:59 user.dat
```

The *user.dat* files are binary configuration files, created automatically by Windows. They can be edited with the Profile Editor on a Windows client, but they can be somewhat tricky to get correct. Samba supports them correctly for all clients up to NT 5.0 beta, but they're still relatively new.

 Hints and HOWTOs for handling logon scripts are available in the Samba documentation tree, in both *docs/textdocs/DOMAIN.txt* and *docs/textdocs/PROFILES.txt*.

Mandatory profiles

Users can also have *mandatory profiles*, which are roaming profiles that they cannot change. For example, with a mandatory profile, if a user adds a command to the Start Menu on Tuesday, it will be gone when he or she logs in again on Wednesday. The mandatory profile is simply a *user.dat* file that has been renamed to *user.man* and made read-only on the Unix server. It normally contains settings that the administrator wishes to ensure the user always executes. For example, if an administrator wants to create a fixed user configuration, he or she can do the following:

1. Create the read-write directory on the Samba server.

2. Set the `logon path` option in the *smb.conf* file to point to this directory.

3. Logon as the user from Windows 95/98 to have the client populate the directory.

4. Rename the resulting *user.dat* to *user.man*.

5. Make the directory and its contents read only.

Mandatory profiles are fairly unusual. Roaming profiles, on the other hand, are one of the more desirable features of Windows that Samba can support.

Logon Script Options

Table 6-10 summarizes the options commonly used in association with Windows domain logon scripts.

Table 6-10. Logon Script Options

Option	Parameters	Function	Default	Scope
`logon script`	string (DOS path)	Name of DOS/NT batch file	None	Global
`logon path`	string (UNC server and share name)	Location of roaming profile for user	`\\%N\%U\ profile`	Global

Table 6-10. Logon Script Options (continued)

Option	Parameters	Function	Default	Scope
logon drive	string (drive letter)	Specifies the logon drive for a home directory (NT only)	Z:	Global
logon home	string (UNC server and share name)	Specifies a location for home directories for clients logging on to the domain	\\%N\%U	Global

logon script

This option specifies a Windows .BAT or .CMD file with lines ending in carriage-return/line feed that will be executed on the client after a user has logged on to the domain. Each logon script should be stored at the base of a share entitled [netlogin] (see the section "Configuring Samba for Windows Domain Logons" for details.) This option frequently uses the %U or %m variables (user or NetBIOS name) to point to an individual script. For example:

```
logon script = %U.bat
```

will execute a script based on the username located at the base of the [netlogin] share. If the user who is connecting is **fred** and the path of the [netlogin] share maps to the directory */export/samba/netlogin*, the script should be */export/samba/netlogin/fred.bat*. Because these scripts are downloaded to the client and executed on the Windows side, they must consist of DOS formatted carriage-return/linefeed characters instead of Unix carriage returns.

logon path

This option provides a location for roaming profiles. When the user logs on, a roaming profile will be downloaded from the server to the client and activated for the user who is logging on. When the user logs off, those contents will be uploaded back on the server until the next time the user connects.

It is often more secure to create a separate share exclusively for storing user profiles:

```
logon path =  \\hydra\profile\%U
```

For more informaiton on this option, see the section "Logon Scripts," earlier in this chapter.

logon drive

This option specifies the drive letter on an NT client to which the home directory specified with the **logon home** option will be mapped. Note that this option will work with Windows NT clients only. For example:

```
logon drive = I:
```

You should always use drive letters that will not conflict with fixed drives on the client machine. The default is Z:, which is a good choice because it is as far away from A:, C:, and D: as possible.

logon home

This option specifies the location of a user's home directory for use by the DOS NET commands. For example, to specify a home directory as a share on a Samba server, use the following:

```
logon home = \\hydra\%U
```

Note that this works nicely with the [homes] service, although you can specify any directory you wish. Home directories can be mapped with a logon script using the following command:

```
NET USE I: /HOME
```

In addition, you can use the User Environment Profile under User Properties in the Windows NT User Manager to verify that the home directory has automatically been set.

Other Connection Scripts

After a user successfully makes a connection to any Samba share, you may want the Samba server to execute a program on its side to prepare the share for use. Samba allows scripts to be executed before and after someone connects to a share. You do not need to be using Windows domains to take advantage of the options. Table 6-11 introduces some of the configuration options provided for setting up users.

Table 6-11. Connection Script Options

Option	Parameters	Function	Default	Scope
root preexec	string (Unix command)	Sets a command to run as root, before connecting to the share.	None	Share
preexec (exec)	string (Unix command)	Sets a Unix command to run as the user before connecting to the share.	None	Share
postexec	string (Unix command)	Sets a Unix command to run as the user after disconnecting from the share.	None	Share
root postexec	string (Unix command)	Sets a Unix command to run as root after disconnecting from the share.	None	Share

root preexec

The first form of the logon command is called **root preexec**. This option specifies a Unix command as its value that will be run *as the root user* before any connection to a share is completed. You should use this option specifically for performing actions that require root privilege. For example, **root preexec** can be used to mount CD-ROMs for a share that makes them available to the clients, or to create necessary directories. If no **root preexec** option is specified, there is no default action. Here is an example of how you can use the command to mount a CD-ROM:

```
[homes]
     browseable = no
     writeable = yes
     root preexec = /etc/mount /dev/cdrom2
```

Remember that these commands will be run as the root user. Therefore, in order to ensure security, users should never be able to modify the target of the **root preexec** command.

preexec

The next option run before logon is the **preexec** option, sometimes just called **exec**. This is an ordinary unprivileged command run by Samba as the user specified by the variable %u. For example, a common use of this option is to perform logging, such as the following:

```
[homes]
     preexec = echo "%u connected to %S from %m (%I)\" >>/tmp/.log
```

Be warned that any information the command sends to standard output will not be seen by the user, but is instead thrown away. If you intend to use a **preexec** script, you should ensure that it will run correctly before having Samba invoke it.

postexec

Once the user disconnects from the share, the command specified with **postexec** is run as the user on the Samba server to do any necessary cleanup. This option is essentially the same as the **preexec** option. Again, remember that the command is run as the user represented by %u and any information sent to standard output will be ignored.

root postexec

Following the **postexec** option, the **root postexec** command is run, if one has been specified. Again, this option specifies a Unix command as its value that will be run *as the root user* before disconnecting from a share. You should use this option specifically for performing actions that require root privilege.

Working with NIS and NFS

Finally, Samba has the ability to work with NIS and NIS+. If there is more than one file server, and each runs Samba, it may be desirable to have the SMB client connect to the server whose disks actually house the user's home directory. It isn't normally a good idea to ship files across the network once via NFS to a Samba server, only to be sent across the network once again to the client via SMB. (For one thing, it's slow—about 30 percent of normal Samba speed). Therefore, there are a pair of options to tell Samba that NIS knows the name of the right server and indicate in which NIS map the information lives.

Table 6-12 introduces some of the other configuration options specifically for setting up users.

Table 6-12. NIS Options

Option	Parameters	Function	Default	Scope
nis homedir	boolean	If **yes**, use NIS instead of */etc/passwd* to look up the path of a user's home directory	no	Global
homedir map	string (NIS map name)	Sets the NIS map to use to look up a user's home directory	None	Global

nis homedir and homedir map

The **nis homedir** and **homedir map** options are for Samba servers on network sites where Unix home directories are provided using NFS, the automounter, and NIS (Yellow Pages).

The **nis homedir** option indicates that the home directory server for the user needs to be looked up in NIS. The **homedir map** option tells Samba what NIS map to look in for the server that has the user's home directory. The server needs to be a Samba server, so the client can do an SMB connect to it, and the other Samba servers need to have NIS installed so they can do the lookup.

For example, if user **joe** asks for a share called **[joe]**, and the **nis homedir** option is set to **yes**, Samba will look in the file specified by **homedir map** for a home directory for **joe**. If it finds one, Samba will return the associated machine name to the client. The client will then try to connect to *that* machine and get the share from there. Enabling NIS lookups looks like the following:

```
[globals]
    nis homedir = yes
    homedir map = amd.map
```

7

Printing and Name Resolution

This chapter tackles two Samba topics: setting up printers for use with a Samba server and configuring Samba to use or become a Windows Internet Name Service (WINS) server. Samba allows client machines to send documents to printers connected to the Samba server. In addition, Samba can also assist you with printing Unix documents to a printer on a Windows machine. In the first part of this chapter, we will discuss how to get printers configured to work on either side.

In the second half of the chapter, we will introduce the Windows Internet Name Service, Microsoft's implementation of a NetBIOS Name Server (NBNS). As mentioned in Chapter 1, *Learning the Samba*, an NBNS allows machines to perform name resolution on a NetBIOS network without having to rely on broadcasts. Instead, each machine knows exactly where the WINS server is and can query it for the IP addresses of other machines on the network.

Sending Print Jobs to Samba

A printer attached to the Samba server shows up in the list of shares offered in the Network Neighborhood. If the printer is registered on the client machine and the client has the correct printer driver installed, the client can effortlessly send print jobs to a printer attached to a Samba server. Figure 7-1 shows a Samba printer as it appears in the Network Neighborhood of a Windows client.

To administer printers with Samba, you should understand the basic process by which printing takes place on a network. Sending a print job to a printer on a Samba server involves four steps:

1. Opening and authenticating a connection to the printer share
2. Copying the file over the network

3. Closing the connection

4. Printing and deleting the copy of the file

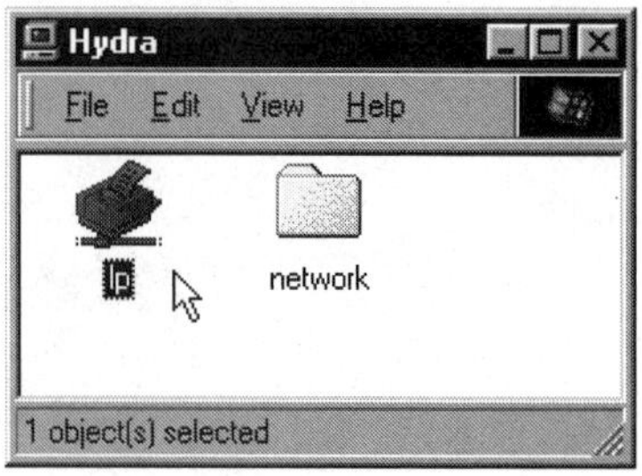

Figure 7-1. A Samba printer in the Network Neighborhood

When a print job arrives at a Samba server, the print data is temporarily written to disk in the directory specified by the **path** option of the printer share. Samba then executes a Unix print command to send that data file to the printer. The job is printed as the authenticated user of the share. Note that this may be the guest user, depending on how the share is configured.

Print Commands

In order to print the document, you'll need to tell Samba what the command is to print and delete a file. On Linux, such a command is:

```
lpr -r -Pprinter file
```

This tells **lpr** to copy the document to a spool area, usually */var/spool*, retrieve the name of the printer in the system configuration file (*/etc/printcap*), and interpret the rules it finds there to decide how to process the data and which physical device to send it to. Note that because the **-r** option has been listed, the file specified on the command line will be deleted after it has been printed. Of course, the file removed is just a copy stored on the Samba server; the original file on the client is unaffected.

Linux uses a Berkeley (BSD) style of printing. However, the process is similar on System V Unix. Here, printing and deleting becomes a compound command:

```
lp -dprinter -s file; rm file
```

With System V, the */etc/printcap* file is replaced with different set of configuration files hiding in */usr/spool/lp*, and there is no option to delete the file. You have to do it yourself, which is why we have added the **rm** command afterward.

Printing Variables

Samba provides four variables specifically for use with printing configuration options. They are shown in Table 7-1.

Table 7-1. Printing Variables

Variable	Definition
%s	The full pathname of the file on the Samba server to be printed
%f	The name of the file itself (without the preceding path) on the Samba server to be printed
%p	The name of the Unix printer to use
%j	The number of the print job (for use with lprm, lppause, and lpresume)

A Minimal Printing Setup

Let's start with a simple but illustrative printing share. Assuming that you're on a Linux system and you have a printer called lp listed in the printer capabilities file, the following addition to your *smb.conf* file will make the printer accessible through the network:

```
[printer1]
    printable = yes
    print command = /usr/bin/lpr -r  %s
    printer = lp
    printing = BSD
    read only = yes
    guest ok = yes
```

This configuration allows anyone to send data to the printer, something we may want to change later. For the moment, what's important to understand is that the variable %s in the **print command** option will be replaced with the name of the file to be printed when Samba executes the command. Changing the **print command** to reflect a different style of Unix machine typically involves only replacing the right side of the **print command** option with whatever command you need for your system and changing the target of the **printing** option.

Let's look at the commands for a System V Unix. With variable substitution, the System V Unix command becomes:

```
print command = lp -d%p -s %s; rm %s
```

As mentioned earlier, the %p variable resolves to the name of the printer, while the %s variable resolves to the name of the file. After that, you can change the **printing** option to reflect that you're using a System V architecture:

```
printing = SYSV
```

If you are using share-level security, pay special attention to the guest account used by Samba. The typical setting, **nobody**, may not be allowed to print by the operating system. If that's true for your operating system, you should place a **guest account** option under the printing share (or even perhaps the global share) specifying an account that can. A popular candidate with the Samba authors is the **ftp** account, which is often preconfigured to be safe for untrusted guest users. You can set it with the following command:

```
guest account = ftp
```

Another common printing issue is that clients may need to request the status of a print job sent to the Samba server. Samba will not reject a document from being sent to an already busy printer share. Consequently, Samba needs the ability to communicate not only the status of the current printing job to the client, but also which documents are currently waiting to be printed on that printer. Samba also has to provide the client the ability to pause print jobs, resume print jobs, and remove print jobs from the printing queue. Samba provides options for each of these tasks. As you might expect, they borrow functionality from existing Unix commands. The options are:

- **lpq command**
- **lprm command**
- **lppause command**
- **lpresume command**

We will cover these options in more detail below. For the most part, however, the value of the **printing** configuration option will determine their values, and you should not need to alter the default values of these options.

Here are a few important items to remember about printing shares:

- You must put **printable = yes** in all printer shares (even **[printers]**), so that Samba will know that they are printer shares. If you forget, the shares will not be usable for printing and will instead be treated as disk shares.
- If you set the **path** configuration option in the printer section, any files sent to the printer(s) will be copied to the directory you specify instead of to the default location of */tmp*. As the amount of disk space allocated to */tmp* can be relatively small in some Unix operating systems, many administrators opt to use */var/spool* or some other directory instead.
- The **read only** option is ignored for printer shares.
- If you set **guest ok = yes** in a printer share and Samba is configured for share-level security, it will allow anyone to send data to the printer as the **guest account** user.

Using one or more Samba machines as a print server gives you a great deal of flexibility on your LAN. You can easily partition your available printers, restricting some to members of one department, or you can maintain a bank of printers available to all. In addition, you can restrict a printer to a selected few by adding the trusty `valid users` option to its share definition:

```
[deskjet]
    printable = yes
    path = /var/spool/samba/print
    valid users = gail sam
```

All of the other share accessibility options defined in the previous chapter should work for printing shares as well. Since the printers themselves are accessed through Samba by name, it's also simple to delegate print services among several servers using familiar Unix commands for tasks such as load balancing or maintenance.

The [printers] Share

Chapter 4, *Disk Shares*, briefly introduced `[printers]`, a special share for automatically creating printing services. Let's review how it works: if you create a share named `[printers]` in the configuration file, Samba will automatically read in your printer capabilities file and create a printing share for each printer that appears in the file. For example, if the Samba server had `lp`, `pcl` and `ps` printers in its printer capabilities file, Samba would provide three printer shares with those names, each configured with the options in the `[printers]` share.

Recall that Samba obeys following rules when a client requests a share that has not been created through the *smb.conf* file:

- If the share name matches a username in the system password file and a `[homes]` share exists, a new share is created with the name of the user and is initialized using the values given in the `[homes]` and `[global]` sections.

- Otherwise, if the name matches a printer in the system printer capabilities file, and a `[printers]` share exists, a new share is created with the name of the printer and initialized using the values given in the `[printers]` section. (Variables in the `[global]` section do not apply here.)

- If neither of those succeed, Samba looks for a `default service` share. If none is found, it returns an error.

This brings to light an important point: be careful that you do not give a printer the same name as a user. Otherwise, you will end up connecting to a disk share when you may have wanted a printer share instead.

Here is an example [printers] share for a Linux (BSD) system. Some of these options are already defaults; however, we have listed them anyway for illustrative purposes:

```
[global]
    printing = BSD
    print command = /usr/bin/lpr -P%p -r %s
    printcap file = /etc/printcap
    min print space = 2000

[printers]
    path = /usr/spool/public
    printable = true
    guest ok = true
    guest account = pcguest
```

Here, we've given Samba global options that specify the printing type (BSD), a print command to send data to the printer and remove a temporary file, our default printer capabilities file, and a minimum printing space of 2 megabytes.

In addition, we've created a [printers] share for each of the system printers. Our temporary spooling directory is specified by the **path** option: */usr/spool/ public*. Each of the shares is marked as printable—this is necessary, even in the [printers] section. The two **guest** options are useful in the event that Samba is using share-level security: we allow guest access to the printer and we specify the guest user that Samba should use to execute print commands.

Test Printing

Here is how you can test printing from the Samba server. Let's assume the most complex case and use a guest account. First, run the Samba *testparm* command on your configuration file that contains the print shares, as we did in Chapter 2, *Installing Samba on a Unix System*. This will tell you if there are any syntactical problems with the configuration file. For example, here is what you would see if you left out the **path** configuration option in the previous example:

```
# testparm
Load smb config files from /usr/local/samba/lib/smb.conf
Processing configuration file "/usr/local/samba/lib/smb.conf"
Processing section "[global]"
Processing section "[homes]"
Processing section "[data]"
Processing section "[printers]"
No path in service printers - using /tmp
Loaded services file OK.
Press enter to see a dump of your service definitions
Global parameters:
    load printers: Yes
    printcap name: /etc/printcap
Default service parameters:
```

```
      guest account: ftp
      min print space: 0
      print command: lpr -r -P%p %s
      lpq command: lpq -P%p
      lprm command: lprm -P%p %j
lppause command:
      lpresume command:
  Service parameters [printers]:
      path: /tmp
      print ok: Yes
      read only: true
      public: true
```

Second, try the command **testprns** *printername*. This is a simple program that verifies that the specified printer is available in your *printcap* file. If your *printcap* file is not in the usual place, you can specify its full pathname as the second argument to the *testprns* command:

```
# testprns lp /etc/printcap
Looking for printer lp in printcap file /etc/printcap
Printer name lp is valid.
```

Next, log on as the guest user, go to the spooling directory, and ensure that you can print using the same command that *testparm* says Samba will use. As mentioned before, this will tell you if you need to change the guest account, as the default account may not be allowed to print.

Finally, print something to the Samba server via **smbclient**, and see if the following actions occur:

- The job appears (briefly) in the Samba spool directory specified by the path.
- The job shows up in your print systems spool directory.
- The job disappears from the spool directory that Samba used.

If *smbclient* cannot print, you can reset the **print command** option to collect debugging information:

```
print command = /bin/cat %s >>/tmp/printlog; rm %s
```

or:

```
print command = echo "printed %s on %p" >>/tmp/printlog
```

A common problem with Samba printer configuration is forgetting to use the full pathnames for commands; simple commands often don't work because the guest account's PATH doesn't include them. Another frequent problem is not having the correct permissions on the spooling directory.

There is more information on debugging printers in the Samba documentation (*Printing.txt*). In addition, the Unix print systems are covered in detail in AEleen Frisch's *Essential Systems Administration* (published by O'Reilly).

Setting Up and Testing a Windows Client

Now that Samba is offering a workable printer, you need to set it up on a Windows client. Look at the Samba server in the Network Neighborhood. It should now show each of the printers that are available. For example, in Figure 7-1, we saw a printer called lp.

Next, you need to have the Windows client recognize the printer. Double-click on the printer icon to get started. If you try to select an uninstalled printer (as you just did), Windows will ask you if it should help configure it for the Windows system. Respond "Yes," which will open the Printer Wizard.

The first thing the wizard will ask is whether you need to print from DOS. Let's assume you don't, so choose No and press the Next button to get to the manufacturer/model window as shown in Figure 7-2.

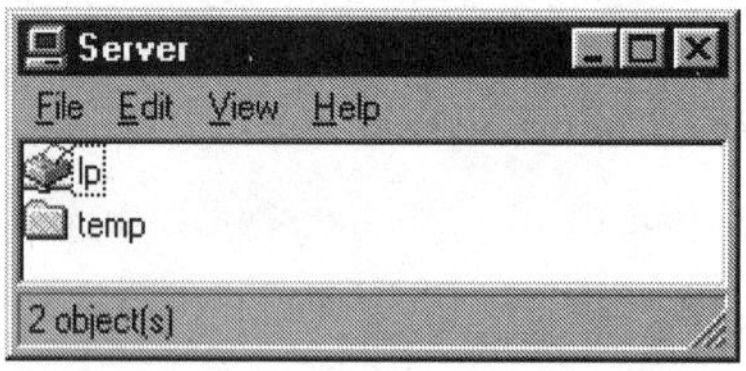

![Server window showing lp printer and temp folder, 2 object(s)]

Figure 7-2. A printer in the Network Neighborhood

In this dialog box, you should see a large list of manufacturers and models for almost every printer imaginable. If you don't see your printer on the list, but you know it's a PostScript printer, select Apple as the manufacturer and Apple Laser-Writer as the model. This will give you the most basic Postscript printer setup, and arguably one of the most reliable. If you already have any Postscript printers attached, you will be asked about replacing or reusing the existing driver. Be aware that if you replace it with a new one, you may make your other printers fail. Therefore, we recommend you keep using your existing printer drivers as long as they're working properly.

Following that, the Printer Wizard will ask you to name the printer. Figure 7-3 shows this example, where the name has defaulted to our second laserwriter.

Here, you rename it from Apple Laserwriter (Copy 2) to "ps on Samba server," so you know where to look for the printouts. In reality, you can name the printer anything you want.

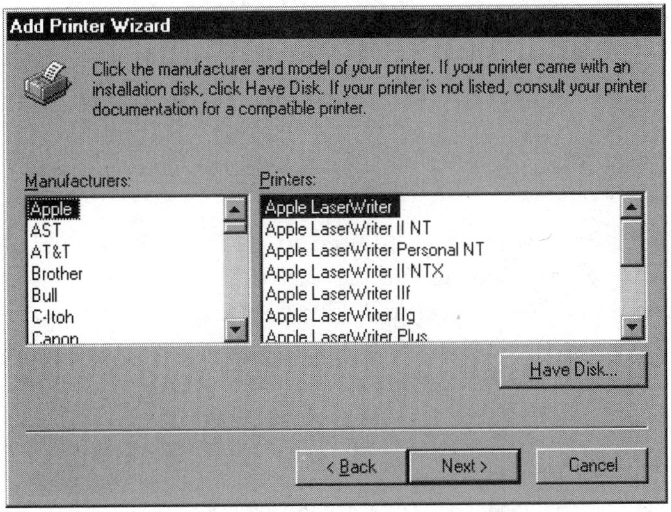

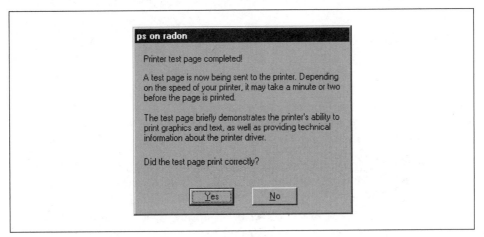

Figure 7-3. Printer manufacturers and models

Finally, the Printing Wizard asks if it should print a test page. Click on Yes, and you should be presented with the dialog in Figure 7-4.

Figure 7-4. Printing successfully completed

If the test printing was unsuccessful, press the No button in Figure 7-4 and the Printing Wizard will walk you through some debugging steps for the client side of the process. If the test printing does work, congratulations! The remote printer will now be available to all your PC applications through the File and Print menu items.

Automatically Setting Up Printer Drivers

The previous section described how to manually configure a printer driver for your Windows system. As a system administrator, however, you can't always guarantee that users can perform such a process without making mistakes. Luckily, however, you can ask Samba to automatically set up the printer drivers for a specific printer.

Samba has three options that can be used to automatically set up printer drivers for clients who are connecting for the first time. These options are `printer driver`, `printer driver file`, and `printer driver location`. This section explains how to use these options to allow users to skip over the Manufacturer dialog in the Add Printer Wizard above.

For more information on how to do this, see the *PRINTER_DRIVER. TXT* file in the Samba distribution documentation.

There are four major steps:

1. Install the drivers for the printer on a Windows client (the printer need not be attached).

2. Create a printer definition file from the information on a Windows machine.

3. Create a `PRINTER$` share where the resulting driver files can be placed.

4. Modify the Samba configuration file accordingly.

Let's go over each of the four steps in greater detail.

Install the drivers on a windows client

Use Windows 95/98 for this step. It doesn't matter which client you choose, as long as it has the ability to load the appropriate drivers for the printer. In fact, you don't even need to have the printer attached to the machine. All you're interested in here is getting the appropriate driver files into the Windows directory. First, go to the Printers window of My Computer and double-click on the Add Printer icon, as shown in Figure 7-5.

At this point, you can follow the Add Printer Wizard dialogs through to select the manufacturer and model of the printer in question. If it asks you if you want to

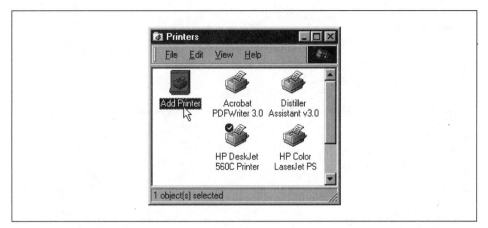

Figure 7-5. The Printers window

print from MS-DOS, answer No. Windows should load the appropriate driver resources from its CD-ROM and ask you if you want to print a test page. Again, respond No and close the Add Printer Wizard dialog.

Create a printer definition file

You can create a printer definition file by using the *make_printerdef* script in the */usr/local/samba/bin* directory. In order to use this script, you need to copy over the following four files from a Windows client:*

> *C:\WINDOWS\INF\MSPRINT.INF*
> *C:\WINDOWS\INF\MSPRINT2.INF*
> *C:\WINDOWS\INF\MSPRINT3.INF*
> *C:\WINDOWS\INF\MSPRINT4.INF*

Once you have the four files, you can create a printer definition file using the appropriate printer driver and its .INF file. If the printer driver starts with the letters A–K, use either the *MSPRINT.INF* file or the *MSPRINT3.INF* file. If it begins with the letters L–Z, use the *MSPRINT2.INF* file or the *MSPRINT4.INF* file. You may need to *grep* through each of the files to see where your specific driver is. For the following example, we have located our driver in *MSPRINT3.INF* and created a printer definition file for a HP DeskJet 560C printer:

```
$grep "HP DeskJet 560C Printer" MSPRINT.INF MSPRINT3.INF
MSPRINT3.INF: "HP DeskJet 560C Printer"=DESKJETC.DRV,HP_DeskJet_ ...

$make_printerdef MSPRINT3.INF "HP DeskJet 560C Printer" >printers.def
FOUND:DESKJETC.DRV
```

---

* Older Windows 95 clients may have only the first two files.

```
End of section found
CopyFiles: DESKJETC,COLOR_DESKJETC
Datasection: (null)
Datafile: DESKJETC.DRV
Driverfile: DESKJETC.DRV
Helpfile: HPVDJC.HLP
LanguageMonitor: (null)

Copy the following files to your printer$ share location:
DESKJETC.DRV
HPVCM.HPM
HPVIOL.DLL
HPVMON.DLL
HPVRES.DLL
HPCOLOR.DLL
HPVUI.DLL
HPVDJCC.HLP
color\HPDESK.ICM
```

Note the files that the script asks you to copy. You'll need those for the next step.

Create a PRINTER$ share

This part is relatively easy. Create a share called [PRINTER$] in your *smb.conf* that points to an empty directory on the Samba server. Once that is done, copy over the files that the *make_printerdef* script requested of you into the location of the path configuration option for the [PRINTER$] share. For example, you can put the following in your configuration file:

```
[PRINTER$]
    path = /usr/local/samba/print
    read only = yes
    browsable = no
    guest ok = yes
```

The files requested by the *make_printerdef* script are typically located in the *C:\ WINDOWS\SYSTEM* directory, although you can use the following commands to find out exactly where they are:

```
cd C:\WINDOWS
dir filename /s
```

In this case, each of the files needs to be copied to the */usr/local/samba/print* directory on the Samba server. In addition, copy the *printers.def* file that you created over to that share as well. Once you've done that, you're almost ready to go.

Modify the Samba configuration file

The last step is to modify the Samba configuration file by adding the following three options:

- `printer driver`

- printer driver file
- printer driver location

The `printer driver file` is a global option that points to the *printers.def* file; place that option in your `[global]` section. The other options should be set in the printer share for which you wish to automatically configure the drivers. The value for `printer driver` should match the string that shows up in the Printer Wizard on the Windows system. The value of the `printer driver location` is the pathname of the PRINTER$ share you set up, not the Unix pathname on the server. Thus, you could use the following:

```
[global]
    printer driver file = /usr/local/samba/print/printers.def
[hpdeskjet]
    path = /var/spool/samba/printers
    printable = yes

    printer driver = HP DeskJet 560C Printer
    printer driver location = \\%L\PRINTER$
```

Now you're ready to test it out. At this point, remove the Windows printer that you "set up" in the first step from the list of printers in the Printers window of My Computer. If Samba asks you to delete unneeded files, do so. These files will be replaced shortly on the client, as they now exist on the Samba server.

Testing the configuration

Restart the Samba daemons and look for the `[hpdeskjet]` share under the machine name in the Network Neighborhood. At this point, if you click on the printer icon, you should begin the printer setup process and come to the dialog shown in Figure 7-6.

This is different from the dialog you saw earlier when setting up a printer. Essentially, the dialog is asking if you wish to accept the driver that is "already installed"—in other words, offered by Samba. Go ahead and keep the existing driver, and press the Next button. At this point, you can give the printer a name and print out a test page. If it works, the setup should be complete. You should be able to repeat the process now from any Windows client.

Printing to Windows Client Printers

If you have printers connected to clients running Windows 95/98 or NT 4.0, those printers can also be accessed from Samba. Samba comes equipped with a tool called *smbprint* that can be used to spool print jobs to Windows-based printers. In order to use this, however, you need to set up the printer as a shared resource on

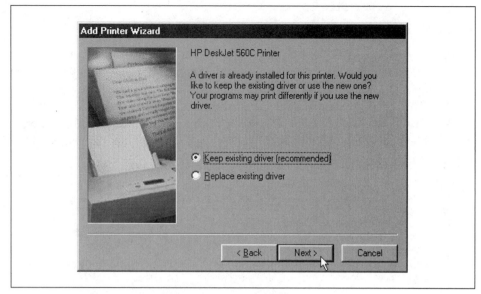

Figure 7-6. Automatically configuring the printer driver

the client machine. If you haven't already done this, you can reset this from the
Printers window, reached from the Start button, as shown in Figure 7-7.

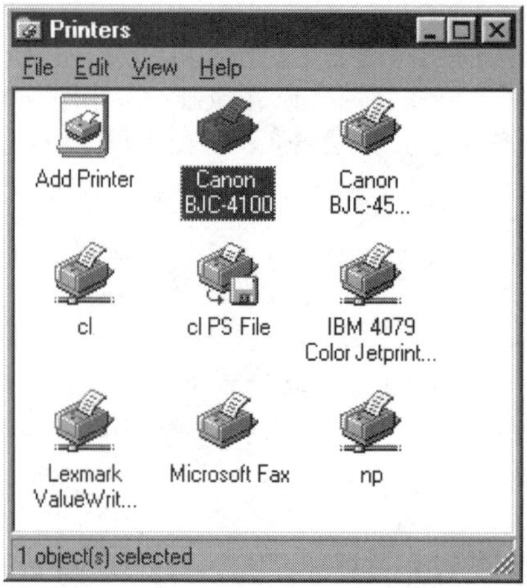

Figure 7-7. The Printers window

Select a printer that's locally connected (for example, ours is the Canon printer),
press the right mouse button to bring up a menu, and select Sharing. This will give

you the Sharing tab of the Printer Properties frame, as shown in Figure 7-8. If you want it available to everybody on your LAN as the Windows guest user, enter a blank password.

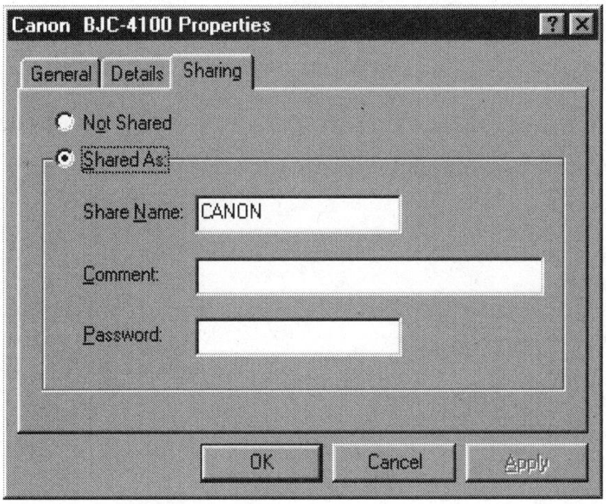

Figure 7-8. The Sharing tab of the printer

Once you've got this working, you can add your printer to the list of standard printers and Samba can make it available to all the other PCs in the workgroup. To make installation on Unix easier, the Samba distribution provides two sample scripts: *smbprint* and *smbprint.sysv*. The first works with BSD-style printers; the second is designed for System V printers.

BSD printers

There are two steps you need to have a BSD Unix recognize a remote printer:

1. Place an entry for the printer in the */etc/printcap* file (or equivalent).

2. Place a configuration file in the */var/spool* directory for the printer.

First, edit your */etc/printcap* file and add an entry for the remote printer. Note that the input filter (if) entry needs to point to the *smbprint* program if the machine is on Windows 95/98. The following set of lines will accomplish on a Linux machine, for example:

```
laserjet:\
   :sd=/var/spool/lpd/laser:\          # spool directory
   :mx#0:\                             # maximum file size (none)
   :sh:\                              # surpress burst header (no)
   :if=/usr/local/samba/bin/smbprint: # text filter
```

After that, you need to create a configuration file in the spool directory that you specified with the **sd** parameter above. (You may need to create that directory.) The file must have the name *.config* and should contain the following information:

- The NetBIOS name of the Windows machine with the printer
- The service name that represents the printer
- The password used to access that service

The last two parameters were set up in the Sharing dialog for the requested resource on the Windows machine. In this case, the *.config* file would have three lines:

```
server = phoenix
service = CANON
password = ""
```

After you've done that, reset the Samba server machine and try printing to it using any standard Unix program.

System V printers

Sending print jobs from a System V Unix system is a little easier. Here, you need to get obtain the *smbprint.sysv* script in the */usr/local/samba/examples/printing* directory and do the following:

1. Change the **server, service,** and **password** parameters in the script to match the NetBIOS machine, its shared printer service, and its password, respectively. For example, the following entries would be correct for the service in the previous example:

   ```
   server = phoenix
   service = CANON
   password = ""
   ```

2. Run the following commands, which create a reference for the printer in the printer capabilities file. Note that the new Unix printer entry **canon_printer** is named:

   ```
   # lpadmin -p canon_printer -v /dev/null -i ./smbprint.sysv
   # enable canon_printer
   # accept canon_printer
   ```

After you've done that, restart the Samba daemons and try printing to it using any standard Unix program. You should now be able to send data to a printer on a Windows client across the network.

Samba Printing Options

Table 7-2 summarizes the Samba printing options.

Table 7-2. Printing Configuration Options

Option	Parameters	Function	Default	Scope
printing	bsd, sysv, hpux, aix, qnx, plp, softq, or lprng	Sets the print system type for your Unix system.	System dependent	Share
printable (print ok)	boolean	Marks a share as a printing share.	no	Share
printer (printer name)	string (Unix printer name)	Sets the name of the printer to be shown to clients.	System dependent	Share
printer driver	string (printer driver name)	Sets the driver name that should be used by the client to send data to the printer.	None	Share
printer driver file	string (fully-qualified pathname)	Sets the name of the printer driver file.	None	Global
printer driver location	string (network pathname)	Specifies the pathname of the share for the printer driver file.	None	Share
lpq cache time	numeric (time in seconds)	Sets the amount of time in seconds that Samba will cache the lpq status.	10	Global
postscript	boolean	Treats all print jobs sent as postscript by prepending %! at the beginning of each file.	no	Share
load printers	boolean	Automatically loads each of the printers in the *printcap* file as printing shares.	no	Global
print command	string (shell command)	Sets the Unix command to perform printing.	See below	Share
lpq command	string (shell command)	Sets the Unix command to return the status of the printing queue.	See below	Share
lprm command	string (shell command)	Sets the Unix command to remove a job from the printing queue.	See below	Share
lppause command	string (shell command)	Sets the Unix command to pause a job on the printing queue.	See below	Share

Table 7-2. Printing Configuration Options (continued)

Option	Parameters	Function	Default	Scope
lpresume command	string (shell command)	Sets the Unix command to resume a paused job on the printing queue.	See below	Share
printcap name (printcap)	string (fully-qualified pathname)	Specifies the location of the printer capabilities file.	System dependent	Global
min print space	numeric (size in kilobytes)	Sets the minimum amount of disk free space that must be present to print.	0	Share
queuepause command	string (shell command)	Sets the Unix command to pause a queue.	See below	Share
queueresume command	string (shell command)	Sets the Unix command to resume a queue.	See below	Share

printing

The **printing** configuration option tells Samba a little about your Unix printing system, in this case which printing parser to use. With Unix, there are several different families of commands to control printing and print statusing. Samba supports seven different types, as shown in Table 7-3.

Table 7-3. Printing Types

Variable	Definition
BSD	Berkeley Unix system
SYSV	System V
AIX	AIX Operating System (IBM)
HPUX	Hewlett-Packard Unix
QNX	QNX Realtime Operating System (QNX)
LPRNG	LPR Next Generation (Powell)
SOFTQ	SOFTQ system
PLP	Portable Line Printer (Powell)

The value for this optio.n will be one of these seven options. For example:

```
printing = SYSV
```

The default value of this option is system dependent and is configured when Samba is first compiled. For most systems, the *configure* script will automatically detect the printing system to be used and configure it properly in the Samba makefile. However, if your system is a PLP, LPRNG, or QNX printing system, you will need to explicitly specify this in the makefile or the printing share.

The most common system types are BSD and SYSV. Each of the printers on a BSD Unix server are described in the printer capabilities file—normally */etc/printcap*.

Setting the `printing` configuration option automatically sets at least three other printing options for the service in question: `print command`, `lpq command`, and `lprm command`. If you are running Samba on a system that doesn't support any of these printing styles, simply set the commands for each of these manually.

printable

The printable option must be set to **yes** in order to flag a share as a printing service. If this option is not set, the share will be treated as a disk share instead. You can set the option as follows:

```
[printer1]
    printable = yes
```

printer

The option, sometimes called **printer name**, specifies the name of the printer on the server to which the share points. This option has no default and should be set explicitly in the configuration file, even though Unix systems themselves often recognize a default name such as `lp` for a printer. For example:

```
[deskjet]
    printer = hpdkjet1
```

printer driver

The `printer driver` option sets the string that Samba uses to tell Windows what the printer is. If this option is set correctly, the Windows Printer Wizard will already know what the printer is, making installation easier for end users by giving them one less dialog to worry about. The string given should match the string that shows up in the Printer Wizard, as shown in Figure 7-9. For example, an Apple LaserWriter typically uses **Apple LaserWriter**; a Hewlett Packard Deskjet 560C uses **HP DeskJet 560C Printer**.

Automatically configuring printer drivers with Samba is explained in greater detail in the section "Automatically Setting Up Printer Drivers," earlier in this chapter.

printer driver file

This global option gives the location of the Windows 95/98 printer driver definition file, which is needed to give printer drivers to clients using a Samba printer. The default value of this option is */usr/local/samba/lib/printers.def*. You can override this default as shown below:

```
[deskjet]
    printer driver file = /var/printers/printers.def
```

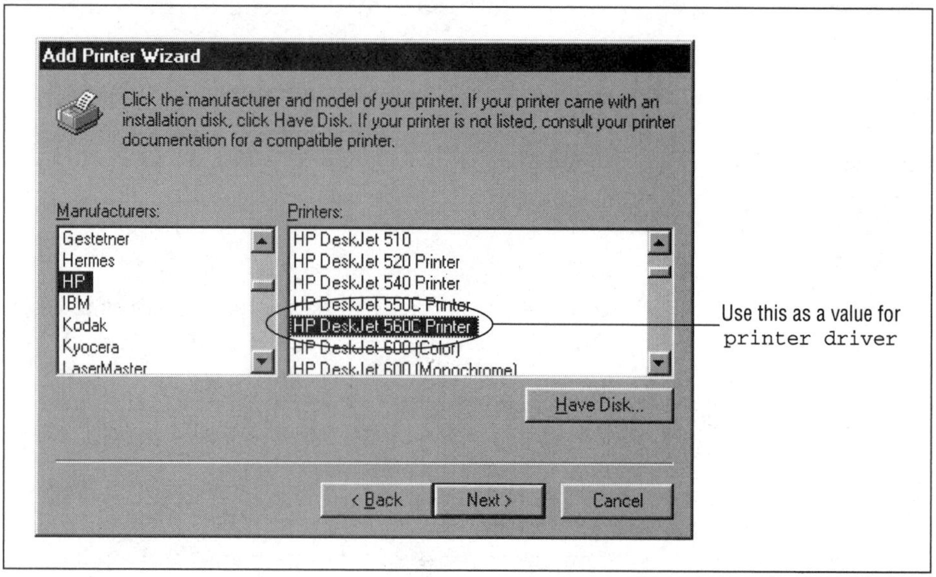

Figure 7-9. The Add Printer Wizard dialog box in Windows 98

This option is explained in greater detail in the section "Automatically Setting Up Printer Drivers," earlier in this chapter.

printer driver location

This option specifies a specific share that contains Windows 95 and 98 printer driver and definition files. There is no default parameter for this value. You can specify the location as a network pathname. A frequent approach is to use a share on your own machine, as shown here:

```
[deskjet]
    printer driver location = \\%L\PRINTER$
```

This option is also explained in greater detail in the section "Automatically Setting Up Printer Drivers," earlier in this chapter.

lpq cache time

The global `lpq cache time` option allows you to set the number of seconds that Samba will remember the current printer status. After this time elapses, Samba will issue an *lpq* command (or whatever command you specify with the `lpq command` option) to get a more up-to-date status. This defaults to 10 seconds, but can be increased if your `lpq command` takes an unusually long time to run or you have lots of clients. The following example resets the time to 30 seconds:

```
[deskjet]
    lpq cache time = 30
```

postscript

The **postscript** option forces the printer to treat all data sent to it as Postscript. It does this by prepending the characters **%!** at the beginning of the first line of each job. It is normally used with PCs that insert a ^D (control-D or "end-of-file mark) in front of the first line of a PostScript file. It will not, obviously, turn a non-PostScript printer into a PostScript one. The default value of this options is **no**. You can override it as follows:

```
[deskjet]
    postscript = yes
```

print command, lpq command, lprm command, lppause command, lpresume command

These options tell Samba which Unix commands used to control and send data to the printer. The Unix commands involved are: *lpr* (send to Line PRinter), *lpq* (List Printer Queue), *lprm* (Line printer ReMove), and optionally *lppause* and *lpresume*. Samba provides an option named after each of these commands, in case you need to override any of the system defaults. For example, consider:

```
lpq command = /usr/ucb/lpq %p
```

This would set the **lpq command** to use */usr/ucb/lpq*. Similarly:

```
lprm command = /usr/local/lprm -P%p %j
```

would set the Samba printer remove command to */usr/local/lprm*, and provide it the print job number using the **%j** variable.

The default values for each of these options are dependent on the value of the **printing** option. Table 7-4 shows the default commands for each of the printing options. The most popular printing system is BSD.

Table 7-4. Default Commands for Various Printing Commands

Option	BSD, AIX, PLP, LPRNG	SYSV, HPUX	QNX	SOFTQ
print command	lpr -r -P%p %s	lp -c -d%p %s; rm %s	lp -r -P%p %s	lp -d%p -s %s; rm %s
lpq command	lpq -P%p	lpstat -o%p	lpq -P%p	lpstat -o%p
lprm command	lprm -P%p %j	cancel %p-%j	cancel %p-%j	cancel %p-%j
lppause command	lp -i %p-%j -H hold (SYSV only)	None	None	None
lpresume command	lp -i %p-%j -H resume (SYSV only)	None	None	qstat -s -j%j -r

It is typically not necessary to reset these options in Samba, with the possible exception of **print command**. This option may need to be explicitly set if your printing system doesn't have a **-r** (remove after printing) option on the printing command. For example:

```
/usr/local/lpr -P%p %s; /bin/rm %s
```

With a bit of judicious programming, these *smb.conf* options can also used for debugging:

```
print command = cat %s >>/tmp/printlog; lpr -r -P%p %s
```

For example, this configuration can verify that files are actually being delivered to the Samba server. If they are, their contents will show up in the */tmp/printlog* file.

After BSD, the next most popular kind of printing system is SYSV (or System V) printing, plus some SYSV variants for IBM's AIX and Hewlett-Packard's HP-UX. These system do not have an */etc/printcap* file. Instead, the **printcap file** option can be set to an appropriate *lpstat* command for the system. This tells Samba to get a list of printers from the *lpstat* command. Alternatively, you can set the global configuration option **printcap name** to the name of a dummy *printcap* file you provide. In the latter case, the file must contain a series of lines such as:

```
lp|print1|My Printer 1
print2|My Printer 2
print3|My Printer 3
```

Each line names a printer, and provides aliases for it. In this example, the first printer is called **lp**, **print1**, or **My Printer 1**, whichever the user prefers to use. The first name will be used in place of **%p** in any command Samba executes for that printer.

Two additional printer types are also supported by Samba: LPRNG (LPR New Generation) and PLP (Public Line Printer). These are public domain and Open Source printing systems, and are used by many sites to overcome problems with vendor-supplied software. In addition, the SOFTQ and QNX realtime operating systems are supported by Samba.

load printers

The **load printers** option tells Samba to create shares for all known printer names and load those shares into the browse list. Samba will create and list a printer share for each printer name in */etc/printcap* (or system equivalent). For example, if your *printcap* file looks like this:*

```
lp:\
  :sd=/var/spool/lpd/lp:\          # spool directory
  :mx#0:\                          # maximum file size (none)
```

---

* We have placed annotated comments off to the side in case you've never dealt with this file before.

```
        :sh:\                              # surpress burst header (no)
        :lp=/dev/lp1:\                     # device name for output
        :if=/var/spool/lpd/lp/filter:      # text filter

    laser:\
        :sd=/var/spool/lpd/laser:\         # spool directory
        :mx#0:\                             # maximum file size (none)
        :sh:\                              # surpress burst header (no)
        :lp=/dev/laser:\                   # device name for output
        :if=/var/spool/lpd/lp/filter:      # text filter
```

and you specify:

```
    load printers = yes
```

the shares [lp] and [laser] will automatically be created as valid print shares when Samba is started. Both shares will borrow the configuration options specified in the [printers] section to configure themselves, and will be available in the browse list for the Samba server.

printcap name

If the printcap name option (also called printcap) appears in a printing share, Samba will use the file specified as the system printer capabilities file. This is normally */etc/printcap*. However, you can reset it to a file consisting of only the printers you want to share over the network. The value must be a fully-qualified filename of a printer capabilities file on the server:

```
    [deskjet]
        printcap name = /usr/local/printcap
```

min print space

The min print space option sets the amount of spool space that must be available on the disk before printing is allowed. Setting it to zero (the default) turns the check off; setting it to any other number sets the amount of free space in kilobytes required. This option helps avoid having print jobs fill up the remaining disk space on the server, which may cause other processes to fail:

```
    [deskjet]
        min print space = 4000
```

queuepause command

This configuration option specifies a command that tells Samba how to pause a print queue entirely, as opposed to a single job on the queue. The default value depends on the printing type chosen. You should not need to alter this option.

queueresume command

This configuration option specifies a command that tells Samba how to resume a paused print queue, as opposed to resuming a single job on the print queue. The default value depends on the printing type chosen. You should not need to alter this option.

Name Resolution with Samba

Before NetBIOS Name Servers (NBNS) came about, name resolution worked entirely by broadcast. If you needed a machine's address, you simply broadcast its name across the network and, in theory, the machine itself would reply. This approach is still possible: anyone looking for a machine named `fred` can still broadcast a query and find out if it exists and what its IP address is. (We use this capability to troubleshoot Samba name services with the `nmblookup` command in Chapter 9, *Troubleshooting Samba.*)

As you saw in the first chapter, however, broadcasting—whether it be browsing or name registration and resolution—does not pass easily across multiple subnets. In addition, many broadcasts tend to bog down networks. To solve this problem, Microsoft now provides the Windows Internet Naming Service (WINS), a cross-subnet NBNS, which Samba supports. With it, an administrator can designate a single machine to act as a WINS server, and can then provide each client that requires name resolution the address of the WINS server. Consequently, name registration and resolution requests can be directed to a single machine from any point on the network, instead of broadcast.

WINS and broadcasting are not the only means of name resolution, however. There are actually four mechanisms that can be used with Samba:

- WINS

- Broadcasting

- Unix */etc/hosts* or NIS/NIS+ matches

- *LMHOSTS* file

Samba can use any or all of these name resolution methods in the order that you specify in the Samba configuration file using the `name resolve order` parameter. However, before delving into configuration options, let's discuss the one that you've probably not encountered before: the *LMHOSTS* file.

The LMHOSTS File

LMHOSTS is the standard LAN Manager *hosts* file used to resolve names into IP addresses on the system. It is the NBT equivalent of the */etc/hosts* file that is standard on all Unix systems. By default, the file is usually stored as */usr/local/samba/ lib/LMHOSTS* and shares a format similar to */etc/hosts*. For example:

```
192.168.220.100    hydra
192.168.220.101    phoenix
```

The only difference is that the names on the right side of the entries are NetBIOS names instead of DNS names. Because they are NetBIOS names, you can assign resource types to them as well:

```
192.168.220.100    hydra#20
192.168.220.100    simple#1b
192.168.220.101    phoenix#20
```

Here, we've assigned the **hydra** machine to be the primary domain controller of the **SIMPLE** domain, as indicated by the resource type <1B> assigned to the name after **hydra**'s IP address in the second line. The other two are standard workstations.

If you wish to place an *LMHOSTS* file somewhere other than the default location, you will need to notify the *nmbd* process upon start up, as follows:

```
nmbd -H /etc/samba/lmhosts -D
```

Setting Up Samba to Use Another WINS Server

You can set up Samba to use a WINS server somewhere else on the network by simply pointing it to the IP address of the WINS server. This is done with the global **wins server** configuration option, as shown here:

```
[global]
    wins server = 192.168.200.122
```

With this option enabled, Samba will direct all WINS requests to the server at 192.168.200.122. Note that because the request is directed at a single machine, we don't have to worry about any of the problems inherent to broadcasting. However, though you have specified an IP address for a WINS server in the configuration file, Samba will not necessarily use the WINS server before other forms of name resolution. The order in which Samba attempts various name-resolution techniques is given with the **name resolve order** configuration option, which we will discuss shortly.

If you have a Samba server on a subnet that still uses broadcasting and the Samba server knows the correct location of a WINS server on another subnet, you can configure the Samba server to forward any name resolution requests with the **wins proxy** option:

```
[global]
    wins server = 192.168.200.12
    wins proxy = yes
```

Use this only in situations where the WINS server resides on another subnet. Otherwise, the broadcast will reach the WINS server regardless of any proxying.

Setting Up Samba as a WINS Server

You can set up Samba as a WINS server by setting two global options in the configuration file, as shown below:

```
[global]
    wins support = yes
    name resolve order = wins lmhosts hosts bcast
```

The **wins support** option turns Samba into a WINS server. Believe it or not, that's all you need to do! Samba handles the rest of the details behind the scenes, leaving you a relaxed administrator. The **wins support=yes** and the **wins server** option are mutually exclusive; you cannot simultaneously offer Samba as the WINS server and point to another system as the server.

If Samba is acting as a WINS server, you should probably get familiar with the **name resolve order** option mentioned earlier. This option tells Samba the order of methods in which it tries to resolve a NetBIOS name. It can take up to four values:

lmhosts

Uses a LAN Manager *LMHOSTS* file

hosts

Uses the standard name resolution methods of the Unix system, */etc/hosts*, DNS, NIS, or a combination (as configured for the system)

wins

Uses the WINS server

bcast

Uses a broadcast method

The order in which you specify them in the value is the order in which Samba will attempt name resolution when acting as a WINS server. For example, let's look at the value specified previously:

```
name resolve order = wins lmhosts hosts bcast
```

This means that Samba will attempt to use its WINS entries first for name resolution, followed by the LAN Manager *LMHOSTS* file on its system. Next, the hosts value causes it to use Unix name resolution methods. The word **hosts** may be misleading; it covers not only the */etc/hosts* file, but also the use of DNS or NIS (as configured on the Unix host). Finally, if those three do not work, it will use a broadcast to try to locate the correct machine.

Finally, you can instruct a Samba server that is acting as a WINS server to check with the system's DNS server if a requested host cannot be found in its WINS database. With a typical Linux system, for example, you can find the IP address of the

DNS server by searching the */etc/resolv.conf* file. In it, you might see an entry such as the following:

```
nameserver 127.0.0.1
nameserver 192.168.200.192
```

This tells us that a DNS server is located at 192.168.220.192. (The 127.0.0.1 is the localhost address and is never a valid DNS server address.)

Use the global **dns proxy** option to alert Samba to use the configured DNS server:

```
[global]
    wins support = yes
    name resolve order = wins lmhosts hosts bcast
    dns proxy = yes
```

Name Resolution Configuration Options

Samba's WINS options are shown in Table 7-5.

Table 7-5. WINS Options

Option	Parameters	Function	Default	Scope
wins support	boolean	If set to yes, Samba will act as a WINS server.	no	Global
wins server	string (IP address or DNS name)	Identifies a WINS server for Samba to use for name registration and resolution.	None	Global
wins proxy	boolean	Allows Samba to act as a proxy to a WINS server on another subnet.	no	Global
dns proxy	boolean	If set to yes, a Samba WINS server will search DNS if it cannot find a name in WINS.	no	Global
name resolve order	lmhosts, hosts, wins, or bcast	Specifies an order of the methods used to resolve NetBIOS names.	lmhosts hosts wins bcast	Global
max ttl	numerical	Specifies the maximum time-to-live in seconds for a requested NetBIOS names.	259200 (3 days)	Global
max wins ttl	numerical	Specifies the maximum time-to-live in seconds for NetBIOS names given out by Samba as a WINS server.	518400 (6 days)	Global
min wins ttl	numerical	Specifies the minimum time-to-live in seconds for NetBIOS names given out by Samba as a WINS server.	21600 (6 hours)	Global

wins support

Samba will provide WINS name service to all machines in the network if you set the following in the [global] section of the *smb.conf* file:

```
[global]
    wins support = yes
```

The default value is **no**, which is typically used to allow another Windows NT server to become a WINS server. If you do enable this option, remember that a Samba WINS server currently cannot exchange data with any backup WINS servers. If activated, this option is mutually exclusive with the **wins server** parameter; you cannot set both to **yes** at the same time or Samba will flag an error.

wins server

Samba will use an existing WINS server on the network if you specify the **wins server** global option in your configuration file. The value of this option is either the IP address or DNS name (not NetBIOS name) of the WINS server. For example:

```
[global]
    wins server = 192.168.220.110
```

or:

```
[global]
    wins server = wins.example.com
```

In order for this option to work, the **wins support** option must be set to **no** (the default). Otherwise, Samba will report an error. You can specify only one WINS server using this option.

wins proxy

This option allows Samba to act as a proxy to another WINS server, and thus relay name registration and resolution requests from itself to the real WINS server, often outside the current subnet. The WINS server can be indicated through the **wins server** option. The proxy will then return the WINS response back to the client. You can enable this option by specifying the following in the [global] section:

```
[global]
    wins proxy = yes
```

dns proxy

If you want the domain name service (DNS) to be used if a name isn't found in WINS, you can set the following option:

```
[global]
    dns proxy = yes
```

This will cause *nmbd* to query for machine names using the server's standard domain name service. You may wish to deactivate this option if you do not have a permanent connection to your DNS server. Despite this option, we recommend using a WINS server. If you don't already have any WINS servers on your network, make one Samba machine a WINS server. Do not, however, make two Samba machines WINS servers (one primary and one backup) as they currently cannot exchange WINS databases.

name resolve order

The global **name resolve order** option specifies the order of services that Samba will use in attempting name resolution. The default order is to use the *LMHOSTS* file, followed by standard Unix name resolution methods (some combination of */etc/hosts*, DNS, and NIS), then query a WINS server, and finally use broadcasting to determine the address of a NetBIOS name. You can override this option by specifying something like the following:

```
[global]
    name resolve order = lmhosts wins hosts bcast
```

This causes resolution to use the *LMHOSTS* file first, followed by a query to a WINS server, the system hosts file, and finally broadcasting. You need not use all four options if you don't want to. This option is covered in more detail in the section "Setting Up Samba as a WINS Server," earlier in this chapter.

max ttl

This option gives the maximum time to live (TTL) during which a NetBIOS name registered with the Samba server will remain active. You should never need to alter this value.

max wins ttl

This option give the maximum time to live (TTL) during which a NetBIOS name resolved from a WINS server will remain active. You should never need to change this value from its default.

min wins ttl

This option give the minimum time to live (TTL) during which a NetBIOS name resolved from a WINS server will remain active. You should never need to alter this value from its default.

8

Additional Samba Information

This chapter wraps up our coverage of the *smb.conf* configuration file with some miscellaneous options that can perform a variety of tasks. We will talk briefly about options for supporting programmers, internationalization, messages, and common Windows bugs. For the most part, you will use these options only in isolated circumstances. We also cover performing automated backups with the *smbtar* command at the end of this chapter. So without further ado, let's jump into our first subject: options to help programmers.

Supporting Programmers

If you have programmers accessing your Samba server, you'll want to be aware of the special options listed in Table 8-1.

Table 8-1. Programming Configuration Options

Option	Parameters	Function	Default	Scope
time server	boolean	If **yes**, *nmbd* announces itself as a SMB time service to Windows clients.	no	Global
time offset	numerical (number of minutes)	Adds a specified number of minutes to the reported time.	0	Global
dos filetimes	boolean	Allows non-owners of a file to change its time if they can write to it.	no	Share
dos filetime resolution	boolean	Causes file times to be rounded to the next even second.	no	Share
fake directory create times	boolean	Sets directory times to avoid a MS *nmake* bug.	no	Share

Time Synchronization

Time synchronization can be very important to programmers. Consider the following options:

```
time server = yes
dos filetimes = yes
fake directory create times = yes
dos filetime resolution = yes
delete readonly = yes
```

If you set these options, Samba shares will provide the kind of compatible file times that Visual C++, *nmake*, and other Microsoft programming tools require. Otherwise, PC *make* programs will tend to think that all the files in a directory need to be recompiled every time. Obviously, this is not the behavior you want.

time server

If your Samba server has an accurate clock, or if it's a client of one of the Unix network time servers, you can instruct it to advertise itself as an SMB time server by setting the **time server** option as follows:

```
[global]
    time server = yes
```

The client will still have to request the correct time with the following DOS command, substituting the Samba server name in at the appropriate point:

```
C:\NET TIME \\server /YES /SET
```

This command can be placed in a Windows logon script (see Chapter 6, *Users, Security, and Domains*).

By default, the **time server** option is normally set to **no**. If you turn this service on, you can use the command above to keep the client clocks from drifting. Time synchronization is important to clients using programs such as *make*, which compile based on the last time the file was changed. Incorrectly synchronized times can cause such programs to either remake all files in a directory, which wastes time, or not recompile a source file that was just modified because of a slight clock drift.

time offset

To deal with clients that don't process daylight savings time properly, Samba provides the **time offset** option. If set, it adds the specified number of minutes to the current time. This is handy if you're in Newfoundland and Windows doesn't know about the 30-minute time difference there:

```
[global]
    time offset = 30
```

dos filetimes

Traditionally, only the root user and the owner of a file can change its last-modified date on a Unix system. The share-level **dos filetimes** option allows the Samba server to mimic the characteristics of a DOS/Windows machine: any user can change the last modified date on a file in that share if he or she has write permission to it. In order to do this, Samba uses its root privileges to modify the timestamp on the file.

By default, this option is disabled. Setting this option to **yes** is often necessary to allow PC *make* programs to work properly. Without it, they cannot change the last-modified date themselves. This often results in the program thinking *all* files need recompiling when they really don't.

dos filetime resolution

dos filetime resolution is share-level option. If set to **yes**, Samba will arrange to have the file times rounded to the closest two-second boundary. This option exists primarily to satisfy a quirk in Windows that prevents Visual C++ from correctly recognizing that a file has not changed. You can enable it as follows:

```
[data]
    dos filetime resolution = yes
```

We recommend using this option only if you are using Microsoft Visual C++ on a Samba share that supports opportunistic locking.

fake directory create times

The **fake directory create times** option exists to keep PC *make* programs sane. VFAT and NTFS filesystems record the creation date of a specific directory while Unix does not. Without this option, Samba takes the earliest recorded date it has for the directory (often the last-modified date of a file) and returns it to the client. If this is not sufficient, set the following option under a share definition:

```
[data]
    fake directory create times = yes
```

If set, Samba will adjust the directory create time it reports to the hardcoded value January 1st, 1980. This is primarily used to convince the Visual C++ *nmake* program that any object files in its build directories are indeed younger than the creation date of the directory itself and need to be recompiled.

Magic Scripts

The following options deal with *magic scripts* on the Samba server. Magic scripts are a method of running programs on Unix and redirecting the output back to the SMB client. These are essentially an experimental hack. However, some users and their programs still rely on these two options for their programs to function correctly. Magic scripts are not widely trusted and their use is highly discouraged by the Samba team. See Table 8-2 for more information.

Table 8-2. Networking Configuration Options

Option	Parameters	Function	Default	Scope
magic script	string (fully-qualified filename)	Sets the name of a file to be executed by Samba, as the logged-on user, when closed.	None	Share
magic output	string (fully-qualified filename)	Sets a file to log output from the magic file.	*scriptname. out*	Share

magic script

If the `magic script` option is set to a filename and the client creates a file by that name in that share, Samba will run the file as soon as the user has opened and closed it. For example, let's assume that the following option was created in the share `[accounting]`:

```
[accounting]
    magic script = tally.sh
```

Samba continually monitors the files in that share. If one by the name of *tally.sh* is closed (after being opened) by a user, Samba will execute the contents of that file locally. The file will be passed to the shell to execute; it must therefore be a legal Unix shell script. This means that it must have newline characters as line endings instead of Windows CR/LFs. In addition, it helps if you use the #! directive at the beginning of the file to indicate under which shell the script should run.

magic output

This option specifies an output file that the script specified by the `magic script` option will send output to. You must specify a filename in a writable directory:

```
[accounting]
    magic script = tally.sh
    magic output = /var/log/magicoutput
```

If this option is omitted, the default output file is the name of the script (as stated in the `magic script` option) with the extension *.out* appended onto it.

Internationalization

Samba has a limited ability to speak foreign tongues: if you need to deal with characters that aren't in standard ASCII, some options that can help you are shown in Table 8-3. Otherwise, you can skip over this section.

Table 8-3. Networking Configuration Options

Option	Parameters	Function	Default	Scope
client code page	Described in this section	Sets a code page to expect from clients	850	Global
character set	Described in this section	Translates code pages into alternate UNIX character sets	None	Global
coding system	Described in this section	Translates code page 932 into an Asian character set	None	Global
valid chars	string (set of characters)	Obsolete: formerly added individual characters to a code page, and had to be used after setting client code page	None	Global

client code page

The character sets on Windows platforms hark back to the original concept of a *code page*. These code pages are used by DOS and Windows clients to determine rules for mapping lowercase letters to uppercase letters. Samba can be instructed to use a variety of code pages through the use of the global `client code page` option in order to match the corresponding code page in use on the client. This option loads a code-page definition file, and can take the values specified in Table 8-4.

Table 8-4. Valid Code Pages with Samba 2.0

Code Page	Definition
437	MS-DOS Latin (United States)
737	Windows 95 Greek
850	MS-DOS Latin 1 (Western European)
852	MS-DOS Latin 2 (Eastern European)
861	MS-DOS Icelandic
866	MS-DOS Cyrillic (Russian)
932	MS-DOS Japanese Shift-JIS
936	MS-DOS Simplified Chinese
949	MS-DOS Korean Hangul
950	MS-DOS Traditional Chinese

You can set the client code page as follows:

```
[global]
    client code page = 852
```

The default value of this option is 850. You can use the *make_smbcodepage* tool that comes with Samba (by default in */usr/local/samba/bin*) to create your own SMB code pages, in the event that those listed earlier are not sufficient.

character set

The global `character set` option can be used to convert filenames offered through a DOS code page (see the previous section, "client code page") to equivalents that can be represented by Unix character sets other than those in the United States. For example, if you want to convert the Western European MS-DOS character set on the client to a Western European Unix character set on the server, you can use the following in your configuration file:

```
[global]
    client code page = 850
    character set = ISO8859-1
```

Note that you must include a `client code page` option to specify the character set from which you are converting. The valid character sets (and their matching code pages) that Samba 2.0 accepts are listed in Table 8-5:

Table 8-5. Valid Character Sets with Samba 2.0

Character Set	Matching Code Page	Definition
ISO8859-1	850	Western European Unix
ISO8859-2	852	Eastern European Unix
ISO8859-5	866	Russian Cyrillic Unix
KOI8-R	866	Alternate Russian Cyrillic Unix

Normally, the `character set` option is disabled completely.

coding system

The `coding system` option is similar to the `character set` option. However, its purpose is to determine how to convert a Japanese Shift JIS code page into an appropriate Unix character set. In order to use this option, the `client code page` option described previously must be set to page 932. The valid coding systems that Samba 2.0 accepts are listed in Table 8-6.

Table 8-6. Valid Coding System Parameters with Samba 2.0

Character Set	Definition
SJIS	Standard Shift JIS
JIS8	Eight-bit JIS codes

Table 8-6. Valid Coding System Parameters with Samba 2.0 (continued)

Character Set	Definition
J8BB	Eight-bit JIS codes
J8BH	Eight-bit JIS codes
J8@B	Eight-bit JIS codes
J8@J	Eight-bit JIS codes
J8@H	Eight-bit JIS codes
JIS7	Seven-bit JIS codes
J7BB	Seven-bit JIS codes
J7BH	Seven-bit JIS codes
J7@B	Seven-bit JIS codes
J7@J	Seven-bit JIS codes
J7@H	Seven-bit JIS codes
JUNET	JUNET codes
JUBB	JUNET codes
JUBH	JUNET codes
JU@B	JUNET codes
JU@J	JUNET codes
JU@H	JUNET codes
EUC	EUC codes
HEX	Three-byte hexidecimal code
CAP	Three-byte hexidecimal code (Columbia Appletalk Program)

valid chars

The **valid chars** option is an older Samba feature that will add individual characters to a code page. However, this option is being phased out in favor of more modern coding systems. You can use this option as follows:

```
valid chars = î
valid chars = 0450:0420 0x0A20:0x0A00
valid chars = A:a
```

Each of the characters in the list specified should be separated by spaces. If there is a colon between two characters or their numerical equivalents, the data to the left of the colon is considered an uppercase character, while the data to the right is considered the lowercase character. You can represent characters both by literals (if you can type them) and by octal, hexidecimal, or decimal Unicode equivalents.

We recommend against using this option. Instead, go with one of the standard code pages listed earlier in this section. If you do use this option, however, it must be listed after the **client code page** to which you wish to add the character. Otherwise, the characters will not be added.

WinPopup Messages

You can use the WinPopup tool (*WINPOPUP.EXE*) in Windows to send messages to users, machines, or entire workgroups on the network. This tool comes standard with Windows for Workgroups and Windows 95/98. With either Windows 95 or 98, however, you need to be running WinPopup to receive and send WinPopup messages. With Windows NT, you can still receive messages without starting such a tool; they will automatically appear in a small dialog box on the screen when received. The WinPopup application is shown in Figure 8-1.

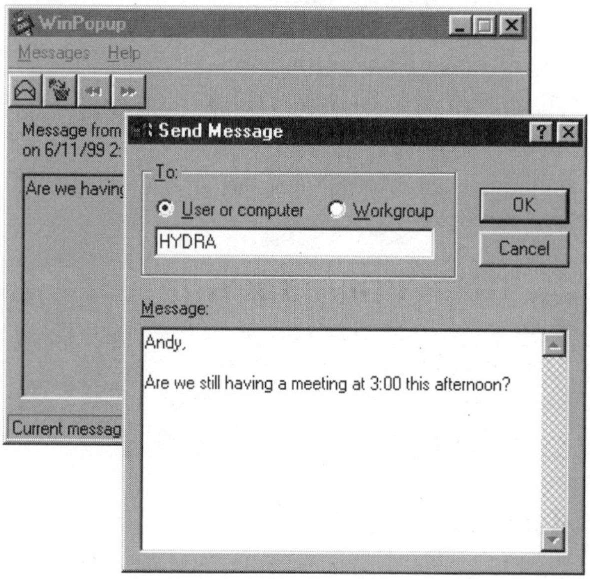

Figure 8-1. The WinPopup application

Samba has a single WinPopup messaging option, **message command**, as shown in Table 8-7.

Table 8-7. WinPopup Configuration Option

Option	Parameter	Function	Default	Scope
message command	string (fully-qualified pathname)	Sets a command to run on Unix when a WinPopup message is received.	None	Global

message command

Samba's `message command` option sets the path to a program that will run on the server when a Windows popup message arrives at the server. The command will be executed using the `guest account` user. What to do with one of these is questionable since it's probably for the Samba administrator, and Samba doesn't know his or her name. If you know there's a human using the console, the Samba team once suggested the following:

```
[global]
     message command = /bin/csh -c 'xedit %s; rm %s' &
```

Note the use of variables here. The `%s` variable will become the file that the message is in. This file should be deleted when the command is finished with it; otherwise, there will be a buildup of pop-up files collecting on the Samba server. In addition, the command must fork its own process (note the & after the command); otherwise the client may suspend and wait for notification that the command was sent successfully before continuing.

In addition to the standard variables, Table 8-8 shows the three unique variables that you can use in a `message command`.

Table 8-8. Message Command Variables

Variable	Definition
%s	The name of the file in which the message resides
%f	The name of the client that sent the message
%t	The name of the machine that is the destination of the message

Recently Added Options

Samba has several options that appeared around the time of Samba 2.0, but are not entirely supported. However, we will give you a brief overview of their workings in this section. These options are shown in Table 8-9.

Table 8-9. Recently Added Options

Option	Parameters	Function	Default	Scope
change notify timeout	numerical (number of seconds)	Sets the interval between checks when a client asks to wait for a change in a specified directory.	60	Global
machine password timeout	numerical (number of seconds)	Sets the renewal interval for NT domain machine passwords.	604,800 (1 week)	Global

Table 8-9. Recently Added Options (continued)

Option	Parameters	Function	Default	Scope
stat cache	boolean	If **yes**, Samba will cache recent name mappings.	**yes**	Global
stat cache size	numerical	Sets the size of the stat cache.	50	Global

change notify timeout

The `change notify timeout` global option emulates a Windows NT SMB feature called *change notification*. This allows a client to request that a Windows NT server periodically monitor a specific directory on a share for any changes. If any changes occur, the server will notify the client.

As of version 2.0, Samba will perform this function for its clients. However, performing these checks too often can slow the server down considerably. This option sets the time period that Samba should wait between such checks. The default is one minute (60 seconds); however, you can use this option to specify an alternate time that Samba should wait between performing checks:

```
[global]
    change notify timeout = 30
```

machine password timeout

The `machine password timeout` global option sets a retention period for NT domain machine passwords. The default is currently set to the same time period that Windows NT 4.0 uses: 604,800 seconds (one week). Samba will periodically attempt to change the *machine account password*, which is a password used specifically by another server to report changes to it. This option specifies the number of seconds that Samba should wait before attempting to change that password. The following example changes it to a single day, by specifying the following:

```
[global]
    machine password timeout = 86400
```

stat cache

The `stat cache` global option turns on caching of recent case-insensitive name mappings. The default is **yes**. The Samba team recommends that you never change this parameter.

stat cache size

The `stat cache size` global option sets the size of the cache entries to be used for the `stat cache` option. The default here is 50. Again, the Samba team recommends that you never change this parameter.

Miscellaneous Options

Many Samba options are present to deal with operating system issues on either Unix or Windows. The options shown in Table 8-10 deal specifically with some of these known problems. We usually don't change these and we recommend the same to you.

Table 8-10. Miscellaneous Options

Option	Parameters	Function	Default	Scope
deadtime	numerical (number of minutes)	Specifies the number of minutes of inactivity before a connection should be terminated.	0	Global
dfree command	string (command)	Used to provide a command that returns disk free space in a format recognized by Samba.	None	Global
fstype	NTFS, FAT, or Samba	Sets the filesystem type reported by the server to the client.	NTFS	Global
keep alive	seconds	Sets the number of seconds between checks for an inoperative client.	0 (none)	Global
max disk size	numerical (size in MB)	Sets the largest disk size to return to a client, some of which have limits. Does not affect actual operations on the disk.	0 (infinity)	Global
max mux	numerical	Sets the maximum number of simultaneous SMB operations that clients may make.	50	Global
max open files	numerical	Limits number of open files to be below Unix limits.	10,000	Global
max xmit	numerical	Specifies the maximum packet size that Samba will send.	65,535	Global
nt pipe support	boolean	Turns off an experimental NT feature, for benchmarking or in case of an error.	yes	Global
nt smb support	boolean	Turns off an experimental NT feature, for benchmarking or in case of an error.	yes	Global
ole locking compatibility	boolean	Remaps out-of-range lock requests used on Windows to fit in allowable range on Unix. Turning it off causes Unix lock errors.	yes	Global
panic action	command	Program to run if Samba server fails; for debugging.	None	Global
set directory	boolean	If yes, allows VMS clients to issue set dir commands.	no	Global

Table 8-10. Miscellaneous Options (continued)

Option	Parameters	Function	Default	Scope
smbrun	string (fully-qualified command)	Sets the command Samba uses as a wrapper for shell commands.	None	Global
status	boolean	If yes, allows Samba to monitor status for smbstatus command.	yes	Global
strict sync	boolean	If no, ignores Windows applications requests to perform a sync-to-disk.	no	Global
sync always	boolean	If yes, forces all client writes to be committed to disk before returning from the call.	no	Global
strip dot	boolean	If yes, strips trailing dots from Unix filenames.	no	Global

deadtime

This global option sets the number of minutes that Samba will wait for an inactive client before closing its session with the Samba server. A client is considered inactive when it has no open files and there is no data being sent from it. The default value for this option is 0, which means that Samba never closes any connections no matter how long they have been inactive. You can override it as follows:

```
[global]
    deadtime = 10
```

This tells Samba to terminate any inactive client sessions after 10 minutes. For most networks, setting this option as such will work because reconnections from the client are generally performed transparently to the user.

dfree command

This global option is used on systems that incorrectly determine the free space left on the disk. So far, the only confirmed system that needs this option set is Ultrix. There is no default value for this option, which means that Samba already knows how to compute the free disk space on its own and the results are considered reliable. You can override it as follows:

```
[global]
    dfree command = /usr/local/bin/dfree
```

This option should point to a script that should return the total disk space in a block, and the number of available blocks. The Samba documentation recommends the following as a usable script:

```
#!/bin/sh
df $1 | tail -1 | awk '{print $2" "$4}'
```

On System V machines, the following will work:

```
#!/bin/sh
/usr/bin/df $1 | tail -1 | awk '{print $3" "$5}'
```

fstype

This share-level option sets the type of filesystem that Samba reports when queried by the client. There are three strings that can be used as a value to this configuration option, as listed in Table 8-11.

Table 8-11. Filesystem Types

Variable	Definition
NTFS	Microsoft Windows NT filesystem
FAT	DOS FAT filesystem
Samba	Samba filesystem

The default value for this option is **NTFS**, which represents a Windows NT filesystem. There probably isn't a need to specify any other type of filesystem. However, if you need to, you can override it per share as follows:

```
[data]
    fstype = FAT
```

keep alive

This global option specifies the number of seconds that Samba waits between sending NetBIOS *keep-alive packets*. These packets are used to ping a client to detect whether it is still alive and on the network. The default value for this option is 0, which means that Samba will not send any such packets at all. You can override it as follows:

```
[global]
    keep alive = 10
```

max disk size

This global option specifies an illusory limit, in megabytes, for each of the shares that Samba is using. You would typically set this option to prevent clients with older operating systems from incorrectly processing large disk spaces, such as those over one gigabyte.

The default value for this option is 0, which means there is no upper limit at all. You can override it as follows:

```
[global]
    max disk size = 1000
```

max mux

This global option specifies the maximum number of concurrent SMB operations that Samba allows. The default value for this option is 50. You can override it as follows:

```
[global]
    max mux = 100
```

max open files

This global option specifies the maximum number of open files that Samba should allow at any given time for all processes. This value must be equal to or less than the amount allowed by the operating system, which varies from system to system. The default value for this option is 10,000. You can override it as follows:

```
[global]
    max open files = 8000
```

max xmit

This global option sets the maximum size of packets that Samba exchanges with a client. In some cases, setting a smaller maximum packet size can increase performance, especially with Windows for Workgroups. The default value for this option is 65535. You can override it as follows:

```
[global]
    max xmit = 4096
```

The section "The TCP receive window," in Appendix B, *Samba Performance Tuning*," shows some uses for this option.

nt pipe support

This global option is used by developers to allow or disallow Windows NT clients the ability to make connections to the NT SMB-specific IPC$ pipes. As a user, you should never need to override the default:

```
[global]
    nt pipe support = yes
```

nt smb support

This global option is used by developers to negotiate NT-specific SMB options with Windows NT clients. The Samba team has discovered that slightly better performance comes from setting this value to no. However, as a user, you should probably not override the default:

```
[global]
    nt smb support = yes
```

ole locking compatibility

This global option turns off Samba's internal byte-range locking manipulation in files, which gives compatibility with Object Linking and Embedding (OLE) applications that use high byte-range locks as a method of interprocess communication. The default value for this option is **yes**. If you trust your Unix locking mechanisms, you can override it as follows:

```
[global]
    ole locking compatibility = no
```

panic action

This global option specifies a command to execute in the event that Samba itself encounters a fatal error when loading or running. There is no default value for this option. You can specify an action as follows:

```
[global]
    panic action = /bin/csh -c
            'xedit <<: "Samba has shutdown unexpectedly";:'
```

set directory

This boolean share-level option allows Digital Pathworks clients to use the **setdir** command to change directories on the server. If you are not using the Digital Pathworks client, you should not need to alter this option. The default value for this option is **no**. You can override it per share as follows:

```
[data]
    set directory = yes
```

smbrun

This option sets the location of the *smbrun* executable, which Samba uses as a wrapper to run shell commands. The default value for this option is automatically configured by Samba when it is compiled. If you did not install Samba to the standard directory, you can specify where the binary is as follows:

```
[global]
    smbrun = /usr/local/bin/smbrun
```

status

This global option indicates whether Samba should log all active connections to a status file. This file is used only by the *smbstatus* command. If you have no intentions of using this command, you can set this option to **no**, which can result in a small increase of speed on the server. The default value for this option is **yes**. You can override it as follows:

```
[global]
    status = no
```

strict sync

This share-level option determines whether Samba honors all requests to perform a disk sync when requested to do so by a client. Many clients request a disk sync when they are really just trying to flush data to their own open files. As a result, this can substantially slow a Samba server down. The default value for this option is **no**. You can override it as follows:

```
[data]
    strict sync = yes
```

sync always

This share-level option decides whether every write to disk should be followed by a disk synchronization before the write call returns control to the client. Even if the value of this option is **no**, clients can request a disk synchronization; see the `strict sync` option above. The default value for this option is **no**. You can override it per share as follows:

```
[data]
    sync always = yes
```

strip dot

This global option determines whether to remove the trailing dot from Unix filenames that are formatted with a dot at the end. The default value for this option is **no**. You can override it per share as follows:

```
[global]
    strip dot = yes
```

This option is now considered obsolete; the user should use the `mangled map` option insead.

Backups with smbtar

Our final topic in this chapter is the *smbtar* tool. One common problem with modem PCs is that floppies and even CD-ROMs are often too small to use for backups. However, buying one tape drive per machine would also be silly.

Consequently, many sites don't back up their PCs at all. Instead, they reinstall them using floppy disks and CD-ROMs when they fail.

Thankfully, Samba provides us with another option: you can back up PCs' data using the *smbtar* tool. This can be done on a regular basis if you keep user data on your Samba system, or only occasionally, to save the local applications and configuration files and thus make repairs and reinstallations quicker.

To back up PCs from a Unix server, you need to do three things:

1. Ensure that File and Printer Sharing is installed on the PC and is bound to the TCP/IP protocol.

2. Explicitly share a disk on the PC so it can be read from the server.

3. Set up the backup scripts on the server.

We'll use Windows 95/98 to illustrate the first two steps. Go to the Networking icon in the Control Panel window, and check that File and Printer Sharing for Microsoft Networks is currently listed in the top window, as shown in Figure 8-2.

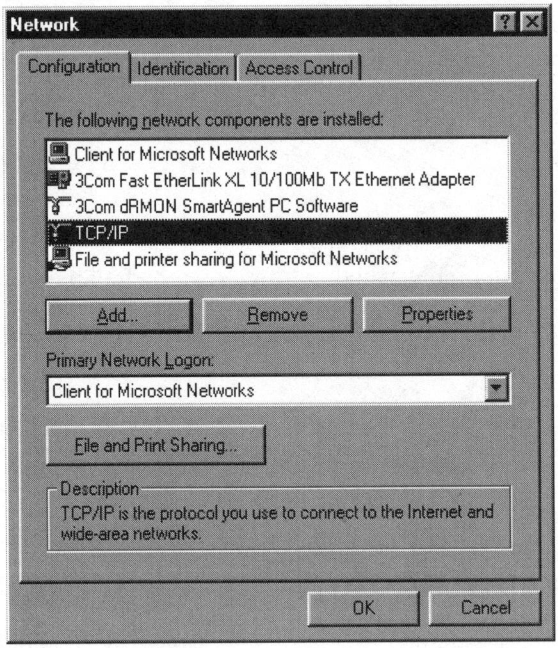

Figure 8-2. The Networking window

If "File and printer sharing for Microsoft Networks" isn't installed, you can install it by clicking on the Add button on the Network panel. After pressing it, you will be asked what service to add. Select Service and move forward, and you will be asked for a vendor and a service to install. Finally, select "File and printer sharing for Microsoft Networks," and click on Done to install the service.

Once you've installed "File and printer sharing for Microsoft Networks," return to the Network panel and select the TCP/IP protocol that is tied to your Samba network adapter. Then, click on the Properties button and choose the Bindings tab at the top. You should see a dialog box similar to Figure 8-3. Here, you'll need to verify that the "File and Printer Sharing" checkbox is checked, giving it access to TCP/IP. At this point you can share disks with other machines on the net.

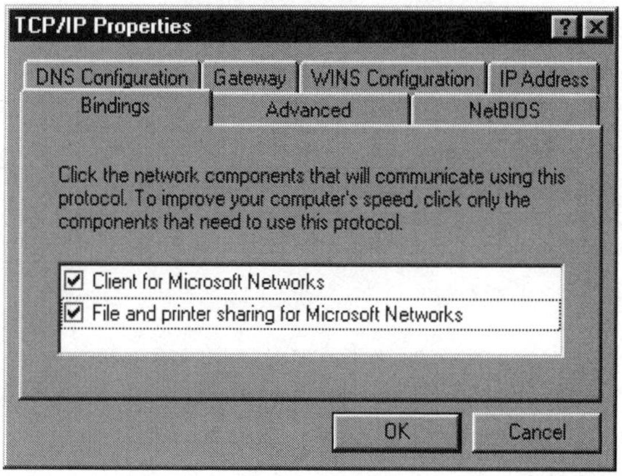

Figure 8-3. TCP/IP Bindings

The next step is to share the disk you want to back up with the tape server. Go to My Computer and select, for example, the My Documents directory. Then right-click on the icon and select its Properties. This should yield the dialog box in Figure 8-4.

Select the Sharing tab and turn file sharing on. You now have the choice to share the disk as read-only, read-write (Full), or either, each with separate password. This is the Windows 95/98 version, so it provides only share-level security. In this example, we made it read/write and set a password, as shown in Figure 8-5. When you enter the password and click on OK, you'll be prompted to re-enter it. After that, you have finished the second step.

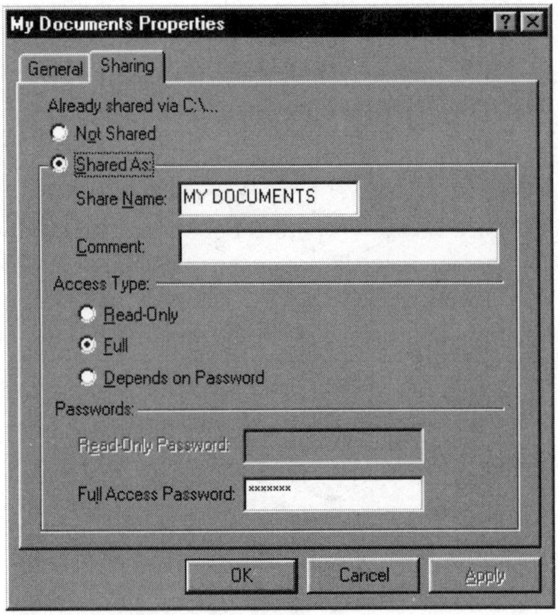

Figure 8-4. My Documents Properties

Finally, the last step is to set up a backup script on the tape server, using the *smbtar* program. The simplest script might contain only a single line and would be something like the following:

```
smbtar -s client -t /dev/rst0 -x "My Documents" -p password
```

This unconditionally backs up the *//client/My Documents* share to the device */dev/ rst0*. Of course, this is excessively simple and quite insecure. What you will want to do will depend on your existing backup scheme.

However, to whet your appetite, here are some possibilities of what *smbtar* can do:

- Back up files incrementally using the DOS archive bit (the −i option). This requires the client share to be accessed read-write so the bit can be cleared by *smbtar*

- Back up only files that have changed since a specified date (using the −N *filename* option)

- Back up entire PC drives, by sharing all of C: or D:, for example, and backing that up

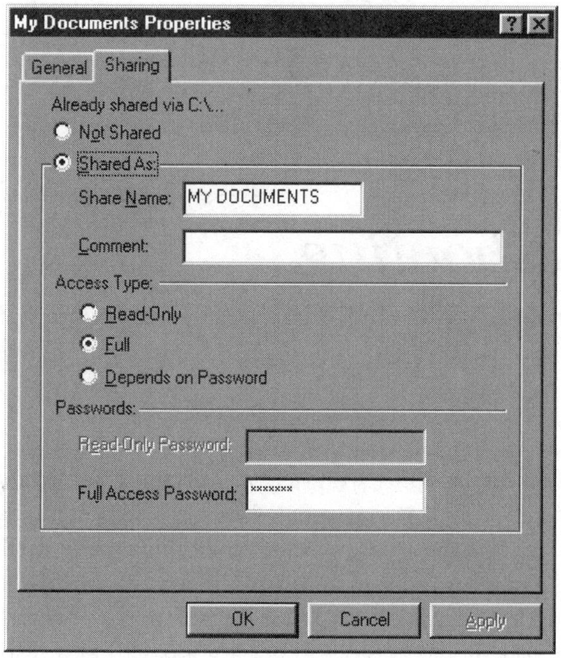

Figure 8-5. MyFiles Properties as shared

Except for the first example, each of these can be done with the PC sharing set to read-only, reducing the security risk of having passwords in scripts and passing them on the command line.

9

Troubleshooting Samba

Samba is extremely robust. Once you've got everything set up the way you want, you'll probably forget that it is running. When trouble occurs, it's typically during installation or when you're trying to add something new to the server. Fortunately, there are a wide variety of resources that you can use to diagnose these troubles. While we can't describe in detail the solution to every problem that you might encounter, you should be able to get a good start at a resolution by following the advice given in this chapter.

The first section of the chapter lists the tool bag, a collection of tools available for troubleshooting Samba; the second section is a detailed how-tó, and the last section lists extra resources you may need to track down particularly stubborn problems.

The Tool Bag

Sometimes Unix seems to be made up of a handful of applications and tools. There are tools to troubleshoot tools. And of course, there are several ways to accomplish the same task. When you are trying to solve a problem related to Samba, a good plan of attack is to check the following:

1. Samba logs

2. Fault tree

3. Unix utilities

4. Samba test utilities

5. Documentation and FAQs

6. Searchable archives

7. Samba newsgroups

Let's go over each of these one by one in the following sections.

Samba Logs

Your first line of attack should always be to check the log files. The Samba log files can help diagnose the vast majority of the problems that beginning to intermediate Samba administrators are likely to face. Samba is quite flexible when it comes to logging. You can set up the server to log as little or as much as you want. Substitution variables that allow you to isolate individual logs for each machine, share, or combination thereof.

By default, logs are placed in *samba_directory/var/smbd.log* and *samba_directory/var/nmbd.log*, where **samba_directory** is the location where Samba was installed (typically, */usr/local/samba*). As we mentioned in Chapter 4, *Disk Shares*, you can override the location and name using the **log file** configuration option in *smb.conf*. This option accepts all of the substitution variables mentioned in Chapter 2, *Installing Samba on a Unix System*, so you could easily have the server keep a separate log for each connecting client by specifying the following in the [global] section of *smb.conf*:

```
log file = %m.log
```

Alternatively, you can specify a log directory to use with the −l flag on the command line. For example:

```
smbd -l /usr/local/var/samba
```

Another useful trick is to have the server keep a log for each service (share) that is offered, especially if you suspect a particular share is causing trouble. Use the %S variable to set this up in the [global] section of the configuration file:

```
log file = %S.log
```

Log levels

The level of logging that Samba uses can be set in the *smb.conf* file using the global **log level** or **debug level** option; they are equivalent. The logging level is an integer which ranges from 0 (no logging), and increases the logging to voluminous by **log level = 3**. For example, let's assume that we are going to use a Windows client to browse a directory on a Samba server. For a small amount of log information, you can use **log level = 1**, which instructs Samba to show only cursory information, in this case only the connection itself:

```
105/25/98 22:02:11 server (192.168.236.86) connect to service public as user
pcguest (uid=503,gid=100) (pid 3377)
```

Higher debug levels produce more detailed information. Usually you won't need any more than level 3; this is more than adequate for most Samba administrators.

Levels above 3 are for use by the developers and dump enormous amounts of cryptic information.

Here is example output at levels 2 and 3 for the same operation. Don't worry if you don't understand the intricacies of an SMB connection; the point is simply to show you what types of information are shown at the different logging levels:

```
/* Level 2 */
Got SIGHUP
Processing section "[homes]"
Processing section "[public]"
Processing section "[temp]"
Allowed connection from 192.168.236.86 (192.168.236.86) to IPC$
Allowed connection from 192.168.236.86 (192.168.236.86) to IPC/


/* Level 3 */
05/25/98 22:15:09 Transaction 63 of length 67
switch message SMBtconX (pid 3377)
Allowed connection from 192.168.236.86 (192.168.236.86) to IPC$
ACCEPTED: guest account and guest ok
found free connection number 105
Connect path is /tmp
chdir to /tmp
chdir to /
05/25/98 22:15:09 server (192.168.236.86) connect to service IPC$ as user pcguest
(uid=503,gid=100) (pid 3377)
05/25/98 22:15:09 tconX service=ipc$ user=pcguest cnum=105
05/25/98 22:15:09 Transaction 64 of length 99
switch message SMBtrans (pid 3377)
chdir to /tmp
trans <\PIPE\LANMAN> data=0 params=19 setup=0
Got API command 0 of form <WrLeh> <B13BWz>
(tdscnt=0,tpscnt=19,mdrcnt=4096,mprcnt=8)
Doing RNetShareEnum
RNetShareEnum gave 4 entries of 4 (1 4096 126 4096)
05/25/98 22:15:11 Transaction 65 of length 99
switch message SMBtrans (pid 3377)
chdir to /
chdir to /tmp
trans <\PIPE\LANMAN> data=0 params=19 setup=0
Got API command 0 of form <WrLeh> <B13BWz>
(tdscnt=0,tpscnt=19,mdrcnt=4096,mprcnt=8)
Doing RNetShareEnum
RNetShareEnum gave 4 entries of 4 (1 4096 126 4096)
05/25/98 22:15:11 Transaction 66 of length 95
switch message SMBtrans2 (pid 3377)
chdir to /
chdir to /pcdisk/public
call_trans2findfirst: dirtype = 0, maxentries = 6, close_after_first=0, close_if_
end = 0 requires_resume_key = 0 level = 260, max_data_bytes = 2432
unix_clean_name [./DESKTOP.INI]
unix_clean_name [desktop.ini]
```

```
unix_clean_name [./]
creating new dirptr 1 for path ./, expect_close = 1
05/25/98 22:15:11 Transaction 67 of length 53
switch message SMBgetatr (pid 3377)
chdir to /

[...]
```

We cut off this listing after the first packet because it runs on for many pages. However, you should be aware that log levels above 3 will quickly fill your disk with megabytes of excruciating detail concerning Samba internal operations. Log level 3 is extremely useful for following exactly what the server is doing, and most of the time it will be obvious where an error is occurring by glancing through the log file.

A word of warning: using a high log level (3 or above) will *seriously* slow down the Samba server. Remember that every log message generated causes a write to disk (an inherently slow operation) and log levels greater than 2 produce massive amounts of data. Essentially, you should turn on logging level 3 only when you're actively tracking a problem in the Samba server.

Activating and deactivating logging

To turn logging on and off, set the appropriate level in the [global] section of *smb.conf.* Then, you can either restart Samba, or force the current daemon to reprocess the configuration file. You also can send the *smbd* process a SIGUSR1 signal to increase its log level by one while it's running, and a SIGUSR2 signal to decrease it by one:

```
# Increase the logging level by 1
kill -SIGUSR1 1234

# Decrease the logging level by 1
kill -SIGUSR2 1234
```

Logging by individual client machines or users

An effective way to diagnose problems without hampering other users is to assign different log levels for different machines in [global] section of the *smb.conf* file. We can do this by building on the strategy we presented earlier:

```
[global]
    log level = 0
    log file = /usr/local/samba/lib/log.%m
    include = /usr/local/samba/lib/smb.conf.%m
```

These options instruct Samba to use unique configuration and log files for each client that connects. Now all you have to do is create an *smb.conf* file for a specific client machine with a **log level = 3** entry in it (the others will pick up the default log level of 0) and use that log file to track down the problem.

Similarly, if only particular users are experiencing a problem, and it travels from machine to machine with them, you can isolate logging to a specific user by adding the following to the *smb.conf* file:

```
[global]
      log level = 0
      log file = /usr/local/samba/lib/log.%u
      include = /usr/local/samba/lib/smb.conf.%u
```

Then you can create a unique *smb.conf* file for each user (e.g., */usr/local/samba/ lib/smb.conf.tim*) files containing the configuration option `log level = 3` and only those users will get more detailed logging.

Samba Test Utilities

A rigorous set of tests that exercise the major parts of Samba are described in various files in the */docs/textdocs* directory of the Samba distribution kit, starting with *DIAGNOSIS.TXT*. The fault tree in this chapter is a more detailed version of the basic tests suggested by the Samba team, but covers only installation and reconfiguration diagnosis, like *DIAGNOSIS.TXT*. The other files in the */docs* subdirectoryies address specific problems (such as Windows NT clients) and instruct you how to troubleshoot items not included in this book. If the fault tree doesn't suffice, be sure to look at *DIAGNOSIS.TXT* and its friends.

Unix Utilities

Sometimes it's useful to use a tool outside of the Samba suite to examine what's happening inside the server. Unix has always been a "kitchen-sink" operating system. Two diagnostic tools can be of particular help in debugging Samba troubles: *trace* and *tcpdump*.

Using trace

The *trace* command masquerades under several different names, depending on the operating system that you are using. On Linux it will be *strace*, on Solaris you'll use *truss*, and SGI will have *padc* and *par*. All have essentially the same function, which is to display each operating system function call as it is executed. This allows you to follow the execution of a program, such as the Samba server, and will often pinpoint the exact call that is causing the difficulty.

One problem that *trace* can highlight is the location of an incorrect version of a dynamically linked library. This can happen if you've downloaded prebuilt binaries of Samba. You'll typically see the offending call at the end of the *trace*, just before the program terminates.

A sample **strace** output for the Linux operating system follows. This is a small section of a larger file created during the opening of a directory on the Samba server. Each line is a system-call name, and includes its parameters and the return value. If there was an error, the error value (e.g., **ENOENT**) and its explanation are also shown. You can look up the parameter types and the errors that can occur in the appropriate **trace** manual page for the operating system that you are using.

```
chdir("/pcdisk/public")                  = 0
stat("mini/desktop.ini", 0xbffff7ec)     = -1 ENOENT (No such file or directory)
stat("mini", {st_mode=S_IFDIR|0755, st_size=1024, ...}) = 0
stat("mini/desktop.ini", 0xbffff7ec)     = -1 ENOENT (No such file or directory)
open("mini", O_RDONLY)                    = 5
fcntl(5, F_SETFD, FD_CLOEXEC)             = 0
fstat(5, {st_mode=S_IFDIR|0755, st_size=1024, ...}) = 0
lseek(5, 0, SEEK_CUR)                     = 0
SYS_141(0x5, 0xbfffdbbc, 0xedc, 0xbfffdbbc, 0x80ba708) = 196
lseek(5, 0, SEEK_CUR)                     = 1024
SYS_141(0x5, 0xbfffdbbc, 0xedc, 0xbfffdbbc, 0x80ba708) = 0
close(5)                                  = 0
stat("mini/desktop.ini", 0xbffff86c)     = -1 ENOENT (No such file or directory)
write(3, "\0\0\0#\377SMB\10\1\0\2\0\200\1\0"..., 39) = 39
SYS_142(0xff, 0xbffffc3c, 0, 0, 0xbffffc08) = 1
read(3, "\0\0\0?", 4)                     = 4
read(3, "\377SMBu\0\0\0\0\0\0\0\0\0\0\0\0"..., 63) = 63
time(NULL)                                = 896143871
```

This example shows several **stat** calls failing to find the files they were expecting. You don't have to be a expert to see that the file *desktop.ini* is missing from that directory. In fact, many difficult problems can be identified by looking for obvious, repeatable errors with *trace*. Often, you need not look farther than the last message before a crash.

Using tcpdump

The *tcpdump* program, written by Van Jacobson, Craig Leres, and Steven McCanne, and extended by Andrew Tridgell, allows you to monitor network traffic in real time. A variety of output formats are available and you can filter the output to look at only a particular type of traffic. The *tcpdump* program lets you examine all conversations between client and server, including SMB and NMB broadcast messages. While its troubleshooting capabilities lie mainly at the OSI network layer, you can still use its output to get a general idea of what the server and client are attempting to accomplish.

A sample *tcpdump* log follows. In this instance, the client has requested a directory listing and the server has responded appropriately, giving the directory names **homes**, **public**, **IPC$**, and **temp** (we've added a few explanations on the right):

```
$tcpdump -v -s 255 -i eth0 port not telnet
SMB PACKET: SMBtrans (REQUEST)                    Request packet
```

```
SMB Command   = 0x25                                    Request was ls or dir.

[000] 01 00 00 10                                       ....


>>> NBT Packet
Outer frame of SMB packet
NBT Session Packet
Flags=0x0
Length=226
[lines skipped]

SMB PACKET: SMBtrans (REPLY)                            Beginning of a reply to
request
SMB Command   = 0x25                                    Command was an ls or dir
Error class   = 0x0
Error code    = 0
No errors
Flags1        = 0x80
Flags2        = 0x1
Tree ID       = 105
Proc ID       = 6075
UID           = 100
MID           = 30337
Word Count    = 10
TotParamCnt=8
TotDataCnt=163
Res1=0
ParamCnt=8
ParamOff=55
Res2=0
DataCnt=163
DataOff=63
Res3=0
Lsetup=0
Param Data: (8 bytes)
[000] 00 00 00 00 05 00 05 00                           ........

Data Data: (135 bytes)
Actual directory contents:
[000] 68 6F 6D 65 73 00 00 00  00 00 00 00 00 00 00 00  homes... ........
[010] 64 00 00 00 70 75 62 6C  69 63 00 00 00 00 00 00  d...publ ic......
[020] 00 00 00 00 75 00 00 00  74 65 6D 70 00 00 00 00  ....u... temp....
[030] 00 00 00 00 00 00 00 00  76 00 00 00 49 50 43 24  ........ v...IPC$
[040] 00 00 00 00 00 00 00 00  00 00 03 00 77 00 00 00  ........ ....w...
[050] 64 6F 6E 68 61 6D 00 00· 00 00 00 00 00 00 00 00  donham.. ........
[060] 92 00 00 00 48 6F 6D 65  20 44 69 72 65 63 74 6F  ....Home Directo
[070] 72 69 65 73 00 00 00 49  50 43 20 53 65 72 76 69  ries...I PC Servi
[080] 63 65 20 28 53 61 6D                              ce (Sam
```

This is more of the same debugging session as with the *trace* command; the listing of a directory. The options we used were **-v** (verbose), **-i eth0** to tell
tcpdump the interface to listen on (an Ethernet port), and **-s 255** to tell it to save

the first 255 bytes of each packet instead of the default: the first 68. The option `port not telnet` is used to avoid screens of telnet traffic, since we were logged in to the server remotely. The *tcpdump* program actually has quite a number of options to filter just the traffic you want to look at. If you've used *snoop* or *etherdump*, they'll look vaguely familiar.

You can download the modified *tcpdump* from the Samba FTP server at *ftp:// samba.anu.edu.au/pub/samba/tcpdump-smb*. Other versions don't include support for the SMB protocol; if you don't see output such as that shown in the example, you'll need to use the SMB-enabled version.

The Fault Tree

The fault tree is for diagnosing and fixing problems that occur when you're installing and reconfiguring Samba. It's an expanded form of a trouble and diagnostic document that is part of the Samba distribution.

Before you set out to troubleshoot any part of the Samba suite, you should know the following information:

- Your client IP address (we use 192.168.236.10)
- Your server IP address (we use 192.168.236.86)
- The netmask for your network (typically 255.255.255.0)
- Whether the machines are all on the same subnet (ours are)

For clarity, we've renamed the server in the following examples to *server.example. com*, and the client machine to *client.example.com*.

How to use the fault tree

Start the tests here, without skipping forward; it won't take long (about five minutes) and may actually save you time backtracking. Whenever a test succeeds, you will be given a section name and page number to which you can safely skip.

Troubleshooting Low-level IP

The first series of tests is that of the low-level services that Samba needs in order to run. The tests in this section will verify that:

- The IP software works
- The Ethernet hardware works
- Basic name service is in place

Subsequent sections will add TCP software, the Samba daemons *smbd* and *nmbd*, host-based access control, authentication and per-user access control, file services, and browsing. The tests are described in considerable detail in order to make them understandable by both technically oriented end users and experienced systems and network administrators.

Testing the networking software with ping

The first command to enter on both the server and the client is `ping 127.0.0.1`. This is the *loopback address* and testing it will indicate whether any networking support is functioning at all. On Unix, you can use `ping 127.0.0.1` with the statistics option and interrupt it after a few lines. On Sun workstations, the command is typically `/usr/etc/ping -s 127.0.0.1`; on Linux, just `ping 127.0.0.1`. On Windows clients, run `ping 127.0.0.1` in an MS-DOS window and it will stop by itself after four lines.

Here is an example on a Linux server:

```
server% ping 127.0.0.1
PING localhost: 56 data bytes 64 bytes from localhost (127.0.0.1):
icmp-seq=0. time=1. ms 64 bytes from localhost (127.0.0.1):
icmp-seq=1. time=0. ms 64 bytes from localhost (127.0.0.1):
icmp-seq=2. time=1. ms ^C
----127.0.0.1 PING Statistics----
3 packets transmitted, 3 packets received, 0% packet loss round-trip (ms)
min/avg/max = 0/0/1
```

If you get "ping: no answer from…" or "100% packet loss," you have no IP networking at all installed on the machine. The address `127.0.0.1` is the internal loopback address and doesn't depend on the computer being physically connected to a network. If this test fails, you have a serious local problem. TCP/IP either isn't installed or is seriously misconfigured. See your operating system documentation if it is a Unix server. If it is a Windows client, follow the instructions in Chapter 3, *Configuring Windows Clients*, to install networking support.

 If *you're* the network manager, some good references are Craig Hunt's *TCP/IP Network Administration*, Chapter 11, and Craig Hunt & Robert Bruce Thompson's new book, *Windows NT TCP/IP Network Administration*, both published by O'Reilly.

Testing local name services with ping

Next, try to ping `localhost` on the Samba server. `localhost` is the conventional hostname for the 127.0.0.1 loopback, and it should resolve to that address. After typing `ping localhost`, you should see output similar to the following:

```
server%  ping localhost
PING localhost: 56 data bytes  64 bytes from localhost (127.0.0.1):
icmp-seq=0. time=0. ms  64 bytes from localhost (127.0.0.1):
icmp-seq=1. time=0. ms  64 bytes from localhost (127.0.0.1):
icmp-seq=2. time=0. ms  ^C
```

If this succeeds, try the same test on the client. Otherwise:

- If you get "unknown host: localhost," there is a problem resolving the host name localhost into a valid IP address. (This may be as simple as a missing entry in a local *hosts* file.) From here, skip down to the section "Troubleshooting Name Services."

- If you get "ping: no answer," or "100% packet loss," but pinging 127.0.0.1 worked, then name services is resolving to an address, but it isn't the correct one. Check the file or database (typically */etc/hosts* on a Unix system) that the name service is using to resolve addresses to ensure that the entry is corrected.

Testing the networking hardware with ping

Next, ping the server's network IP address from itself. This should get you exactly the same results as pinging 127.0.0.1:

```
server%  ping 192.168.236.86
PING 192.168.236.86: 56 data bytes 64 bytes from 192.168.236.86 (192.168.236.86):
icmp-seq=0. time=1. ms 64 bytes from 192.168.236.86 (192.168.236.86):
icmp-seq=1. time=0. ms 64 bytes from 192.168.236.86 (192.168.236.86):
icmp-seq=2. time=1. ms ^C
----192.168.236.86 PING Statistics----
3 packets transmitted, 3 packets received, 0% packet loss round-trip (ms)
min/avg/max = 0/0/1
```

If this works on the server, repeat it for the client. Otherwise:

- If ping *network_ip* fails on either the server or client, but ping 127.0.0.1 works on that machine, you have a TCP/IP problem that is specific to the Ethernet network interface card on the computer. Check with the documentation for the network card or the host operating system to determine how to correctly configure it. However, be aware that on some operating systems, the *ping* command appears to work even if the network is disconnected, so this test doesn't always diagnose all hardware problems.

Testing connections with ping

Now, ping the server by name (instead of its IP address), once from the server and once from the client. This is the general test for working network hardware:

```
server%  ping server
PING server.example.com: 56 data bytes 64 bytes from server.example.com (192.168.
236.86):
```

```
icmp-seq=0. time=1. ms 64 bytes from server.example.com (192.168.236.86):
icmp-seq=1. time=0. ms 64 bytes from server.example.com (192.168.236.86):
icmp-seq=2. time=1. ms ^C
----server.example.com PING Statistics----
3 packets transmitted, 3 packets received, 0% packet loss round-trip (ms)
min/avg/max = 0/0/1
```

On Microsoft Windows, a ping of the server would look like Figure 9-1.

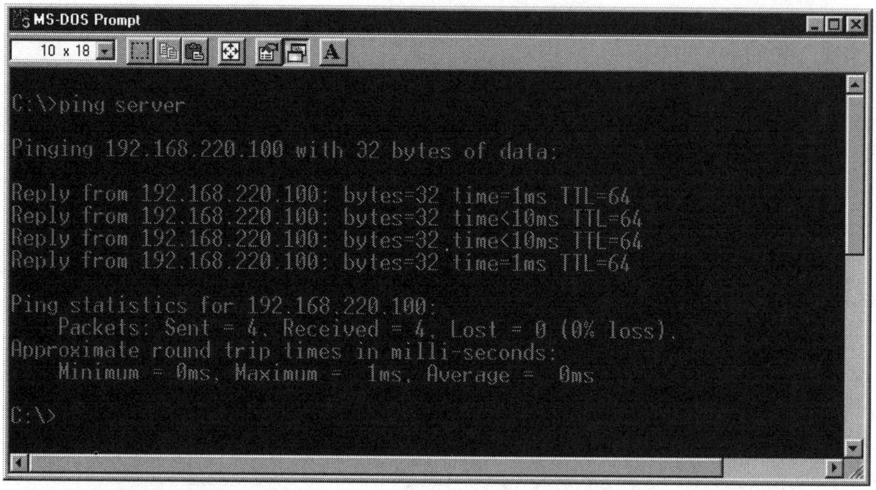

Figure 9-1. Pinging the Samba server from a Windows client

If successful, this test tells us five things:

1. The hostname (e.g., "server") is being found by your local nameserver.

2. The hostname has been expanded to the full name (e.g., *server.example.com*).

3. Its address is being returned (192.168.236.86).

4. The client has sent the Samba server four 56-byte UDP/IP packets.

5. The Samba server has replied to all four packets.

If this test isn't successful, there can be one of several things wrong with the network:

- First, if you get "ping: no answer," or "100% packet loss," you're not connecting to the network, the other machine isn't connecting, or one of the addresses is incorrect. Check the addresses that the **ping** command reports on each machine, and ensure that they match the ones you set up initially.

  If not, there is at least one mismatched address between the two machines. Try entering the command **arp -a**, and see if there is an entry for the other machine. The `arp` command stands for the Address Resolution Protocol. The `arp -a` command lists all the addresses known on the local machine. Here are some things to try:

— If you receive a message like "192.168.236.86 at (incomplete)," the Ethernet address of 192.168.236.86 is unknown. This indicates a complete lack of connectivity, and you're likely having a problem at the very bottom of the TCP/IP protocol stack, at the Ethernet-interface layer. This is discussed in Chapters 5 and 6 of *TCP/IP Network Administration* (O'Reilly).

— If you receive a response similar to "server (192.168.236.86) at 8:0:20:12:7c:94," then the server has been reached at some time, or another machine is answering on its behalf. However, this means that *ping* should have worked: you may have an intermittent networking or ARP problem.

— If the IP address from ARP doesn't match the addresses you expected, investigate and correct the addresses manually.

• If each machine can ping itself but not another, something is wrong on the network between them.

• If you get "ping: network unreachable" or "ICMP Host Unreachable," then you're not receiving an answer and there is likely more than one network involved.

In principle, you shouldn't try to troubleshoot SMB clients and servers on different networks. Try to test a server and client on the same network. The three tests that follow assume you might be testing between two networks:

a. First, perform the tests for no answer described earlier in this section. If this doesn't identify the problem, the remaining possibilities are the following: an address is wrong, your netmask is wrong, a network is down, or just possibly you've been stopped by a firewall.

b. Check both the address and the netmasks on source and destination machines to see if something is obviously wrong. Assuming both machines really are on the same network, they both should have the same netmasks and *ping* should report the correct addresses. If the addresses are wrong, you'll need to correct them. If they're right, the programs may be confused by an incorrect netmask. See "Netmasks," later in this chapter.

c. If the commands are still reporting that the network is unreachable and neither of the previous two conditions is in error, one network really may be unreachable from the other. This, too, is a network manager issue.

- If you get "ICMP Administratively Prohibited," you've struck a firewall of some sort or a misconfigured router. You will need to speak to your network security officer.

- If you get "ICMP Host redirect," and *ping* reports packets getting through, this is generally harmless: you're simply being rerouted over the network.

- If you get a host redirect and no *ping* responses, you are being redirected, but no one is responding. Treat this just like the "Network unreachable" response and check your addresses and netmasks.

- If you get "ICMP Host Unreachable from gateway *gateway_name*," ping packets are being routed to another network, but the other machine isn't responding and the router is reporting the problem on its behalf. Again, treat this like a "Network unreachable" response and start checking addresses and netmasks.

- If you get "ping: unknown host *hostname*," your machine's name is not known. This tends to indicate a name-service problem, which didn't affect `localhost`. Have a look at "Troubleshooting Name Services," later in this chapter.

- If you get a partial success, with some pings failing but others succeeding, you either have an intermittent problem between the machines or an overloaded network. Ping for longer, and see if more than about 3 percent of the packets fail. If so, check it with your network manager: a problem may just be starting. However, if only a few fail, or if you happen to know some massive network program is running, don't worry unduly. Ping's ICMP (and UDP) are designed to drop occasional packets.

- If you get a response like "smtsvr.antares.net is alive" when you actually pinged *client.example.com*, you're either using someone else's address or the machine has multiple names and addresses. If the address is wrong, name service is clearly the culprit; you'll need to change the address in the name service database to refer to the right machine. This is discussed in "Troubleshooting Name Services," later in this chapter.

Server machines are often *multihomed*: connected to more than one network, with different names on each net. If you are getting a response from an unexpected name on a multihomed server, look at the address and see if it's on your network (see the section "Netmasks," later in this chapter). If so, you should use that address, rather than one on a different network, for both performance and reliability reasons.

Servers may also have multiple names for a single Ethernet address, especially if they are web servers. This is harmless, if otherwise startling. You probably will want to use the official (and permanent) name, rather than an alias which may change.

- If everything works, but the IP address reported is 127.0.0.1, you have a name service error. This typically occurs when a operating system installation program generates an */etc/hosts* line similar to 127.0.0.1 localhost *hostname-domainname*. The localhost line should say 127.0.0.1 localhost or 127.0.0.1 localhost loghost. Correct it, lest it cause failures to negotiate who is the master browse list holder and who is the master browser. It can, also cause (ambiguous) errors in later tests.

If this worked from the server, repeat it from the client.

Troubleshooting TCP

Now that you've tested IP, UDP, and a name service with *ping*, it's time to test TCP. *ping* and browsing use ICMP and UDP; file and print services (shares) use TCP. Both depend on IP as a lower layer and all four depend on name services. Testing TCP is most conveniently done using the FTP (file transfer protocol) program.

Testing TCP with FTP

Try connecting via FTP, once from the server to itself, and once from the client to the server:

```
server% ftp server
Connected to server.example.com.
220 server.example.com FTP server (Version 6.2/OpenBSD/Linux-0.10) ready.
 Name (server:davecb):
331 Password required for davecb.
Password:
230 User davecb logged in.
 ftp> quit
221 Goodbye.
```

If this worked, skip to the section "Troubleshooting Server Daemons." Otherwise:

- If you received the message "server: unknown host," then nameservice has failed. Go back to the corresponding *ping* step, "Testing local name services with ping," and rerun those tests to see why name lookup failed.

- If you received "ftp: connect: Connection refused," the machine isn't running an FTP daemon. This is mildly unusual on Unix servers. Optionally, you might try this test by connecting to the machine using telnet instead of FTP; the messages are very similar and telnet uses TCP as well.

- If there was a long pause, then "ftp: connect: Connection timed out," the machine isn't reachable. Return to the section "Testing connections with ping."

- If you received "530 Logon Incorrect," you connected successfully, but you've just found a different problem. You likely provided an incorrect username or password. Try again, making sure you use your username from the Unix server and type your password correctly.

Troubleshooting Server Daemons

Once you've confirmed that TCP networking is working properly, the next step is to make sure the daemons are running on the server. This takes three separate tests because no single one of the following will decisively prove that they're working correctly.

To be sure they're running, you need to find out if:

1. The daemon has started

2. The daemons are registered or bound to a TCP/IP port by the operating system

3. They're actually paying attention

Before you start

First, check the logs. If you've started the daemons, the message "smbd version *some_number* started" should appear. If it doesn't, you will need to restart the Samba daemons.

If the daemon reports that it has indeed started, look out for "bind failed on port 139 socket_addr=0 (Address already in use)". This means another daemon has been started on port 139 (*smbd*). Also, *nmbd* will report a similar failure if it cannot bind to port 137. Either you've started them twice, or the *inetd* server has tried to provide a daemon for you. If it's the latter, we'll diagnose that in a moment.

Looking for daemon processes with ps

Next, you need to see if the daemons have been started. Use the **ps** command on the server with the **long** option for your machine type (commonly **ps ax** or **ps -ef**), and see if you have either *smbd* and *nmbd* already running. This often looks like the following:

```
server% ps ax
  PID TTY STAT TIME    COMMAND
  1   ?   S    0:03    init [2]
  2   ?   SW   0:00    (kflushd)
(...many lines of processes...)
  234 ?   S    0:14    nmbd -D3
  237 ?   S    0:11    smbd -D3
(...more lines, possibly including more smbd lines...)
```

This example illustrates that *smbd* and *nmbd* have already started as stand-alone daemons (the -D option) at log level 3.

Looking for daemons bound to ports

Next, the daemons have to be registered with the operating system so they can get access to TCP/IP ports. The `netstat` command will tell you if this has been done. Run the command `netstat -a` on the server, and look for lines mentioning netbios, 137 or 139:

```
server% netstat -a
Active Internet connections (including servers)
Proto Recv-Q Send-Q  Local Address        Foreign Address      (state)
udp    0      0       *.netbios-           *.*
tcp    0      0       *.netbios-           *.*
LISTEN
tcp    8370   8760    server.netbios-      client.1439
ESTABLISHED
```

or:

```
server% netstat -a
Active Internet connections (including servers)
Proto Recv-Q Send-Q  Local Address        Foreign Address      (state)
udp    0      0       *.137                *.*
tcp    0      0       *.139                *.*
LISTEN
tcp    8370   8760    server.139           client.1439
ESTABLISHED
```

Among many similar lines, there should be at least one UDP line for `*.netbios-` or `*.137`. This indicates that the *nmbd* server is registered and (we hope) is waiting to answer requests. There should also be at least one TCP line mentioning `*.netbios-` or `*.139`, and it will probably be in the LISTENING state. This means that *smbd* is up and listening for connections.

There may be other TCP lines indicating connections from *smbd* to clients, one for each client. These are usually in the ESTABLISHED state. If there are *smbd* lines in the ESTABLISHED state, *smbd* is definitely running. If there is only one line in the LISTENING state, we're not sure yet. If both of the lines is missing, a daemon has not succeeded in starting, so it's time to check the logs and then go back to Chapter 2.

If there is a line for each client, it may be coming either from a Samba daemon or from the master IP daemon, *inetd*. It's quite possible that your *inetd* startup file contains lines that start Samba daemons without your realizing it; for instance, the lines may have been placed there if you installed Samba as part of a Linux distribution. The daemons started by *inetd* prevent ours from running. This problem typically produces log messages such as "bind failed on port 139 socket_addr=0 (Address already in use)."

Check your */etc/inetd.conf*; unless you're intentionally starting the daemons from
there, there *must not* be any `netbios-ns` (udp port 137) or `netbios-ssn` (tcp
port 139) servers mentioned there. *inetd* is a daemon that provides numerous services, controlled by entries in */etc/inetd.conf*. If your system is providing an SMB
daemon via *inetd*, there will be lines like the following in the file:

```
netbios-ssn stream tcp nowait root /usr/local/samba/bin/smbd smbd
netbios-ns dgram udp wait root /usr/local/samba/bin/nmbd nmbd
```

Checking smbd with telnet

Ironically, the easiest way to test that the *smbd* server is actually working is to
send it a meaningless message and see if it rejects it. Try something like the
following:

```
echo hello | telnet localhost 139
```

This sends an erroneous but harmless message to *smbd*. The `hello` message is
important. Don't try telneting to the port and typing just anything; you'll probably
just hang your process. `hello`, however, is generally a harmless message.

```
server% echo "hello" | telnet localhost 139
Trying
Trying 192.168.236.86 ...
Connected to localhost. Escape character is '^]'.
Connection closed by foreign host.
```

If you get a "Connected" message followed by a "Connection closed" message, the
test was a success. You have an *smbd* daemon listening on the port and rejecting
improper connection messages. On the other hand, if you get "telnet: connect:
Connection refused," there is probably no daemon present. Check the logs and go
back to Chapter 2.

Regrettably, there isn't an easy test for *nmbd*. If the `telnet` test and the `netstat`
test both say that there is an *smbd* running, there is a good chance that `netstat`
will also be correct about *nmbd* running.

Testing daemons with testparm

Once you know there's a daemon, you should always run `testparm`, in hopes of
getting:

```
server% testparm
Load smb config files from /opt/samba/lib/smb.conf
Processing section "[homes]"
Processing section "[printers]" ...
Processing section "[tmp]"
Loaded services file OK. ...
```

The `testparm` program normally reports processing a series of sections, and responds with "Loaded services file OK" if it succeeds. If not, it will report one or more of the following messages, which will also appear in the logs as noted:

"Allow/Deny connection from account (n) to service"

A *testparm*-only message produced if you have valid/invalid user options set in your *smb.conf.* You will want to make sure that you are on the valid user list, and that root, bin, etc., are on the invalid user list. If you don't, you will not be able to connect, or folks who shouldn't *will* be able to.

"Warning: You have some share names that are longer than eight chars"

For anyone using Windows for Workgroups and older clients. They will fail to connect to shares with long names, producing an overflow message that sounds confusingly like a memory overflow.

"Warning: [name] service MUST be printable!"

A printer share lacks a `printable = yes` option.

"No path in service name using [name]"

A file share doesn't know which directory to provide to the user, or a print share doesn't know which directory to use for spooling. If no path is specified, the service will try to run with a path of */tmp*, which may not be what you want.

"Note: Servicename is flagged unavailable"

Just a reminder that you have used the `available = no` option in a share.

"Can't find include file [name]"

A configuration file referred to by an `include` option did not exist. If you were including the file unconditionally, this is an error and probably a serious one: the share will not have the configuration you intended. If you were including it based one of the `%` variables, such as `%a` (architecture), you will need to decide if, for example, a missing Windows for Workgroups configuration file is a problem. It often isn't.

"Can't copy service name, unable to copy to itself"

You tried to copy a *smb.conf* section into itself.

"Unable to copy service—source not found: [name]"

Indicates a missing or misspelled section in a `copy =` option.

"Ignoring unknown parameter name"

Typically indicates an obsolete, misspelled or unsupported option.

"Global parameter name found in service section"

Indicates a global-only parameter has been used in an individual share. Samba will ignore the parameter.

After the `testparm` test, repeat it with (exactly) three parameters: the name of your *smb.conf* file, the name of your client, and its IP address:

```
testparm samba_directory/lib/smb.conf client 192.168.236.10
```

This will run one more test that checks the host name and address against `host allow` and `host deny` options and may produce the "Allow/Deny connection from account account_name" to service message for the client machine. This message indicates you have valid/invalid host options in your *smb.conf,* and they prohibit access from the client machine. Entering `testparm /usr/local/lib/experimental.conf` is also an effective way to test an experimental *smb.conf* file before putting it into production.

Troubleshooting SMB Connections

Now that you know the servers are up, you need to make sure that they're running properly. We start with the *smb.conf* file in the *samba_directory/lib* directory.

A minimal smb.conf file

In the following tests, we assume you have a `[temp]` share suitable for testing, plus at least one account. An *smb.conf* file that includes just these is:

```
[global]
    workgroup = EXAMPLE
    security = user
    browsable = yes
    local master = yes
[homes]
    guest ok = no
    browseble = no
[temp]
    path = /tmp
    public = yes
```

A word of warning: the `public = yes` option in the `[temp]` share is just for testing. You probably don't want people without accounts to be able to store things on your Samba server, so you should comment it out when you're done.

Testing locally with smbclient

The first test is to ensure the server can list its own services (shares). Run the command `smbclient` with a `-L` option of `localhost` to connect to itself, and a `-U` option of just `%` to specify the guest user. You should see the following:

```
server% smbclient -L localhost -U%
Server time is Wed May 27 17:57:40 1998 Timezone is UTC-4.0
Server=[localhost]
User=[davecb]
```

```
Workgroup=[EXAMPLE]
Domain=[EXAMPLE]
    Sharename        Type      Comment
    ---------        -----     ----------
    temp             Disk
    IPC$             IPC       IPC Service (Samba 1.9.18)
    homes            Disk      Home directories
This machine does not have a browse list
```

If you received this output, move on to the next test, "Testing connections with smbclient." On the other hand, if you receive an error, check the following:

- If you get "Get_hostbyname: unknown host localhost," either you've spelled its name wrong or there actually is a problem (which should have been seen back in "Testing local name services with ping") In the latter case, move on to "Troubleshooting Name Services."

- If you get "Connect error: Connection refused," the server machine was found, but it wasn't running an *nmbd* daemon. Skip back to "Troubleshooting Server Daemons," and retest the daemons.

- If you get the message "Your server software is being unfriendly," the initial session request packet got a garbage response from the server. The server may have crashed or started improperly. The common causes of this can be discovered by scanning the logs for:

    — Invalid command-line parameters to *smbd*; see the *smbd* manual page.

    — A fatal problem with the *smb.conf* file that prevents the startup of *smbd*. Always check your changes, as was done in the section "Testing daemons with testparm."

    — The directories where Samba keeps its log and lock files are missing.

    — There is already a server on the port (139 for *smbd*, 137 for *nmbd*), preventing it from starting.

- If you're using *inetd* instead of stand-alone daemons, check your */etc/inetd. conf* and */etc/services* entries against their manual pages for errors as well.

- If you get a **Password:** prompt, your guest account is not set up properly. The **%U** option tells *smbclient* to do a "null login," which requires that the guest account be present but does not require it to have any privileges.

- If you get the message "SMBtconX failed. ERRSRV—ERRaccess," you aren't permitted access to the server. This normally means you have a **valid hosts** option that doesn't include the server, or an **invalid hosts** option that does. Recheck with the command **testparm smb.conf** *your_hostname your_ip_address* (see the section "Testing daemons with testparm") and correct any unintended prohibitions.

Testing connections with smbclient

Run the command smbclient *server*\temp, which connects to your server's
/tmp share, to see if you can connect to a file service. You should get the following response:

```
server% smbclient '\\server\temp'
Server time is Tue May  5 09:49:32 1998 Timezone is UTC-4.0 Password:
smb: \> quit
```

- If you get "Get_Hostbyname: Unknown host name," "Connect error: Connection refused," or "Your server software is being unfriendly," see the section
  "Testing locally with smbclient" for the diagnoses.

- If you get the message "servertemp: Not enough '\' characters in service," you
  likely didn't quote the address, so Unix stripped off backslashes. You can also
  write the command:

  ```
  smbclient \\\\server\\temp
  ```

or:

```
smbclient //server/temp
```

Now, provide your Unix account password to the **Password** prompt. If you then
get an smb\> prompt, it worked. Enter quit, and continue on to "Testing connections with NET USE." If you then get "SMBtconX failed. ERRSRV—ERRinvnet-
name," the problem can be any of the following:

- A wrong share name: you may have spelled it wrong, it may be too long, it
  may be in mixed case, or it may not be available. Check that it's what you
  expect with testparm (see the section "Testing daemons with testparm.")

- security = share, in which you may have to add -U *your_account* to the
  smbclient command, or know the password of a Unix account named temp.

- An erroneous username.

- An erroneous password.

- An invalid users or valid users option in your *smb.conf* file that doesn't
  allow your account to connect. Recheck with testparm smb.conf *your_
  hostname your_ip_address* (see "Testing daemons with testparm").

- A valid hosts option that doesn't include the server, or an invalid hosts
  option that does. Also test this with *testparm*.

- A problem in authentication, such as if shadow passwords or the PAM (Password Authentication Module) is used on the server, but Samba is not compiled to use it. This is rare, but occasionally happens when a SunOS 4 Samba
  binary (no shadow passwords) is run without recompilation on a Solaris system (with shadow passwords).

- The `encrypted passwords = yes` option in the configuration file, but no password for your account in the *smbpasswd* file.

- You have a null password entry, either in Unix */etc/passwd* or in the *smbpasswd* file.

- You are connecting to [`temp`], and you do not have the `guest ok = yes` option in the [`temp`] section of the *smb.conf* file.

- You are connecting to [`temp`] before connecting to your home directory, and your guest account isn't set up correctly. If you can connect to your home directory and then connect to [`temp`], that's the problem. See Chapter 2 for more information on creating a basic Samba configuration file.

  A bad guest account will also prevent you from printing or browsing until after you've logged in to your home directory.

There is one more reason for this failure that has nothing at all to do with passwords: the `path =` line in your *smb.conf* file may point somewhere that doesn't exist. This will not be diagnosed by *testparm*, and most SMB clients can't tell it from other types of bad user accounts. You will have to check it manually.

Once you have connected to [`temp`] successfully, repeat the test, this time, logging in to your home directory (e.g., map network drive *server\davecb*) looking for failures in doing that. If you have to change anything to get that to work, re-test [`temp`] again afterwards.

Testing connections with NET USE

Run the command `net use * \server\temp` on the DOS or Windows client to see if it can connect to the server. You should be prompted for a password, then receive the response "The command was completed successfully," as shown in Figure 9-2.

If that succeeded, continue with the steps in the section "Testing connections with Windows Explorer." Otherwise:

- If you get "The specified shared directory cannot be found," or "Cannot locate specified share name," the directory name is either misspelled or not in the *smb.conf* file. This message can also warn of a name in mixed case, including spaces, or is longer than eight characters.

- If you get "The computer name specified in the network path cannot be located," or "Cannot locate specified computer," the directory name has been misspelled, the name service has failed, there is a networking problem, or the `hosts deny =` option includes your host.

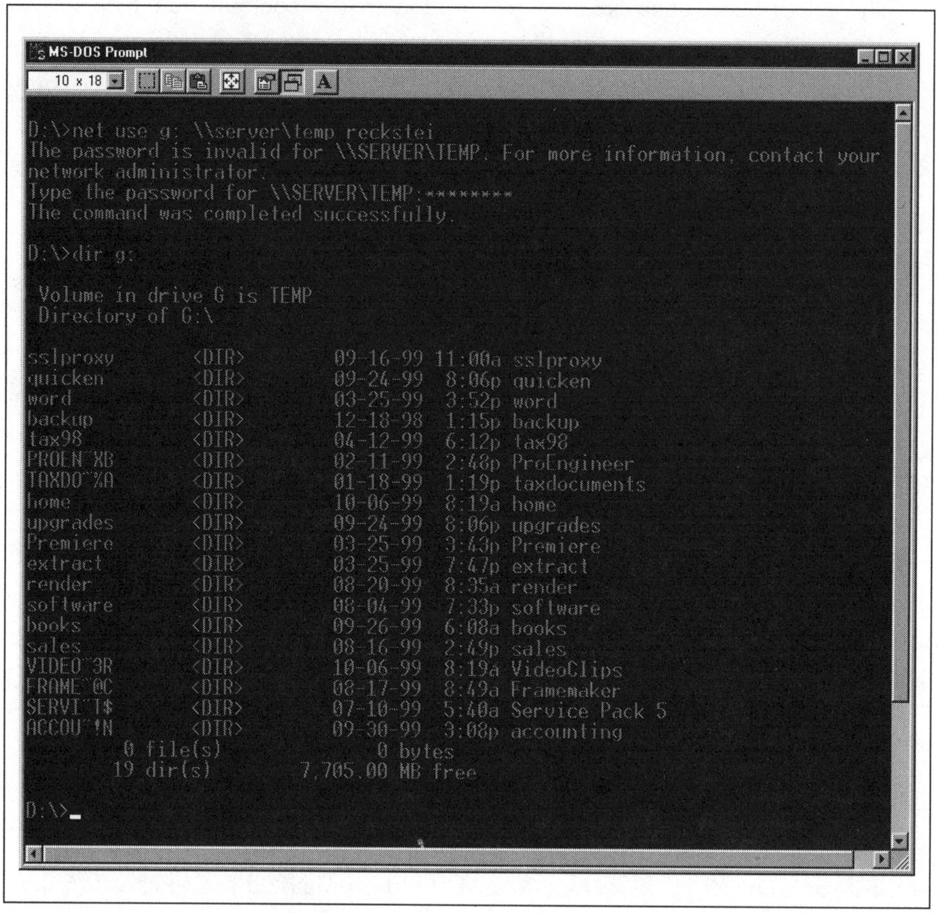

Figure 9-2. Results of the NET USE command

— If it is not a spelling mistake, you need to double back to at least the section "Testing connections with smbclient," to investigate why it doesn't connect.

— If *smbclient* does work, it's a name service problem with the client name service, and you need to go forward to the section "Testing the server with nmblookup," and see if you can look up both client and server with *nmblookup*.

- If you get "The password is invalid for **\server\username**," your locally cached copy on the client doesn't match the one on the server. You will be prompted for a replacement.

Windows 95 and 98 clients keep a local *password* file, but it's really just a cached copy of the password it sends to Samba and NT servers to authenticate you. That's what is being prompted for here. You can still log on to a Windows machine without a password (but not to NT).

If you provide your password, and it still fails, your password is not being matched on the server, you have a `valid users` or `invalid users` list denying you permission, NetBEUI is interfering, or the encrypted password problem described in the next paragraph exists.

- If your client is NT 4.0, NT 3.5 with Patch 3, Windows 95 with Patch 3, Windows 98 or any of these with Internet Explorer 4.0, these default to using Microsoft encryption for passwords (discussed in Chapter 6's "Passwords" section, along with the alternatives). In general, if you have installed a major Microsoft product recently, you may have applied an update and turned on encrypted passwords.

Because of Internet Explorer's willingness to honor URLs such as *file://somehost/somefile* by making SMB connections, clients up to and including Windows 95 Patch Level 2 would happily send your password, in plaintext, to SMB servers anywhere on the Internet. This was considered a bad idea, and Microsoft quite promptly switched to using only encrypted passwords in the SMB protocol. All subsequent releases of their products have included this correction. Encrypted passwords aren't actually needed unless you're using Internet Explorer 4.0 without a firewall, so it's reasonable to keep using unencrypted passwords on your own networks.

- If you have a mixed-case password on Unix, the client is probably sending it in all one case. If changing your password to all one case works, this was the problem. Regrettably, all but the oldest clients support uppercase passwords, so Samba will try once with it in uppercase and once in lower case. If you wish to use mixed-case passwords, see the `password level` option in Chapter 6 for a workaround.

- You may have a `valid users` problem, as tested with *smbclient* (see "Testing connections with smbclient").

- You may have the NetBEUI protocol bound to the Microsoft client. This often produces long timeouts and erratic failures, and is known to have caused failures to accept passwords in the past.

The term "bind" is used to mean connecting a piece of software to another in this case. The Microsoft SMB client is "bound to" TCP/IP in the bindings section of the TCP/IP properties panel under the Windows 95/98 Network icon in the Control Panel. TCP/IP in turn is bound to an Ethernet card. This is not the same sense of the word as binding an SMB daemon to a TCP/IP port.

Testing connections with Windows Explorer

Start Windows Explorer or NT Explorer (not Internet Explorer), select Tools→Map Network Drive and specify *server*\temp to see if you can make Explorer connect to the */tmp* directory. You should see a screen similar to the one in Figure 9-3. If so, you've succeeded and can skip to "Troubleshooting Browsing."

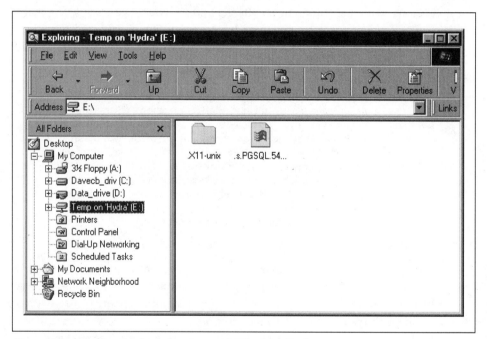

Figure 9-3. Accessing the /tmp directory with Windows Explorer

A word of caution: Windows Explorer and NT Explorer are rather poor as diagnostic tools: they do tell you that something's wrong, but rarely what it is. If you get a failure, you'll need to track it down with the NET USE command, which has far superior error reporting:

• If you get "The password for this connection that is in your password file is no longer correct," you may have any of the following:

— Your locally cached copy on the client doesn't match the one on the server.

— You didn't provide a username and password when logging on to the client. Most Explorers will continue to send a username and password of null, even if you provide a password.

— You have misspelled the password.

— You have an `invalid users` or `valid users` list denying permission.

— Your client is NT 4.0, NT 3.5 with Patch 3, Windows 95 with Patch 3, Windows 98, or any of these with Internet Explorer 4. They will all want encrypted passwords.

— You have a mixed-case password, which the client is supplying in all one case.

- If you get "The network name is either incorrect, or a network to which you do not have full access," or "Cannot locate specified computer," you may have any of the following:

— Misspelled name

— Malfunctioning service

— Failed share

— Networking problem

— Bad `path` line

— `hosts deny` line that excludes you

- If you get "You must supply a password to make this connection," the password on the client is out of synchronization with the server, or this is the first time you've tried from this client machine and the client hasn't cached it locally yet.

- If you get "Cannot locate specified share name," you have a wrong share name or a syntax error in specifying it, a share name longer than eight characters, or one containing spaces or in mixed case.

Once you can reliably connect to the [temp] directory, try once again, this time using your home directory. If you have to change something to get home directories working, then retest with [temp], and vice versa, as we showed in the section "Testing connections with NET USE." As always, if Explorer fails, drop back to that section and debug it there.

Troubleshooting Browsing

Finally, we come to browsing. This was left to last, not because it is hardest, but because it's both optional and partially dependent on a protocol that doesn't

guarantee delivery of a packet. Browsing is hard to diagnose if you don't already
know all the other services are running.

Browsing is purely optional: it's just a way to find the servers on your net and the
shares that they provide. Unix has nothing of the sort and happily does without.
Browsing also assumes all your machines are on a local area network (LAN) where
broadcasts are allowable.

First, the browsing mechanism identifies a machine using the unreliable UDP protocol; then it makes a normal (reliable) TCP/IP connection to list the shares the
machine provides.

Testing browsing with smbclient

We'll start with testing the reliable connection first. From the server, try listing its
own shares via *smbclient* with a –L option of your server's name. You should get:

```
server% smbclient -L server
Added interface ip=192.168.236.86 bcast=192.168.236.255 nmask=255.255.255.0 Server
time is Tue Apr 28 09:57:28 1998 Timezone is UTC-4.0
Password:
Domain=[EXAMPLE]
OS=[Unix]
Server=[Samba 1.9.18]
Server=[server]
User=[davecb]
Workgroup=[EXAMPLE]
Domain=[EXAMPLE]
    Sharename      Type        Comment
    ---------      ----        -------
    cdrom          Disk        CD-ROM
    cl             Printer     Color Printer 1
    davecb         Disk        Home Directories

This machine has a browse list:
    Server         Comment
    ---------      -------
    SERVER         Samba 1.9.18

This machine has a workgroup list:
    Workgroup      Master
    ---------      -------
    EXAMPLE        SERVER
```

- If you didn't get a Sharename list, the server is not allowing you to browse
  any shares. This should not be the case if you've tested any of the shares with
  Windows Explorer or the NET USE command. If you haven't done the
  `smbclient -L localhost -U%` test yet (see "Testing locally with smbclient"),
  do it now. An erroneous guest account can prevent the shares from being
  seen. Also, check the *smb.conf* file to make sure you do not have the option
  `browsable = no` anywhere in it: we suggest a minimal *smb.conf* file (see "A

minimal smb.conf file") for you to steal from. You need to have `browseable` enabled in order to be able to see at least the [`temp`] share.

- If you didn't get a browse list, the server is not providing information about the machines on the network. At least one machine on the net must support browse lists. Make sure you have `local master = yes` in the *smb.conf* file if you want Samba be the local master browser.

- If you got a browse list but didn't get */tmp*, you probably have a *smb.conf* problem. Go back to "Testing daemons with testparm."

- If you didn't get a workgroup list with your workgroup name in it, it is possible that your workgroup is set incorrectly in the *smb.conf* file.

- If you didn't get a workgroup list at all, ensure that `workgroup =EXAMPLE` is present in the *smb.conf* file.

- If you get nothing, try once more with the options `-I` *ip_address* `-n` *netbios_name* `-W` *workgroup* `-d3` with the NetBIOS and workgroup name in uppercase. (The `-d 3` option sets the log/debugging level to 3.)

If you're still getting nothing, you shouldn't have gotten this far. Double back to at least "Testing TCP with FTP," or perhaps "Testing connections with ping." On the other hand:

- If you get "SMBtconX failed. ERRSRV—ERRaccess," you aren't permitted access to the server. This normally means you have a `valid hosts` option that doesn't include the server, or an invalid hosts option that does.

- If you get "Bad password," then you presumably have one of the following:

  — An incorrect `hosts allow` or `hosts deny` line

  — An incorrect `invalid users` or `valid users` line

  — A lowercase password and OS/2 or Windows for Workgroups clients

  — A missing or invalid guest account

  Check what your guest account is (see "Testing locally with smbclient") and verify your *smb.conf* file with `testparm smb.conf` *your_hostname your_ip_address* (see "Testing daemons with testparm") and change or comment out any `hosts allow`, `hosts deny`, `valid users` or `invalid users` lines.

- If you get "Connection refused," the *smbd* server is not running or has crashed. Check that it's up, running, and listening to the network with *netstat*, see step "Testing daemons with testparm."

- If you get "Get_Hostbyname: Unknown host name," you've made a spelling error, there is a mismatch between Unix and NetBIOS hostname, or there is a name service problem. Start nameservice debugging with "Testing connections with NET USE." If this works, suspect a name mismatch and go to step "Troubleshooting NetBIOS Names."

- If you get "Session request failed," the server refused the connection. This usually indicates an internal error, such as insufficient memory to fork a process.

- If you get "Your server software is being unfriendly," the initial session request packet received a garbage response from the server. The server may have crashed or started improperly. Go back to "Testing locally with smbclient," where the problem is first analyzed.

- If you suspect the server is not running, go back to "Looking for daemon processes with ps" to see why the server daemon isn't responding.

Testing the server with nmblookup

This will test the "advertising" system used for Windows name services and browsing. Advertising works by broadcasting one's presence or willingness to provide services. It is the part of browsing that uses an unreliable protocol (UDP), and works only on broadcast networks like Ethernets. The *nmblookup* program broadcasts name queries for the hostname you provide, and returns its IP address and the name of the machine, much like *nslookup* does with DNS. Here, the -d (debug- or log-level) option, and the -B (broadcast address) options direct queries to specific machines.

First, we check the server from itself. Run *nmblookup* with a -B option of your server's name to tell it to send the query to the Samba server, and a parameter of _ _SAMBA_ _ as the symbolic name to look up. You should get:

```
server% nmblookup -B server _ _SAMBA_ _
Added interface ip=192.168.236.86 bcast=192.168.236.255 nmask=255.255.255.0
Sending queries to 192.168.236.86 192.168.236.86 _ _SAMBA_ _
```

You should get the IP address of the server, followed by the name _ _SAMBA_ _, which means that the server has successfully advertised that it has a service called _ _SAMBA_ _, and therefore at least part of NetBIOS nameservice works.

- If you get "Name_query failed to find name _ _SAMBA_ _" you may have specified the wrong address to the -B option, or *nmbd* is not running. The -B option actually takes a broadcast address: we're using a machine-name to get a unicast address, and to ask server if it has claimed _ _SAMBA_ _.

- Try again with -B *ip_address*, and if that fails too, *nmbd* isn't claiming the name. Go back briefly to "Testing daemons with testparm" to see if *nmbd* is running. If so, it may not claiming names; this means that Samba is not providing the browsing service—a configuratiuon problem. If that is the case, make sure that *smb.conf* doesn't contain the option browsing = no.

Testing the client with nmblookup

Next, check the IP address of the client from the server with *nmblookup* using **-B** option for the client's name and a parameter of `'*'` meaning "anything," as shown here:

```
server% nmblookup -B client '*'
Sending queries to 192.168.236.10 192.168.236.10 *
Got a positive name query response from 192.168.236.10 (192.168.236.10)
```

- If you receive "Name-query failed to find name *," you have made a spelling mistake, or the client software on the PC isn't installed, started, or bound to TCP/IP. Double back to Chapter 2 or Chapter 3 and ensure you have a client installed and listening to the network.

Repeat the command with the following options if you had any failures:

- If nmblookup **-B** *client_IP_address* succeeds but **-B** *client_name* fails, there is a name service problem with the client's name; go to "Troubleshooting Name Services."

- If nmblookup **-B** `127.0.0.1'*'` succeeds, but **-B** *client_IP_address* fails, there is a hardware problem and ping should have failed. See your network manager.

Testing the network with nmblookup

Run the command *nmblookup* again with a **-d** option (debug level) of 2 and a parameter of `'*'` again. This time we are testing the ability of programs (such as *nmbd*) to use broadcast. It's essentially a connectivity test, done via a broadcast to the default broadcast address.

A number of NetBIOS/TCP-IP hosts on the network should respond with "got a positive name query response" messages. Samba may not catch all of the responses in the short time it listens, so you won't always see all the SMB clients on the network. However, you should see most of them:

```
server% nmblookup -d 2 '*'
Added interface ip=192.168.236.86 bcast=192.168.236.255 nmask=255.255.255.0
Sending queries to 192.168.236.255
Got a positive name query response from 192.168.236.191 (192.168.236.191)
Got a positive name query response from 192.168.236.228 (192.168.236.228)
Got a positive name query response from 192.168.236.75 (192.168.236.75)
Got a positive name query response from 192.168.236.79 (192.168.236.79)
Got a positive name query response from 192.168.236.206 (192.168.236.206)
Got a positive name query response from 192.168.236.207 (192.168.236.207)
Got a positive name query response from 192.168.236.217 (192.168.236.217)
Got a positive name query response from 192.168.236.72 (192.168.236.72) 192.168.
236.86 *
```

However:

- If this doesn't give at least the client address you previously tested, the default broadcast address is wrong. Try **nmblookup -B 255.255.255.255 -d 2 '*'**, which is a last-ditch variant (a broadcast address of all ones). If this draws responses, the broadcast address you've been using before is wrong. Troubleshooting these is discussed in the "Broadcast addresses" section, later in this chapter.

- If the address 255.255.255.255 fails too, check your notes to see if your PC and server are on different subnets, as discovered in "Testing connections with ping." You should try to diagnose this with a server and client on the same subnet, but if you can't, you can try specifying the remote subnet's broadcast address with **-B**. Finding that address is discussed in the same place as troubleshooting broadcast addresses, in the section "Broadcast addressess," later in this chapter. The **-B** option will work if your router supports directed broadcasts; if it doesn't, you may be forced to test with a client on the same network.

Testing client browsing with net view

On the client, run the command *net view \\server* in a DOS window to see if you can connect to the client and ask what shares it provides. You should get back a list of available shares on the server, as shown in Figure 9-4.

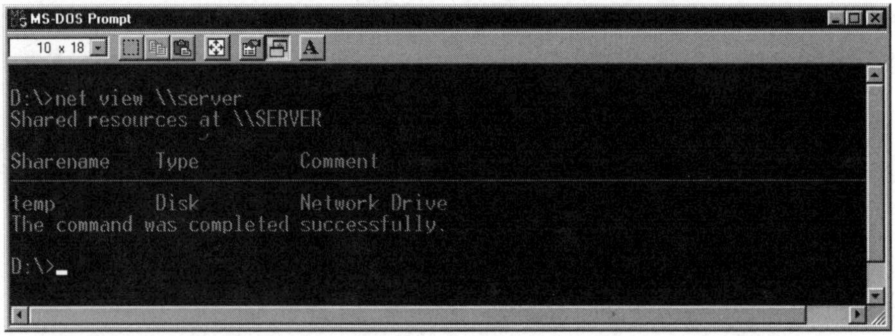

Figure 9-4. Using the net view command

If you received this, continue with the section "Other Things that Fail."

- If you get "Network name not found" for the name you just tested in the section "Testing the client with nmblookup," there is a problem with the client software itself. Double-check this by running *nmblookup* on the client; if it works and NET VIEW doesn't, the client is at fault.

- Of course, if *nmblookup* fails, there is a NetBIOS nameservice problem, as discussed in the section "Troubleshooting NetBIOS Names."

- If you get "You do not have the necessary access rights," or "This server is not configured to list shared resources," either your guest account is misconfigured (see "Testing locally with smbclient"), or you have a hosts allow or hosts deny line that prohibits connections from your machine. These problems should have been detected by the *smbclient* tests starting in the section "Testing browsing with smbclient."

- If you get "The specified computer is not receiving requests," you have misspelled the name, the machine is unreachable by broadcast (tested in "Testing the network with nmblookup"), or it's not running *nmbd*.

- If you get "Bad password error," you're probably encountering the Microsoft-encrypted password problem, as discussed in Chapter 6, with its corrections.

Browsing the server from the client

From the Network Neighborhood (File Manager in older releases), try to browse the server. Your Samba server should appear in the browse list of your local workgroup. You should be able to double click on the name of the server and get a list of shares, as illustrated in Figure 9-5.

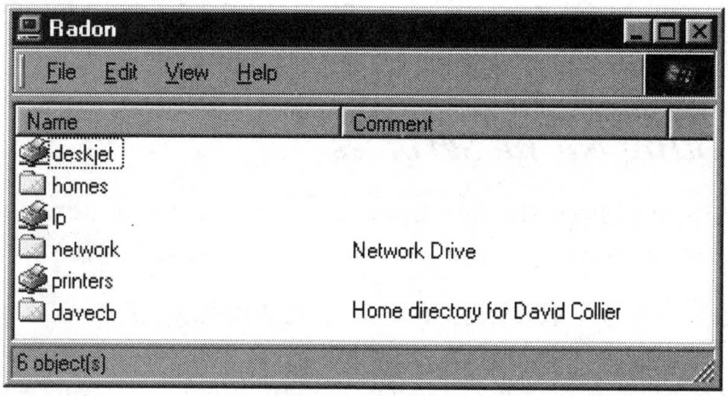

Figure 9-5. List of shares on a server

- If you get an "Invalid password" error with NT 4.0, NT 3.5 with Patch 3, Windows 95 with Patch 3, Windows 98 or any of these with Internet Explorer 4.0, it's most likely the encryption problem again. All of these clients default to using Microsoft encryption for passwords (see Chapter 6).

- If you receive an "Unable to browse the network" error, one of the following has ocurred:

   — You have looked too soon, before the broadcasts and updates have completed; try waiting 30 seconds before re-attempting.

— There is a network problem you've not yet diagnosed.

— There is no browse master. Add the configuration option `local master = yes` to your *smb.conf* file.

— No shares are marked **browsable** in the *smb.conf* file.

• If you receive the message "\\server is not accessible," then:

— You have the encrypted password problem

— The machine really isn't accessible

— The machine doesn't support browsing

Other Things that Fail

If you've made it here, either the problem is solved or it's not one we've seen. The next sections cover troubleshooting tasks that are required to have the infrastructure to run Samba, not Samba itself.

Not logging on

An occasional problem is forgetting to log in to the client or logging in as a wrong (account-less) person. The former is not diagnosed at all: Windows tries to be friendly and lets you on. Locally! The only warning of the latter is that Windows welcomes you and asks about your new account. Either of these leads to repeated refusals to connect and endless requests for passwords. If nothing else seems to work, try logging out or shutting down and logging in again.

Troubleshooting Name Services

This section looks at simple troubleshooting of all the name services that you will encounter, but only for the common problems that affect Samba.

There are several good references for troubleshooting particular name services: Paul Albitz and Cricket Liu's *DNS and Bind* covers the Domain Name Service (DNS), Hal Stern's *NFS and NIS* (both from O'Reilly) covers NIS ("Yellow pages") while WINS (Windows Internet Name Service), *hosts/LMHOSTS* files and NIS+ are best covered by their respective vendor's manuals.

The problems addressed in this section are:

• Identifying name services

• A hostname can't be looked up

• The long (FQDN) form of a hostname works but the short form doesn't

• The short form of the name works, but the long form doesn't

• A long delay ocurrs before the expected result

Identifying what's in use

First, see if both the server and the client are using DNS, WINS, NIS, or *hosts* files to look up IP addresses when you give them a name. Each kind of machine will have a different preference:

- Windows 95 and 98 machines will look in WINS and *LMHOSTS* files first, then broadcast, and finally try DNS and *hosts* files.

- NT will look in WINS, then broadcast, LMHOSTS files, and finally *hosts* and DNS.

- Windows programs using the WINSOCK standard (like PC-NFSs) will use hosts files, DNS, WINS, and then broadcast. Don't assume that if a different program's name service works, the SMB client program's name service will!

- Samba daemons will use *LMHOSTS*, WINS, the Unix host's preference, and then broadcast.

- Unix hosts can be configured to use any combination of DNS, *hosts* files, and NIS and NIS+, generally in any order.

We recommend that the client machines be configured to use WINS and DNS, the Samba daemons to use WINS and DNS, and the Unix server to use DNS. You'll have to look at your notes and the actual machines to see which is in use.

On the clients, the name services are all set in the TCP/IP Properties panel of the Networking Control Panel, as discussed in Chapter 3. You may need to check there to see what you've actually turned on. On the server, see if an */etc/resolv. conf* file exists. If it does, you're using DNS. You may be using the others as well, though. You'll need to check for NIS and combinations of services.

Check for an */etc/nsswitch.conf* file on Solaris and other System V Unix operating systems. If you have one, look for a line that begins `host:`, followed by one or more of `files`, `bind`, `nis` or `nis+`. These are the name services to use, in order, with optional extra material in square brackets. *files* stands for using *hosts* files, while *bind* (the Berkeley Internet Name Daemon) stands for using DNS.

If the client and server differ, the first thing to do is to get them in sync. Clients can only use only DNS, WINS, *hosts* files and *lmhosts* files, not NIS or NIS+. Servers can use *hosts* files, DNS, and NIS or NIS+, but not WINS—even if your Samba server provides WINS services. If you can't get all the systems to use the same services, you'll have to carefully check the server and the client for the same data.

Samba 2.0 (and late 1.9 versions) added a -R (resolve order) option to *smbclient*. If you want to troubleshoot WINS, for example, you'd say:

```
smbclient -L server -R wins
```

The possible settings are `hosts` (which means whatever the Unix machine is using, not just */etc/hosts* files), `lmhosts`, `wins` and `bcast` (broadcast).

In the following sections, we use the term *long name* for a fully-qualified domain name (FQDN), like `server.example.com`, and the term *short name* for the host part of a FQDN, like `server`.

Cannot look up hostnames

Try the following:

- In DNS:

   Run `nslookup` *name*. If this fails, look for a *resolv.conf* error, a downed DNS server, or a short/long name problem (see the next section). Try the following:

   — Your */etc/resolv.conf* should contain one or more name-server lines, each with an IP address. These are the addresses of your DNS servers.

   — ping each of the server addresses you find. If this fails for one, suspect the machine. If it fails for each, suspect your network.

   — Retry the lookup using the full domain name (e.g., *server.example.com*) if you tried the short name first, or the short name if you tried the long name first. If results differ, skip to the next section.

- In Broadcast/WINS:

   Broadcast/WINS does only short names such as `server`, (not long ones, such as `server.example.com`). Run `nmblookup -S` *server*. This reports everything broadcast has registered for the name. In our example, it looks like this:

```
Looking up status of 192.168.236.86
received 10 names
        SERVER          <00> -          M <ACTIVE>
        SERVER          <03> -          M <ACTIVE>
        SERVER          <1f> -          M <ACTIVE>
        SERVER          <20> -          M <ACTIVE>
        .._ _MSBROWSE_ _.<01> - <GROUP> M <ACTIVE>
        MYGROUP         <00> - <GROUP>  M <ACTIVE>
        MYGROUP         <1b> -          M <ACTIVE>
        MYGROUP         <1c> - <GROUP>  M <ACTIVE>
        MYGROUP         <1d> -          M <ACTIVE>
        MYGROUP         <1e> - <GROUP>  M <ACTIVE>
```

The required entry is `SERVER <00>`, which identifies *server* as being this machine's NetBIOS name. You should also see your workgroup mentioned one or more times. If these lines are missing, Broadcast/WINS cannot look up names and will need attention.

The numbers in angle brackets in the previous output identify Net-
BIOS names as being workgroups, workstations, and file users of the
messenger service, master browsers, domain master browsers,
domain controllers and a plethora of others. We primarily use <00>
to identify machine and workgroup names and <20> to identify
machines as servers. The complete list is available at *http://support.
microsoft.com/support/kb/articles/q163/4/09.asp*.

- In NIS:

    Try **ypmatch name hosts**. If this fails, NIS is down. Find out the NIS server's
    name by running *ypwhich*, and ping the machine it to see if it's accessible.

- In NIS+:

    If you're running NIS+, try **nismatch name hosts**. If this fails, NIS is down.
    Find out the NIS server's name by running *niswhich*, and ping that machine to
    see if it's accessible.

- In *hosts* files:

    Inspect */etc/hosts* on the client (C:\WINDOWS\HOSTS). Each line should have
    an IP number and one or more names, the primary name first, then any
    optional aliases. An example follows:

    ```
    127.0.0.1           localhost
    192.168.236.1       dns.svc.example.com
    192.168.236.10      client.example.com client
    192.168.236.11      backup.example.com loghost
    192.168.236.86      server.example.com server
    192.168.236.254     router.svc.example.com
    ```

    On Unix, `localhost` should always be 127.0.0.1, although it may be just an
    alias for a hostname on the PC. On the client, check that there are no #XXX
    directives at the ends of the lines; these are LAN Manager/NetBIOS directives,
    and should appear only in *LMHOSTS* files (C:\WINDOWS\LMHOSTS).

- In *LMHOSTS* files:

    This file is a local source for LAN Manager (NetBIOS) names. It has a format
    very similar to */etc/hosts* files, but does not support long-form domain names
    (e.g., server.example.com), and may have a number of optional #XXX direc-
    tives following the names. Note there usually is a *lmhosts.sam* (for sample) file
    in C:\WINDOWS, but it's not used unless renamed to C:\WINDOWS\LMHOSTS.

Long and short hostnames

Where the long (FQDN) form of a hostname works but the short name doesn't (for example, `client.example.com` works but `client` doesn't), consider the following:

- DNS:

  This usually indicates there is no default domain in which to look up the short names. Look for a `default` line in */etc/resolv.conf* on the Samba server with your domain in it, or a `search` line with one or more domains in it. One or the other may need to be present to make short names usable; which one depends on vendor and version of the DNS resolver. Try adding `domain` *your domain* to *resolv.conf* and ask your network or DNS administrator what should have been in the file.

- Broadcast/WINS:

  Broadcast/WINS doesn't support long names; it won't suffer from this problem.

- NIS:

  Try the command `ypmatch hostname hosts`. If you don't get a match, your tables don't include short names. Speak to your network manager; short names may be missing by accident, or may be unsupported as a matter of policy. Some sites don't ever use (ambiguous) short names.

- NIS+ :

  Try `nismatch` *hostname* `hosts`, and treat failure exactly as with NIS above.

- *hosts:*

  If the short name is not in */etc/hosts*, consider adding it as an alias. Avoid, if you can, short names as primary names (the first one on a line). Have them as aliases if your system permits.

- *LMHOSTS:*

  LAN Manager doesn't support long names, so it won't suffer from this problem.

On the other hand, if the short form of the name works and the long doesn't, consider the following:

- DNS:

  This is bizarre; see your network or DNS administrator, as this is probably a DNS setup bug.

- Broadcast/WINS:

  This is a normal bug; Broadcast/WINS can't use the long form. Optionally, consider DNS. Microsoft has stated that they will switch to DNS, though it's not providing name types like <00>.

- NIS:

  If you can use **ypmatch** to look up the short form but not the long, consider adding the long form to the table as at least an alias.

- NIS+:

  Same as NIS, except you use **nismatch** instead of **ypmatch** to look up names.

- *hosts:*

  Add the long name as at least an alias, and preferably as the primary form. Also consider using DNS if it's practical.

- *LMHOSTS:*

  This is a normal bug. LAN Manager can't use the long form; consider switching to DNS or *hosts*.

Unusual delays

When there is a long delay before the expected result:

- DNS:

  Test the same name with the *nslookup* command on the machine (client or server) that is slow. If *nslookup* is also slow, you have a DNS problem. If it's slower on a client, you have too many protocols bound to the Ethernet card. Eliminate NetBEUI, which is infamously slow, and optionally, Novel, assuming you don't need them. This is especially important on Windows 95, which is particularly sensitive to excess protocols.

- Broadcast/WINS:

  Test the client using **nmblookup**, and if it's faster, you probably have the protocols problem as mentioned in the previous item.

- NIS:

  Try **ypmatch**, and if it's slow, report the problem to your network manager.

- NIS+:

  Try **nismatch**, similarly.

- *hosts:*

  hosts files, if of reasonable size, are always fast. You probably have the protocols problem mentioned under DNS, above.

- *LMHOSTS:*

  This is not a name lookup problem; *LMHOSTS* files are as fast as *hosts* files.

Localhost issues

When a localhost isn't 127.0.0.1, try the following:

- DNS:

    There is probably no record for `localhost. A 127.0.0.1`. Arrange to add one, and a reverse entry, `1.0.0.127.IN-ADDR.ARPA PTR 127.0.0.1`.

- Broadcast/WINS:

    Not applicable.

- NIS:

    If `localhost` isn't in the table, add it.

- NIS+:

    If `localhost` isn't in the table, add it.

- *hosts:*

    Add a line is the *hosts* file that says `127.0.0.1 localhost`

- *LMHOSTS:*

    Not applicable.

Troubleshooting Network Addresses

A number of common problems are caused by incorrect Internet address routing or the incorrect assignment of addresses. This section helps you determine what your addresses are.

Netmasks

The netmasks tell each machine which addresses can be reached directly (are on your local network) and which addresses require forwarding packets through a router. If the netmask is wrong, the machines will make one of two mistakes. One is to try to route local packets via a router, which is an expensive way to waste time—it may work reasonably fast, it may run slowly, or it may fail utterly. The second mistake is to fail to send packets for a remote machine to the router, which will prevent them from being forwarded to the remote machine.

The netmask is a number like an IP address, with one-bits for the network part of an address and zero-bits for the host portion. The netmask is literally used to mask off parts of the address inside the TCP/IP code. If the mask is 255.255.0.0, the first 2 bytes are the network part and the last 2 are the host part. More common is 255. 255.255.0, in which the first 3 bytes are the network part and the last one is the host part.

For example, let's say your IP address is 192.168.0.10 and the Samba server is 192.168.236.86. If your netmask happens to be 255.255.255.0, the network part of the addresses is the first 3 bytes and the host part is the last byte. In this case, the network parts are different, and the machines are on different networks:

Network Part	Host Part
192 168 000	10
192 168 235	86

If your netmask happens to be 255.255.0.0, the network part is just the first two bytes. In this case, the network parts match and so the two machines are on the same network:

Network Part	Host Part
192 168	000 10
192 168	236 86

Of course, if your netmask says one thing and your network manager says another, the netmask is wrong.

Broadcast addresses

The broadcast address is a normal address, with the hosts part all one-bits. It means "all hosts on your network." You can compute it easily from your netmask and address: take the address and put one-bits in it for all the bits that are zero at the end of the netmask (the host part). The following table illustrates this:

	Network Part	Host Part
IP address	192 168 236	86
Netmask	255 255 255	000
Broadcast	192 168 236	255

In this example, the broadcast address on the 192.168.236 network is 192.168.236.255. There is also an old "universal" broadcast address, 255.255.255.255. Routers are prohibited from forwarding these, but most machines on your local network will respond to broadcasts to this address.

Network address ranges

A number of address ranges have been reserved for testing and for non-connected networks; we use one of these for the book. If you don't have an address yet, feel free to use one of these to start with. They include one class A (large) network, 10.*.*.*, and 254 class C (smaller) networks, 192.168.1.* through to 192.168.254.*. In this book we use one of the latter, 192.168.236.*. The domain *example.com* is also reserved for unconnected networks, explanatory examples, and books.

If you're actually connecting to the Internet, you'll need to get a real network and a domain name, probably through the same company that provides your connection.

Finding your network address

If you haven't recorded your IP address, it will be displayed by the *ifconfig* command on Unix or by the IPCONFIG command on Windows 95 and NT. (Check your manual pages for any options required by your brand of Unix: Sun wants `ifconfig -a`). You should see output similar to the following:

```
server% ifconfig -a
le0: flags=63<UP,BROADCAST,NOTRAILERS,RUNNING >
        inet 192.168.236.11 netmask ffffff00 broadcast 192.168.236.255
lo0: flags=49<&lt>UP,LOOPBACK,RUNNING<&gt>
        inet 127.0.0.1 netmask ff000000
```

One of the interfaces will be loopback (in our examples `lo0`), and the other will be the regular IP interface. The flags should show that the interface is running, and Ethernet interfaces will also say they support broadcasts (PPP interfaces don't). The other places to look for IP addresses are */etc/hosts* files, Windows *HOSTS* files, Windows *LMHOSTS* files, NIS, NIS+ and DNS.

Troubleshooting NetBIOS Names

Historically, SMB protocols have depended on the NetBIOS name system, also called the LAN Manager name system. This was a simple scheme where each machine had a unique 20-character name and broadcast it on the LAN for everyone to know. With TCP/IP, we tend to use names like *client.example.com* stored in */etc/hosts* files, through DNS or WINS.

The usual mapping to domain names such as *server.example.com* simply uses the *server* part as the NetBIOS name and converts it to uppercase. Alas, this doesn't always work, especially if you have a machine with a 21-character name; not everyone uses the same NetBIOS and DNS names. For example, *corpvm1* along with *vm1.corp.com* is not unusual.

A machine with a different NetBIOS name and domain name is confusing when you're troubleshooting; we recommend that you try to avoid this wherever possible. NetBIOS names are discoverable with *smbclient*:

- If you can list shares on your Samba server with *smbclient* and a `-L` option (list shares) of ***short_name_of_server***, the short name is the NetBIOS name.

- If you get "Get_Hostbyname: Unknown host name," there is probably a mismatch. Check in the *smb.conf* file to see if the NetBIOS name is explicitly set.

- Try again, specifying -I and the IP address of the Samba server (e.g., smbclient -L server -I 192.168.236.86). This overrides the name lookup and forces the packets to go to the IP address. If this works, there was a mismatch.

- Try with -I and the full domain name of the server (e.g., smbclient -L server -I server.example.com). This tests the lookup of the domain name, using whatever scheme the Samba server uses (e.g., DNS). If it fails, you have a name service problem. You should reread the section "Troubleshooting Name Services" after you finish troubleshooting the NetBIOS names.

- Try with -n (NetBIOS name) and the name you expect to work (e.g., smbclient -n server -L server-12) but without overriding the IP address through -I. If this works, the name you specified with -n is the actual NetBIOS name of the server. If you receive "Get-Hostbyname: Unknown host MARY," it's not the right server yet.

- If nothing is working so far, repeat the tests specifying -U *username* and -W *workgroup*, with the username and workgroup in uppercase, to make sure you're not being derailed by a user or workgroup mismatch.

- If nothing works still and you had evidence of a name service problem, troubleshoot name service in the section "Troubleshooting Name Services," and then return to NetBIOS name service.

Extra Resources

At some point during your Samba career, you will want to turn to online or printed resources for news, updates, and aid.

Documentation and FAQs

It's okay to read the documentation. Really. Nobody can see you, and we won't tell. In fact, Samba ships with a large set of documentation files, and it is well worth the effort to at least browse through them, either in the distribution directory on your computer under */docs*, or online at the Samba web site: *http://samba. anu.edu.au/samba/*. The most current FAQ list, bug information, and distribution locations are located at the web site, with links to all of the Samba manual pages and HOW-TOs.

Samba Newsgroups

Usenet newsgroups have always been a great place to get advice on just about any topic. In the past few years, though, this vast pool of knowledge has developed something that has made it into an invaluable resource: a memory. Archival and search sites such as DejaNews (*http://www.dejanews.com*) have made sifting through years of valuable solutions on a topic as simple as a few mouse clicks.

The primary newsgroup for Samba is *comp.protocols.smb*. This should always be your first stop when there's a problem. More often than not, spending five minutes researching an error here will save hours of frustration while trying to debug something yourself.

When searching a newsgroup, try to be as specific as possible, but not too wordy. Searching on actual error messages is best. If you don't find an answer immediately in the newsgroup, resist the temptation to post a request for help until you've done a bit more work on the problem. You may find that the answer is in a FAQ or one of the many documentation files that ships with Samba, or a solution might become evident when you run one of Samba's diagnostic tools. If nothing works, post a request in *comp.protocols.smb*, and be as specific as possible about what you have tried and what you are seeing. Include any error messages that appear. It may be several days before you receive help, so be patient and keep trying things while you wait.

Once you post a request for help, keep poking at the problem yourself. Most of us have had the experience of posting a Usenet article containing hundreds of lines of intricate detail, only to solve the problem an hour later after the article has blazed its way across several continents. The rule of thumb goes something like this: the more folks who have read your request, the simpler the solution. Usually this means that once everyone in the Unix community has seen your article, the solution will be something simple like, "Plug the computer into the wall socket."

Samba Mailing Lists

The following are mailing lists for support with Samba. See the Samba homepage, *http://www.samba.org/* for information on subscribing and unsubscribing to these mailing lists:

samba-binaries@samba.org
> This mailing list has information on precompiled binaries for the Samba platform.

samba-bugs@samba.org
> This mailing list is the place to report suspected bugs in Samba.

samba-ntdom@samba.org
> This mailing list has information on support for domains (particularly Windows NT) with the Samba product.

samba-technical@samba.org
> This mailing list maintains debate about where the future of Samba is headed.

samba@samba.org

> This is the primary Samba mailing list that contains general questions and HOW-TO information on Samba.

http://kt.linuxcare.com/KC/samba/

> This is an edited commentary on the Samba development lists, much like the Linux "Kernel Traffic" site. Reading this site is an easy way to keep current with Samba changes.

Samba Discussion Archives

There is a search service for the primary Samba mailing list. At the time this book was written, it was listed under "searchable" in the Sources paragraph on the first page of the Samba site and its mirrors, *http://samba.anu.edu.au/listproc/ghindex. html*.

Further Reading

Craig Hunt; *TCP/IP Network Administration, 2nd Edition.* Sebastopol, CA: O'Reilly and Associates, 1997 (ISBN 1-56592-322-7).

Hunt, Craig, and Robert Bruce Thompson; *Windows NT TCP/IP Network Administration.* Sebastopol, CA: O'Reilly and Associates, 1998 (*ISBN* 1-56592-377-4).

Albitz, Paul, and Cricket Liu; *DNS and Bind, 3rd Edition.* Sebastopol, CA: O'Reilly & Associates, 1998 (ISBN 1-56592-512-2).

Stern, Hal; *Managing NFS and NIS.* Sebastopol, CA: O'Reilly & Associates, 1991 (ISBN 0-937175-75-7).

A

Configuring Samba with SSL

This appendix describes how to set up Samba to use secure connections between the Samba server and its clients. The protocol used here is Netscape's Secure Sockets Layer (SSL). For this example, we will establish a secure connection between a Samba server and a Windows NT workstation.

Before we begin, we will assume that you are familiar with the fundamentals of public-key cryptography and X.509 certificates. If not, we highly recommend Bruce Schneier's *Applied Cryptography, 2nd Edition* (Wiley) as the premiere source for learning the many secret faces of cryptography.

 If you would like more information on Samba and SSL, be sure to look at the document *SSLeay.txt* in the *docs/textdocs* directory of the Samba distribution, which is the basis for this appendix.

About Certificates

Here are a few quick questions and answers from the *SSLeay.txt* file in the Samba documentation, regarding the benefits of SSL and certificates. This text was written by Christian Starkjohann for the Samba projects.

What is a Certificate?

A certifcate is issued by an issuer, usually a *Certification Authority* (CA), who confirms something by issuing the certificate. The subject of this confirmation depends on the CA's policy. CAs for secure web servers (used for shopping malls, etc.) usually attest only that the given public key belongs the given domain name. Company-wide CAs might attest that you are an employee of the company, that you have permissions to use a server, and so on.

What is an X.509 certificate, technically?

Technically, the certificate is a block of data signed by the certificate issuer (the CA). The relevant fields are:

- Unique identifier (name) of the certificate issuer
- Time range during which the certificate is valid
- Unique identifier (name) of the certified object
- Public key of the certified object
- The issuer's signature over all the above

If this certificate is to be verified, the verifier must have a table of the names and public keys of trusted CAs. For simplicity, these tables should list certificates issued by the respective CAs for themselves (self-signed certificates).

What are the implications of this certificate structure?

Four implications follow:

- Because the certificate contains the subjects's public key, the certificate and the private key together are all that is needed to encrypt and decrypt.
- To verify certificates, you need the certificates of all CAs you trust.
- The simplest form of a dummy-certificate is one that is signed by the subject.
- A CA is needed. The client can't simply issue local certificates for servers it trusts because the server determines which certificate it presents.

Requirements

To set up SSL connections, you will need to download two programs in addition to Samba:

SSLeay

> Eric Young's implementation of the Secure Socket's Layer (SSL) protocol as a series of Unix programming libraries

SSL Proxy

> A freeware SSL application from Objective Development, which can be used to proxy a secure link on Unix or Windows NT platforms

These two products assist with the server and client side of the encrypted SSL connection. The SSLeay libraries are compiled and installed directly on the Unix system. SSL Proxy, on the other hand, can be downloaded and compiled (or downloaded in binary format) and located on the client side. If you intend to have a Windows NT client or a Samba client on the other end of the SSL connection, you will not require a special setup.

SSL Proxy, however, does not work on Windows 95/98 machines. Therefore, if you want to have a secure connection between a Samba server and Windows 95/98 client, you will need to place either a Unix server or a Windows NT machine on the same subnet with the Windows 9x clients and route all network connections through the SSL-Proxy-enabled machine. See Figure A-1.

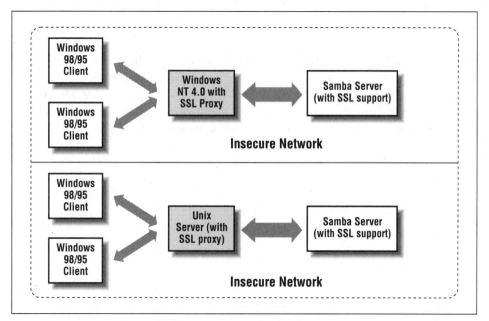

Figure A-1. Two possible ways of proxying Windows 95/98 clients

For the purposes of this chapter, we will create a simple SSL connection between the Samba server and a Windows NT client. This configuration can be used to set up more complex networks at the administrator's discretion.

Installing SSLeay

Samba uses the SSLeay package, written by Eric Young, to provide Secure Sockets Layer support on the server side. Because of U.S. export law, however, the SSLeay package cannot be shipped with Samba distributions that are based in the United States. For that reason, the Samba creators decided to leave it as a separate package entirely. You can download the SSLeay distribution from any of the following sites:

- *ftp://ftp.psy.uq.oz.au/pub/Crypto/SSL/*
- *ftp://ftp.uni-mainz.de/pub/internet/security/ssl*
- *ftp://ftp.cert.dfn.de/pub/tools/crypt/sslapps*
- *ftp://ftp.funet.fi/pub/crypt/mirrors/ftp.psy.uq.oz.au*
- *ftp://ftp.sunet.se/ftp/pub/security/tools/crypt/ssleay*

The latest version as of this printing is 0.9.0b. Download it to the same server as the Samba distribution, then uncompress and untar it. You should be left with a directory entitled *SSLeay-0.9.0b*. After changing to that directory, you will need to configure and build the SSL encryption package in the same way that you did with Samba.

SSLeay uses a Perl-based *configure* script. This script modifies the Makefile that constructs the utilities and libraries of the SSLeay package. However, the default script is hardcoded to find Perl at */usr/local/bin/perl*. You may need to change the *configure* script to point to the location of the Perl executable file on your Unix system. For example, you can type the following to locate the Perl executable:

```
# which perl
/usr/bin/perl
```

Then modify the first line of the *configure* script to force it to use the correct Perl executable. For example, on our Red Hat Linux system:

```
#!/usr/bin/perl
#
# see PROBLEMS for instructions on what sort of things to do
# when tracking a bug -tjh
...
```

After that, you need to run the *configure* script by specifying a target platform for the distribution. This target platform can be any of the following:

BC-16	BC-32	FreeBSD	NetBSD-m86
NetBSD-sparc	NetBSD-x86	SINIX-N	VC-MSDOS
VC-NT	VC-W31-16	VC-W31-32	VC-WIN16
VC-WIN32	aix-cc	aix-gcc	alpha-cc
alpha-gcc	alpha400-cc	cc	cray-t90-cc
debug	debug-irix-cc	debug-linux-elf	dgux-R3-gcc
dgux-R4-gcc	dgux-R4-x86-gcc	dist	gcc
hpux-cc	hpux-gcc	hpux-kr-cc	irix-cc
irix-gcc	linux-aout	linux-elf	ncr-scde
nextstep	purify	sco5-cc	solaris-sparc-cc
solaris-sparc-gcc	solaris-sparc-sc4	solaris-usparc-sc4	solaris-x86-gcc
sunos-cc	sunos-gcc	unixware-2.0	unixware

For our system, we would enter the following:

```
# ./Configure linux-elf
CC              =gcc
CFLAG           =-DL_ENDIAN -DTERMIO -DBN_ASM -O3 -fomit-frame-pointer
EX_LIBS         =
BN_MULW         =asm/bn86-elf.o
DES_ENC         =asm/dx86-elf.o asm/yx86-elf.o
BF_ENC          =asm/bx86-elf.o
CAST_ENC        =asm/cx86-elf.o
RC4_ENC         =asm/rx86-elf.o
RC5_ENC         =asm/r586-elf.o
MD5_OBJ_ASM     =asm/mx86-elf.o
SHA1_OBJ_ASM    =asm/sx86-elf.o
RMD160_OBJ_ASM=asm/rm86-elf.o
THIRTY_TWO_BIT mode
DES_PTR used
DES_RISC1 used
DES_UNROLL used
BN_LLONG mode
RC4_INDEX mode
```

After the package has been configured, you can build it by typing **make**. If the build did not successfully complete, consult the documentation that comes with the distribution or the FAQ at *http://www.cryptsoft.com/ssleay/* for more information on what may have happened. If the build did complete, type **make install** to install the libraries on the system. Note that the makefile installs the package in */usr/local/ssl* by default. If you decide to install it in another directory, remember the directory when configuring Samba to use SSL.

Configuring SSLeay for Your System

The first thing you need to do is to set the **PATH** environment variable on your system to include the */bin* directory of the SSL distribution. This can be done with the following statement:

```
PATH=$PATH:/usr/local/ssl/bin
```

That's the easy part. Following that, you will need to create a random series of characters that will be used to prime SSLeay's random number generator. The random number generator will be used to create key pairs for both the clients and the server. You can create this random series by filling a text file of a long series of random characters. For example, you can use your favorite editor to create a text file with random characters, or use this command and enter arbitrary characters at the standard input:

```
cat >/tmp/private.txt
```

The Samba documentation recommends that you type characters for longer than a minute before interrupting the input stream by hitting Control-D. Try not to type only the characters that are under your fingers on the keyboard; throw in some symbols and numbers as well. Once you've completed the random file, you can prime the random number generator with the following command:

```
# ssleay genrsa -rand /tmp/private.txt >/dev/null
2451 semi-random bytes loaded
Generating RSA private key, 512 bit long modulus
..+++++
...............................+++++
e is 65537 (0x10001)
```

You can safely ignore the output of this command. After it has completed, remove the series of characters used to create the key because this could be used to recreate any private keys that were generated from this random number generator:

```
rm -f /tmp/private.txt
```

The result of this command is the hidden file *.rnd*, which is stored in your home directory. SSLeay will use this file when creating key pairs in the future.

Configuring Samba to use SSL

At this point, you can compile Samba to use SSL. Recall that in Chapter 2, *Installing Samba on a Unix System*, we said you have to first run the configure script, which initializes the makefile, before you compile Samba. In order to use SSL with Samba, you will need to reconfigure the makefile:

```
./configure --with-ssl
```

After that, you can compile Samba with the following commands:

```
# make clean
# make all
```

If you encounter an error that says the *smbd* executable is missing the file *ssl.h*, you probably didn't install SSLeay in the default directory. Use the configure option `--with-sslinc` to point to the base directory of the SSL distribution—in this case, the directory that contains *include/ssl.h*.

On the other hand, if you have a clean compile, you're ready to move on to the next step: creating certificates.

Becoming a Certificate Authority

The SSL protocol requires the use of X.509 certificates in the protocol handshake to ensure that either one or both parties involved in the communication are indeed who they say they are. Certificates in real life, such as those use for SSL connections on public web sites, can cost in the arena of $300 a year. This is because the certificate must have a digital signature placed on it by a *certificate authority*. A certificate authority is an entity that vouches for the authenticity of a digital certificate by signing it with its own private key. This way, anyone who wishes to check the authenticity of the certificate can simply use the certificate authority's public key to check the signature.

You are allowed to use a public certificate authority with SSLeay. However, you don't have to. Instead, SSLeay will allow you to declare yourself a trusted certificate authority—specifying which clients you choose to trust and which clients you do not. In order to do this, you will need to perform several tasks with the SSLeay distribution.

The first thing you need to do is specify a secure location where the certificates of the clients and potentially the server will be stored. We have chosen */etc/certificates* as our default. Execute the following commands as **root**:

```
# cd /etc
# mkdir certificates
# chmod 700 certificates
```

Note that we shut out all access to users other than **root** for this directory. This is very important.

Next, you need to set up the SSLeay scripts and configuration files to use the certificates stored in this directory. In order to do this, first modify the *CA.sh* script located at */usr/local/ssl/bin/CA.sh* to specify the location of the directory you just created. Find the line that contains the following entry:

```
CATOP=./demoCA
```

Then change it to:

```
CATOP=/etc/certificates
```

Next, you need to modify the */usr/local/ssl/lib/ssleay.cnf* file to specify the same directory. Find the entry:

```
[ CA_default ]
dir     = ./demoCA          # Where everything is kept
```

Then change it to:

```
[ CA_default ]
dir     = /etc/certificates  # Where everything is kept
```

Next, run the certificate authority setup script, *CA.sh*, in order to create the certificates. Be sure to do this as the same user that you used to prime the random number generator above:

```
/usr/local/ssl/bin/CA.sh -newca
mkdir: cannot make directory '/etc/certificates': File exists
CA certificate filename (or enter to create)
```

Press the Enter key to create a certificate for the CA. You should then see:

```
Making CA certificate ...
Using configuration from /usr/local/ssl/lib/ssleay.cnf
Generating a 1024 bit RSA private key
...........................+++++
....................+++++
writing new private key to /etc/certificates/private/cakey.pem
Enter PEM pass phrase:
```

Enter a new pass phrase for your certificate. You will need to enter it twice correctly before SSLeay will accept it:

```
Enter PEM pass phrase:
Verifying password - Enter PEM pass phrase:
```

Be sure to remember this pass phrase. You will need it to sign the client certificates in the future. Once SSLeay has accepted the pass phrase, it will continue on with a series of questions for each of the fields in the X509 certificate:

```
You are about to be asked to enter information that will be
incorporated into your certificate request.
What you are about to enter is what is called a Distinguished
Name or a DN.
There are quite a few fields but you can leave some blank
For some fields there will be a default value,
If you enter '.', the field will be left blank.
```

Fill out the remainder of the fields with information about your organization. For example, our certificate looks like this:

```
Country Name (2 letter code) [AU]:US
State or Province Name (full name) [Some-State]:California
Locality Name (eg, city) []:Sebastopol
Organization Name (eg, company) []:O'Reilly
Organizational Unit Name (eg, section) []:Books
Common Name (eg, YOUR name) []:John Doe
Email Address []:doe@ora.com
```

After that, SSLeay will be configured as a certificate authority and can be used to sign certificates for client machines that will be connecting to the Samba server.

Creating Certificates for Clients

It's simple to create a certificate for a client machine. First, you need to generate a public/private key pair for each entity, create a certificate request file, and then use *SSLeay* to sign the file as a trusted authority.

For our example client **phoenix**, this boils down to three SSLeay commands. The first generates a key pair for the client and places it in the file *phoenix.key*. The private key will be encrypted, in this case using triple DES. Enter a pass phrase when requested below—you'll need it for the next step:

```
# ssleay genrsa -des3 1024 >phoenix.key
1112 semi-random bytes loaded
Generating RSA private key, 1024 bit long modulus
........................................+++++
.............+++++
e is 65537 (0x10001)
Enter PEM pass phrase:
Verifying password - Enter PEM pass phrase:
```

After that command has completed, type in the following command:

```
# ssleay req -new -key phoenix.key -out phoenix-csr
Enter PEM pass phrase:
```

Enter the pass phrase for the client certificate you just created (not the certificate authority). At this point, you will need to answer the questionnaire again, this time for the client machine. In addition, you must type in a challenge password and an optional company name—those do not matter here. When the command completes, you will have a certificate request in the file *phoenix-csr*.

Then, you must sign the certificate request as the trusted certificate authority. Type in the following command:

```
# ssleay ca -days 1000 -inflies phoenix-csr >phoenix.pem
```

This command will prompt you to enter the PEM pass phrase of the *certificate authority*. Be sure that you do not enter the PEM pass phrase of the client certificate that you just created. After entering the correct pass phrase, you should see the following:

```
Check that the request matches the signature
Signature ok
The Subjects Distinguished Name is as follows:
...
```

This will be followed by the information that you just entered for the client certificate. If there is an error in the fields, the program will notify you. On the other hand, if everything is fine, SSLeay will confirm that it should sign the certificate and commit it to the database. This adds a record of the certificate to the */etc/certificates/newcerts* directory.

The operative files at the end of this exercise are the *phoenix.key* and *phoenix.pem* files, which reside in the current directory. These files will be passed off to the client with whom the SSL-enabled Samba server will interact, and will be used by SSL Proxy.

Configuring the Samba Server

The next step is to modify the Samba configuration file to include the following setup options. These options assume that you created the certificates directory for the certificate authority at */etc/certificates*:

```
[global]
    ssl = yes
    ssl server cert = /etc/certificates/cacert.pem
    ssl server key = /etc/certificates/private/cakey.pem
    ssl CA certDir = /etc/certificates
```

At this point, you will need to kill the Samba daemons and restart them manually:

```
# nmbd -D
# smbd -D
Enter PEM pass phrase:
```

You will need to enter the PEM pass phrase of the certificate authority to start up the Samba daemons. Note that this may present a problem in terms of starting the program using ordinary means. However, you can get around this using advanced scripting languages, such as Expect or Python.

Testing with smbclient

A good way to test whether Samba is working properly is to use the *smbclient* program. On the Samba server, enter the following command, substituting the appropriate share and user for a connection:

```
# smbclient //hydra/data -U tom
```

You should see several debugging statements followed by a line indicating the negotiated cipher, such as:

```
SSL: negotiated cipher: DES-CBC3-SHA
```

After that, you can enter your password and connect to the share normally. If this works, you can be sure that Samba is correctly supporting SSL connections. Now, on to the client setup.

Setting Up SSL Proxy

The SSL Proxy program is available as a standalone binary or as source code. You can download it from *http://obdev.at/Products/sslproxy.html*.

Once it is downloaded, you can configure and compile it like Samba. We will configure it on a Windows NT system. However, setting it up for a Unix system involves a nearly identical series of steps. Be sure that you are the superuser (administrator) for the next series of steps.

If you downloaded the binary for Windows NT, you should have the following files in a directory:

- *cygwinb19.dll*
- *README.TXT*
- *sslproxy.exe*
- *dummyCert.pem*

The only one that you will be interested in is the SSL Proxy executable. Copy over the *phoenix.pem* and *phoenix.key* files that you generated earlier for the client to the same directory as the SSL proxy executable. Make sure that the directory is secure from the prying eyes of other users.

The next step is to ensure that the Windows NT machine can resolve the NetBIOS name of the Samba server. This means that you should either have a WINS server up and running (the Samba server can perform this task with the `wins support = yes` option) or have it listed in the appropriate *hosts* file of the system. See Chapter 7, *Printing and Name Resolution*, for more information on WINS server.*

Finally, start up SSL Proxy with the following command. Here, we assume that `hydra` is the name of the Samba server:

```
# C:\SSLProxy>sslproxy -l 139 -R hydra -r 139 -n -c phoenix.pem -k phoenix.key
```

This tells SSL Proxy to listen for connections to port 139 and relay those requests to port 139 on the NetBIOS machine `hydra`. It also instructs SSL Proxy to use the *phoenix.pem* and *phoenix.key* files to generate the certificate and keys necessary to initiate the SSL connection. SSL Proxy responds with:

```
Enter PEM pass phrase:
```

Enter the PEM pass phrase of the client keypair that you generated, *not* the certificate authority. You should then see the following output:

```
SSL: No verify locations, trying default
proxy ready, listening for connections
```

That should take care of the client. You can place this command in a startup sequence on either Unix or Windows NT if you want this functionality available at all times. Be sure to set any clients you have connecting to the NT server (including the NT server itself) to point to this server instead of the Samba server.

After you've completed setting this up, try to connect using clients that proxy through the NT server. You should find that it works almost transparently.

---

* If you are running SSL Proxy on a Unix server, you should ensure that the DNS name of the Samba server can be resolved.

SSL Configuration Options

Table A-1 summarizes the configuration options introduced in the previous section for using SSL. Note that all of these options are global in scope; in other words, they must appear in the [global] section of the configuration file.

Table A-1. SSL Configuration Options

Option	Parameters	Function	Default	Scope
ssl	boolean	Indicates whether SSL mode is enabled with Samba.	no	Global
ssl hosts	string (list of addresses)	Specifies a list of hosts that must always connect using SSL.	None	Global
ssl hosts resign	string (list of addresses)	Specifies a list of hosts that never connect using SS.	None	Global
ssl CA certDir	string (fully-qualified pathname)	Specifies the directory where the certificates are stored.	None	Global
ssl CA certFile	string (fully-qualified pathname)	Specifies a file that contains all of the certificates for Samba.	None	Global
ssl server cert	string (fully-qualified pathname)	Specifies the location of the server's certificate.	None	Global
ssl server key	string (fully-qualified pathname)	Specifies the location of the server's private key.	None	Global
ssl client cert	string (fully-qualified pathname)	Specifies the location of the client's certificate.	None	Global
ssl client key	string (fully-qualified pathname)	Specifies the location of the client's private key.	None	Global
ssl require clientcert	boolean	Indicates whether Samba should require each client to have a certificate.	no	Global
ssl require servercert	boolean	Indicates whether the server itself should have a certificate.	no	Global
ssl ciphers	String	Specifies the cipher suite to use during protocol negotiation.	None	Global
ssl version	ssl2or3, ssl3, or tls1	Specifies the version of SSL to use.	ssl2or3	Global

Table A-1. SSL Configuration Options (continued)

Option	Parameters	Function	Default	Scope
ssl compatibility	boolean	Indicates whether compatibility with other implementations of SSL should be activated.	no	Global

ssl

This global option configures Samba to use SSL for communication between itself and clients. The default value of this option is no. You can reset it as follows:

```
[global]
    ssl = yes
```

Note that in order to use this option, you must have a proxy for Windows 95/98 clients, such as in the model presented earlier in this chapter.

ssl hosts

This option specifies the hosts that will be forced into using SSL. The syntax for specifying hosts and addresses is the same as the hosts allow and the hosts deny configuration options. For example:

```
[global]
    ssl = yes
    ssl hosts = 192.168.220.
```

This example specifies that all hosts that fall into the 192.168.220 subnet must use SSL connections with the client. This type of structure is useful if you know that various connections will be made by a subnet that lies across an untrusted network, such as the Internet. If neither this option nor the ssl hosts resign option has been specified, and ssl is set to yes, Samba will allow only SSL connections from all clients.

ssl hosts resign

This option specifies the hosts that will *not* be forced into SSL mode. The syntax for specifying hosts and addresses is the same as the hosts allow and the hosts deny configuration options. For example:

```
[global]
    ssl = yes
    ssl hosts resign = 160.2.310. 160.2.320.
```

This example specifies that all hosts that fall into the 160.2.310 or 160.2.320 subnets will not use SSL connections with the client. If neither this option nor the ssl hosts option has been specified, and ssl is set to yes, Samba will allow only SSL connections from all clients.

ssl CA certDir

This option specifies the directory containing the certificate authority's certificates that Samba will use to authenticate clients. There must be one file in this directory for each certificate authority, named as specified earlier in this chapter. Any other files in this directory are ignored. For example:

```
[global]
    ssl = yes
    ssl hosts = 192.168.220.
    ssl CA certDir = /usr/local/samba/cert
```

There is no default for this option. You can alternatively use the option `ssl CA certFile` if you wish to place all the certificate authority information in the same file.

ssl CA certFile

This option specifies a file that contains the certificate authority's certificates that Samba will use to authenticate clients. This option differs from `ssl CA certDir` in that there is only one file used for all the certificate authorities. An example of its usage follows:

```
[global]
    ssl = yes
    ssl hosts = 192.168.220.
    ssl CA certFile = /usr/local/samba/cert/certFile
```

There is no default for this option. You can also use the option `ssl CA certDir` if you wish to have a separate file for each certificate authority that Samba trusts.

ssl server cert

This option specifies the location of the server's certificate. This option is mandatory; the server must have a certificate in order to use SSL. For example:

```
[global]
    ssl = yes
    ssl hosts = 192.168.220.
    ssl CA certFile = /usr/local/samba/cert/certFile
    ssl server cert = /usr/local/samba/private/server.pem
```

There is no default for this option. Note that the certificate may contain the private key for the server.

ssl server key

This option specifies the location of the server's private key. You should ensure that the location of the file cannot be accessed by anyone other than `root`. For example:

```
[global]
    ssl = yes
    ssl hosts = 192.168.220.
    ssl CA certFile = /usr/local/samba/cert/certFile
    ssl server key = /usr/local/samba/private/samba.pem
```

There is no default for this option. Note that the private key may be contained in the certificate for the server.

ssl client cert

This option specifies the location of the client's certificate. The certificate may be requested by the Samba server with the `ssl require clientcert` option; the certificate is also used by *smbclient.* For example:

```
[global]
    ssl = yes
    ssl hosts = 192.168.220.
    ssl CA certFile = /usr/local/samba/cert/certFile
    ssl server cert = /usr/local/ssl/private/server.pem
    ssl client cert= /usr/local/ssl/private/clientcert.pem
```

There is no default for this option.

ssl client key

This option specifies the location of the client's private key. You should ensure that the location of the file cannot be accessed by anyone other than **root**. For example:

```
[global]
    ssl = yes
    ssl hosts = 192.168.220.
    ssl CA certDir = /usr/local/samba/cert/
    ssl server key = /usr/local/ssl/private/samba.pem
    ssl client key = /usr/local/ssl/private/clients.pem
```

There is no default for this option. This option is only needed if the client has a certificate.

ssl require clientcert

This option specifies whether the client is required to have a certificate. The certificates listed with either the `ssl CA certDir` or the `ssl CA certFile` will be searched to confirm that the client has a valid certificate and is authorized to connect to the Samba server. The value of this option is a simple boolean. For example:

```
[global]
    ssl = yes
    ssl hosts = 192.168.220.
    ssl CA certFile = /usr/local/samba/cert/certFile
```

```
ssl require clientcert = yes
```

We recommend that you require certificates from all clients that could be connecting to the Samba server. The default value for this option is **no**.

ssl require servercert

This option specifies whether the server is required to have a certificate. Again, this will be used by the *smbclient* program. The value of this option is a simple boolean. For example:

```
[global]
    ssl = yes
    ssl hosts = 192.168.220.
    ssl CA certFile = /usr/local/samba/cert/certFile
    ssl require clientcert = yes
    ssl require servercert = yes
```

Although we recommend that you require certificates from all clients that could be connecting to the Samba server, a server certificate is not required. It is, however, recommended. The default value for this option is **no**.

ssl ciphers

This option sets the ciphers on which SSL will decide during the negotiation phase of the SSL connection. Samba can use any of the following ciphers:

```
DEFAULT
DES-CFB-M1
NULL-MD5
RC4-MD5
EXP-RC4-MD5
RC2-CBC-MD5
EXP-RC2-CBC-MD5
IDEA-CBC-MD5
DES-CBC-MD5
DES-CBC-SHA
DES-CBC3-MD5
DES-CBC3-SHA
RC4-64-MD5
NULL
```

It is best not to set this option unless you are familiar with the SSL protocol and want to mandate a specific cipher suite.

ssl version

This global option specifies the version of SSL that Samba will use when handling encrypted connections. The default value is **ssl2or3**, which specifies that either version 2 or 3 of the SSL protocol can be used, depending on which version is negotiated in the handshake between the server and the client. However, if you want Samba to use only a specific version of the protocol, you can specify the following:

```
[global]
    ssl version = ssl3
```

Again, it is best not to set this option unless you are familiar with the SSL protocol and want to mandate a specific version.

ssl compatibility

This global option specifies whether Samba should be configured to use other versions of SSL. However, because no other versions exist at this writing, the issue is moot and the variable should always be left at the default.

B

Samba Performance Tuning

This appendix discusses various ways of performance tuning and system sizing with Samba. *Performance tuning* is the art of finding bottlenecks and adjusting to eliminate them. *Sizing* is the practice of eliminating bottlenecks by spending money to avoid having them in the first place. Normally, you won't have to worry about either with Samba. On a completely untuned server, Samba will happily support a small community of users. However, on a properly tuned server, Samba will support at least twice as many users. This chapter is devoted to outlining various performance-tuning and sizing techniques that you can use if you want to stretch your Samba server to the limit.

A Simple Benchmark

How do you know if you're getting reasonable performance? A simple benchmark is to compare Samba with FTP. Table B-1 shows the throughput, in kilobytes per second, of a pair of servers: a medium-size Sun SPARC Ultra and a small Linux Pentium server. Numbers are reported in kilobytes per second (KB/s).

Table B-1. Sample Benchmark Benchmarks

Command	FTP	Untuned Samba	Tuned Samba
Sparc get	1014.5	645.3	866.7
Sparc put	379.8	386.1	329.5
Pentium get	973.27	N/A	725
Pentium put	1014.5	N/A	1100

If you run the same tests on your server, you probably won't see the same numbers. However, you *should* see similar ratios of Samba to FTP, probably in the range of 68 to 80 percent. It's not a good idea to base *all* of Samba's throughput against FTP. The golden rule to remember is this: if Samba is much slower than FTP, it's time to tune it.

You might think that an equivalent test would be to compare Samba to NFS. In reality, however, it's much less useful to compare their speeds. Depending entirely on whose version of NFS you have and how well it's tuned, Samba can be slower or faster than NFS. We usually find that Samba is faster, but watch out; NFS uses a different algorithm from Samba, so tuning options that are optimal for NFS may be detrimental for Samba. If you run Samba on a well-tuned NFS server, Samba may perform rather badly.

A more popular benchmark is Ziff-Davis' *NetBench,* a simulation of many users on client machines running word processors and accessing data on the SMB server. It's not a prefect measure (each NetBench client does about ten times the work of a normal user on our site), but it is a fair comparison of similar servers. In tests performed by Jeremy Allison in November 1998, Samba 2.0 on a SGI multiprocessor outperformed NT Server 4.0 (Patch Level 2) on an equivalent high-end Compaq. This was confirmed and strengthened by a Sm@rt Reseller test of NT and Linux on identical hardware in February 1999.

In April 1999, the Mindcraft test lab released a report about a test showing that Samba on a four-processor Linux machine was significantly slower than native file serving on the same machine running Windows NT. While the original report was slammed by the Open Source community because it was commissioned by Microsoft and tuned the systems to favor Windows NT, a subsequent test was fairer and generally admitted to reveal some areas where Linux needed to improve its performance, especially on multiprocessors. Little was said about Samba itself. Samba is known to scale well on multiprocessors, and exceeds 440MB/s on a four-processor SGI O200, beating Mindcraft's 310MB/s.

Relative performance will probably change as NT and PC hardware get faster, of course, but Samba is improving as well. For example, Samba 1.9.18 was faster only with more than 35 clients. Samba 2.0, however, is faster regardless of the number of clients. In short, Samba is very competitive with the best networking software in the industry, and is only getting better.

As we went to press, Andrew Tridgell released the alpha-test version suite of benchmarking programs for Samba and SMB networks. Expect even more work on performance from the Samba team in the future.

Samba Tuning

That being said, let's discuss how you can take an already fast networking package and make it even faster.

Benchmarking

Benchmarking is an arcane and somewhat black art, but the level of expertise needed for simple performance tuning is fairly low. Since the Samba server's goal in life is to transfer files, we will examine only throughput, not response time to particular events, under the benchmarking microscope. After all, it's relatively easy to measure file transfer speed, and Samba doesn't suffer too badly from response-time problems that would require more sophisticated techniques.

Our basic strategy for this work will be:

- Find a reasonably-sized file to copy and a program that reports on copy speeds, such as *smbclient*.

- Find a quiet (or typical) time to do the test.

- Pre-run each test a few times to preload buffers.

- Run tests several times and watch for unusual results.

- Record each run in detail.

- Compare the average of the valid runs to expected values.

After establishing a baseline using this method, we can adjust a single parameter and do the measurements all over again. An empty table for your tests is provided at the end of this chapter.

Things to Tweak

There are literally thousands of Samba setting combinations that you can use in search of that perfect server. Those of us with lives outside of system administration, however, can narrow down the number of options to those listed in this section, which are the most likely to affect overall throughput. They are presented roughly in order of impact.

Log level

This is an obvious one. Increasing the logging level (`log level` or `debug level` configuration options) is a good way to debug a problem, unless you happen to be searching for a performance problem! As mentioned in Chapter 4, *Disk Shares*, Samba produces a ton of debugging messages at level 3 and above, and writing them to disk or syslog is a slow operation. In our *smbclient/ftp* tests, raising the log level from 0 to 3 cut the untuned `get speed` from 645.3 to 622.2KB/s, or roughly 5 percent. Higher log levels were even worse.

Socket options

The next thing to look at are the `socket options` configuration options. These are really host system tuning options, but they're set on a per-connection basis, and can be reset by Samba on the sockets it employs by adding `socket options = option` to the `[global]` section of your *smb.conf* file. Not all of these options are supported by all vendors; check your vendor's manual pages on *setsockopt*(1) or *socket*(5) for details.

The main options are:

`TCP_NODELAY`

Have the server send as many packets as necessary to keep delay low. This is used on telnet connections to give good response time, and is used—somewhat counter-intuitively—to get good speed even when doing small requests or when acknowledgments are delayed (as seems to occur with Microsoft TCP/IP). This is worth a 30–50 percent speedup by itself. Incidentally, in Samba 2.0.4, `socket options = TCP_NODELAY` became the default value for that option.

`IPTOS_LOWDELAY`

This is another option that trades off throughput for lower delay, but which affects routers and other systems, not the server. All the IPTOS options are new; they're not supported by all operating systems and routers. If they are supported, set `IPTOS_LOWDELAY` whenever you set `TCP_NODELAY`.

`SO_SNDBUF` and `SO_RCVBUF`

The send and receive buffers can often be the reset to a value higher than that of the operating system. This yields a marginal increase of speed (until it reaches a point of diminishing returns).

`SO_KEEPALIVE`

This initiates a periodic (four-hour) check to see if the client has disappeared. Expired connections are addressed somewhat better with Samba's `keepalive` and `dead time` options. All three eventually arrange to close dead connections, returning unused memory and process-table entries to the operating system.

There are several other socket options you might look at, (e.g., `SO_SNDLOWAT`), but they vary in availability from vendor to vendor. You probably want to look at *TCP/IP Illustrated* if you're interested in exploring more of these options for performance tuning with Samba.

read raw and write raw

These are important performance configuration options; they enable Samba to use large reads and writes to the network, of up to 64KB in a single SMB request. They also require the largest SMB packet structures, `SMBreadraw` and `SMBwriteraw`, from which the options take their names. Note that this is not the same as a Unix *raw read*. This Unix term usually refers to reading disks without using the files system, quite a different sense from the one described here for Samba.

In the past, some client programs failed if you tried to use **read raw**. As far as we know, no client suffers from this problem any more. Read and write raw default to **yes**, and should be left on unless you find you have one of the buggy clients.

Opportunistic locking

Opportunistic locks, or *oplocks*, allow clients to cache files locally, improving performance on the order of 30 percent. This option is now enabled by default. For read-only files, the **fake oplocks** provides the same functionality without actually doing any caching. If you have files that cannot be cached, *oplocks* can be turned off.

Database files should never be cached, nor should any files that are updated both on the server and the client and whose changes must be immediately visible. For these files, the **veto oplock files** option allows you to specify a list of individual files or a pattern containing wildcards to avoid caching. *oplocks* can be turned off on a share-by-share basis if you have large groups of files you don't want cached on clients. See Chapter 5, *Browsing and Advanced Disk Shares*, for more information on opportunistic locks.

IP packet size (MTU)

Networks generally set a limit to the size of an individual transmission or packet This is called the Maximum Segment Size, or if the packet header size is included, the Maximum Transport Unit (MTU). This MTU is not set by Samba, but Samba needs to use a **max xmit** (write size) bigger than the MTU, or throughput will be reduced. This is discussed in further detail in the following note. The MTU is normally preset to 1500 bytes on an Ethernet and 4098 bytes on FDDI. In general, having it too low cuts throughput, and having it too high causes a sudden performance dropoff due to fragmentation and retransmissions.

If you are communicating over a router, some systems will assume the router is a serial link (e.g., a T1) and set the MTU to more or less 536 bytes. Windows 95 makes this mistake, which causes nearby clients to perform well, but clients on the other side of the router to be noticeably slower. If the client makes the opposite error and uses a large MTU on a link which demands a small one, the packets will be broken up into fragments. This slows transfers slightly, and any networking errors will cause multiple fragments to be retransmitted, which slows Samba significantly. Fortunately, you can modify the Windows MTU size to prevent either error.

The TCP receive window

TCP/IP works by breaking down data into small packets that can be transmitted from one machine to another. When each packet is transmitted, it contains a checksum that allows the receiver to check the packet data for potential errors in transmission. Theoretically, when a packet is received and verified, an acknowledgment packet should be sent back to the sender that essentially says, "Everything arrived intact: please continue."

In order to keep things moving, however, TCP accepts a range (window) of packets that allows a sender to keep transmitting without having to wait for an acknowledgment of every single packet. (It can then bundle a group of acknowledgments and transmit them back to the sender at the same time.) In other words, this receive window is the number of bytes that the sender can transmit before it has to stop and wait for a receiver's acknowledgment. Like the MTU, it is automatically set based on the type of connection. Having the window too small causes a lot of unnecessary waiting for acknowledgment messages. Various operating systems set moderate buffer sizes on a per-socket basis to keep one program from hogging all the memory.

The buffer sizes are assigned in bytes, such as `SO_SNDBUF=8192` in the `socket options` line. Thus, an example `socket options` configuration option is:

```
socket options = SO_SNDBUF=8192
```

Normally, one tries to set these socket options higher than the default: 4098 in SunOS 4.1.3 and SVR4, and 8192–16384 in AIX, Solaris, and BSD. 16384 has been suggested as a good starting point: in a non-Samba test mentioned in Stevens' book, it yielded a 40 percent improvement. You'll need to experiment, because performance will fall off again if you set the sizes too high. This is illustrated in Figure B-1, a test done on a particular Linux system.

Setting the socket options `O_SNDBUF` and `SO_RCVBUF` to less than the default is inadvisable. Setting them higher improves performance, up to a network-specific limit. However, once you exceed that limit, performance will abruptly level off.

max xmit

In Samba, the option that is directly related with the MTU and window size is `max xmit`. This option sets the largest block of data Samba will try to write at any one time. It's sometimes known as the *write size*, although that is not the name of the Samba configuration option.

Because the percentage of each block required for overhead falls as the blocks get larger, max xmit is conventionally set as large as possible. It defaults to the

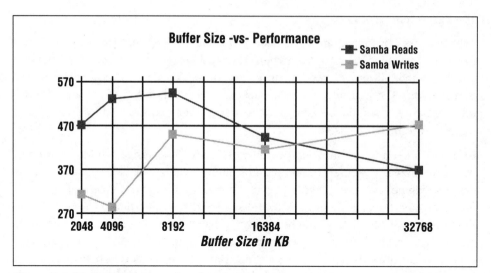

Figure B-1. SO_SNDBUF size and performance

protocol's upper limit, which is 64 kilobytes. The smallest value that doesn't cause significant slowdowns is 2048. If it is set low enough, it will limit the largest packet size that Samba will be able to negotiate. This can be used to simulate a small MTU if you need to test an unreliable network connection. However, such a test should not be used in production for reducing the effective MTU.

read size

If **max xmit** is commonly called the write size, you'd expect **read size** to be the maximum amount of data that Samba would want to read from the client via the network. Actually, it's not. In fact, it's an option to trigger *write ahead*. This means that if Samba gets behind reading from the disk and writing to the network (or vice versa) by the specified amount, it will start overlapping network writes with disk reads (or vice versa).

The read size doesn't have a big performance effect on Unix, unless you set its value quite small. At that point, it causes a detectable slowdown. For this reason, it defaults to 2048 and can't be set lower than 1024.

read prediction

Besides being counterintuitive, this option is also obsolete. It enables Samba to read ahead on files opened read only by the clients. The option is disabled in Samba 2.0 (and late 1.9) Because it interferes with opportunistic locking.

Other Samba Options

The following Samba options will affect performance if they're set incorrectly, much like the debug level. They're mentioned here so you will know what to look out for:

hide files

>Providing a pattern to identify files hidden by the Windows client **hide files** will result in any file matching the pattern being passed to the client with the DOS hidden attribute set. It requires a pattern match per file when listing directories, and slows the server noticeably.

lpq cache time

>If your **lpq** (printer queue contents) command takes a long time to complete, you should increase **lpq cache time** to a value higher than the actual time required for **lpq** to execute, so as to keep Samba from starting a new query when one's already running. The default is 10 seconds, which is reasonable.

strict locking

>Setting the **strict locking** option causes Samba to check for locks on every access, not just when asked to by the client. The option is primarily a bug-avoidance feature, and can prevent ill-behaved DOS and Windows applications from corrupting shared files. However, it is slow and should typically be avoided.

strict sync

>Setting **strict sync** will cause Samba to write each packet to disk and wait for the write to complete whenever the client sets the sync bit in a packet. Windows 98 Explorer sets the bit in all packets transmitted, so if you turn this on, anyone with Windows 98 will think Samba servers are horribly slow.

sync always

>Setting **sync always** causes Samba to flush every write to disk. This is good if your server crashes constantly, but the performance costs are immense. SMB servers normally use oplocks and automatic reconnection to avoid the ill effects of crashes, so setting this option is not normally necessary.

wide links

>Turning off **wide links** prevents Samba from following symbolic links in one file share to files that are not in the share. It is turned on by default, since following links in Unix is not a security problem. Turning it off requires extra processing on every file open. If you do turn off wide links, be sure to turn on **getwd cache** to cache some of the required data.

There is also a `follow symlinks` option that can be turned off to prevent following any symbolic links at all. However, this option does not pose a performance problem.

`getwd cache`

This option caches the path to the current directory, avoiding long tree-walks to discover it. It's a nice performance improvement on a printer server or if you've turned off `wide links`.

Our Recommendations

Here's an *smb.conf* file that incorporates the recommended performance enhancements so far. Comments have been added on the right side.

```
[global]
    log level = 1                          # Default is 0
    socket options = TCP_NODELAY IPTOS_LOWDELAY
    read raw = yes                         # Default
    write raw = yes                        # Default
    oplocks = yes                          # Default
    max xmit = 65535                       # Default
    dead time = 15                         # Default is 0
    getwd cache = yes
    lpq cache = 30
[okplace]
    veto oplock files = this/that/theotherfile
[badplace]
    oplocks = no
```

Sizing Samba Servers

Sizing is a way to prevent bottlenecks before they occur. The preferred way to do this is to know how many requests per second or how many kilobytes per second the clients will need, and ensure that all the components of the server provide at least that many.

The Bottlenecks

The three primary bottlenecks you should worry about are CPU, disk I/O, and the network. For most machines, CPUs are rarely a bottleneck. A single Sun SPARC 10 CPU can start (and complete) between 700 and 800 I/O operations a second, giving approximately 5,600 to 6,400KB/s of throughput when the data averages around 8KBs (a common buffer size). A single Intel Pentium 133 can do less only because of somewhat slower cache and bus interfaces, not due to lack of CPU power. Purpose-designed Pentium servers, like some Compaq servers, will be able to start 700 operations per CPUs, on up to four CPUs.

Too little memory, on the other hand, can easily be a bottleneck; each Samba process will use between 600 and 800KB on Intel Linux, and more on RISC CPUs. Having less will cause an increase in virtual memory paging and therefore a performance hit. On Solaris, where it has been measured, *smbd* will use 2.6 MB for program and shared libraries, plus 768KB for each connected client. *nmbd* occupies 2.1 MB, plus 496KB extra for its (single) auxiliary process.

Hard disks will always bottleneck at a specific number of I/O operations per second: for example, each 7200 RPM SCSI disk is capable of performing 70 operations per second, for a throughput of 560KB/s; a 4800 RPM disk will perform fewer than 50, for a throughput of 360KB/s. A single IDE disk will do still fewer. If the disks are independent, or striped together in a RAID 1 configuration, they will each peak out at 400 to 560KB/s and will scale linearly as you add more. Note that this is true only of RAID 1. RAID levels other than 1 (striping) add extra overhead.

Ethernets (and other networks) are obvious bottleneck: a 10 Mb/s (mega*bits*/second) Ethernet will handle around 1100KB/s (kilo*bytes*/s) using 1500-byte packets A 100 Mb/s Fast Ethernet will bottleneck below 6,500KB/s with the same packet size. FDDI, at 155 Mb/s will top out at approximately 6,250KB/s, but gives good service at even 100 percent load and transmits much larger packets (4KB).

ATM should be much better, but as of the writing of this book it was too new to live up to its potential; it seems to deliver around 7,125 Mb/s using 9KB packets.

Of course, there can be other bottlenecks: more than one IDE disk per controller is not good, as are more than three 3600 SCSI-I disks per slow/narrow controller, or more than three 7200 SCSI-II disks per SCSI-II fast/wide controller. RAID 5 is also slow, as it requires twice as many writes as independent disks or RAID 1.

After the second set of Ethernets and the second disk controller, start worrying about bus bandwidth, especially if you are using ISA/EISA buses.

Reducing Bottlenecks

From the information above we can work out a model that will tell us the maximum capability of a given machine. The data is mostly taken from Brian Wong's *Configuration and Capacity Planning for Solaris Servers*,[*] so there is a slight Sun bias to our examples.

A word of warning: this is not a complete model. Don't assume that this model will predict every bottleneck or even be within 10 percent in its estimates. A model to predict performance instead of one to warn you of bottlenecks would be

---

[*] See Wong. Brian L, *Configuration and Capacity Planning for Solaris Servers*, Englewood Cliffs, NJ (Sun/ Prentice-Hall), 1997, ISBN 0-13-349952-9.

much more complex and would contain rules like "not more than three disks per SCSI chain". (A good book on real models is Raj Jain's *The Art of Computer Systems Performance Analysis.**) With that warning, we present the system in Figure B-2.

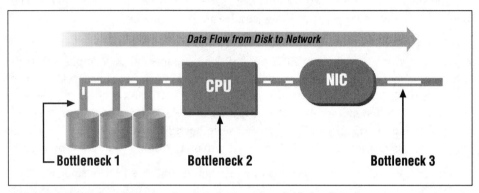

Figure B-2. Data flow through a Samba server, with possible bottlenecks

The flow of data should be obvious. For example, on a read, data flows from the disk, across the bus, through or past the CPU, and to the network interface card (NIC). It is then broken up into packets and sent across the network. Our strategy here is to follow the data through the system and see what bottlenecks will choke it off. Believe it or not, it's rather easy to make a set of tables that list the maximum performance of common disks, CPUs, and network cards on a system. So that's exactly what we're going to do.

Let's take a concrete example: a Linux Pentium 133 MHz machine with a single 7200 RPM data disk, a PCI bus, and a 10-Mb/s Ethernet card. This is a perfectly reasonable server. We start with Table B-2, which describes the hard drive—the first potential bottleneck in the system.

Table B-2. Disk Throughput

Disk RPM	I/O Operations/second	KB/second
7200	70	560
4800	60	480
3600	40	320

Disk throughput is the number of kilobytes of data that a disk can transfer per second. It is computed from the number of 8KB I/O operations per second a disk can perform, which in turn is strongly influenced by disk RPM and bit density. In

---

* See Jain. Raj, *The Art of Computer Systems Performance Analysis*, New York, NY (John Wiley and Sons), 1991, ISBN 0-47-150336-3.

effect, the question is: how much data can pass below the drive heads in one second? With a single 7200 RPM disk, the example server will give us 70 I/O operations per second at roughly 560KB/s.

The second possible bottleneck is the CPU. The data doesn't actually flow through the CPU on any modern machines, so we have to compute throughput somewhat indirectly.

The CPU has to issue I/O requests and handle the interrupts coming back, then transfer the data across the bus to the network card. From much past experimentation, we know that the overhead that dominates the processing is consistently in the filesystem code, so we can ignore the other software being run. We compute the throughput by just multiplying the (measured) number of file I/O operations per second that a CPU can process by the same 8K average request size. This gives us the results shown in Table B-3.

Table B-3. CPU Throughput

CPU	I/O Operations/second	KB/second
Intel Pentium 133	700	5,600
Dual Pentium 133	1,200	9,600
Sun SPARC II	660	5,280
Sun SPARC 10	750	6,000
Sun Ultra 200	2,650	21,200

Now we put the disk and the CPU together: in the Linux example, we have a single 7200 RPM disk, which can give us 560KB/s, and a CPU capable of starting 700 I/O operations, which could give us 5600KB/s. So far, as you would expect, our bottleneck is clearly going to be the hard disk.

The last potential bottleneck is the network. If the network speed is below 100 Mb/s, the bottleneck will be the network speed. After that, the design of the network card is more likely to slow us down. Table B-4 shows us the average throughput of many types of data networks. Although network speed is conventionally measured in bits per second, Table B-4 lists bytes per second to make comparison with the disk and CPU (Table B-2 and Table B-3) easier.

Table B-4. Network Throughput

Network Type	KB/second
ISDN	16
T1	197
Ethernet 10m	1,113
Token ring	1,500

Table B-4. Network Throughput (continued)

Network Type	KB/second
FDDI	6,250
Ethernet 100m	6,500[a]
ATM 155	7,125[a]

[a] These will increase. For example, Crays, Sun Ultras, and DEC/Compaq Alphas already have bettered these figures.

In the running example, we have a bottleneck at 560KB/s due to the disk. Table B-4 shows us that a standard 10 megabit per second Ethernet (1,113KB/s) is far faster than the disk. Therefore, the hard disk is still the limiting factor. (This scenario, by the way, is very common.) Just by looking at the tables, we can predict that small servers won't have CPU problems, and that large ones with multiple CPUs will support striping and multiple Ethernets long before they start running out of CPU power. This, in fact, is exactly what happens.

Practical Examples

An example from *Configuration and Capacity Planning for Solaris Servers* (Wong) shows that a dual-processor SPARCstation 20/712 with four Ethernets and six 2.1 GB disks will spend all its time waiting for the disks to return some data. If it was loaded with disks (Brian Wong suggests as many as 34 of them), it would still be held below 1,200KB/s by the Ethernet cards. To get the performance the machine is capable of, we would need to configure multiple Ethernets, 100 Mbps Fast Ethernet, or 155 Mbps FDDI.

The progression you'd work through to get that conclusion looks something like Table B-5.

Table B-5. Tuning a Medium-Sized Server

Machine	Disk Throughput	CPU Throughput	Network Throughput	Actual Throughput
Dual SPARC 10, 1 disk	560	6000	1,113	560
Add 5 more disks	3,360	6000	1,113	1,113
Add 3 more Ethernets	3,360	6000	4,452	3,360
Change to using a 20-disk array	11,200	6000	4,452	4,452
Use dual 100 Mbps ether	11,200	6000	13,000	11,200

Initially, the bottleneck is the disk with only 560 KB/s of throughput available. Our solution is to add five more disks. This gives us more throughput on the disks than on the Ethernet, so then the Ethernet becomes the problem. Consequently, as we continue to expand, we go back and forth several times between these two. As you add disks, CPUs, and network cards, the bottleneck moves. Essentially, the strategy is to add more equipment to try to avoid each bottleneck until you reach your target performance, or (unfortunately) you either can't add any more or run out of money.

Our experience bears out this kind of calculation; a large SPARC 10 file server that one author maintained was quite capable of saturating an Ethernet plus about a third of an FDDI ring when using two processors. It did nearly as well with a single processor, albeit with a fast operating system and judicious over-optimization.

The same process applies to other brands of purpose-designed servers. We found the same rules applied to DECstation 2100s as to the newest Alphas or Compaqs, old MIPS 3350s and new SGI O2s. In general, a machine offering multi-CPU server configurations will have enough bus bandwidth and CPU power to reliably bottleneck on hard disk I/O when doing file service. As one would hope, considering the cost!

How Many Clients Can Samba Handle?

Well, that depends entirely on how much data each user consumes. A small server with three SCSI-1 disks, which can serve about 960KB/s of data, will support between 36 and 80 clients in an ordinary office environment where they are typically loading, and saving equal-sized spreadsheets or word processing documents (36 clients $\times$ 2.3 transfers/second $\times$ 12k file=1 MB/s).

On the same server in a development environment with programmers running a fairly heavy edit-compile-test cycle, one can easily see requests for 1 MB/s, limiting the server to 25 or fewer clients. To take this a bit further, an imaging system whose clients each require 10 MB/s will perform poorly no matter how big a server is if they're all on a 10 MB/s Ethernet. And so on.

If you don't know how much data an average user consumes, you can size your Samba servers by patterning them after existing NFS, Netware, or LAN Manager servers. You should be especially careful that the new servers have as many disks and disk controllers as the ones you've copied. This technique is appropriately called "punt and hope."

If you know how many clients an existing server can support, you're in *much* better shape. You can analyze the server to see what its maximum capacity is and use that to estimate how much data they must be demanding. For example, if serving home directories to 30 PCs from a PC server with two IDE disks is just too slow, and 25 clients is about right, then you can safely assume you're bottlenecked on

Ethernet I/O (approximately 375KB) rather than disk I/O (up to 640KB). If so, you can then conclude that the clients are demanding 15 (that is, 375/25)KB/s on average.

Supporting a new lab of 75 clients will mean you'll need 1,125KB/s, spread over multiple (preferably three) Ethernets, and a server with at least three 7200 RPM disks and a CPU capable of keeping up. These requirements can be met by a Pentium 133 or above with the bus architecture to drive them all at full speed (e.g., PCI).

A custom-built PC server or a multiprocessor-capable workstation like a Sun Sparc, a DEC/Compaq Alpha, an SGI, or the like, would scale up easier, as would a machine with fast Ethernet, plus a switching hub to drive the client machines on individual 10 MB/s Ethernets.

How to guess

If you have no idea at all what you need, the best thing is to try to guess based on someone else's experience. Each individual client machine can average from less than 1 I/O per second (normal PC or Mac used for sales/accounting) to as much as 4 (fast workstation using large applications). A fast workstation running a compiler can happily average 3-4 MB/s in data transfer requests, and an imaging system can demand even more.

Our recommendation? Spy on someone with a similar configuration and try to estimate their bandwidth requirements from their bottlenecks and the volume of the screams from their users. We also recommend Brian Wong's *Configuration and Capacity Planning for Solaris Servers*. While he uses Sun Solaris foremost in his examples, his bottlenecks are disks and network cards, which are common among all the major vendors. His tables for FTP servers also come very close to what we calculated for Samba servers, and make a good starting point.

Measurement Forms

Table B-6 and Table B-7 are empty tables that you can use for copying and recording data. The bottleneck calculation in the previous example can be done in a spreadsheet, or manually with Table B-8. If Samba is as good as or better than FTP, and if there aren't any individual test runs that are much different from the average, you have a well-configured system. If loopback isn't much faster than anything else, you have a problem with your TCP/IP software. If both FTP and Samba are slow, you probably have a problem with your networking: a faulty Ethernet card will produce this, as will accidentally setting an Ethernet card to half-duplex when it's not connected to a half-duplex hub. Remember that CPU and disk speeds are commonly measured in bytes, network speeds in bits.

We've included columns for both bytes and bits in the tables. In the last column, we compare results to 10 Mb/s because that's the speed of a traditional Ethernet.

Table B-6. Ethernet Interface to Same Host: FTP

Run No	Size in Bytes	Time (sec)	Bytes/sec	Bits/sec	% of 10 Mb/s
1					
2					
3					
4					
5					
Average:					
Deviation:					

Table B-7. Ethernet Interface to Same Host: FTP

Run No	Size in Bytes	Time, sec	Bytes/sec	Bits/sec	% of 10 Mb/s
1					
2					
3					
4					
5					
Average:					
Deviation:					

Table B-8. Bottleneck Calculation Table

CPU	CPU Throughput	Number of Disks	Disk Throughput	Number of Networks	Network Throughput	Total Throughput

In Table B-8:

- CPU throughput = (KB/second from Figure 6-5) × (number of CPUs)
- Disk throughput = (KB/second from Figure 6-4) × (number of disks)
- Network throughput = (KB/second from Figure 6-6) × (number of networks)
- Total throughput = min (Disk, CPU, and Network throughput)

A typical test, in this case for an FTP `get`, would be entered as in Table B-9:

Table B-9. Ethernet Interface to Same Host: FTP

Run No	Size in Bytes	Time, sec	Bytes/sec	Bits/sec	% of 10 Mb/s
1	1812898	2.3	761580		
2		2.3	767820		
3		2.4	747420		
4		2.3	760020		
5		2.3	772700		
Average:		2.32	777310	6218480	62
Deviation:		0.04			

The Sparc example we used earlier would look like Table B-10.

Table B-10. Sparc 20 Example, Redux

CPU	CPU Throughput	Number of Disks	Disk Throughput	Number of Networks	Network Throughput	Total Throughput
2	6,000	1	560	1 10base2	1,113	560
2	6,000	6	3,360	1	1,113	1,113
2	6,000	6	3,360	4 10base2	4,452	3,360
2	6,000	20	11,200	4	4,452	4,452
2	6,000	20	11,200	2 100base2	13,000	11,200

C

Samba Configuration Option Quick Reference

The following pages list each of the Samba configuration options. If an option is applicable only to the global section, "[global]" will appear before its name. Any lists mentioned are space separated, except where noted. A glossary of terms follows the options.

admin users = user list

allowable values: user list   *default:* NULL

List of users who will be granted root permissions on the share by Samba.

allow hosts = host list

allowable values: any   *default:* NULL

Synonym for `hosts allow`. List of machines that may connect to a share.

alternate permissions = boolean

allowable values: YES, NO   *default:* NO

Obsolete. Has no effect in Samba 2. Files will be shown as read-only if the owner can't write them. In Samba 1.9 and earlier, setting this option would set the DOS filesystem read-only attribute on any file the user couldn't read. This in turn required the `delete readonly` option.

[global] announce as = system type

allowable values: NT, Win95, WfW   *default:* NT

Have Samba announce itself as something other than an NT server. Discouraged because it interferes with serving browse lists.

[global] announce version = number.number

allowable values: any   *default:* 4.2

Instructs Samba to announce itself as an older version SMB server. Discouraged.

[global] auto services = share list

allowable values: any shares   *default:* NULL

List of shares that will always appear in browse lists. A synonym is `preload`.

available = boolean

allowable values: YES, NO   *default:* YES

If set to NO, denies access to a share. Doesn't affect browsing.

[global] bind interfaces only = boolean

allowable values: YES, NO   *default:* NO

If set to YES, shares and browsing will be provided only on interfaces in an interfaces list (see `interfaces`). New in Samba 1.9.18. If you set this option to YES, be sure to add 127. 0.0.1 to the interfaces list to allow *smbpasswd* to connect to the local machine to change passwords. This is a convienence option; it does not improve security.

browsable = boolean

allowable values: YES, NO   *default:* YES

Allows a share to be announced in browse lists.

blocking locks = boolean

allowable values: YES, NO   *default:* YES

If YES, honors byte range lock requests with time limits for queuing the request and retrying it until the time period expires. New in Samba 2.0.

[global] browse list = boolean

allowable values: YES, NO   *default:* YES

Turns on/off `browse list` from this server. Avoid changing.

[global] case sensitive = boolean

allowable values: YES, NO   *default:* NO

If YES, uses exactly the case the client supplied when trying to resolve a filename. If NO, matches either upper- or lowercase name. Avoid changing.

[global] case sig names = boolean

allowable values: YES, NO   *default:* NO

Synonym for `case sensitive`.

[global] change notify timeout = number

allowable values: positive number   *default:* 60

Sets the number of seconds between checks when a client asks for notification of changes in a directory. Introduced in Samba 2.0 to limit the performance cost of the checks. Avoid lowering.

character set = name

allowable values: ISO8859-1, ISO8859-2, ISO8859-5, KOI8-R   *default:* NULL

If set, translates from DOS code pages to the Western European (ISO8859-1), Eastern European (ISO8859-2), Russian Cyrillic (ISO8859-5), or Alternate Russian (KOI8-R) character set. The `client code page` must be set to 850.

client code page = name

allowable values: See Table 8-4   *default:* 437 (US MS-DOS)

Sets the DOS code page explicitly, overriding any previous `valid chars` settings. Examples of values are 850 for European, 437 is the US standard, and 932 for Japanese Shift-JIS. Introduced in Samba 1.9.19.

coding system = code

allowable values: euc, cap, hex, hexN, sjis, j8bb, j8bj, jis8, j8bh, j8@b, j8@j, j8@h, j7bb, j7bj, jis7, j7bh, j7@b, j7@j, j7@h, jubb, jubj, junet, jubh, ju@b, ju@j, ju@h   *default:* NULL

Sets the coding system used, notably for Kanji. This is employed for filenames and should correspond to the code page in use. The `client code page` option must be set to 932 (Japanese Shift-JIS). Introduced in Samba 2.0.

comment = text

allowable values: a text string or NULL   *default:* NULL

Sets the comment that appears beside a share in a NET VIEW or the details list of a Microsoft directory window. See also the `server string` configuration option.

[global] config file = pathname

allowable values: Unix pathname   *default:* NULL

Selects an additional Samba configuration file to read instead of the current one. Used to relocate the configuration file, or used with %-variables to select custom configuration files for some users or machines.

copy = section name

allowable values: existing section's name   *default:* NULL

Copies the configuration of a previously seen share into the share where it appears. Used with %-variables to select custom configurations for machines, architectures and users. The copied section must be earlier in the configuration file. Copied options are of lesser priority than those explicitly listed in the section.

create mask = octal value

allowable values: octal permission bits, 0-0777   *default:* 0744

Also called `create mode`. Sets the maximum allowable permissions for new files (e.g., 0755). See also `directory mask`. To require certain permissions to be set, see `force create mask/force directory mask`. This option stopped affecting directories in Samba 1.9.17, and the default value changed in Samba 2.0.

create mode = octal permission bits

allowable values: octal permission bits, 0-0777   *default:* 0744

Synonym for `create mask`.

[global] deadtime = minutes

allowable values: minutes   *default:* 0

The time in minutes before an unused connection will be terminated. Zero means forever. Used to keep clients from tying up server resources forever. If used, clients will have to auto-reconnect after minutes of inactivity. See also `keepalive`.

[global] debug level = number

allowable values: number   *default:* 0

Sets the logging level used. Values of 3 or more slow Samba noticeably. A synonym is `log level`. Recommended value: 1.

[global] debug timestamp = boolean

allowable values: YES, NO   *default:* YES

Timestamps all log messages. Can be turned off when it's not useful (e.g., in debugging). New in Samba 2.0.

[global] default = name

allowable values: share name   *default:* NULL

Also called `default service`. The name of a service (share) to provide if someone requests a service they don't have permission to use or which doesn't exist. As of Samba 1.9.14, the path will be set from the name the client specified, with any "_" characters changed to "/" characters, allowing access to any directory on the Samba server. Use is strongly discouraged.

default case = case

allowable values: LOWER, UPPER   *default:* LOWER

Sets the case in which to store new filenames. LOWER indicates mixed case, UPPER indicates uppercase letters.

[global] default service = share name

allowable values: share name   *default:* NULL

Synonym for `default`.

delete readonly = boolean

allowable values: NO, YES   *default:* NO

Allow delete requests to remove read-only files. This is not allowed in DOS/Windows, but is normal in Unix, which has separate directory permissions. Used with programs like RCS, or with the older `alternate permissions` option.

delete veto files = boolean

allowable values: NO, YES   *default:* NO

Allow delete requests for a directory containing files or subdirectories the user can't see due to the `veto files` option. If set to NO, the directory will not be deleted and will still contain invisible files.

deny hosts = host list

allowable values: host list   *default:* NULL

A synonym is `hosts deny`. Specifies a list of machines from which to refuse connections or shares.

[global] dfree command = command

allowable values: shell command   *default:* varies

A command to run on the server to return disk free space. Not needed unless the OS command does not work properly.

directory = pathname

allowable values: pathname   *default:* NULL

Synonym for `path`. A directory provided by a file share, or used by a printer share. Set automatically in the [`homes`] share to user's home directory, otherwise defaults to */tmp*.

directory mask = octal permission bits

allowable values: octal value from 0 to 0777　　　　　　　*default:* 0755

Also called `directory mode`. Sets the maximum allowable permissions for newly created directories. To require certain permissions be set, see the `force create mask` and `force directory mask` options.

directory mode = octal permission bits

allowable values: octal value from 0 to 0777　　　　　　　*default:* 0755

Synonym for `directory mask`.

[global] dns proxy = boolean

allowable values: YES, NO　　　　　　　*default:* YES

If set to YES, and if `wins server = YES`, look up hostnames in DNS if they are not found using WINS.

[global] domain logons = boolean

allowable values: YES, NO　　　　　　　*default:* NO

Allow Windows 95/98 or NT clients to log on to an NT-like domain.

[global] domain master = boolean

allowable values: YES, NO　　　　　　　*default:* NO

Become a domain master browser list collector if possible for the entire workgroup/domain.

dont descend = comma-list

allowable values: comma-separated list of paths　　　　　　　*default:* NULL

Does not allow a change directory or search in the directories specified. This is a browsing convenience option; it doesn't provide any extra security.

dos filetimes = boolean

allowable values: YES, NO　　　　　　　*default:* NO

Allow non-owners to change file times if they can write to the file. See also `dos filetime resolution`.

dos filetime resolution = boolean

allowable values: YES, NO　　　　　　　*default:* NO

Set file times on Unix to match DOS standards (round to next even second). Recommended if using Visual C++ or a PC *make* program to avoid remaking the programs unnecesarily. Use with the `dos filetimes` option.

[global] encrypt passwords = boolean

allowable values: YES, NO   *default:* NO

Uses Windows NT-style password encryption. Requires an *smbpasswd* on the Samba server.

exec = command

allowable values: shell command   *default:* NULL

Synonym of **preexec**, a command to run as the user just before connecting to the share.

fake directory create times = boolean

allowable values: YES, NO   *default:* NO

Bug fix for users of Microsoft *nmake*. If set, Samba will set directory create times such that *nmake* won't remake all files every time.

fake oplocks = boolean

allowable values: YES, NO   *default:* NO

Return YES whenever a client asks if it can lock a file and cache it locally, but does not enforce lock on the server. Use only for read-only disks, as Samba now supports real **oplocks** and has per-file overrides. See also **oplocks** and **veto oplock files**.

follow symlinks = boolean

allowable values: YES, NO   *default:* YES

If YES, Samba will follow symlinks in a file share or shares. See the **wide links** option if you want to restrict symlinks to just the current share.

force create mask = octal permission bits

allowable values: octal value from 0 to 0777   *default:* 0

Provides bits that will be ORed into the permissions of newly created files. Used with the **create mode** configuration option.

force create mode = octal permission bits

allowable values: octal value from 0 to 0777   *default:* 0

Synonym for **force create mask**.

force directory mask = octal permission bits

allowable values: octal value from 0 to 0777   *default:* 0

Provides bits that will be ORed into the permissions of newly created directories, forcing those bits to be set. Used with **directory mode**.

force directory mode = octal permission bits

allowable values: octal value from 0 to 0777　　　　　　　　　　　　*default:* 0

Synonym for `force directory mask`.

force group = unix group

allowable values: group　　　　　　　　　　　　　　　　　　　　　*default:* NULL

Sets the effective group name assigned to all users accessing a share. Used to override user's normal groups.

force user = name

allowable values: username　　　　　　　　　　　　　　　　　　　*default:* NULL

Sets the effective username assigned to all users accessing a share. Discouraged.

fstype = string

allowable values: NTFS, FAT, Samba　　　　　　　　　　　　　　　*default:* NTFS

Sets the filesystem type reported to the client.

[global] getwd cache = boolean

allowable values: YES, NO　　　　　　　　　　　　　　　　　　　*default:* NO

Cache current directory for performance. Recommended with the `wide links` option.

group = group

allowable values: unix group　　　　　　　　　　　　　　　　　　*default:* NULL

An obsolete form of `force group`.

guest account = user

allowable values: username　　　　　　　　　　　　　　　　　　　*default:* NULL

Sets the name of the unprivileged Unix account to use for tasks like printing and for accessing shares marked with `guest ok`.

guest ok = boolean

allowable values: YES, NO　　　　　　　　　　　　　　　　　　　*default:* NO

If YES, passwords are not needed for this share. Synonym of `public`.

guest only = boolean

allowable values: YES, NO　　　　　　　　　　　　　　　　　　　*default:* NO

Forces user of a share to do so as the guest account. Requires `guest ok` or `public` to be `yes`.

hide dot files = boolean

allowable values: YES, NO   *default:* YES

Treats files beginning with a dot in a share as if they had the DOS/Windows hidden attribute set.

hide files = slash-separated list

allowable values: list of patterns, separated by / characters   *default:* NULL

List of file or directory names to set the DOS hidden attribute on. Names may contain ? or * pattern-characters and %-variables. See also `hide dot files` and `veto files`.

[global] homedir map = NIS map name

allowable values: NIS map name   *default:* auto.home

Used with `nis homedir` to locate user's Unix home directory from Sun NIS (not NIS+).

hosts allow = host list

allowable values: list of hostnames   *default:* NULL

Synonym of `allow hosts`, a list of machines that can access a share or shares. If NULL (the default) any machine can access the share unless there is a `hosts deny` option.

hosts deny = host list

allowable values: list of hostnames   *default:* NULL

Synonym of `deny hosts`, a list of machines that cannot connect to a share or shares.

[global] hosts equiv = pathname

allowable values: pathname   *default:* NULL

Path to a file of trusted machines from which password-less logins are allowed. Strongly discouraged, because Windows/NT users can always override the user name, the only security in this scheme.

include = pathname

allowable values: pathname   *default:* NULL

Include the named file in *smb.conf* at the line where it appears. This option does not understand the variables %u (user), %P (current share's root directory), or %S (current share name), because they are not set at the time the file is read.

[global] interfaces = interface list

allowable values: IP addresses separated by spaces   *default:* NULL

Sets the interfaces to which Samba will respond. The default is the machine's primary interface only. Recommended on multihomed machines or to override erroneous addresses and netmasks.

invalid users = user list

allowable values: list of users   *default:* NULL

List of users that will not be permitted access to a share or shares.

[global] keepalive = number

allowable values: number of seconds   *default:* 0

Number of seconds between checks for a crashed client. The default of 0 causes no checks to be performed. Recommended if you want checks more often than every four hours. 3600 (10 minutes) is reasonable. See also **socket options** for another approach.

[global] kernel oplocks = boolean

allowable values: YES, NO   *default:* automatic

Break oplock when a Unix process accesses an *oplocked* file, preventing corruption. Set to YES on operating systems supporting this, otherwise set to NO. New in Samba 2.0; supported on SGI, and hopefully soon on Linux and BSD. Avoid changing.

[global] ldap filter = various

allowable values: various   *default:* varies

Options beginning with **ldap** are part of an experimental (circa Samba 2.0) use of the Lightweight Directory Access Protocol (LDAP) general directory/distributed database for user, name, and host information. This option is reserved for future use.

[global] ldap port = various

allowable values: various   *default:* various

Options beginning with **ldap** are part of an experimental (circa Samba 2.0) use of the Lightweight Directory Access Protocol (LDAP) general directory/distributed database for user, name, and host information. This option is reserved for future use.

[global] ldap root = various

allowable values: various   *default:* various

Options beginning with **ldap** are part of an experimental (circa Samba 2.0) use of the Lightweight Directory Access Protocol (LDAP) general directory/distributed database for user, name, and host information. This option is reserved for future use.

[global] ldap server = various

allowable values: various   *default:* various

Options beginning with `ldap` are part of an experimental (circa Samba 2.0) use of the Lightweight Directory Access Protocol (LDAP) general directory/distributed database for user, name, and host information. This option is reserved for future use.

[global] ldap suffix = various

allowable values: various   *default:* various

Options beginning with `ldap` are part of an experimental (circa Samba 2.0) use of the Lightweight Directory Access Protocol (LDAP) general directory/distributed database for user, name, and host information. This option is reserved for future use.

[global] load printers = boolean

allowable values: YES, NO   *default:* YES

Load all printer names from the system printer capabilities into browse list. Uses configuration options from the `[printers]` section.

[global] local master = boolean

allowable values: YES, NO   *default:* YES

Stands for election as the local master browser. See also `domain master` and `os level`.

[global] lm announce = value

allowable values: AUTO, YES, NO   *default:* AUTO

Produce OS/2 SMB broadcasts at an interval specified by the `lm interval` option. YES/NO turns them on/off unconditionally. AUTO causes the Samba server to wait for a LAN Manager announcement from another client before sending one out. Required for OS/2 client browsing.

[global] lm interval = seconds

allowable values: number   *default:* 60

Sets the time period, in seconds, between OS/2 SMB broadcast announcements.

[global] lock directory = pathname

allowable values: pathname   *default:* /usr/local/samba/var/locks

Set a directory to keep lock files in. The directory must be writable by Samba, readable by everyone.

locking = boolean

allowable values: YES, NO   *default:* YES

Perform file locking. If set to NO, Samba will accept lock requests but will not actually lock resources. Recommended only for read-only file systems.

[global] log file = pathname

allowable values: pathname   *default:* varies

Set name and location of the log file. Allows all %-variables.

[global] log level = number

allowable values: number   *default:* 0

A synonym of `debug level`. Sets the logging level used. Values of 3 or more slow the system noticeably.

[global] logon drive = drive

allowable values: DOS drive name   *default:* None

Sets the drive on Windows NT (only) of the `logon path`.

[global] logon home = path

allowable values: Unix pathname   *default:* \\%N\%U

Sets the home directory of a Windows 95/98 or NT Workstation user. Allows `NET USE H:/HOME` from the command prompt.

[global] logon path = pathname

allowable values: Windows pathname   ·   *default:* \\%N\%U*profile*

Sets path to Windows profile directory. This contains *USER.MAN* and/or *USER.DAT* profile files and the Windows 95 Desktop, Start Menu, Network Neighborhood, and programs folders.

[global] logon script = pathname

allowable values: pathname   *default:* NULL

Sets pathname relative to [netlogin] share of a DOS/NT script to run on the client at login time. Allows all %-variables.

lppause command = /absolute_path/command

allowable values: fully-qualfied Unix shell command   *default:* varies

Sets the command to pause a print job. Honors the %p (printer name) and %j (job number) variables.

lpresume command = /absolute_path/command

allowable values: fully-qualified Unix shell command   *default:* varies

Sets the command to resume a paused print job. Honors the **%p** (printer name) and **%j** (job number) variables.

[global] lpq cache time = seconds

allowable values: number of seconds   *default:* 10

Sets how long to keep print queue (**lpq**) status is cached, in seconds.

lpq command = /absolute_path/command

allowable values: fully-qualfied Unix shell command   *default:* varies

Sets the command used to get printer status. Usually initialized to a default value by the **printing** option. Honors the **%p** (printer name) variable.

lprm command = /absolute_path/command

allowable values: fully-qualified Unix shell command   *default:* varies

Sets the command to delete a print job. Usually initialized to a default value by the **printing** option. Honors the **%p** (printer name) and **%j** (job number) variables.

machine password timeout = seconds

allowable values: number of seconds   *default:* 604,800

Sets the period between (NT domain) machine password changes. Default is 1 week, or 604,800 seconds.

magic output = pathname

allowable values: Unix pathname   *default: script.out*

Sets the output file for the discouraged **magic scripts** option. Default is the script name, followed by the extension *.out.*

magic script = pathname

allowable values: Unix pathname   *default:* NULL

Sets a filename for execution via a shell whenever the file is closed from the client, to allow clients to run commands on the server.

mangle case = boolean

allowable values: allowable values: YES, NO   *default:* NO

Mangle a name if it is in mixed case.

mangled map = map list

allowable values: list of to-from pairs   *default:* NULL

Set up a table of names to remap (e.g., *.html* to *.htm*).

mangled names = boolean

allowable values: YES, NO   *default:* YES

Sets Samba to abbreviate names that are too long or have unsupported characters to the DOS 8.3 style.

mangling char = character

allowable values: character   *default:* ~

Sets the unique mangling character used in all mangled names.

[global] mangled stack = number

allowable values: number   *default:* 50

Sets the size of a cache of recently-mangled filenames.

map aliasname = pathname

allowable values: Unix pathname   *default:* NULL

Points to a file of Unix group/NT group pairs, one per line. This is used to map NT aliases to Unix group names. See also the configuration options `username map` and `map groupname`. Introduced in Samba 2.0.

map archive = boolean

allowable values: YES, NO   *default:* YES

If YES, Samba sets the executable-by-user (0100) bit on Unix files if the DOS archive attribute is set. Recommended: if used, the `create mask` must contain the 0100 bit.

map hidden = boolean

allowable values: YES, NO   *default:* NO

If YES, sets executable-by-other (0001) bit on Unix files if the DOS hidden attribute is set. If used, the `create mask` option must contain the 0001 bit.

map groupname = pathname

allowable values: pathname   *default:* NULL

Points to a file of Unix group/NT group, one per line. This is used to map NT group names to Unix group names. See also the configuration options `username map` and `map aliasname`. Introduced in Samba 2.0.

map system = boolean

allowable values: YES, NO   *default:* NO

If YES, Samba sets the executable-by-group (0010) bit on Unix files if the DOS system attribute is set. If used, the `create mask` must contain the 0010 bit.

max connections = number

allowable values: number   *default:* 0 (infinity)

Set maximum number of connections allowed to a share from each individual client machine.

[global] max disk size = number

allowable values: size in MB   *default:* 0 (unchanged)

Sets maximum disk size/free-space size (in megabytes) to return to client. Some clients or applications can't understand large maximum disk sizes.

[global] max log size = number

allowable values: size in KB   *default:* 5000

Sets the size (in kilobytes) at which Samba will start a new log file. The current log file will be renamed with an *.old* extension, replacing any previous file with that name.

[global] max mux = number

allowable values: number   *default:* 50

Sets the number of simultaneous operations that Samba clients may make. Avoid changing.

[global] max packet = number

allowable values: number   *default:* N/A

Synonym for `packet size`. Obsolete as of Samba 1.7. Use `max xmit` instead.

[global] max open files = number

allowable values: number   *default:* 10,000

Limits the number of files a Samba process will try to keep open at one time. Samba allows you to set this to less than the Unix maximum. This option is a workaround for a separate problem. Avoid changing. This option was introduced in Samba 2.0.

[global] max ttl = seconds

allowable values: time in seconds   *default:* 14400 (4 hrs)

Sets the time to keep NetBIOS names in *nmbd* cache while trying to perform a lookup on it. Avoid changing.

[global] max wins ttl = seconds

allowable values: time in seconds   *default:* 259200 (3 days)

Limits time-to-live of a NetBIOS name in *nmbd* WINS cache, in seconds. Avoid changing.

[global] max xmit = bytes

allowable values: size in bytes   *default:* 65535

Sets maximum packet size that will be negotiated by Samba. Tuning parameter for slow links and older client bugs. Values less than 2048 are discouraged.

[global] message command = /absolute_path/command

allowable values: shell command   *default:* NULL

Sets the command on the server to run when a WinPopup message arrives from a client. The command must end in "&" to allow immediate return. Honors all %-variables except %u (user), and supports the extra variables %s (filename the message is in), %t (destination machine), and %f (from).

min print space = kilobytes

allowable values: space in KB   *default:* 0 (unlimited)

Sets minimum spool space required before accepting a print request.

[global] min wins ttl = seconds

allowable values: time in seconds   *default:* 21600 (6 hrs)

Sets minimum time-to-live of a NetBIOS name in *nmbd* WINS cache, in seconds. Avoid changing.

name resolve order = list

allowable values: list of lmhosts, wins, hosts and bcast   *default:* lmhosts wins hosts bcast

Sets order of lookup when trying to get IP address from names. The hosts parameter carrries out a regular name look up using the server's normal sources: */etc/hosts*, DNS, NIS, or a combination of them. Introduced in Samba 1.9.18p4.

[global] netbios aliases = list

allowable values: list of netbios names   *default:* NULL

Adds additional NetBIOS names by which a Samba server will advertise itself.

netbios name = hostname

allowable values: host name   *default:* varies

Sets the NetBIOS name by which a Samba server is known, or primary name if NetBIOS aliases exist.

[global] networkstation user login = boolean

allowable values: YES, NO   *default:* YES

If set to NO, clients will not do a full login when `security = server`. Avoid changing. Turning it off is a temporary workaround (introduced in Samba 1.9.18p3) for NT trusted domains bug. Automatic correction was introduced in Samba 1.9.18p10; the parameter may eventually be removed.

[global] nis homedir = boolean

allowable values: YES, NO   *default:* NO

If YES, the `homedir map` will be used to look up the user's home-directory server name and return it to the client. The client will contact that machine to connect to the share. This avoids mounting from a machine that doesn't actually have the disk. The machine with the home directories must be an SMB server.

[global] nt pipe support = boolean

allowable values: YES, NO   *default:* YES

Allows turning off NT-specific pipe calls. This is a developer/benchmarking option and may be removed in the future. Avoid changing.

[global] nt smb support = boolean

allowable values: YES, NO   *default:* YES

If YES, allow NT-specific SMBs to be used. This is a developer/benchmarking option and may be removed in the future. Avoid changing.

[global] null passwords = boolean

allowable values: YES, NO   *default:* NO

If YES, allows access to accounts that have null passwords. Strongly discouraged.

ole locking compatibility = boolean

allowable values: YES, NO   *default:* YES

If YES, locking ranges will be mapped to avoid Unix locks crashing when Windows uses locks above 32KB. You should avoid changing this option. Introduced in Samba 1.9.18p10.

only guest = boolean

allowable values: YES, NO   *default:* NO

A synonym for `guest only`. Forces user of a share to login as the guest account.

only user = boolean

allowable values: YES, NO   *default:* NO

Requires that users of the share be on a **username** = list.

oplocks = boolean

allowable values: YES, NO   *default:* YES

If YES, support local caching of *opportunistic* locked files on client. This option is recommended because it improves performance by about 30%. See also **fake oplocks** and **veto oplock files**.

[global] os level = number

allowable values: number   *default:* 0

Sets the candidacy of the server when electing a browse master. Used with the **domain master** or **local master** options. You can set a higher value than a competing operating system if you want Samba to win. Windows for Workgroups and Windows 95 use 1, Windows NT client uses 17, and Windows NT Server uses 33.

[global] packet size = bytes

allowable values: number in bytes   *default:* 65535

Obsolete. Discouraged synonym of **max packet**. See **max xmit**.

[global] passwd chat debug = boolean

allowable values: YES, NO   *default:* NO

Logs an entire password chat, including passwords passed, with a log level of 100. For debugging only. Introduced in Samba 1.9.18p5.

[global] passwd chat = command sequence

allowable values: Unix server commands   *default:* compiled-in value

Sets the command used to change passwords on the server. Supports the variables **%o** (old password) and **%n** (new password) and allows \r \n \t and \s (space) escapes in the sequence.

[global] passwd program = program

allowable values: Unix server program   *default:* NULL

Sets the command used to change user's password. Will be run as **root**. Supports **%u** (user).

[global] password level = number

allowable values: number   *default:* 0

Specifies the number of uppercase letter permutations used to match passwords. Workaround for clients that change passwords to a single case before sending them to the Samba server. Causes repeated login attempts with passwords in different cases, which can trigger account lockouts.

[global] password server = netbios names

allowable values: list of NetBIOS names   *default:* NULL

A list of SMB servers that will validate passwords for you. Used with an NT password server (PDC or BDC) and the `security = server` or `security = domain` configuration options. Caution: an NT password server must allow logins from the Samba server.

panic action = /absolute_path/command

allowable values: fully-qualfied Unix shell command   *default:* NULL

Sets the command to run when Samba panics. For Samba developers and testers, `/usr/bin/X11/xterm –display :0 -e gdb /samba/bin/smbd %d` is a possible value.

path = pathname

allowable values: pathname   *default:* varies

Sets the path to the directory provided by a file share or used by a printer share. Set automatically in `[homes]` share to user's home directory, otherwise defaults to */tmp*. Honors the `%u` (user) and `%m` (machine) variables.

postexec = /absolute_path/command

allowable values: fully-qualified Unix shell command   *default:* NULL

Sets a command to run as the user after disconnecting from the share. See also the options `preexec`, `root preexec`, and `root postexec`.

postscript = boolean

allowable values: YES, NO   *default:* NO

Flags a printer as PostScript to avoid a Windows bug by inserting `%!` as the first line. Works only if printer actually is PostScript compatible.

preexec = /absolute_path/command

allowable values: fully-qualified Unix shell command   *default:* NULL

Sets a command to run as the user before connecting to the share. See also the options `postexec`, `root preexec`, and `root postexec`.

[global] preferred master = boolean

allowable values: YES, NO   *default:* NO

If YES, Samba is preferred to become the master browser. Causes Samba to call a browsing election when it comes online.

preload = share list

allowable values: list of services   *default:* NULL

Synonym of `auto services`. Specifies a list of shares that will always appear in browse lists.

preserve case = boolean

allowable values: YES, NO   *default:* NO

If set to YES, this option leaves filenames in the case sent by client. If no, it forces filenames to the case specified by the `default case` option. See also `short preserve case`.

print command = /absolute_path/command

allowable values: fully-qualified Unix shell command   *default:* varies

Sets the command used to send a spooled file to the printer. Usually initialized to a default value by the `printing` option. This option honors the `%p` (printer name), `%s` (spool file) and `%f` (spool file as a relative path) variables. Note that the command in the value of the option must include file deletion of the spool file.

print ok = boolean

allowable values: YES, NO   *default:* NO

Synonym of `printable`.

printable = boolean

allowable values: YES, NO   *default:* NO

Sets a share to be a print share. Required for all printers.

[global] printcap name = pathname

allowable values: pathname   *default:* /etc/printcap

Sets the path to the printer capabilities file used by the `[printers]` share. The default value changes to */etc/qconfig* under AIX and *lpstat* on System V.

printer = name

allowable values: printer name   *default:* `lp`

Sets the name of the Unix printer.

printer driver = printer driver name

allowable values: exact printer driver string used by Windows   *default:* NULL

Sets the string to pass to Windows when asked what driver to use to prepare files for a printer share. Note that the value is case sensitive.

[global] printer driver file = path

allowable values: Unix pathname   *default: samba-lib/printers.def*

Sets the location of a *msprint.def* file, usable by Windows 95/98.

printer driver location = path

allowable values: Windows network path   *default:* **server***PRINTER$*

Sets the location of the driver for a particular printer. The value is a pathname for a share that stores the printer driver files.

printer name = name

allowable values: name   *default:* NULL

Synonym of `printer`.

printing = style

allowable values: bsd, sysv, hpux, aix, qnx, plp, lprng   *default:* bsd

Sets printing style to one of the above, instead of the compiled-in value. This sets initial values of at least the `print command`, `print command`, `lpq command`, and `lprm command`.

[global] protocol = protocol

allowable values: NT1, LANMAN2, LANMAN1, COREPLUS, CORE   *default:* NT1

Sets SMB protocol version to one of the allowable values. Resetting is highly discouraged. Only for backwards compatibility with older-client bugs.

public = boolean

allowable values: YES, NO   *default:* NO

If YES, passwords are not needed for this share. A synonym is `guest ok`.

queuepause command = /absolute_path/command

allowable values: valid Unix command   *default:* varies

Sets the command used to pause a print queue. Usually initialized to a default value by the `printing` option. Introduced in Samba 1.9.18p10.

queueresume command = /absolute_path/command

allowable values: valid Unix command   *default:* varies

Sets the command used to resume a print queue. Usually initialized to a default value by the `printing` option. Introduced in Samba 1.9.18p10.

read bmpx = boolean

allowable values: YES, NO   *default:* NO

Obsolete. Do not change.

read list = comma-separated list

allowable values: comma-separated list of users   *default:* NULL

Specifies a list of users given read-only access to a writeable share.

read only = boolean

allowable values: YES, NO   *default:* NO

Sets a share to read-only. Antonym of `writable` and `write ok`.

[global] read prediction = boolean

allowable values: YES, NO   *default:* NO

Reads ahead data for read-only files. Obsolete; removed in Samba 2.0.

[global] read raw = boolean

allowable values: YES, NO   *default:* YES

Allows fast streaming reads over TCP using 64K buffers. Recommended.

[global] read size = bytes

allowable values: size in bytes   *default:* 2048

Sets a buffering option for servers with mismatched disk and network speeds. Requires experimentation. Avoid changing. Should not exceed 65536.

[global] remote announce = remote list

allowable values: list of remote addresses   *default:* NULL

Adds workgroups to the list on which the Samba server will announce itself. Specified as IP address/workgroup (for instance, 192.168.220.215/SIMPLE) with multiple groups separated by spaces. Allows directed broadcasts. The server will appear on those workgroup's browse lists. Does not require WINS.

[global] remote browse sync = address list

allowable values: IP-address list   *default:* NULL

Enables Samba-only browse list synchronization with other Samba local master browsers. Addresses can be specific addresses or directed broadcasts (i.e., *###.###.###*.255). The latter will cause Samba to hunt down the local master.

revalidate = boolean

allowable values: YES, NO   *default:* NO

If set to YES, requires users to re-enter passwords even after a successful initial logon to a share with a password.

[global] root = pathname

allowable values: Unix pathname   *default:* NULL

Synonym for `root directory`.

[global] root dir = pathname

allowable values: Unix pathname   *default:* NULL

Synonym for `root directory`.

[global] root directory = pathname

allowable values: Unix pathname   *default:* NULL

Specifies a directory to `chroot()` to before starting daemons. Prevents any access below that directory tree. See also the `wide links` configuration option.

root postexec = /absolute_path/command

allowable values: fully-qualified Unix shell command   *default:* NULL

Sets a command to run as root after disconnecting from the share. See also `preexec`, `postexec`, and `root preexec` configuration options. Runs after the user's `postexec` command. Use with caution.

root preexec = /absolute_path/command

allowable values: fully-qualified Unix shell command   *default:* NULL

Sets a command to run as root before connecting to the share. See also `preexec`, `postexec`, and `root postexec` configuration options. Runs before the user's `preexec` command. Use with caution.

[global] security = value

allowable values: share, user, server, domain   *default:* share in Samba 1.0, user in 2.0

Sets password-security policy. If `security = share`, services have a shared password, available to everyone. If `security = user`, users have (Unix) accounts and passwords. If security = server, users have accounts and passwords and a separate machine authenticates them for Samba. If security = domain, full NT-domain authentication is done. See also the password server and encrypted passwords configuration options.

[global] server string = text

allowable values: string   *default:* Samba %v in 2.0

Sets the name that appears beside a server in browse lists. Honors the %v (Samba version number) and %h (hostname) variables.

set directory = boolean

allowable values: YES, NO   *default:* NO

Allows DEC Pathworks client to use the *set dir* command.

[global] shared file entries = number

allowable values: number   *default:* 113

Obsolete; do not use.

shared mem size = bytes

allowable values: size in bytes   *default:* 102400

If compiled with FAST_SHARE_MODES (mmap), sets the shared memory size in bytes. Avoid changing.

[global] smb passwd file = path

allowable values: Unix pathname   *default:* /usr/local/samba/private/smbpasswd

Overrides compiled-in path to password file if encrypted passwords = yes.

[global] smbrun = /absolute_path/command

allowable values: smbrun command   *default:* compiled-in value

Overrides compiled-in path to *smbrun* binary. Avoid changing.

share modes = boolean

allowable values: YES, NO   *default:* YES

If set to YES, this option supports Windows-style whole-file (deny mode) locks.

short preserve case = boolean

allowable values: YES, NO   *default:* NO

If set to YES, leaves mangled 8.3-style filenames in the case sent by client. If no, it forces the case to that specified by the default case option. See also preserve case.

[global] socket address = IP address

allowable values: IP address   *default:* NULL

Sets address on which to listen for connections. Default is to listen to all addresses. Used to support multiple virtual interfaces on one server. Highly discouraged.

[global] socket options = socket option list

allowable values: list   *default:* NULL

Sets OS-specific socket options. SO_KEEPALIVE has TCP check clients every 4 hours to see if they are still accessible. TCP_NODELAY sends even tiny packets to keep delay low. Recommended wherever the operating system supports them. See Appendix B, *Samba Performance Tuning*, for more information.

[global] status = boolean

allowable values: YES, NO   *default:* YES

If YES, logs connections to a file (or shared memory) accessible to *smbstatus.*

strict sync = boolean

allowable values: YES, NO   *default:* NO

If set to YES, Samba will synchronize to disk whenever the client sets the sync bit in a packet. If set to NO, Samba flushes data to disk whenever buffers fill. Defaults to NO because Windows 98 Explorer sets the bit (incorrectly) in all packets. Introduced in Samba 1.9.18p10.

strict locking = boolean

allowable values: YES, NO   *default:* NO

If set to YES, Samba checks locks on every access, not just on demand and at open time. Not recommended.

[global] strip dot = boolean

allowable values: YES, NO   *default:* NO

Removes trailing dots from filenames. Use `mangled map` instead.

[global] syslog = number

allowable values: number   *default:* 1

Sets number of Samba log messages to send to *syslog.* Higher is more verbose. The *syslog.conf* file must have suitable logging enabled.

[global] syslog only = boolean

allowable values: YES, NO   *default:* NO

If set to YES, log only to *syslog,* not standard Samba log files.

sync always = boolean

allowable values: YES, NO   *default:* NO

If set to YES, Samba calls *fsync(3)* after every write. Avoid except for debugging crashing servers.

[global] time offset = minutes

allowable values: minutes   *default:* 0

Sets number of minutes to add to system time zone calculation. Provided to fix a client daylight-savings bug; not recommended.

[global] time server = boolean

allowable values: YES, NO   *default:* NO

If YES, *nmbd* will provide time service to its clients.

unix password sync = boolean

allowable values: YES, NO   *default:* NO

If set, will attempt to change the user's Unix password whenever the user changes his or her SMB password. Used to ease synchronization of Unix and Microsoft password databases. Added in Samba 1.9.18p4. See also `passwd chat`.

unix realname = boolean

allowable values: YES, NO   *default:* NO

If set, will provide the GCOS field of */etc/passwd* to the client as the user's full name.

update encrypted = boolean

allowable values: YES, NO   *default:* NO

Updates the Microsoft-format password file when a user logs in with unencrypted passwords. Provided to ease conversion to encryped passwords for Windows 95/98 and NT. Added in Samba 1.9.18p5.

user = comma-separated list

allowable values: comma-separated list of user names   *default:* NULL

Synonym for `username`.

username = comma-separated list

allowable values: comma-separated list of user names   *default:* NULL

Sets a list of users to try to log in as for a share or shares with share-level security. Synonyms are `user` and `users`. Discouraged. Use `NET USE \\`*server*`\`*share*`%`*user* from the client instead.

username level = number

allowable values: number   *default:* 0

Number of uppercase letter permutations allowed to match Unix usernames. Workaround for Windows feature (single-case usernames). Use is discouraged.

[global] username map = pathname

allowable values: pathname   *default:* NULL

Names a file of Unix-to-Windows name pairs; used to map different spellings of account names and those Windows usernames longer than eight characters.

valid chars = list

allowable values: list of numeric values   *default:* NULL

Semi-obsolete. Adds national characters to a character set map. Overridden by `client code page`.

valid users = user list

allowable values: list of users   *default:* NULL (everyone)

List of users that can log in to a share.

veto files = slash-list

allowable values: slash-separated list of filenames   *default:* NULL

List of files not to allow the client to see when listing a directory's contents. See also `delete veto files`.

veto oplock files = slash-list

allowable values: slash-separated list of filenames   *default:* NULL

List of files not to oplock (and cache on clients). See also `oplocks` and `fake oplocks`.

volume = share name

allowable values: string   *default:* NULL

Sets the volume label of a disk share, notably a CD-ROM.

wide links = boolean

allowable values: YES, NO   *default:* YES

If set to YES, Samba will follow symlinks out of the current disk share(s). See also the `root dir` and `follow symlinks` options.

[global] wins proxy = boolean

allowable values: YES, NO   *default:* NO

If set to YES, *nmbd* will proxy resolution requests to WINS servers on behalf of old clients, which use broadcasts. WINS server is typically on another subnet.

[global] wins server = host

allowable values: hostname   *default:* NULL

Sets the DNS name or IP address of the WINS server.

[global] wins support = boolean

allowable values: YES, NO   *default:* NO

If set to YES, Samba activates WINS service. The `wins server` option must not be set if `wins support = yes`.

[global] workgroup = name

allowable values: workgroup name   *default:* compiled-in

Sets the workgroup to which things will be served. Overrides compiled-in value. Choosing a name other than `WORKGROUP` is strongly recommended.

writable = boolean

allowable values: YES, NO   *default:* YES

Antonym for `read only`; synonym of `write ok`.

write list = comma-separated list

allowable values: comma-separated list of users   *default:* NULL (everyone)

List of users that are given read-write access to a read-only share. See also `read list`.

write ok = boolean

allowable values: YES, NO   *default:* YES

Synonym of the `writable` configuration option.

[global] write raw = boolean

allowable values: YES, NO   *default:* YES

Allows fast streaming writes over TCP, using 64KB buffers. Recommended.

Glossary of Configuration Values

Address list

A space-separated list of IP addresses in *###.###.###.###* format.

Comma-separated list

A list of items separated by commas.

Command

A Unix command, with full path and parameters.

Host list

A space-separated list of hosts. Allows IP addresses, address masks, domain names, ALL, and EXCEPT

Interface list

A space-separated list of interfaces, in either address/netmask or address/n-bits format. For example, 192.168.2.10/24 or 192.168.2.10/255.255.255.0

Map list

A space-separated list of file-remapping strings such as (*.html *.htm).

Remote list

A space-separated list of subnet-broadcast-address/workgroup pairs. For example, 192.168.2.255/SERVERS 192.168.4.255/STAFF.

Service (share) list

A space-separated list of share names, without the enclosing square brackets.

Slash-list

A list of filenames, separated by "/" characters to allow embedded spaces. For example, /.*/fred flintstone/*.frk/.

Text

One line of text.

User list

A space-separated list of usernames. In Samba 1.9, @group-name will include everyone in Unix group group-name. In Samba 2.0, @group-name includes whomever is in the NIS netgroup group_name if one exists, otherwise whomever is in the Unix group group_name. In addition, +group_name is a Unix group, &group_name is an NIS netgroup, and &+ and +& cause an ordered search of both Unix and NIS groups.

Configuration File Variables

Table C-1 lists of Samba configuration file variables.

Table C-1. Variables in Alphabetic Order

Name	Meaning
%a	Client's architecture (one of Samba, WfWg, WinNT, Win95, or UNKNOWN)
%d	Current server process's processID
%f	Print-spool file as a relative path (printing only)
%f	User from which a message was sent (messages only)
%G	Primary group name of %U (requested username)
%g	Primary group name of %u (actual username)
%H	Home directory of %u (actual username)
%h	Samba server's (Internet) hostname
%I	Client's IP address
%j	Print job number (printing only)
%L	Samba server's NetBIOS name (virtual servers have multiple names)
%M	Client's (Internet) hostname
%m	Client's NetBIOS name
%n	New password (password change only)
%N	Name of the NIS home directory server (without NIS, same as %L)
%o	Old password (password change only)
%P	Current share's root directory (actual)
%p	Current share's root directory (in an NIS homedir map)
%p	Print filename (printing only)
%R	Protocol level in use (one of CORE, COREPLUS, LANMAN1, LANMAN2, or NT1)
%S	Current share's name
%s	Filename the message is in (messages only)
%s	Print-spool file name (printing only)
%T	Current date and time
%t	Destination machine (messages only)
%u	Current share's username
%U	Requested username for current share
%v	Samba version

D

Summary of Samba Daemons and Commands

This appendix is a reference listing of command-line options and other information to help you use the executables that come with Samba distribution.

Samba Distribution Programs

The following sections provide information about the command-line parameters for Samba programs.

smbd

The *smbd* program provides Samba's file and printer services, using one TCP/IP stream and one daemon per client. It is controlled from the default configuration file, *samba_dir/lib/smb.conf,* and can be overridden by command-line options.

The configuration file is automatically re-evaluated every minute. If it has changed, most new options are immediately effective. You can force Samba to immediately reload the configuration file if you send a SIGHUP to *smbd.* Reloading the configuration file, however, will not affect any clients that are already connected. To escape this "grandfather" configuration, a client would need to disconnect and reconnect, or the server itself would have to be restarted, forcing all clients to reconnect.

Other signals

To shut down a *smbd* process, send it the termination signal SIGTERM (-15) which allows it to die gracefully instead of a SIGKILL (-9). To increment the debug logging level of *smbd* at runtime, send the program a SIGUSR1 signal. To decrement it at runtime, send the program a SIGUSR2 signal.

Command-line options

–D The *smbd* program is run as a daemon. This is the recommended way to use *smbd* (it is also the default action). In addition, *smbd* can also be run from *inetd*.

–d *debuglevel*
Sets the debug (sometimes called logging) level. The level can range from 0 all the way to 10. Specifying the value on the command line overrides the value specified in the *smb.conf* file. Debug level 0 logs only the most important messages; level 1 is normal; levels 3 and above are primarily for debugging and slow *smbd* considerably.

–h Prints command-line usage information for the *smbd* program.

Testing/debugging options

–a If this is specified, each new connection to the Samba server will append all logging messages to the log file. This option is the opposite of **–o**, and is the default.

–i *scope*
This sets a NetBIOS scope identifier. Only machines with the same identifier will communicate with the server. The scope identifier was a predecessor to workgroups, and this option is included only for backwards compatibility.

–l *log_file*
Send the log messages to somewhere other than the location compiled in or specified in the *smb.conf* file. The default is often */usr/local/samba/var/log.smb*, */usr/samba/var/log.smb*, or */var/log/log.smb*. The first two are strongly discouraged on Linux, where */usr* may be a read-only filesystem.

–O *socket_options*
This sets the TCP/IP socket options, using the same parameters as the **socket options** configuration option. It is often used for performance tuning and testing.

–o This option is the opposite of **–a**. It causes log files to be overwritten when opened. Using this option saves hunting for the right log entries if you are performing a series of tests and inspecting the log file each time.

–P This option forces *smbd* not to send any network data out. This option is typically used only by Samba developers.

–P This option forces *smbd* not to send any network data out. This option is typically used only by Samba developers.

–p *port_number*
This sets the TCP/IP port number that the server will accept requests from. Currently, all Microsoft clients send only to the default port: 139.

-s *configuration_file*
>   Specifies the location of the Samba configuration file. Although the file defaults to */usr/local/samba/lib/smb.conf,* you can override it here on the command line, typically for debugging.

nmbd

The *nmbd* program is Samba's NetBIOS name and browsing daemon. It replies to broadcast NetBIOS over TCP/IP (NBT) name-service requests from SMB clients and optionally to Microsoft's Windows Internet Name Service (WINS) requests. Both of these are versions of the name-to-address lookup required by SMB clients. The broadcast version uses UDP/IP broadcast on the local subnet only, while WINS uses TCP/IP, which may be routed. If running as a WINS server, *nmbd* keeps a current name and address database in the file *wins.dat* in the samba_dir/ *var/locks* directory.

An active *nmbd* program can also respond to browsing protocol requests used by the Windows Network Neighborhood. Browsing is a combined advertising, service announcement, and active directory protocol. This protocol provides a dynamic directory of servers and the disks and printers that the servers are providing. As with WINS, this was initially done by making UDP/IP broadcasts on the local subnet. Now, with the concept of a local master browser, it is done by making TCP/IP connections to a server. If *nmbd* is acting as a local master browser, it stores the browsing database in the file *browse.dat* in the samba_dir/*var/locks* directory.

Signals

Like *smbd,* the *nmbd* program responds to several Unix signals. Sending *nmbd* a SIGHUP signal will cause it to dump the names it knows about to the file *namelist.debug* in the samba_dir/*locks* directory and its browsing database to the *browse.dat* file in the same directory. To shut down a *nmbd* process send it a SIGTERM (-15) signal instead of a SIGKILL (-9) to allow it to die gracefully. You can increment the debug logging level of *nmbd* by sending it a SIGUSR1 signal; you can decrement it by sending a SIGUSR2 signal.

Command-line options

-D Instructs the *nmbd* program to run as a daemon. This is the recommended way to use *nmbd.* In addition, *nmbd* can also be run from *inetd.*

-d *debuglevel*
>   Sets the debug (sometimes called logging) level. The level can range from 0, all the way to 10. Specifying the value on the command line overrides the value specified in the *smb.conf* file. Debug level 0 logs only the most impor-

tant messages; level 1 is normal; level 3 and above are primarily for debugging, and slow *nmbd* considerably.

-h Prints command-line usage information for the *nmbd* program (also -?).

Testing/debugging options

-a If this is specified, each new connection to the Samba server will append all logging messages to the log file. This option is the opposite of -o, and is the default.

-H *hosts_file*

This option loads a standard *hosts* file for name resolution.

-i *scope*

This sets a NetBIOS scope identifier. Only machines with the same identifier will communicate with the server. The scope identifier was a predecessor to workgroups, and this option is included only for backward compatibility.

-l *log_file*

Sends the log messages to somewhere other than the location compiled-in or specified in the *smb.conf* file. The default is often */usr/local/samba/var/log.nmb*, */usr/samba/var/log.nmb*, or */var/log/log.nmb*. The first two are strongly discouraged on Linux, where */usr* may be a read-only filesystem.

-n *NetBIOS_name*

This option allows you to override the NetBIOS name by which the daemon will advertise itself. Specifying the option on the command line overrides the netbios name option in the Samba configuration file.

-O *socket_options*

This sets the TCP/IP socket options, using the same parameters as the socket options configuration option. It is often used for performance tuning and testing.

-o This option is the opposite of -a. It causes log files to be overwritten when opened. Using this option saves hunting for the right log entries if you are performing a series of tests and inspecting the log file each time.

-p *port_number*

This sets the UDP/IP port number from which the server will accept requests. Currently, all Microsoft clients send only to the default port: 137.

-s *configuration_file*

Specifies the location of the Samba configuration file. Although the file defaults to */usr/local/samba/lib/smb.conf*, you can override it here on the command line, typically for debugging.

-v

This option prints the current version of Samba.

Samba Startup File

Samba is normally started by running it from your Unix system's *rc* files at boot time. For systems with a System V-like set of */etc/rcN.d* directories, this can be done by placing a suitably named script in the */rc* directory. Usually, the script starting Samba is called *S91samba*, while the script stopping or "killing" Samba is called *K91samba*. On Linux, the usual subdirectory for the scripts is */etc/rc2.d*. On Solaris, the directory is */etc/rc3.d*. For machines with */etc/rc.local* files, you would normally add the following lines to that file:

```
/usr/local/samba/bin/smbd -D
/usr/local/samba/bin/nmbd -D
```

The following example script supports two extra commands, **status** and **restart**, in addition to the normal **start** and **stop** for System V machines:

```
#!/bin/sh
#
# /etc/rc2.d./S91Samba  --manage the SMB server in a System V manner
#
OPTS="-D"
#DEBUG=-d3
PS="ps  ax"
SAMBA_DIR=/usr/local/samba
case "$1" in
'start')
    echo "samba "
    $SAMBA_DIR/bin/smbd $OPTS $DEBUG
    $SAMBA_DIR/bin/nmbd $OPTS $DEBUG
    ;;
'stop')
    echo "Stopping samba"
    $PS | awk '/usr.local.samba.bin/ { print $1}' |\
    xargs kill
    ;;
'status')
    x=`$PS | grep -v grep | grep '$SAMBA_DIR/bin'`
    if [ ! "$x" ]; then
        echo "No samba processes running"
    else
        echo "  PID TT STAT  TIME COMMAND"
        echo "$x"
    fi
    ;;
'restart')
    /etc/rc2.d/S91samba stop
    /etc/rc2.d/S91samba start
    /etc/rc2.d/S91samba status
    ;;
*)
    echo "$0: Usage error -- you must say $0 start,  stop, status or restart ."
    ;;
```

```
        esac
        exit
```

You'll need to set the actual paths and **ps** options to suit the machine you're using. In addition, you might want to add additional commands to tell Samba to reload its *smb.conf* file or dump its *nmbd* tables, depending on your actual needs.

smbsh

The *smbsh* program lets you use a remote Windows share on your Samba server as if the share was a regular Unix directory. When it's run, it provides an extra directory tree under */smb*. Subdirectories of */smb* are servers, and subdirectories of the servers are their individual disk and printer shares. Commands run by *smbsh* treat the */smb* filesystem as if it were local to Unix. This means that you don't need *smbmount* in your kernel to mount Windows filesystems the way you mount with NFS filesystems. However, you do need to configure Samba with the **--with-smbwrappers** option to enable *smbsh*.

Options

-d *debuglevel*

Sets the debug (sometimes called logging) level. The level can range from 0, the default, all the way to 10. Debug level 0 logs only the most important messages; level 1 is normal; level 3 and above are primarily for debugging, and slow *smbsh* considerably.

-l *logfile*

Sets the name of the logfile to use.

-P *prefix*

Sets the root directory to mount the SMB filesystem. The default is */smb*.

-R *resolve order*

Sets the resolve order of the name servers. This option is similar to the **resolve order** configuration option, and can take any of the four parameters, **lmhosts**, **host**, **wins**, and **bcast**, in any order.

-U *user*

Supports *user%password.*

-W *workgroup*

Sets the NetBIOS workgroup to which the client will connect.

smbclient

The *smbclient* program is the maid-of-all-work of the Samba suite. Initially intended as a testing tool, it has become a full command-line Unix client, with an

FTP-like interactive client. Some of its options are still used for testing and tuning, and it makes a simple tool for ensuring that Samba is running on a server.

It's convenient to look at *smbclient* as a suite of programs:

- FTP-like interactive file transfer program

- Interactive printing program

- Interactive tar program

- Command-line message program

- Command-line *tar* program (but see *smbtar* later)

- "What services do you have" query program

- Command-line debugging program

General command-line options

The program has the usual set of *smbd*-like options, which apply to all the interactive and command-line use. The syntax is:

```
smbclient //server_name/share_name [password] [-options]
```

Here is an explanation of each of the command-line options:

-d *debug_level*
> Sets the debug (logging) level, from 0 to 10, with A for all. Overrides the value in *smb.conf*. Debug level 0 logs only the most important messages; level 1 is normal; debug level 3 and above are for debugging, and slow *smbclient* considerably.

-h Prints the command-line help information (usage) for smbclient.

-n *NetBIOS_name*
> Allows you to override the NetBIOS name by which the program will advertise itself.

Smbclient operations

Running smbclient //*server_name*/*share* will cause it to prompt you for a username and password. If the login is successful, it will connect to the share and give you a prompt much like an FTP prompt (the backslash in the prompt will be replaced by the current directory within the share as you move around the filesystem):

```
smb:\>
```

From this command line, you can use several FTP-like commands, as listed in Table D-1. Arguments in square brackets are optional.

Table D-1. smbclient Commands

Command	Description
? *command*	Provides list of commands or help on specified command.
help [*command*]	Provides list of commands or help on specified command.
! [*command*]	If a command is specified, it will be run in a local shell. If not, you will be placed into a local shell on the client.
dir [*filename*]	Displays any files matching *filename* in the current directory on the server, or all files if *filename* is omitted.
ls [*filename*]	Displays any files matching *filename* in the current directory on the server, or all files if *filename* is omitted.
cd [*directory*]	If *directory* is specified, changes to the specified directory on the remote server. If not, reports the current directory on the remote machine.
lcd [*directory*]	If *directory* is specified, the current directory on the local machine will be changed. If not, the name of the current directory on the local machine will be reported.
get *remotefile* [*localfile*]	Copies the file *remotefile* to the local machine. If a *localfile* is specified, uses that name to copy the file to. Treats the file as binary; does *not* do LF to CR/LF conversions.
put *localfile* [*remotefile*]	Copies *localfile* to the remote machine. If a *remotefile* is specified, uses that as the name to copy to on the remote server. Treats the file as binary; does *not* do LF to CR/LF conversions.
mget *pattern*	Gets all files matching *pattern* from the remote machine.
mput *pattern*	Places all local files matching *pattern* on the remote machine.
prompt	Toggles interactive prompting on and off for mget and mput.
lowercase ON (or OFF)	If lowercase is on, *smbclient* will convert filenames to lowercase during an mget or get (but not a mput or put).
del *filename*	Delete a file on the remote machine.
md *directory*	Create a directory on the remote machine.
mkdir *directory*	Create a directory on the remote machine.
rd *directory*	Remove the specified directory on the remote machine.
rmdir *directory*	Remove the specified directory on the remote machine.
setmode *filename* [+|-]rsha	Set DOS filesystem attribute bits, using Unix-like modes. r is read-only, s is system, h is hidden, and a is archive.
exit	Exits *smbclient*.
quit	Exits *smbclient*.

There are also mask and recursive commands for large copies; see the *smbclient* manual page for details on how to use these. With the exception of mask, recursive, and the lack of an ASCII transfer mode, *smbclient* works exactly the same as FTP. Note that because it does binary transfers, Windows files copied to Unix will have lines ending in carriage-return and linefeed (\r\n), not Unix's linefeed (\n).

Printing commands

The *smbclient* program can also be used for access to a printer by connecting to a print share. Once connected, the commands shown in Table D-2 can be used to print.

Table D-2. smbclient Printing Commands

Command	Description
print *filename*	Prints the file by copying it from the local machine to the remote one and then submitting it as a print job there.
printmode *text* | *graphics*	Instructs the server that the following files will be plain text (ASCII) or the binary graphics format that the printer requires. It's up to the user to ensure that the file is indeed the right kind.
queue	Displays the queue for the print share you're connected to, showing job ID, name, size, and status.

Finally, to print from the *smbclient*, use the **-c** option:

```
cat printfile | smbclient //server/printer_name  -c "print -"
```

Tar commands

smbclient can tar up files from a file share. This is normally done from the command line using the *smbtar* command, but the commands shown in Table D-3 are also available interactively.

Table D-3. smbclient Printing Commands

Command	Description
tar c|x[IXbgNa] *operands*	Performs a creation or extraction *tar* similar to the command-line program.
blocksize *size*	Sets the block size to be used by *tar*, in 512-byte blocks.
tarmode full|inc|reset| noreset	Makes *tar* pay attention to DOS archive bit for all following commands. In **full** mode (the default), *tar* will back up everything. In **inc** (incremental) mode, *tar* will back up only those files with the archive bit set. In **reset** mode, *tar* will reset the archive bit on all files it backs up. (this requires the share to be writable), and in **noreset** mode the archive bit will not be reset even after the file has been backed up.

Command-line message program options

-M *NetBIOS_machine_name*

This option allows you to send immediate messages using the WinPopup protocol to another computer. Once a connection is established, you can type your message, pressing control-D to end. If WinPopup is not running on the receiving machine, the program returns an error.

-U *user*

This option allows you to indirectly control the FROM part of the message.

Command-line tar program options

The -T (tar), -D (starting directory), and -c (command) options are used together to tar up files interactively. This is better done with *smbtar*, which will be discussed shortly. We don't recommend using *smbclient* directly as a *tar* program.

-D *initial_directory*

Changes to initial directory before starting.

-c *command_string*

Passes a command string to the *smbclient* command interpreter, which treats it as a semicolon-separated list of commands to be executed. This is handy to say things such as **tarmode inc**, for example, which forces **smbclient -T** to back up only files with the archive bit set.

-T *command filename*

Runs the *tar* driver, which is *gtar* compatible. The two main commands are: c (create) and x (extract), which may be followed by any of:

a   Resets archive bits once files are saved.

b *size*

    Sets blocksize in 512-byte units.

g   Backs up only files with the archive bit set.

I *file*

    Includes files and directories (this is the default). Does not do pattern-matching.

N *filename*

    Backs up only those files newer than *filename.*

q   Does not produce diagnostics.

X *file*

    Excludes files.

Command-line query program

If *smbclient* is run as:

```
smbclient -L server_name
```

it will list the shares and other services that machine provides. This is handy if you don't have *smbwrappers*. It can also be helpful as a testing program in its own right.

Command-line debugging/diagnostic program options

Any of the various modes of operation of *smbclient* can be used with the debugging and testing command-line options:

-B *IP_addr*
> Sets the broadcast address.

-d *debug_level*
> Sets the debug (sometimes called logging) level. The level can range from 0 all the way to 10. In addition, you can specify A for all debugging options. Debug level 0 logs only the most important messages; level 1 is normal; level 3 and above are primarily for debugging and slow operations considerably.

-E Sends all messages to stderr instead of stdout.

-I *IP_address*
> Sets the IP address of the server to which it connects.

-i *scope*
> This sets a NetBIOS scope identifier. Only machines with the same identifier will communicate with the server. The scope identifier was a predecessor to workgroups, and this option is included only for backward compatibility.

-l *log_file*
> Sends the log messages to the specified file.

-N Suppresses the password prompt. Unless a password is specified on the command line or this parameter is specified, the client will prompt for a password.

-n *NetBIOS_name*
> This option allows you to override the NetBIOS name by which the daemon will advertise itself.

-O *socket_options*
> Sets the TCP/IP socket options using the same parameters as the **socket options** configuration option. It is often used for performance tuning and testing.

-p *port_number*
> Sets the port number from which the client will accept requests.

-R *resolve_order*

Sets the resolve order of the name servers. This option is similar to the
resolve order configuration option, and can take any of the four parameters, lmhosts, host, wins, and bcast, in any order .

-s *configuration_file*

Specifies the location of the Samba configuration file. Used for debugging.

-t *terminal_code*

Sets the terminal code for Asian languages.

-U *username*

Sets the username and optionally password (e.g., -U fred%secret).

-W *workgroup*

Specifies the workgroup that you want the client to connect as.

If you want to test a particular name service, run *smbclient* with -R and just the
name of the service. This will force *smbclient* to use only the service you gave.

smbstatus

The *smbstatus* program lists the current connections on a Samba server. There are
three separate sections. The first section lists various shares that are in use by specific users. The second section lists the locked files that Samba currently has on all
of its shares. Finally, the third section lists the amount of memory usage for each
of the shares. For example:

```
# smbstatus
Samba version 2.0.3
Service      uid      gid      pid      machine
-------------------------------------------------
network      davecb   davecb   7470     phoenix  (192.168.220.101) Sun May 16
network      davecb   davecb   7589     chimaera (192.168.220.102) Sun May 16

Locked files:
Pid    DenyMode    R/W       Oplock          Name
-------------------------------------------------------
7589   DENY_NONE   RDONLY    EXCLUSIVE+BATCH  /home/samba/quicken/inet/common/
system/help.bmp    Sun May 16 21:23:40 1999
7470   DENY_WRITE  RDONLY    NONE            /home/samba/word/office/findfast.exe
Sun May 16 20:51:08 1999
7589   DENY_WRITE  RDONLY    EXCLUSIVE+BATCH /home/samba/quicken/1fbmp70n.dll
Sun May 16 21:23:39 1999
7589   DENY_WRITE  RDWR      EXCLUSIVE+BATCH /home/samba/quicken/inet/qdata/
runtime.dat    Sun May 16 21:23:41 1999
7470   DENY_WRITE  RDONLY    EXCLUSIVE+BATCH /home/samba/word/office/osa.exe
Sun May 16 20:51:09 1999
7589   DENY_WRITE  RDONLY    NONE            /home/samba/quicken/qversion.dll
Sun May 16 21:20:33 1999
```

```
7470    DENY_WRITE RDONLY     NONE          /home/samba/quicken/qversion.dll
Sun May 16 20:51:11 1999


Share mode memory usage (bytes):
   1043432(99%) free + 4312(0%) used + 832(0%) overhead = 1048576(100%) total
```

Options

-b Forces *smbstatus* to produce brief output. This includes the version of Samba and auditing information about the users that have logged into the server.

-d Gives verbose output, including each of the three reporting sections listed in the previous example. This is the default.

-L Forces *smbstatus* to print only the current file locks it has. This corresponds to the second section in a verbose output.

-p Prints a list of *smbd* process IDs only. This is often used for scripts.

-S Prints only a list of shares and their connections. This corresponds to the first section in a verbose output.

-s *configuration_file*
    Sets the Samba configuration file to use when processing this command.

-u *username*
    Limits the *smbstatus* report to the activity of a single user.

smbtar

The *smbtar* program is a shell script on top of *smbclient* that gives the program more intelligible options when doing tar operations. Functionally, it is equivalent to the Unix *tar* program.

Options

-a
    Resets the archive bit mode

-b *blocksize*
    Blocking size. Defaults to 20.

-d *directory*
    Changes to initial directory before restoring or backing up files.

-i Incremental mode; tar files are backed up only if they have the DOS archive bit set. The archive bit is reset after each file is read.

-l *log_level*
    Sets the logging level.

-N *filename*

Backs up only the files newer than the last modification date of *filename*. For incremental backups.

-p *password*

Specifies the password to use to access a share.

-r Restores files to the share from the tar file.

-s *server*

Specifies the SMB/CIFS server in which the share resides.

-t *tape*

Tape device or file. Default is the value of the environment variable $TAPE, or *tar.out* if $TAPE isn't set.

-u *user*

Specifies the user to connect to the share as. You can specify the password as well, in the format *username%password*.

-v Specifies the use of verbose mode.

-X *file*

Tells *smbtar* to exclude the specified file from the *tar* create or restore.

-x *share*

States the share name on the server to connect to. The default is **backup**, which is a common share name to perform backups with.

For example, a trivial backup command to archive the data for user **sue** is:

```
# smbtar -s pc_name -x sue -u sue -p secret -t sue.tar
```

nmblookup

The *nmblookup* program is a client program that exercises the NetBIOS-over-UDP/IP name service for resolving NBT machine names into IP addresses. The command works by broadcasting its queries on the local subnet until a machine with that name responds. You can think of it as a Windows *nslookup(1)* or *dig(1)*. This is useful for looking up both normal NetBIOS names, and the odd ones like _ _MSBROWSE_ _ that the Windows name services use to provide directory-like services. If you wish to query for a particular type of NetBIOS name, add the NetBIOS <type> to the end of the name.

The command line is:

```
nmblookup [-options] name
```

The options supported are:

-A Interprets *name* as an IP address and do a node-status query on this address.

-B *broadcast _address*

Sends the query to the given broadcast address. The default is to send the query to the broadcast address of the primary network interface.

-d *debuglevel*

Sets the debug (sometimes called logging) level. The level can range from 0 all the way to 10. Debug level 0 logs only the most important messages; level 1 is normal; level 3 and above are primarily for debugging and slow the program considerably.

-h Prints command-line usage information for the program.

-i *scope*

Sets a NetBIOS scope identifier. Only machines with the same identifier will communicate with the server. The scope identifier was a predecessor to workgroups, and this option is included only for backward compatibility.

-M Searches for a local master browser. This is done with a broadcast searching for a machine that will respond to the special name _ _MSBROWSE_ _, and then asking that machine for information, instead of broadcasting the query itself.

-R Sets the recursion desired bit in the packet. This will cause the machine that responds to try to do a WINS lookup and return the address and any other information the WINS server has saved.

-r Use the root port of 137 for Windows 95 machines.

-S Once the name query has returned an IP address, does a node status query as well. This returns all the resource types that the machine knows about, with their numeric attributes. For example:

```
% nmblookup -d 4 -S elsbeth
received 6 names
        ELSBETH             <00> - <GROUP> B <ACTIVE>
        ELSBETH             <03> -         B <ACTIVE>
        ELSBETH             <1d> -         B <ACTIVE>
        ELSBETH             <1e> - <GROUP> B <ACTIVE>
        ELSBETH             <20> -         B <ACTIVE>
        .._ _MSBROWSE_ _..  <01> - <GROUP> B <ACTIVE>
```

-s *configuration_file*

Specifies the location of the Samba configuration file. Although the file defaults to */usr/local/samba/lib/smb.conf,* you can override it here on the command-line, normally for debugging.

-T This option can be used to translate IP addresses into resolved names.

-U *unicast_address*

Performs a unicast query to the specified address. Used with **-R** to query WINS servers.

Note that there is no workgroup option for *nmblookup*; you can get around this by putting `workgroup = workgroup_name` in a file and passing it to *nmblookup* with the `-s smb.conf_file` option.

smbpasswd

The *smbpasswd* password has two distinct sets of functions. When run by users, it changes their encrypted passwords. When run by `root`, it updates the encrypted password file. When run by an ordinary user with no options, it connects to the primary domain controller and changes his or her Windows password.

The program will fail if *smbd* is not operating, if the `hosts allow` or `hosts deny` configuration options will not permit connections from localhost (IP address 127.0. 0.1), or the `encrypted passwords = no` option is set.

Regular user options

`-D debug_level`

Sets the debug (also called logging) level. The level can range from 0 to 10. Debug level 0 logs only the most important messages; level 1 is normal; level 3 and above are primarily for debugging and slow the program considerably.

`-h` Prints command-line usage information for the program.

`-r remote_machine_name`

Specifies on which machine the password should change. The remote machine must be a primary domain controller (PDC).

`-R resolve_order`

Sets the resolve order of the name servers. This option is similar to the `resolve order` configuration option, and can take any of the four parameters, `lmhosts`, `host`, `wins`, and `bcast`, in any order.

`-U username`

Used only with `-r`, to modify a username that is spelled differently on the remote machine.

Root-only options

`-a username`

Adds a user to the encrypted password file.

`-d username`

Disables a user in the encrypted password file.

`-e username`

Enables a disabled user in the encrypted password file.

−m *machine_name*

> Changes a machine account's password. The machine accounts are used to authenticate machines when they connect to a primary or backup domain controller.

−j *domain_name*

> Adds a Samba server to a Windows NT Domain.

−n Sets no password for the user.

−s *username*

> Causes *smbpasswd* to be silent and to read its old and new passwords from standard input, rather than from */dev/tty*. This is useful for writing scripts.

testparm

The *testparm* program checks an *smb.conf* file for obvious errors and self-consistency. Its command line is:

```
testparm [options] configfile_name [hostname IP_addr]
```

If the configuration file is not specified, the file at **samba_dir/lib/smb.conf** is checked by default. If you specify a hostname and an IP address, an extra check will be made to ensure that the specified machine would be allowed to connect to Samba. If a hostname is specified, an IP address should be present as well.

Options

−h Prints command-line information for the program.

−L *server_name*

> Resets the %L configuration variable to the specified server name.

−s This option prevents the *testparm* program from prompting the user to press the Enter key before printing a list of the configuration options for the server.

testprns

The *testprns* program checks a specified printer name against the system printer capabilities (*printcap*) file. Its command line is:

```
testprns printername [printcapname]
```

If the **printcapname** isn't specified, Samba attempts to use one located in the *smb.conf* file. If one isn't specified there, Samba will try */etc/printcap*. If that fails, the program will generate an error.

rpcclient

This is a new client that exercises the RPC (remote procedure call) interfaces of an SMB server. Like *smbclient*, *rpcclient* started its life as a test program for the Samba developers and will likely stay that way for a while. Its command line is:

```
rpcclient //server/share
```

The command-line options are the same as the Samba 2.0 *smbclient*, and the operations you can try are listed in Table D-4.

Table D-4. rpcclient commands

Command	Description
regenum keyname	Registry Enumeration (keys, values)
regdeletekey keyname	Registry Key Delete
regcreatekey keyname [keyvalue]	Registry Key Create
regquerykey keyname	Registry Key Query
regdeleteval valname	Registry Value Delete
regcreateval valname valtype value	Registry Key Create
reggetsec keyname	Registry Key Security
regtestsec keyname	Test Registry Key Security
ntlogin [username] [password]	NT Domain Login Test
wksinfo	Workstation Query Info
srvinfo	Server Query Info
srvsessions	List Sessions on a Server
srvshares	List shares on a server
srvconnections	List connections on a server
srvfiles	List files on a server
lsaquery	Query Info Policy (domain member or server)
lookupsids	Resolve names from SIDs
ntpass	NT SAM Password Change

tcpdump

The *tcpdump* utility, a classic system administration tool, dumps all the packet headers it sees on an interface that match an expression. The version included in the Samba distribution is enhanced to understand the SMB protocol. The *expression* is a logical expression with "and," "or," and "not," although sometimes it's very simple. For example, host escrime would select every packet going to or from escrime. The expression is normally one or more of:

- host *name*
- net *network_number*
- port *number*
- src *name*
- dst *name*

The most common options are src (source), dst (destination), and port. For example, in the book we used the command:

```
tcpdump port not telnet
```

This dumps all the packets except telnet; we were logged-in via telnet and wanted to see only the SMB packets.

Another *tcpdump* example is selecting traffic between server and either sue or joe:

```
tcpdump host server and \( sue or joe \)
```

We recommend using the -s 1500 option so that you capture all of the SMB messages sent, instead of just the header information.

Options

There are many options, and many other kinds of expressions that can be used with *tcpdump*. See the manual page for details on the advanced options. The most common options are as follows:

-c *count*

Forces the program to exit after receiving the specified number of packets.

-F *file*

Reads the expression from the specified file and ignores expressions on the command line.

-i *interface*

Forces the program to listen on the specified interface.

-r *file*

Reads packets from the specified file (captured with -w).

-s *length*

Saves the specified number of bytes of data from each packet (rather than 68 bytes).

-w *file*

Writes the packets to the specified file.

E

Downloading Samba with CVS

This appendix contains information on how to download the latest source version of Samba using the Concurrent Versions System (CVS). CVS is a freely available configuration management tool available from Cyclic Software and is distributed under the GNU General Public License. You can download the latest copy from *http://www.cyclic.com/*. The Samba team describes various ways to access its CVS site at *http://cvs.samba.org/cvs.html*.

CVS works on top of the GNU Revision Control System (RCS). Many Unix systems come preinstalled with RCS. However, if you want to download the latest version of RCS, you can find it at *http://ftp.gnu.org/gnu/rcs/*.

One of the nicest things about CVS is its ability to handle remote logins. This means that people across the globe on the Internet can download and update various source files for any project that uses a CVS repository. Such is the case with Samba. Once you have RCS and CVS installed on your system, you must first log in to the Samba source server with the following command:

```
cvs -d :pserver:cvs@cvs.samba.org:/cvsroot login
```

This tells CVS to connect to the CVS server at *cvs.samba.org*. Once you are connected, you can download the latest source tree with the following command:

```
cvs -d :pserver:cvs@cvs.samba.org:/cvsroot co samba
```

This will download the entire Samba distribution (file by file) into a directory entitled */samba*, which it will create on your hard drive. This directory will have the same structure as the Samba source distribution described in Chapter 2, *Installing Samba on a Unix System*. It includes source and header files, documentation, and sample configuration files to help get you started. After that is completed, you can follow the instructions in Chapter 2 to configure and compile Samba on your server.

F

Sample Configuration File

This appendix gives an example of a production *smb.conf* file and looks at how many of the options are used in practice. The following is a slightly disguised version of one we used at a corporation with five Linux servers, five Windows for Workgroups clients and three NT Workstation clients:

```
# smb.conf -- File Server System for: 1 Example.COM  BSC & Management Office
[globals]
    workgroup = 1EG_BSC
    interfaces = 10.10.1.14/24
```

We provide this service on only one of the machine's interfaces. The **interfaces** option sets its address and netmask, where **/24** is the same as using the netmask 255.255.255.0:

```
    comment = Samba ver. %v
    preexec = csh -c `echo /usr/samba/bin/smbclient \
                    -M %m -I %I` &
```

We use the *preexec* command to log information about all connections by machine name (**%m**) and IP address (**%I**):

```
    # smbstatus will output various info on current status
    status = yes
    browseable = yes
    printing = bsd

    # the username that will be used for access to services
    # specified with 'guest = ok'
    guest account = samba
```

The default guest account was **nobody**, uid -1, which produced log messages on one of our machines saying "your server is being unfriendly," so we created a specific Samba guest account for browsing and printing:

```
# superuser account - admin privilages to shares, with no
# restrictions
# WARNING - use this with care: files can be modified,
# regardless of file permissions
admin users = root

# who is NOT allowed to connect to ANY service
invalid users = @wheel, mail, deamon, adt
```

Daemons can't use Samba, only people. The **invalid users** option closes a security hole; it prevents intruders from breaking in by pretending to be a daemon process.

```
# hosts that are ALLOWED or DENIED from connecting to ANY service
hosts allow = 10.10.1.
hosts deny = 10.10.1.6

# where the lock files will be located
lock directory = /var/lock/samba/locks

# debug log files
# %m = separate log for each NetBIOS-name (each machine)
log file = /var/log/samba/log.%m

# We send priority 0, 1 and 2 messages to the system logs
syslog = 2

# If a WinPopup message is sent to the server,
# redirect it to a user via e-mail

message command = /bin/mail -s 'message from #% on %m' \
                        pkelly < %s; rm %s

# ----------------------------------------------------
# [globals] Performance Tuning
# ----------------------------------------------------

# caching algorithm to reduce time doing getwd() calls.
getwd cache = yes

socket options = TCP_NODELAY

# tell the server whether the client is present and
# responding in seconds
keep alive = 60

# num minutes of inactivity before a connection is
# considered dead
dead time = 30

read prediction = yes
share modes = yes
max xmit = 17384
read size = 512
```

The **share modes**, **max**, **xinit**, and **read size** options are machine-specific (see Appendix B, *Samba Performance Tuning*):

```
# locking is done by the server
locking = yes

# control whether dos style attributes should be mapped
# to unix execute bits
map hidden = yes
map archive = yes
map system = yes
```

The three **map** options will work only on shares with a create mode that includes the execute bits (0111). Our **homes** and **printers** shares won't honor them, but the [www] share will:

```
# ----------------------------------------------------------
# [globals] Security and Domain Logon Services
# ----------------------------------------------------------
# connections are made with UID and GID, not as shares
    security = user

# boolean variable that controls whether passwords
# will be encrypted
    encrypt passwords = yes
    passwd chat = "*New password:*" %n\r "*New password (again):*" %n\r \
"*Password changed*"
    passwd program = /usr/bin/passwd %u

# Always become the local master browser
    domain master = yes
    preferred master = yes
    os level = 34

# For domain logons to work correctly. Samba acts as a
# primary domain controller.
    domain logons = yes

# Logon script to run for user off the server each time
# username (%U) logs in.  Set the time, connect to shares,
# virus checks, etc.
    logon script = scripts\%U.bat

[netlogon]
    comment = "Domain Logon Services"
    path = /u/netlogon
    writable = yes
    create mode = 444
    guest ok = no
    volume = "Network"
```

This share, discussed in Chapter 6, *Users, Security, and Domains*, is required for Samba to work smoothly in a Windows NT domain:

```
# -------------------------------------------------------------
# [homes] User Home Directories
# -------------------------------------------------------------
[homes]
    comment = "Home Directory for : %u "
    path = /u/users/%u
```

The password file of the Samba server specifies each person's home directory as */home/machine_name/person*, which NFS converts to point to the actual physicl location under */u/users*. The `path` option in the `[homes]` share tells Samba the actual (non-NFS) location:

```
    guest ok = no
    read only = no
    create mode = 644
    writable = yes
    browseable = no


# -------------------------------------------------------------
# [printers] System Printers
# -------------------------------------------------------------
[printers]
    comment = "Printers"
    path = /var/spool/lpd/samba
    printcap name = /etc/printcap
    printable = yes
    public = no
    writable = no

    lpq command = /usr/bin/lpq -P%p
    lprm command = /usr/bin/lprm -P%p %j
    lppause command = /usr/sbin/lpc stop %p
    lpresume command = /usr/sbin/lpc start %p

    create mode = 0700

    browseable = no
    load printers = yes

# -------------------------------------------------------------
# Specific Descriptions: [programs] [data] [retail]
# -------------------------------------------------------------
[programs]
    comment = "Shared Programs %T"
    volume = "programs"
```

Shared Programs shows up in the Network Neighborhood, and `programs` is the volume name you specify when an installation program wants to know the label of the CD-ROM from which it thinks it's loading:

```
    path = /u/programs
    public = yes
    writeable = yes
    printable = no
    create mode = 664
```

```
[cdrom]
    comment = "Unix CDROM"
    path = /u/cdrom
    public = no
    writeable = no
    printable = no
    volume = "cdrom"

[data]
    comment =  "Data Directories %T"
    path = /u/data
    public = no
    create mode = 770
    writeable = yes
    volume = "data"

[nt4]
    comment =  "NT4 Server"
    path = /u/systems/nt4
    public = yes
    create mode = 770
    writeable = yes
    volume = "nt4_server"

[www]
    comment =  "WWW System"
    path = /usr/www/http
    public = yes
    create mode = 775
    writeable = yes
    volume = "www_system"
```

The [www] share is the directory used on the Unix server to serve web pages.
Samba makes the directory available to local PC users so the art department can
update web pages.

Index

About the Author

Robert Eckstein enjoys dabbling with just about anything related to computers. From rendering to electronic commerce to compiler construction to fuzzy logic, most of his friends agree that Robert spends far too much time in front of a computer screen. At O'Reilly, Robert works mostly on Java books (notably *Java Swing*) and is also responsible for the *XML Pocket Reference* and *Webmaster in a Nutshell, 2nd Edition*. In his spare time he has been known to provide online coverage for popular conferences. He also writes articles for JavaWorld magazine. Robert holds bachelor's degrees in computer science and communications from Trinity University. In the past, he has worked for the USAA insurance company and, more recently, has spent four years with Motorola's cellular software division. He now lives in Austin, Texas, with his newlywed Michelle—they hope to adopt a talking puppy soon.

David Collier-Brown is a consulting systems integrator, currently working for the performance and engineering group at Sun Opcom in Toronto. In his spare time he reads assiduously, keeps score for his wife's baseball team and, in the two weeks of the local summer, sails from Toronto's outer harbor.

Peter Kelly works on his own as a Systems Consultant in Toronto, Canada, specializing in Internet and network security. Peter is currently finishing exams to be an MCSE, but prefers to work with Linux when he can. When Peter is not working, he enjoys playing golf and reading about security, networking, and Calvin & Hobbes.

Colophon

Our look is the result of reader comments, our own experimentation, and feedback from distribution channels. Distinctive covers complement our distinctive approach to technical topics, breathing personality and life into potentially dry subjects.

The animal on the cover of *Using Samba* is a African ground hornbill (*Bucorvus cafer*). This type of bird is one of fifty hornbill species. The African ground hornbill is a medium to large sized bird characterized by a bright red waddle under a very long beak, dark-colored body and wings, long eyelashes, and short legs. Like all hornbills, it has a casque, a large but lightweight growth on the top of its beak, which grows more folds as the bird ages. It is the only ground-dwelling species of hornbill, though it is able to fly when necessary. It lives in the grasslands of southern and eastern Africa, and nests in the foliage of dense trees, not in nest holes in the ground as other hornbills do. Its diet includes mostly fruit, as well as large insects and small mammals. The African ground hornbill is considered to be sacred by many Africans, and as such this bird is part of many legends and superstitions.

Sarah Jane Shangraw was the production editor and proofreader for *Using Samba*. Sarah Lemaire copyedited the text. Maureen Dempsey and Claire Cloutier LeBlanc provided quality control. Brenda Miller wrote the index.

Edie Freedman designed the cover of this book based on her own series design. The cover image of an African ground hornbill is a 19th-century engraving from the Dover Pictorial Archive. Kathleen Wilson produced the cover layout with QuarkXPress 3.32 using Adobe's ITC Garamond font. Kathleen Wilson also created the CD design.

Alicia Cech designed the interior layout based on a series design by Nancy Priest. Mike Sierra implemented the design in FrameMaker 5.5. The text and heading fonts are ITC Garamond Light and Garamond Book. The illustrations that appear in the book were produced by Robert Romano and Rhon Porter using Macromedia FreeHand 8 and Adobe Photoshop 5. Interior composition was done by Sarah Jane Shangraw, Sebastian Banker, Jeff Holcolmb, and Abigail Myers. This colophon was written by Nicole Arigo.

Whenever possible, our books use RepKover™, a durable and flexible lay-flat binding. If the page count exceeds RepKover's limit, perfect binding is used.